THE LONGEST STREET

By the Same Author

SOME DAYS WERE HAPPY

SIX LOST WOMEN

ALONG THE BROADWAY BEAT

THE LONGEST STREET

A MEMOIR

by

louis sobol

Foreword by Jim Bishop

CROWN PUBLISHERS, INC., NEW YORK

To Peggy, for whom the excitement of "the longest street," its events and its characters, past and present, has never abated

Library of Congress Catalog Card Number: 68–20479
Manufactured in the United States of America
Published simultaneously in Canada by
General Publishing Company Limited
Grateful acknowledgment is made to *Cosmopolitan* for permission to use excerpts from a series of articles entitled "Speakeasy."

Designed by Leonard Cascioli

Contents

FOREWORD

For the Record

by Jim Bishop

The street was a crooked X. It died every morning at 5:00 A.M. and there was nothing to see except the fat water trucks trailing plumes, glistening macadam, and cold electric lights hanging everywhere. A blind man tapping a cane could smell it. A policeman on a tired horse could see it. A kid like George Raft could time-step his way across town to a flat in Hell's Kitchen and feel the excitement in his toes. Soon dawn came up pale green and canary yellow. It streaked the big sky and made Broadway smaller. The lines began to show. The gutter gurgled with dirty water. The drunks curled up in vestibules. Good girls did their penance dozing on cold tables at the Automat.

The light of day was an *exposé*. Everybody became nobody. It was as though an enchanting game had been played all night and some mystic figure from the heavens had come at this hour to strip the masks, to muffle the diamonds, to gray the complexions, to still the laughter, to impale the heart on the laser beam of the sun. Broadway was a fake. It was another street with double-ended trolleys, sight-seeing buses, subway kiosks, newsstand dealers, cops and beggars.

Broadway—the real Broadway—slept all day. It consisted of people, and people, like dollar windup dolls, run down. Arduously, they screened out the sun with heavy drapes and eye pads, and they slid wearily between sheets to shut out the pain of reality. It was not a thing that could wait. Sleep must be nearly instantaneous, and Broadway learned that it could be ensured with a pill, a potion or a shot glass. The merciful limbo of darkness arrived as other people were leaving home. This darkness—also spurious—lasted until the real thing arrived.

The street was resurrected every night at 8:40. The lights were on and they stabbed a silver knife into the sky. This was the call to the faithful. It was curtain time. Waiters hurried with the dinner checks. Bartenders softened vats of ice with baseball bats. The third drink was on the house. Thomas Mitchell, in the mustiness of The Lambs Club, told Joe Laurie, Jr., that he would play one more rack of pool. One more. At the Palais D'Or, amid the dusty drapes which hung from the ceiling, a diamond ring of mirrors reflected B. A. Rolfe a hundred times, a fat man with a horn. On West Fifty-fourth Street, over a garage, a thin man with a horn, Jimmy Durante, punched ragtime from a protesting upright piano.

The day went down and the lights came up. The play to see tonight, if you haven't already heard, is *The Royal Family*. The man to see is Osgood Perkins in *The Front Page*. The woman to see—ah, no. The women to see, you see, are Lynn Fontanne in *The Guardsman*, Belle Baker at the Palace, a beef stew of beauties in the *Follies*, the *Vanities*, the *Scandals*; Helen Morgan on a piano, Sophie Tucker off, Ethel Barrymore snorting with regality, Edna Best in *Charlie's Aunt*, Lady Diana Cooper in *The Miracle*, Marion Davies in *Chu Chin Chow*, Dorothy Gish, Ruth Gordon, Gilda Gray, Julie Harris, June Havoc, Gladys Glad, Gladys Cooper—they were women beyond measure.

Without people, there would be no plays, no musicals, no revues, no nightclubs, no motion pictures, no strip houses—no Broadway. A Florenz Ziegfeld was a definite requirement. But then, so was A. H. Woods and his French bedroom farces. Victor Herbert gave the street melody, and so did Vincent Youmans, and a trio of jazzy gabbers named De Sylva, Brown and Henderson. If you wanted a cheap night, you could walk down to the brand new Paramount and listen to the organist play Irving Berlin's sentimental nosegay, "Remember." For the same price, Clara Bow was there in *Three Weeks*. It was early for Texas Guinan's place and nothing moved except the booze before Larry Fay showed up.

It was people and places and lights, a mile of make-believe. It had its historians: Karl Kitchen and Don Marquis and Mark Hellinger and Walter Winchell and Sime Silverman and Beau

Broadway and Abel Green and Percy Hammond and Alexander Woollcott. It also had Louis Sobol. The others drew a talented finger across the face of Broadway and left a scar. Sobol was the only one who remained to nurse the dying harridan and say a prayer over the remains. The only one.

His weakness was that he had a heart. It could weep for the afflicted, enthuse for the lucky, sympathize with the losers, laugh with the amusing, and hope for the hopeless. He hid the pump behind an unremarkable face and wrote notes to himself about the street he loved. He roamed from Barney Gallant's to Billingsley's Stork Club; from the Paradise to The Tavern. Lou knew every place, every face. The irony of writing a great Broadway column like Sobol's is that, after forty years, one can name his enemies on the fingers of one thumb.

I have known Sobol for a great number of years. He writes syncopated hymns. There was never a time when he hated the street. He is not a hit-and-run lover. He was one of the first, and, ironically, the last of the kings of Broadway. If you want to know the street—and by this I mean the people who made it, as the street made them—you may as well get the story straight. Louis Sobol has it. It lies between these covers.

For the last time, the sun goes down. The lights are up. The clock behind Father Duffy's cross points to 8:40. Curtain time.

1

I Start My Love Affair with Broadway

THE AFTERNOON OF MAY 29, 1929, seemed no different from any other typical warm afternoon. Yet a decision made in an office about a hundred feet distant from the windowless cubicle in which I labored daily was to alter the entire course of my life and project me into the turbulent arena of Broadway.

A few spoken words ended my humdrum routine editorial chores. I was to be thrust into the role of an observer of what was then considered the most exciting pageantry in the world—to watch producers, stage and vaudeville stars, topflight songwriters, mob emirs, nightclub impresarios and headliners, political potentates, society debutantes and dowagers, millionaire playboys parade past and to cheer or groan, depending upon the mood of the moment. I was to become a licensed historian of the wild, bewildering, fascinating, often sanguinary Prohibition era during which sedate mansions of conservative families were converted into plush speakeasies—a run of years during which the moral fiber of otherwise law-abiding citizens disintegrated.

In brief, an apparently impulsive decision by a newspaper

executive was to open wide the portals for a run-of-the-mill newspaperman into a domain where he now would be able to mingle on equal terms with personalities whose names dominated news pages, feature and magazine stories and conversation in the pubs and drawing rooms. Awesome figures to a small-town yokel not long emerged from the quieter pastures of newspapers in Connecticut, I was to become part of the glittering assemblies at First Nights—to have open sesame to the resplendent oases of the period and to receive warmly beckoning fingers of welcome from aloof headwaiters.

Basically a timid soul, I was to be flung into a snarl of some of the most ruthless cutthroats spawned in the lawless era prodded by the Prohibition laws—mob kings and underlings—a terrifying army whose ranks included "Dutch" Schultz, Jack "Legs" Diamond, Louis "Lepke" Buchwalter, Louis "Pretty" Amberg, Charles "Chink" Sherman and others—all to die the hard, hard way.

To repeat, it all started on that mild May afternoon in 1929 when Emile H. Gauvreau, editor of the *New York Evening Graphic,* phoned commanding an immediate visit to his office. He didn't invite me to sit down. He simply stared at me for a spell, grinned weakly, and then snapped: "Do you think you can handle Winchell's job?"

Before, in my befuddlement, I could stammer a reply, Gauvreau continued in his staccato manner: "I want you to write the column for a few days. If it goes over, you've got the job—permanent."

Still bewildered, I started to ask what was this all about, but before I was able to mumble the first few words, Gauvreau was speaking again.

"Winchell in?"

I nodded. (He occupied the tiny, equally windowless office adjoining mine.)

"Okay, you tell him he's to go on vacation tomorrow. Tomorrow, get me. Now go tell him."

Still in a semidaze, I left Gauvreau's office bound for Winchell with the message I had been ordered to convey. Walter was just finishing a conversation over the phone. "That was Alec Woollcott," he announced, as he hung up the receiver. "Ever meet Alec?"

I said I had seen him but couldn't say I had actually met him, although I had good reason to remember him, which I shall explain later.

Winchell went on, "Good guy. I get great stories from him."

I nodded, appropriately awed, and came to the business at hand.

"Walter," I said, "Guv just told me to tell you you can start your vacation right away—tomorrow. He said to tell you I'm going to take over your spot, and if I do all right, he's going to let you go to the *Journal.* That's what the man said, Walter."

Winchell stared at me in disbelief. He fiddled with some clips on his desk and then, rather subdued for him, asked, "When did he tell you that?"

"Why—just now. I've just come from his office. He told me to tell you just what I've told you."

Winchell was silent for a few seconds, and then he exploded. "Why, the little son of a bitch." And then, silent again, unlike the self-confident, vehemently assertive chap those of us on the *Graphic* and folks generally around Broadway had come to know, he asked, almost boyishly timid: "Do you think I ought to go and see him about this? What do you think?"

"Sure, Walter," I replied, brightly. "Sure, why don't you?"

Less than five minutes later, Winchell was back. "It's like you said," he announced. "Look, here's some releases just in—you can use them if you want to for the column tomorrow. See you later."

And he was off—never to return to the *Graphic* again.

At this point, perhaps I should explain why Gauvreau took this peculiar method for informing Walter Winchell, one of the outstanding circulation attractions of the *Graphic,* that the flaming gazette was prepared to continue its news merchandizing without his unique services.

It was no secret that Winchell and the editor were not on speaking terms. The columnist, at that time an indefatigable superambitious reporter who had lured a tremendous following with his uninhibited colorful writing style and originality in coining provocative phrases, added to an uncanny ability to ferret out deep, dark secrets in the lives of citizens in the limelight, had smoldered in increasing resentment over what he considered unwarranted interference by Gauvreau in the conduct of his column. There had been many heated verbal duels between the two, and on one occasion, Winchell, in unrestrained rage, had hurled a sneering remark about the editor's crippled leg. Gauvreau never forgave him.

Then when the news leaked out that Winchell had signed a contract guaranteeing him a substantial bonus in addition to a weekly salary of $500 to move his department over to the dominant *New York Evening Journal,* with its superior circulation and reputation, Gauvreau had pointed out grimly that the piece of paper was worthless and that he expected Winchell to finish out his contract, which still had a couple of years to run.

What influenced a sudden change of mind on Gauvreau's part was to remain a dark secret. But later when Winchell had moved on to the *Daily Mirror* (and not to the *Journal*) and shortly after, when Gauvreau, too, shifted over to the *Mirror* as editor, there were whispers in newspaper circles that it had all been prearranged—that *Mirror* publisher A. J. Kobler, who had convinced William Randolph Hearst that he needed Winchell's column more than did the successful *Journal,* had also dangled the tempting executive job to Gauvreau if he could arrange to have Winchell released from his contract.

So on May 31 (Winchell had already submitted the column for May 30), I took over the department, *Your Broadway and Mine* and the drama critic's chores—as a substitute.

Underneath the heading was a box announcing that "Walter Winchell is holidaying for two weeks. Until Mr. Winchell returns, his department here will be conducted by Louis Sobol." The following day, June 1, without any other announcement my name replaced Winchell's in the boxed heading. I was now officially Broadway columnist and drama critic for the *New York Evening Graphic,* a flamboyant, never too ethical tabloid, which was convinced that if folks liked to read chalked obscenities in the men's room, then certainly they would welcome them if decorated in neat wordage in print.

"Sex," according to the founder, a physical culture fanatic, Bernarr Macfadden, was "the sirloin steak of true living."

Actually, no one regarded too seriously this sordid little sheet which defied most accepted protocol of newspapers. Nevertheless, the *Graphic*'s circulation was booming, and several of its features were regarded highly not only on Broadway but even in loftier circles, though many of the more conservative readers probably hid their copies between the pages of *The New York Times* or the *Tribune.*

The dominant features to which I refer were Winchell's column, which had produced many newsbeats that eventually had found their way to the front pages of other newspapers, and Ed Sullivan's sports column—the same Ed Sullivan who was in later years to get his message over to wider audiences. Incidentally, shortly after I took over my Broadway chores, two other bright young men were added to the staff: Jerry Wald who was to become a top Hollywood film producer, and Norman Krasna, who climbed into his own rewarding niche as a playwright, scenarist, movie producer and director. These two in later years spread the legend that they both had worked for me as office boys, although the truth is, they never did. Krasna occasionally assisted me as a second-string drama critic when there was more than one opening on the same night; and Wald, who had assumed the duties of radio columnist, was awarded space in the little anteroom leading to my office.

While on the subject, another graduate from the *Graphic* ranks was William Robinson, who went on to become the business manager of the *Herald Tribune* and later president of the Coca-Cola company. He became, too, an intimate and often golfing partner of Dwight D. Eisenhower during his White House reign.

As for me, there seemed to be no more unlikely candidate to step into Winchell's well-polished shoes. I had been a small-time Connecticut newspaperman-reporter, state editor and assistant city editor of the *Waterbury Republican*; then later city editor and sports editor of the *New London Day* before being summoned to New York to become city editor eventually of Macfadden's new trade paper, the *Automotive Daily News*.

My chief claim to dubious prestige thereafter was that I had ghosted some of Queen Marie of Romania's pieces distributed by Famous Features Syndicate, as well as revising Helen Keller's little sermonettes. Also, I had turned out the Peaches and Daddy Browning confessionals and some allegedly first-person revelations by two sad figures in the notorious Hall-Mills murder case: Charlotte Mills, daughter of the slain woman, and James Mills, janitor husband of the victim.

And I had written a farce, *The High Hatters,* starring the then comparatively unknown young actor Robert Montgomery and featuring an equally obscure performer named Brian Donlevy. It was not a play that brought me any particular distinction.

The late Burns Mantle delivered this melancholy opinion: "It is rather to be regretted that while Mr. Isquith was carrying *The High Hatters* around the theater district, looking for some place to lay it down, he did not pass a manhole at the moment of explosion."

Richard Watts, Jr., insisted: "What is easily one of the lowest points reached by the current—or for that matter, any past dramatic season was achieved at the Klaw Theater." And the late Alexander Woollcott dismissed my sweat and toil (actually I had written the play in some three weeks) in this fashion: "A May bug called *The High Hatters* which zoomed and buzzed for a time last evening at the Klaw Theater is so palpable a candidate for the ephemeridae that nothing shall be said about it in the kindly jottings of this department."

And then he proceeded to annihilate it!

While I had derived no comfort from these appraisals by the professional aisle assassins, I did now in my new status experience the glowing warmth of satisfaction that here I was to be on equal footing with these dictators—a full-fledged drama critic myself.

As the years trooped by, Winchell, Sullivan and I were to have our respective careers dovetailing through the vagaries of circumstances. Thus, not only did I step into Winchell's post when he moved on to the *Mirror* (and two years later to the *Evening Journal*, which had first sought W. W.'s services); but some years after, when Winchell, harassed by an incipient nervous breakdown was forced to relinquish his Lucky Strike radio hour —a thrice-weekly session which boasted the largest network coverage in the world at the time—I was tapped to replace him.

And when I was graduated from the *Graphic* to the *Journal*, Ed Sullivan was thrust into the *Graphic* post to succeed me. Ed at this period of his career had found his star in the descendant because of differences with the Macfadden higher echelon. In fact his sports column had been denigrated until it was allotted merely a few inches of space. Acquiring the Broadway department gave him a new lift. Similarly, when the *Graphic* expired in an agony of drooping circulation and advertising revenue, Ed was extended another lifeline by the *Daily News*, whose bid for a column a year or so previously I had rejected.

Incidentally, though this was not planned to be a columnar history, when in 1938, after the death of O. O. McIntyre, the Hearst organization decided I might well be equipped to carry on in his homespun tradition, the way was paved for a girl reporter to enter the field—Dorothy Kilgallen. And when Dorothy met her tragic end November 8, 1965, Jack O'Brian was asked to surrender his television and radio column and take over the Kilgallen spot.

I have wandered a bit from the excitement of that momentous day when I became aware that I now had been handed the dual portfolio of Broadway columnist and drama critic. By coincidence it was our tenth wedding anniversary, and so Lee Sobol and I had some extra gratifying reasons for a real celebration, especially since I had been notified that my salary was to be $250 weekly—quite a leap from the $90 my pay envelope had yielded to that point. We had about $400 in our savings account, painfully accumulated through the skillful budgeting by my wife. I urged her to go out and splurge—we were really going to put it on big that evening. "Buy yourself some fancy duds," I pressed. "The Sobols are beginning to ride."

But Lee could not break the frugal habits of a decade of marriage to an impecunious newspaperman. Nor could she quite believe that my rose-colored glasses weren't a bit blurred by excess enthusiasm. So she was content to wear her one good dress that night, an inexpensive little affair—and no jewelry, because she had none. As for me, I boasted two suits *in toto*— the better one, a shiny blue serge.

Thus, the shabby Sobols set out that night to survey their new domain. At Sardi's, we had the first inkling of what was in store. A press agent, Irving Strouse, introduced us to folks whose very names thrilled us. William Gaxton, Ed Wynn, Will Rogers, Georgie Jessel, a fellow columnist, Sidney Skolsky, and finally the owner of the famed theatrical restaurant—Vincent Sardi, Sr.

The flattery oozed out. Jessel promptly told me a story, vowing it was exclusive. Skolsky kindly suggested I ought to join the daily noonday group at Sardi's for laughs and for copy. And the Big Moment came at dinner's end. "Compliments of Mr. Sardi," the captain of waiters announced as I asked nervously for the check, hoping I had sufficient funds to cover.

I recall wondering what, in my new exalted status, I should tip. We had done little dining out before this, and then only occasionally on Sunday afternoons when we would journey down to Second Avenue for midday dinner at one of the restaurants where a table d'hôte meal rarely exceed ninety cents per person. My

The Diamond Horseshoe was Billy Rose's tribute to nostalgia—although the shrewd little showman never ignored the lure of up-to-the-minute beauties in scanty attire. On the stage among the assembly of old-time stars you may spot Nita Naldi, the first woman on the left, one of the original silent movie vamps. The third from the left is Joe Howard, the songwriter who gave us, among other numbers, "I Wonder Who's Kissing Her Now." The other veteran in tails is Carlyle Blackwell, another of the silent movie stars, and next to him, Gilda Gray, colorful figure of an earlier era.
Photo by United Press International

customary lagniappe on these occasions never topped fifty cents for the two of us.

I beckoned to Strouse and explained my dilemma.

"Leave two dollars for the waiter," he suggested, "and a buck to the captain. That'll be ample."

Lee and I looked at each other, rather grimly.

Three dollars, just for the tips!! And we had scarcely started the evening. Was it to be like this every night? Money going out at this extravagant pace! And what if there were no "compliments of the house?"

A bit shaken, nevertheless, and with Strouse as our guide, we invaded Texas Guinan's rowdy haunt and viewed our first night-club girly show, as well as receiving our initiation to Guinan's raucous greetings and quips. Then Texas halted the proceedings to make an announcement. "And now, suckers, I want you to meet someone you'll get to know better soon—you better get to know him soon. The fellow who's taking over Walter Winchell's column on the *Graphic*. Give Louis Sobol a nice big hand—make him feel at home. Get up, Louis, let all these suckers see what you look like. Go on, get up!" The spotlight illuminated our table. In embarrassment I rose and sat down quickly. The applause was perfunctory. From a table away came a vocal expression of amusement and disdain. "He's taking Winchell's place? Oh, no!" Again I asked for the check, and again was informed there was no check—not this time. Texas came over to the table and chatted affably with Lee and myself, offering a few gags she was certain I would like to use (I learned later they were not new), and suggested I call on her anytime I was short of material.

Again I left two dollars for the waiter, who picked it up from the table rather gingerly and somewhat disdainfully, and one dollar to the captain, who also did not seem too enthusiastic.

Our next and final stop was at Reuben's, a favorite after-midnight eating place for the notables of the town, and we were properly awed as we recognized various celebrities. Studying the menu, I wondered whether someday, a sandwich would be named after me, too. (P.S. It was.)

Strouse had left us, so no one knew us at Reuben's. The check for our sandwiches and coffee came to something like three dollars—and this time I got the tab. Having been briefed about tipping, I followed the pattern— two dollars to the waiter, one dollar to the captain. The waiter seemed surprised—he thanked us profusely, and so did the captain.

As we rode home that evening to Jackson Heights, splurging again by taking a taxi instead of the usual subway, Lee, who had been making a mental recapitulation of the evening's expenses, turned to me and remarked rather dubiously: "Do you think we're going to be able to afford this new job of yours?"

2

"The Flamboyant Floodway"

ENDOWED WITH THE PRECIOUS franchise of Broadway historian, I now set out to survey what promised to be a thrilling thoroughfare, and promptly adhering to the silly columnar tradition of the day, I labeled it the Flamboyant Floodway.

Forty-second Street, especially the stretch between Times Square and Eighth Avenue—with its theatres offering the musical extravaganzas of Florenz Ziegfeld, George White, Charles Dillingham and other impresarios, and nonmusical goodies as well, thrust forth all the allure I had anticipated. Nor was I shocked by the fact that Minsky's burlesque with its rowdy attractions was on the street, too. The marquee lights spelled out the impressive names of Will Rogers, Marilyn Miller, Fred and Adele Astaire, Ethel Barrymore, Lunt and Fontanne and so many others. It was an exciting theatre row with such houses as the Eltinge, Liberty, New Amsterdam, Selwyn, Apollo, Lyric nudging each other neighborly.

In more recent years, Forty-second Street has deteriorated

into a haven for pornographic literature, tawdry sex movies, little secondhand stores, shops retailing lethal weapons—with homosexuals, hippies, dope-saturated thugs parading the street—as well as *filles de joie,* some in their teens. I couldn't resist renaming it Bawdy Second Street.

The Big Show, of course, as I started on those initial night rounds, was Broadway itself and its side arteries. Even before I got on speaking terms with them, there was a thrill in encountering, strolling along, perhaps the original fun-loving mayor, Jimmy Walker, or eminent songwriters like Irving Berlin, Cole Porter, Jerome Kern, dominant producers like Ziegfeld, David Belasco or one of the Shubert brothers, famed folks from theatre—William Gaxton, Al Jolson, Fred Stone, Helen Hayes, Katharine Cornell —and always the pretty trim little models with their kits, or chorus girls and show girls rushing to their matinee chores.

A rare photo when Healy's on Broadway was a popular rendezvous. This gathering was a "welcome back to freedom" for Hype Igoe, famed Hearst sports columnist who had been jailed for some minor infraction of the law. Among the assembly: bottom row, starting with the fourth from the left, we spot Wilson Mizner, noted raconteur oft profiled man-about-town of the twenties; then "Tad" (T. A. Dorgan), famed Hearst sports cartoonist, Hype Igoe, composer Irving Berlin, cartoonist Tom McNamara ("Us Boys"), also cartoonists Walter Hoban, Hal Coffman, Cliff Sterett ("Polly and Her Pals"). In the row above, we lead off with Victor Watson, Hearst editor who committed suicide, then third from left, cartoonist Winsor McCay ("Nemo" and "Lady Bountiful"). Fifth from right, cartoonist Jimmy Swinnerton, and third from right, cartoonist humorist Harry Hershfield.
Healy's has long joined the Tombs of Broadway—and for that matter Hype Igoe has passed on. And so have most of those in this gay assembly, although Hershfield and Berlin long beyond the threescore-and-ten mark remain very much alive and active.

You never knew, for instance, whom you might run into as you entered the lobby of the Astor Hotel—noted Broadwayites, illustrious statesmen, visiting foreign notables. Often I was able to chat with those fine veteran slapstick comedians Joe Weber and Lew Fields who used to lunch in the Astor's Hunt Room, or in later years with Jimmy Durante, who lodged at the famed old inn when he was in town. At the Claridge, that amiable, literate, self-styled "rogue," promoter and wit Wilson Mizner, and also newsman-author Gene Fowler were lads to cultivate in the hopes of luring a paragraph for the column.

The Palace Theatre, then at the height of its prestige as the Queen House of Vaudeville, was a must on the beat, if not for the imposing array of star attractions in the show itself, at least for the daily congregation in front of the theatre, prior to the show time, of big-timers and small-timers.

And so I became one of the few troubadours singing the song of Broadway, each of us changing our lyrics from day to day but maintaining the central theme to attest to its perpetually luminous appeal. We dipped into our sack of descriptive chords to weave around the minor byplays, humorous or tragic episodes, romances in the making and the breaking, the rise and fall of its citizens. There was no other thoroughfare in the world, it seemed to us, that boasted such dedicated minnesingers who sent their songs out through the syndicated channels to big cities in far-off places, to the small towns and tiny hamlets, and even overseas.

Although I, for one, wandered into areas away from Broadway, it is a truth that I, as did the others, sang a minor hymn of tribute (and occasionally disdain) chiefly to the minute oblong of spectacular activity—the section that encompassed for our purposes about ten city blocks from north to south on the Broadway highway and not more than perhaps half a dozen blocks east and west.

We ignored the Bronx though not Harlem. Rarely was there a mention of Washington Heights or Brooklyn or Queens. Occasionally I did have my sessions in Greenwich Village or the Lower East Side with its historic name streets, Essex, Delancey, Ludlow, Monroe.

But for the most part, I confess now that what intrigued me were the theatres, the little and big night-spots, the popular eating places, the song ateliers. My cantatas were about the success and the failure, the star and the embryonic hopeful, the playboy and his mistress, the personality saloonkeeper and the occasional cop who popped out of anonymity. A new face sprinkled with stardust appearing before the footlights for the first time, a new voice in which we detected something different and saleable, a comedian evidencing signs of originality in his routine, a new writer showing promise for the theatre or literature—these inspired our hallelujahs.

And of course, for a mayor we had a chap who had been a songwriter, who loved the theatre and its folks, who had divorced his wife of many years to wed a vivacious musical comedy star, Betty Compton. Perhaps remembering him with affection despite his later involvement in a political scandal and temporary fall from grace, I recall at this point when Jimmy Walker, merely a private citizen then, stood with me on Broadway at Fifty-second Street. It was a hot, hot afternoon in August of 1944 and Walker had removed his broad-brimmed, floppy Bangkok, wiped beads of sweat from a brow that, despite his age, was still unwrinkled.

He stopped me from crossing the street. "The light is red," he said. "I put those traffic lights in when I was mayor, and I'm not going to go against them now, and neither are you."

So we waited for the green and walked to the ice-cream parlor next door to the Capitol Theatre, and the girl told us politely, even sadly, that they were all out of peach ice cream but the strawberry was fresh. We ordered the strawberry and then the girl came back, hesitated a second, smiled uncertainly and mumbled, "You Mr. Jimmy Walker?"

The former mayor of the City of New York brushed at his sharp thin Irish nose, smiled wanly and said: "There are people who still call me that," and he scrawled his name across the proferred napkin.

Several hours later in cracked, one-note voices that refused to blend, we "harmonized" his song, "Will You Love Me in December as You Do in May?"—sang it over the mikes—for this was my radio show. Those in the theatre where I conducted the broadcasts laughed unfeelingly, not caring, or perhaps unaware, that this beautiful nostalgic torcher had been written back in 1905 by the then young man who was hovering between two careers, songwriting and the law, and had been fitted with its contagious melody by none other than a beginner named Ernest R. Ball, who was later to compose such tender classics as "Mother Machree" and "When Irish Eyes Are Smiling."

Oh, yes, they laughed when we stood there and sang but I'm sure the years rolled back for Jimmy Walker as he remembered those earlier dreams of a songwriting career. But I just couldn't remember anything except that I had another guest to go on. We parted after the song as the still dapper, slim chap in the floppy Bangkok and the bluish shirt told me that he had to hurry off to kiss three youngsters good-night.

He was fulfilling Betty Compton's dying request that the two children she and Jimmy had adopted after their elopement should be brought up together with the child to whom she had given birth after her divorce from Walker and subsequent marriage to Ten Krappen. Both men saw to it that the wish was carried out—and because of these three babies, the two who had called the musical comedy star "wife" became close friends, and remained so until Jimmy Walker died on November 19, 1946.

Jimmy Walker's favorite haunt was the Central Park Casino, and it was among the restaurants frequented by Winchell, O. O. McIntyre, Hellinger, Sullivan and myself, for it rarely failed to yield copy for the columns. Here it was that Jimmy wooed Betty Compton. Here, too, a young pianist in Phil Reisman's orchestra won high favor among the Casino's elite patrons—Eddy Duchin, who later was to preside over its band and eventually wed one of its social young customers, beautiful Marjorie Oelrichs, who was to die shortly after the birth of their son, Peter Duchin, currently a society bandleader, himself.

Not the least of the attractions at the Casino was a young personable couple, graceful ballroom dancers, George and Julie Murphy. Who was to suspect that Murphy would eventually become a cinema star, branch into politics and finally land in the United States Senate?

Getting back to my beat, I also began to encounter the pathetic young girls I referred to as Creep Janes. Little girls with wistful eyes, with brazen eyes, with disillusioned eyes. They had barged in on New York to taste the sweets of Broadway. They lived two, three and even four in squalid little rooms in dinky hotels. Very few of them ever reached the dizzy pinnacle they sought, but they rarely gave up trying. Some remained on, ashamed to go back home. Others were luckier and became housewives, and still others took to the streets. I came to know so many of them, listened to their heartbreaking stories, and finally wrote a novel about them which was published under the title of *Six Lost Women*.

The theatre was at its glorious zenith. As an authorized drama critic, I had now become an official First Nighter. Still new to my exalted post, I was not so blasé that I didn't experience an anticipatory thrill every time the apron lights went on and the curtain rose on a Ziegfeld, George White, Earl Carroll, Shubert, Dillingham or Morris Gest musical extravaganza. Or for that matter a drama or comedy under the aegis of one of the distinguished producers of the era—David Belasco, for instance, or Gilbert Miller or Charles or Daniel Frohman.

Opening nights were a big show in themselves as Banker Otto Kahn would enter, flinging off his Inverness cape and doffing his high hat, or millionaire Jules Brulatour would follow his glamorous bride, Hope Hampton, down the aisle to their seats in Row A. Never missing were Ira and Rita Katzenberg, who even until recently remained habitual First Nighters, usually occupying front-row pews. O. O. McIntyre and his charming wife—O.O. always affecting that high stiff collar—Merchant Prince Hiram Bloomingdale, George Jean Nathan, Robert Benchley were others of the select group. And when on occasion some star, temporarily at liberty, was one of the First Nighters, what a buzz would go up! It might be Ethel or John Barrymore, Katharine Cornell or even a visitor from then booming Hollywood, Mary Pickford, Douglas Fairbanks or Gloria Swanson.

As to what I had to offer to the reading public in those first few months, here are a few samples:

> May 31, 1929: Broadway wept yesterday over Ed Gallagher who died in a sanitarium the other day. Enough tears were shed to fill every orange juice tank along the Incandescent Highway [please note, how we used to strive for nomenclature for Broadway] by the very people who had neglected and forgotten the former vaudeville star when he lay in his bed of pain spouting incoherencies. But yesterday Broadway remembered that Ed wasn't a bad fellow. And someone recalled that just before the "Gallagher and Shean" chants shoved him and his partner into the Big Money, Gallagher had once remarked: "I don't care where my bookings carry me when I quit this racket—I want my last appearance to be on Broadway." Ed "quit" the racket the other day. And he took his final bow yesterday as he always wanted to—right on Broadway in Campbell's Funeral Chapel.

> June 19, 1929: As a matter of fact, I didn't know until yesterday that David Belasco rarely attends public banquets or

dinners in private homes. The reason, it appears, is his passionate fondness for cold cuts, a dish rarely served at public functions or private dinners. His favorite libation is benedictine but he does take a glass of beer occasionally. Everyone knows, I suppose, that he has what is probably the finest collection of Napoleonic relics in this country, including what he claims to be a genuine lock of the Corsican's hair. Morris Gest is said to have remarked on one occasion that he knew several people who possess one or two Napoleonic hairs which inspired Belasco to retort: "If all Napoleon's hair owned by collectors were heaped together, you and I and the Shuberts would have the finest hair mattress in the world."

July 8, 1930: It was a merry shindig the New York Athletic Club tossed for Admiral Byrd last week and a good time was had by all, including invited celebrities who indulged in soup as we used to observe back in our cub reporter days. Among the principal speakers was Al Smith. He remarked: "Admiral Byrd and I have much in common. He started out for the South Pole about the time I started toward the White House. The only difference is that I returned two years sooner."

On October 22, 1929, I inaugurated a new weekly column purporting to cover the scene—"Snapshots at Random" was the label, and in this department I let loose with God-awful descriptives. Samples: "Brooklyn Bridge at 5 a.m.—a dinosaur skeleton in a veil of mist . . . the Woolworth Building, argus-eyed, rearing its gaunt neck at us . . . Lower Broadway at noon: alive, boisterous as a Dodger fan . . . the cemetery surrounding Trinity Church—quiet haven for the ancient dead—and the modern lunch eater."

I became a pub crawler because I learned folks ease up over a tumbler of Scotch or gin. A fellow will spill out his love for some unattainable girl or reveal how he forged a check when he was an adolescent (a chap who became a dominant Hollywood producer once made this confession to me as we sat in "21"). He will even divulge what he was supposed to keep secret, some maneuver that was to send a certain stock skyrocketing.

It was in saloons that I met for the first time statesmen, cinema beauties, generals, mobsters, society queens, chorus girls —even a future President of the United States. That was Harry S. Truman, then Vice-President, who was in Toots Shor's when I was introduced to him and who probably had a better time that night than he had after donning the Presidential toga. If I had had any idea that he was to step up shortly to the White House throne, I might have lured a paragraph or two out of him that very night that might have made history. Who can tell? As it was I merely said mildly: "I hear, sir, you're going to the fight tonight," and his momentous reply was, "Yes, I am. Looking forward to it."

It was at the Stork Club that I had my first meeting with J. Edgar Hoover and his aide Clyde Tolson that led to a firm friendship. In "21," I first met the then young Henry Ford, and all three of the Roosevelt boys, Elliott, Franklin, Jr., and John—and in the old Hollywood restaurant, I sat down and conversed with a slightly cracked gent with a cowlick riding his narrow forehead—fellow named Talmadge, then Governor of Georgia.

One night at a party in Lüchow's, that nostalgia-steeped eating place once the favorite rendezvous of Diamond Jim Brady and Lillian Russell, of Enrico Caruso and Victor Herbert and of notables from all parts of the world these nights, I sat with Al Steele, then bossman of Pepsi-Cola and his attractive wife, Lillian. Someone lured Lillian onto the dance floor, and Al and I were alone at the table. Suddenly, he inquired, "Do you know Joan Crawford?"

"Know her?" I said, "I knew her when she was a fat dancing kid who called herself Lucille LeSueur—had it changed from her real name, Billie Cassin. In fact, I broke the first announcement of the split-up of her marriage with Doug Fairbanks, Jr., and of her elopement with Franchot Tone. Once, at a party in Hollywood at Otto Preminger's home, I listened to her sound off bitterly about the smash-up of her romance with Greg Bautzer. Know her?—Say, I was practically brought up with her."

"What do you think of her?" Steele wanted to know.

"A swell egg," I said. "She's real glamor—the way movie stars ought to be. But, brother, I wouldn't want to be her husband. She's too much an individualist and she'd want to be boss."

A week later, Lillian Steele called me to tell me she was off to Mexico for a divorce. Shortly after, came the flash that Steele and Joan Crawford had become Mr. and Mrs. I encountered the newlyweds some time later at a little hoedown in Paris hosted by Earl Blackwell. Around 1:00 A.M., Steele suddenly got up and said to Joan, "Honey, it's late. Let's go."

Did the girl I had accused of being bossy freeze him with an icy stare. Did she snap: "I want to stay"? Not on your life. Meekly, she rose. Sweetly she purred, "Of course, darling," and off they went.

And, as far as I know personally, until Steele's death, Joan and the soft-drink executive continued to be happily married.

I had never flown but I came close to settling the deal for my first airplane ride while sharing a snack with a gentleman I had met through the courtesy of publicist Steve Hannagan in Dinty Moore's—Captain Eddie Rickenbacker. And later that night, when he accompanied me to the Hollywood restaurant, I managed to wrest a story from him that had never been told: It was suspected when we first entered World War I that his sympathies were with the Kaiser's Germany.

And it was in Jack Dempsey's restaurant then on Eighth Avenue that I had the first opportunity to have a chat with a taciturn citizen, Charles A. Lindbergh. If I recall, my rather banal question at one point was: "What was your greatest thrill during that flight over the ocean?" And his reply: "I was too busy to notice any thrill—and too tired, too."

One night, I settled down for a drink (this was again at Dinty Moore's) with Colonel Charles (Chuck) Wayne Kerwood, a World War I hero who had served with that colorful flying ace, Raoul Lufberry, in the Lafayette Escadrille. As we sat chatting, Kerwood suddenly interrupted to point to a familiar figure at a distant table.

I've got to tell you a story about him and another fellow," he said. "It might be good for your column. A buddy and I were in Paris, real beat. Our leave was coming to an end and there didn't seem to be a hotel room available. We pleaded with the hotel clerk at one of the hotels—I can't even remember which one —slipped him some francs and finally he told us if we cared to take a chance there was a suite we might be able to use because the chaps who had it were away. Of course, if they came back unexpectedly, we were told, we'd have to vamoose.

"Well, we just plopped into the beds and were snoring away in no time. Around three in the morning, two guys came into the bedroom, pulled at the blankets and roared for us to get out. This was their suite. I barked at them and told them to screw—we needed the sleep.

"Those two fellows just looked us over and without another word, believe me, left. When we got up in the morning, there was a note reading: 'Chums, this room is ours, bought and paid for. The least you can do is have a drink with us this afternoon at the Continental bar and we'll fight it out.'

"We kept the appointment and met the guys we had dispossessed. That"— and Kerwood pointed again over to Floyd Gibbons whose presence in the restaurant had inspired the memory, "was one of them. The other was Ring Lardner. So Louie, I've got to go over now and buy Gibbons a drink."

Public enemies, songwriters, authors, politicians—it was chiefly in the restaurants or night spots that I first came to know them. My initial meeting with Irving Berlin was at Lindy's. Big lumbering Primo Carnera—one of the more vivid recollections I have of him is when he got up on the tiny floor of the old Silver Slipper to dance with a diminutive Dresden doll, and to my amazement, he guided her around with skill and delicacy and grace. It was a wonder to me how that huge fellow could drag those colossal feet of his around with less effort than he used to display on the canvas of the roped arena.

It was at the Stork Club that I sat at the next table to a distinguished financier and the girl he was wooing, to the dismay of his equally prominent society wife. I heard the girl whisper hoarsely: "You'll tell her tomorrow, or I swear I'm going to come over and kill you and myself, too." I shuddered and for the next few days watched the front pages, but no report of the shooting appeared. The next time I encountered the man, he was with his own wife. As for the girl, she took up with a bandleader and later married him.

There, too, is the memory of the beautiful, ill-fated Jean Harlow—her platinum hair tumbling to her bare shoulders, dancing madly in Johnny Carey's Breakfast Club with a ne'er-do-well, and then there was the night when Actor Richard Bennett, rising in Texas Guinan's famous place of gaity, recited—as on another occasion in the past century in another spot, Edgar Allan Poe did —the Lord's Prayer and then was led away.

I recall the night I sat with George Jean Nathan and Orson Welles in "21" and film producer Alexander Korda entered. I hailed him and asked him to sit with us. "You and George Jean Nathan and Orson Welles know each other, of course," I said. Korda smiled. "I have never met Mr. Nathan personally," he said, "it's a pleasure," and stuck out his hand. Nathan stared at him icily and barked: "It is no pleasure to know you. I have never had any high regard for you or your pictures. In fact, I have no high regard for any pictures." Korda blanched visibly, then snapped: "You are a boorish man." Welles chuckled all through the little incident, and I personally felt deep embarrassment.

Some six months before his assassination, I sat in a group with Huey Long at the Park Avenue Club which had been taken over by Joe Zelli. What I recall chiefly is that Long said if he were elected President, he would increase the Cabinet so that every minority in America would have a representative in the seat of government. I asked Long, so definitely totalitarian and segregationist in his ideology, did that mean Negroes, too? And he replied, "Why, of course," and went on to explain that he would separate the country, if he had his way, into racial groups and have Congressmen and Senators proportioned from these groups instead of from States. It was only then I realized the Louisiana Governor was not quite the benign statesman after all.

And it was at the Park Avenue Club, too, that I had an enjoyable and rewarding conversation with a gentleman linked to a Broadway I had been too young to know—a ruddy-cheeked, white-haired citizen, George Rector, who enthralled me as he recalled the heyday of famed Rector's. "I was the first," he insisted, "to bring dancing into a night spot. I offered the Castles, Irene and Vernon, $200 a week for one week and hired Rudolph Valentino on as a dancing man. His job was to dance with lady patrons for a couple of hours each night. Then after each dance, he'd come over to get his slip okayed—for two dollars! That's right—two dollars. Back in 1904 Lillian Russell sang 'Come Down My Evening Star' at our place. So you see, we really started the modern nightclub.

"And the characters that used to drift in, like Death Valley Scott and Coal Oil Johnny. What high spenders! We had a poker game in the place after hours with Johnny "Bet-a-Million" Gates, Johnny Drake and Alphonse Hudson among the players. Hudson was Gates's personal broker and he dropped $74,000 in a single hour's play. I felt real sorry for him, but he said: 'Don't worry about me, George. I'll make it up tomorrow on Gates in commissions.' And the bettors? Davey Johnson, the gambler, wanted to make an election bet. He came into Rector's and told me he had $98,000 in cash and would I lend him $2,000 to make it an even $100,000. Well, he lost. And when I phoned to find out how he was feeling, I was told Davey was napping. How about that? After losing $100,000.

"The showmen that used to come into our place—Flo Ziegfeld, Dillingham, Erlanger. Where have you showmen like that today?

Flo once told me how he approached Erlanger for a bigger cut in the Follies because he was doing all the hard work, picking the principals, costumes, scenery and conducting the long rehearsals. 'My percentage,' he said to Erlanger, 'is all out of proportion to the earnings of the show. You're a rich man and you can afford to make my bit larger. Why, you're worth $40,000,000 if you're worth a nickel.' Erlanger, according to Ziggy snapped: 'Stop right there—I am worth $60,000,000 and a flock of nickels besides."

Shortly after World War II had ended, while I was dining in "21," Jack Kriendler asked me to accompany him to the bar. He wanted me to meet an interesting person. He introduced a tall, handsome chap, Captain Jim Lewis, still in uniform, and I engaged him in a casual conversation which the young officer suddenly interrupted. "You're wearing a suit with a pencil stripe,"

All the skinny lad at the top of the picture fretted about in those earlier days was whether he'd ever make the full grade in movies. Politics to him, then, was just a word in the dictionary. Ronald Reagan has his arms about Jane Wyman (then his wife), and Susan Hayward. *Below, left to right,* are Louella Parsons, the late William A. Curley (editor of *Journal-American*), humorist Arthur "Bugs" Baer, and the debonair author caught posing with one of his three unphotogenic sides. And that's Arleen Whelan gazing down affectionately at Bugs Baer.

he remarked, apropos of nothing. I was puzzled but resumed the conversation. A few seconds later Lewis said, "You're wearing a bow tie." I began to feel uneasy—and annoyed. It seemed the Captain was chaffing me. I sensed what I thought was a sneer and belligerency. I started to walk away but he grabbed me by an arm and snapped: "You're wearing a white handkerchief in your coat pocket." This time I broke loose and walked back to my table. Kriendler came over. "That's a wonderful boy—real guts, don't you think?" he asked.

"Why did you get me into it, and what do you mean, guts?" I stormed. "He's either had too much to drink or he's a menace in your place."

Jack said: "I guess you didn't catch on. He's 90 percent blind. It's only a matter of weeks—maybe a couple of months at most—and his sight'll be all gone. That's why he keeps testing himself—to find out how much he can still see."

In Whyte's restaurant on West Fifty-seventh Street, a plaque over one of the tables proclaims proudly: PRESIDENTIAL TABLE USED BY HARRY S. TRUMAN. And it is true, the former President had a meal at this table in January of 1964 while he was in town in connection with a TV documentary over CBS. When he returned for the dedication of the Singer Bowl at the World's Fair in April, he dined again at Whyte's and was assigned the same table. On this occasion, chatting with the general manager of the restaurant, George Macris, he chuckled as he recounted a little incident earlier in the day. "Don't I know you from somewhere?" he had remarked to the citizen standing next to him—and stuck out his hand to Thomas E. Dewey, his opponent in the memorable election of 1948!

Speaking of plaques, there are several of them at "21" over tables where favorite patrons sat—patrons who have now passed on. One is over the corner table that was always occupied by George Jean Nathan and another which Robert Benchley preferred—and indeed he was at this table when he was stricken by the attack which ended in his death. Former man-about-town William Seeman and film attorney Wilbur McKay are others who have these plaques placed in their memory.

And in the Plaza's Oak Room, there is one designating where George M. Cohan usually sat.

Veteran film producer Samuel Goldwyn was flirting with a

soft drink when I settled down with him at the Stork Club one night. As the conversation progressed, we came to the subject of his alleged hilarious malaprops. He said: "I try hard sometimes when I think of it to talk the way the boys who want to write funny pieces like to have me talk. I remember when this fellow Alva Johnston came to me and said he was going to write about me in the *Saturday Evening Post*. I said to him, 'Okay, but I would appreciate seeing the copy before you send it in.'"

" 'Why certainly, Mr. Goldwyn,' " he said. " 'That's your privilege.' Then I heard nothing more about it until I picked up the first installment in the *Post*, and I don't mind telling you I saw red. So I called up my lawyer, Max Steuer, long-distance in New York and said: 'Max read that stupid article and then tell me what I ought to do about it right away. It's awful.'

"A week passed and no word from Steuer. Then one day, by special-delivery airmail, I got a letter from him—four solid typewritten pages and when you added it all up, Steuer said he thought it was a good piece and he couldn't see why I should object.

"The fifth page had only a little writing on it. It was Steuer's bill—$750 for professional services—$750 he charged me to tell me it was a good piece and I should be satisfied.

"That's when I maybe should have said something funny like what Johnston credited me."

Another night back in 1940 at "21," I sat with surrealist Salvador Dali, composer Vernon Duke and choreographer George Balanchine. Dali at that time affected a pencil-line moustache in contrast with the more extensive handlebars of later years. He spoke rapidly in French, emphasizing with eloquent gestures. Composer Duke, translating, explained apologetically in slightly Russian-accented words, "He speaks not even one word of English—yes, Dal-ee?" and Dali shook his head in negative confirmation.

What Dali was telling us was that, despite the newspaper stories, he had not undergone a single day of prison confinement when he returned to Spain. Although he had publicly denounced Franco and the Falangists and had fully expected to meet either death or imprisonment upon his return, to his surprise he had been accorded gentle, even cordial treatment.

"Almost like a hero," he said. "I couldn't understand it but Franco, himself—all of them, were very nice to me."

Dali confessed he was still puzzled but that nevertheless he would like to remain in the United States for good. And as a matter of fact, the artist has spent most of his time here since.

For Britons on the night of February 25, 1959, memories came back as the emotion-charged thinnish voice of the man who once was their monarch sounded out over the British Broadcasting network. They heard again—and some undoubtedly heard for the first time—the poignant abdication speech which the radio stations had carried slightly over twenty-two years previously, the explanation by King Edward VIII of why he was giving up the throne for the sake of love—love for Mrs. Wallis Warfield Simpson who was to be his wife.

Even while the radio re-creation of those seven historic minutes was coming through the home sets, abroad and relayed to the United States, the Duke of Windsor was at supper in the softly

The one-time monarch who decided the crown wasn't worth wearing if he couldn't be with the woman he loved. The Duke and Duchess of Windsor entering the Savoy Theatre in Nassau, March 22, 1941, for the world premiere of George Bernard Shaw's *Major Barbara,* produced and directed by Gabriel Pascal, who is to be seen peering over the Duchess' right shoulder.

lighted El Morocco with his wife, surrounded by a few intimates. And I was at an adjoining table studying him closely and wondering what might be passing through his mind.

He was in a dinner suit, and the woman for whom he had given up an empire wore a simple black dress and seemed the most animated person in the party. Among those at the table were playwright Noël Coward, veteran producer Gilbert Miller and his wife, the Prince and Princess Dmitri of Russia and several others. For the most part, the Duke seemed pensive—almost as if he had bridged the present to the past. That, of course, may have been my imagination, just as if it may have been my fancy that he might be whispering to himself the words that were coming over the air those very few moments—"I have found it impossible to carry the heavy burden of responsibility and to discharge my duties as King, the way I would wish to do, without the help and support of the woman I love. . . ."

At midnight, the Duke suddenly rose, kissed his Duchess. She murmured, "Take care of yourself"—and he bade quiet adieus to others in the party and left.

The Duchess remained on, rising shortly after, not to go home, but to dance with Noël Coward.

And I just happened to be in El Morocco the evening when Peggy Hopkins Joyce, nettled by publicity proclaiming Mabel Boll as the "most jeweled woman in America," arrived looking like a display case playing hooky from Tiffany's or Cartier's. Peggy danced a few steps on the crowded floor, then dragged her escort to a point near the banquette where Mabel was seated. Here she halted and then casually began stripping off her gems—necklaces, bracelets, rings and a diamond brooch the size of a cauliflower.

One by one she handed them to her bewildered and embarrassed escort. Now, denuded of her gems, Peggy patted the back of her blond coiffure and then calmly leaned over as if to chat with Mabel—and, as if by accident, tipped over a glass of wine, drenching her rival's lap.

"Darling" chirped Peggy, sweetly, but loud enough to be heard above the band's music, "I hear you had such a horrible time with your last face-lift."

It was in El Morocco, too, in September of 1949 when Humphrey Bogart and canned foods tycoon Billy Seeman came in, escorting a couple of stuffed pandas—and I watched as a furious melee took place when pretty model-actress Robin Harris and banker's daughter Peggy Rabe snatched the toys but before they could walk off with them, Bogart shoved the girls, and Robin went down on the floor. Johnny Jelke who was to figure later in unsavory headlines, came to their rescue, and a donnybrook ensued in which fists flew, plates were thrown, and the usually imperturbable John Perona showed signs of annoyance (although most of us thought it was a great show) and had Bogart and Seeman tossed out of the place.

It made a beautiful Page One story.

Come to think of it, none of us suspected some years ago that though they were seated on opposite sides of the zebra-striped room, there might already have been brewing the ingredients for a rather confused romantic plot. The Greek shipping tycoon Aristotle Onassis, short, somber-looking—almost, in his dark-tinted glasses, like a character out of an E. Phillips Oppenheim novel or even one of those James Bond thrillers, sat with his attractive wife, Tina, herself an heiress to shipping millions. And across the room in a gay party of five, the volatile, temperamental operatic star Maria Callas and her husband. Of course, it was far from the soft lights and chattering tumult of El Morocco that the story developed and the world began following the explosive courtship of the Greek millionaire and the Brooklyn-bred diva.

John Perona, who founded El Morocco after his successful Prohibition days venture, the Bath Club, did not live long enough to enjoy the fruition of his big dream—a larger, more elaborate El Morocco in his own building a few blocks east on Fifty-fourth Street. After his death, his son Edwin was to operate the plush haunt, but Edwin never cared for the business, and big, Polish-born John Mills, already famed as the host of the exclusive Les Ambassadeurs in London, took over. But even Mills could not make a go of the place—the elite remained away—and finally the current owner, Maurice Uchitel, a millionaire manufacturer and realty developer, came into possession.

It was rugged going for him, too, but gradually El Morocco regained its allure, and it is once again the glittering rendezvous where your table neighbors may be Onassis and Mme Callas, the Duke and Duchess of Windsor, South American multimillionaires, visiting film notables or international figures.

The Jet Set assembles at El Morocco—the original El Morocco, not the new plush haunt farther down the street where Maurice Uchitel is the current host-owner. The late John Perona, sauve founder of the supper club when this picture was taken in the fifties, is to be spotted smiling out at us—third from the left, seated against the zebra-striped banquette, and next to him is surrealist artist Salvador Dali of the impressive mustachios with Joyce Mathews (before her marriage to Billy Rose) rewarding him with her smile. The first patron on the left, in semi-profile, is one-time Argentinian millionaire playboy, Macoco (Martin Alzaga) once married to musical comedy star Kathryn Ray and then to Kay Williams, who later was to become Mrs. Clark Gable.
Dominant in front is ex-teen-age columnist Betty Betz, now the wife of multimillionaire Frank McMahon. She is one of the most publicized hostesses among the Palm Beach set. The other smiling lad on the banquette is society chronicler and photographer Jerome Zerbe, and facing him, with only nose, forehead and part of an ear exposed, is the late Broadway columnist Danton Walker.

It was in a restaurant, Billy LaHiff's Tavern, that an important event in my life took place. Jack Lait, then a top executive with King Features Syndicate (later he was to become editor of the *Mirror* and co-author with Lee Mortimer of the series of best-selling *Confidential* books) had invited me to lunch with him. Frankly, it wasn't my congenial companionship he sought. He had been authorized to sound me out on my willingness to bring my column over from the *Graphic* to the *New York Evening Journal.* This was a follow-up on a bid made a few days previously by William A. Curley, editor of the *Journal.* Lait suggested that perhaps if I looked over an attractive contract that had been drawn up, which he now wanted me to study, the matter might be settled there and then. It was. On the following day, I submitted my resignation to the *Graphic*—and two weeks later, on June 1, 1931, I became a member of the Hearst newspaper family.

My pub-crawling wasn't confined solely to Manhattan. I took to traveling, in quest of column fodder, whether in Hollywood or Paris, Miami Beach or Rio de Janeiro, Chicago, Madrid, New Orleans or Rome, Acapulco or London. And in some cafe or restaurant, I was fortunate enough to find a newsworthy person. He might be one of the movie or stage stars or a political figure, or some outstanding female star or literary luminary.

It didn't matter where—but in a cafe or restaurant, anywhere in the world, people, I discovered, were the same—more self-revealing, willing and even eager to talk. So I offer no apologies for having spent so many of my lunch hours and evenings in the saloons and eating places in what I considered diligent research for columnar paragraphs.

In brief, I was privileged to be where the action was, to be on the scene and part of it—on the longest street, for Broadway stretches not only from border to border of Manhattan but across the nation and to points abroad—wherever show business in all its forms prevails and performers gather. Indeed, the longest street reaches into Rome and Madrid, London and Paris, Africa—even to Vietnam.

3

"The Flaming Witch"

PAUL YAWITZ, WHO FOR A TIME was a Broadway columnist for the *Daily Mirror* before deserting Manhattan's razzmatazz to join the Hollywood gold rush, occasionally contributed to my department. Once in a disillusioned mood he burst forth with an explosive effusion in which he insisted that Greenwich Village was "a flaming witch who rides high on the wings of promise and brushes blinding siroccos into the eyes of those who would put faith in her."

The Sobols lived in the Village for a couple of decades, and I cannot in all honesty say that we ever encountered the delicious wickedness the section was reputed to have in those days. I went ferreting about here and there, in the nooks and crannies, highways and byways of Christopher Street and Sheridan Square, of Macdougal Alley and Sullivan Street, West Eighth and West Tenth, and never that I can recall had an experience with the "flaming witch" or was blinded by a "sirocco."

I did meet some eccentric and even brilliant personalities, and many of them, true enough, figured as protagonists in bizarre escapades which perhaps brushed the Village in dripping hues of crimson, but it was my ill luck—or good—never to be on the scene when newsworthy trouble erupted.

I don't dismiss the folks I came to know with a shrug and a sneer. They were a colorful lot—from the turbulent poet and novelist Maxwell Bodenheim, who was to meet such a sorry and tragic end, and the belligerent iconoclast Harry ("Tramp Poet") Kemp to the forthright Max Eastman and the moody Eugene O'Neill. There were those philanthropic Strunskys, the philosophic hedonist and saloonkeeper Barney Gallant—yes, Noël Coward, too.

There was a time when I sublet an apartment which had been the home of Edna St. Vincent Millay, and not far from where I dwelt on Christopher Street, Edgar Allan Poe in the long ago had written some of his memorable stories and poems.

Night life boiled in colorful little places like Romany Marie's, a favorite hangout then of historian Will Durant; in Barney Gallant's, where Walter O'Keefe used to chant his lugubrious lament over the man on the flying trapeze; Meyer Horowitz's Village Grove Nut Club where Joe E. Lewis was to be a frequent attraction, and a sawed-off little clown named Lou Dolgoff shouted out his little jokes; Jimmy Kelly's, where shapely lasses titillated the gatherings with what would be considered mild stripping in these *avant-garde* days, and where your table neighbor might be a well-known politician or a formidable mob leader.

It was in Barney Gallant's place on West Third Street that Mark Hellinger beguiled me into my first taste of brandy and kept me indulging as he proposed toasts to my wife, to my daughter, to my mother and father, to my future, etc.—with temporarily disastrous results.

We wandered through quaint Patchin Place, recalling with some awe that among residents of the past had been John Masefield, later to become Poet Laureate of England, Theodore Dreiser, actor Dudley Digges and even, for a brief spell, Eugene O'Neill who it was said had written most of *Emperor Jones* here.

There, too, was Macdougal Alley—something out of a picture book of ancient Britain—a narrow lane flanked by tiny houses, a lane from which emanated such an air of serenity and aloofness from the city's hubbub that we used to invade it for the surcease it seemed to offer.

It was fascinating and exciting, but I never found it wicked in the Village though pretty girls went roaming about wearing dungarees and corduroy pants, and some of the boys neglected to go to the barber. Often I dropped into Benito Collada's El Chico, one of the more authentic Spanish eating places of the era, and I recall how enthralled with the place were two gentlemen I brought in one night—FBI Chief J. Edgar Hoover and his aide, Clyde Tolson.

I kept on the quest for studio bacchanalias and cellar orgies but never was present at any of the saturnalias—if they ever did take place.

Oh, yes, there was a shooting or a suicide or two—usually run-of-the-mill stuff, with the exception of the Maxwell Bodenheim slaying and Harold Sullivan murder.

Sullivan operated a little night-spot, Sully's Showboat, where a happy-go-lucky atmosphere prevailed. I turned out for the opening night, and among those who were also present for the festivities were Christopher Morley, playwright Samson Raphaelson, designer Cleon Throckmorton, Norman Bel Geddes, Texas Guinan, Peggy Joyce and Mark Hellinger. The Village was shocked when one day there came the news that Sullivan (he was a brother-in-law of novelist Thorne Smith) had been shot to death in the hallway of an apartment house.

The Hammers, Victor and Armand, had luxurious digs on West Fourth Street, and hosted lively parties for guests from all walks of life—literary biggies, theatrical stars, political emirs. They were to emerge as operators of one of the great art galleries in New York, and Armand went on to become a multimillionaire financier, head of Occidental Petroleum which rose from a low of one dollar when it was listed on the stock market, to far above a hundred dollars as this was being written, and made millionaires of many who kept the faith. (At one time, I am unhappy to report, I possessed 2,000 shares of Occidental, having paid two dollars per share. When it dropped to $1.50, I sold out. It still makes a melancholy conversation-piece for me.)

For a change of pace, we would dine occasionally in the plush restaurants of the historic Brevoort and the staid Lafayette hotels. Both gone now, high-rise apartment houses having been built on their sites.

It was in January of 1952 that the wreckers began the execution of the Brevoort, the colorful old veteran which had withstood the blasts and scorch of 106 winters and summers before its doom.

It had watched the neighborhood change from an uptown seat of Manhattan's aristocracy to the gin-lit but exciting Bohemian center of the twenties, and something of a renaissance that gave the section a new lift in the late forties. But all through the transition periods, the Brevoort remained as a proud exemplar of gracious living.

Back in 1942, the little hotel did try an excursion into modernity with a gay cafe and merry supper club, frankly endeavoring to lure the tourists as well as the sophisticates. I remember dropping in to catch the Amazonian comedianne Hope Emerson, later to become a featured actress in the films. She sang a sad little ballad, I recall, addressed to Dorothy Dix—about trying to snare a man.

Decades before that, the owner of the hotel, Albert Clark, used no such bait. He enticed customers by bribing ship officers to warn wealthy travelers, new to these shores, that they must stop at the Brevoort because beyond Fourteenth Street was a wilderness infested with scalp-seeking Indians.

In the early days of the hotel's existence, Washington Irving, then in his final days, was a regular patron, stopping in usually after a visit to his pal James Fenwick at No. 21 Fifth Avenue. Mark Twain moved into the Fenwick house in 1904 and usually took his occasional house guest, Robert Louis Stevenson, to dinner at the Brevoort. That conservative ice-queen of American letters, Edith Wharton, often graced the dining room with her frigid and aloofish presence. Later, novelist Henry James, before exiling himself to England, strolling on pleasant evenings from the family home on the Square would drop in for an aperitif. William Dean Howells, Brander Matthews, F. Hopkinson Smith and Ellen Glasgow were consistent patrons.

Dinner at the Brevoort in those calmer years of the late nineteenth and early twentieth centuries would assemble notables from all countries. Presidents Garfield and Arthur were diners whenever they visited New York. So were Theodore Roosevelt and William Howard Taft. The Duke of Marlborough, Winston Churchill's ancestor, was just another customer to the elderly waiters who could remember dowdy Queen Emma of the Sandwich Islands, who moved her entire regal entourage into the hotel.

When King Edward was Prince of Wales, it was at the Brevoort he preferred to dine on the occasion of his visit to Manhattan and another Britisher had a similar preference—the Marquis of Queensbury. Poetess Edna St. Vincent Millay, red-haired tempest who swept out of a sterile New England town into the high-dome literary set of the Village, wrote her lyrics at first in a Rivington Street attic and then spent the meager royalties at Cafe Brevoort. Dancer Isadora Duncan of the flowing veils and barefoot bacchanals bowed to respectability and even put on shoes long enough to enjoy one of the Brevoort's renowned bouillabaisses.

Occasionally I would drop into the Pepper Pot where a handsome lunch was available for sixty cents. In a neighboring building, so the legend went, a gangling girl from the ranch country of Iowa, much too pretty for her drab surroundings, occupied a little furnished room, and often her voice sounded out in sweet song. Two dollars a week was her rent for that room. She was destined to go on to world fame in later years, for her name was Lillian Russell.

Then there was Lee Chumley's rendezvous on Bedford Street. Tall, picturesque, white-haired Lee was my pal, and on several occasions I spent holidays at his ranch up Stony Creek way in the Adirondacks, where at twilight a lake of mist hovered over the marshlands, and at full night the powdered velvet skies hung low, and at dawn deer dipped their beautiful heads into the waters that caressed the back porch of the ranch house.

Chumley's restaurant was as unique as its adventurous founder. Instead of pictures of celebrities, the walls were decorated with the jackets of books authored by patrons. Here I would run into Floyd Dell, John Dos Passos, Theodore Dreiser and heavy-set, silvery-haired Gil Patten who, under the nom de plume of Burt L. Standish, had turned out those precious Frank and Dick Merriwell stories, to say nothing of countless other nickel and dime novels.

On one occasion, the moody young illustrator Hans Stengel was urged by Chumley to come to a special party he was planning for the following night. Stengel sent him a brief note of apology. "I can't come—much as I'd like to for your sake. I'm going away."

Even as Lee was reading the note, Stengel was dead—a suicide hanging from the top of a bathroom door with neck noosed by a belt.

Once, Chumley brought a sharp-looking chap over to my table and introduced him as Walter Liggett. Liggett at the time was writing a series of denunciatory magazine articles which were disturbing Washington. "I am more concerned with the gangsters who run our country," he said, that night, "than with the small-fry thugs you and Winchell and Hellinger write about. I think you're a spineless bunch or you'd do something about the Washington official hoodlums. I wish I had your column for just about a month."

Several years later, Liggett was killed by political mobsters in Minneapolis because he had not been afraid to have his say in print.

Harry Kemp, Dawn Powell, Samuel Ortiz, author of *Haunch, Paunch and Jowl,* and cartoonist Milt Gross were others who frequented the place as were songwriter Harry Woods and chess champion Ed Lasker.

Almost nightly, two newspapermen would huddle at a corner table, always in what seemed earnest conversation. They were Heywood Broun and Carl Randau, and out of their discussions emerged the plans for organizing the Newspaper Guild.

I used to notice on one of the walls a peculiar book-jacket standing out prominently among the hundreds of covers on display. It was a hand-drawn affair lettered: *The Unknown Book by the Unknown Author.* I asked Chumley to explain. He grinned. "Most of the people who come in here," he said, "ask me to reserve a space for their books when they're published. The months go by—and the years—and they never write the first chapter. So that cover represents the books that were never written."

I keep remembering Big Lee, his red or blue shirt open at the collar, his corduroy pants, baggy at the knees, moving from table to table to mix in with the chatter about current plays, books, poems and characters.

One early morning, after the final guest had departed, Lee Chumley put out the lights, latched the doors and went upstairs to his tiny apartment. He never awakened.

Back in the early thirties, I used to pass an unlovely boxlike structure on West Third Street and labeled it the House of Frustration when I came to learn its history. Its landlord was Albert Strunsky, an eccentric but philanthropic gentleman. In the drab little building had lodged at one time or other many who had aspired for a foothold in the literary or art world—and had encountered only defeat. The building had become to them a symbol of despair, especially since they knew some previous occupants had achieved recognition: Eugene O'Neill, for instance; Maxwell Bodenheim (even though toward the end his was a sullied reputation) ; poet Eli Siegel and others.

The young and ambitious hopefuls had tumbled into the Village, fresh perhaps, from minor local triumphs in literary or art circles of Decatur or Nogales, of Jacksonville or Waterbury, convinced that Manhattan and especially the Village was God's personally supervised Paradise for struggling artists and writers. Sooner or later, when their meager hoards dwindled, they came to the House of Frustration, where they could rent a room for as low as two dollars a week. There was no elevator—there were only communal bathrooms on each floor and one telephone, a coin phone on the second floor. They froze in the winter's chill, sweltered in the summer's heat but gradually their hopes vanished. They vacated the cheap little rooms and other hopefuls succeeded them.

I think one of the affairs I miss most was the annual Greenwich Village Ball, of which Cynthia White was the founder and moving spirit. Usually it was conducted on New Year's Eve in Webster Hall. Here, mingling with gents in armor, pretty girls in leotards, lads in clown suits and lasses in ballet skirts, would be more sedate intruders. One night my guests were Marie Harriman, later to become New York State's First Lady, and my literary agent, the late Mark Hanna, and among the familiar faces we spotted those of Douglas Fairbanks, Jr., Theodore Dreiser, Dorothy Parker, Margaret Bourke-White, James Montgomery Flagg, Russell Patterson, Otto Soglow—about a dozen others who seemed to be enticing as much fun out of watching the revelry as we did.

Occasionally at Romany Marie's, I would run into a beautiful young Russian girl, Tamara Dreisen, who sang delightfully and who showed promise of becoming someone in show business. I still recall one conversation with her during which she gazed at me out of her dark brown soulful eyes and commented in melancholy tones: "I don't understand some of the men I meet—they care for nothing more important than fun. You ask them a simple question: 'What is life?' and can they answer?"

Ill-fated Tamara was later to star in Jerome Kern's *Roberta* in which she introduced that poignant little ballad, "Smoke Gets in Your Eyes." She was to be one of the victims of the fatal plane crash off Lisbon during World War II days, the disaster in which other performers lost their lives, and which left Jane Froman and Gypsy Markoff crippled for years.

A favorite gathering place was Mori's, operated by Ma Mori

and her sons Edmund and Albert. Situated in drab Bleecker Street, it was like a sapphire in a rusty tin brooch. The dismal exterior afforded no hint to the opulence, vastness and warmth of the bustling interior and its oftimes elegant patrons of the upper stratum. One night, in the late thirties, sitting around in "21" with film producers Darryl Zanuck and Hal Wallis and caricaturist Irving Hoffman, someone suggested that for a nightcap we journey into the Village. I offered to be the cicerone, and I promised that Mori's was just the place. So we taxied down—only to find a little sign on the door announcing that Mori's had folded two nights previously.

It was at El Chico that Host Benito Collada introduced me to a handsome young man, the Count of Covadonga, who also bore the title of the Prince of Asturias. Later, Collada briefed me. This was the eldest son of ex-King Alfonso of Spain—Crown Prince and heir to the throne—a claim he had abandoned. The royal young man had inherited the curse of the Hapsburgs, the dread blood disease, hemophilia, and had to undergo blood transfusions constantly. "One cut—and poof—he can be dead," Collada explained gloomily.

As the months passed, the Count and I became friendly. I admired his pluck as he kidded about his ailment, remarking: "You see why I'm out for a good time. It always may be my last."

One night in El Morocco, Macoco, a well known playboy from Argentina, showed up with a slight nick on his chin, and settled down with the Count and his fiancée, actress Marta Rocafort (they were married shortly after). Pointing to the cut, he said: "The razor slipped."

Covadonga murmured: "With me that one little cut would be the finger of death."

Divorced later from Marta, he was driving in Miami Beach on September 6, 1938, with a pretty nightclub cigarette girl when the car crashed. Covadonga's injuries were comparatively slight, merely some lacerations but the physicians were helpless in view of his ailment and he was dead within a few hours.

One of the characters I often encountered as I would walk to or from my home on Christopher Street in the early postmidnight hours, sometimes in front of Nick's at Tenth Street and Seventh Avenue, sometimes near the Vanguard, occasionally near Delaney's, was a shriveled little old woman. She never seemed to mind how drunk a person was or how shabby the clothes or how elegant. Her approach was always the same. A quick smile, a plaintive query: "Wouldn't you like to buy my poems, mister?" I was told she wrote as many as a dozen a day and sold them at night, preferring to get ten cents or a quarter, or sometimes even a dollar in cash than a magazine's non-negotiable rejection slips.

Then came weeks when I didn't see her. One night while dining in the Little Venice, I was told she had been found in her tiny room on Bleecker Street—apparently dead for two days before another lodger, not having seen her, thought to look in on the old lady. On a table were four freshly written poems and one that was half completed.

There is no street so drab by day or night as Sullivan slashing across the Village. Because of several of its nightclubs, more particularly Jimmy Kelly's, most of New York's diversion seekers at some time or other had been on the street and forgotten it, I guess, as soon as possible. Yet once this was the heart of the French quarter, harboring refugees from the Commune. No trace left, of course, where a score or more highwaymen in an earlier century were noosed and their bodies permitted to hang for days as a warning. It was on Sullivan that Edwin Forrest, the famed actor, meeting a newspaperman who had written some derogatory comments on his divorce, thrashed the fellow soundly. Although the records do not reveal it, the scoundrel was undoubtedly among the first of Manhattan's gossip columnists.

I never used to pass by Loew's Sheridan Theatre on Seventh Avenue and Twelfth Street without pausing to study the small bronze plaque at the corner of the building. For here I was advised once stood the house where an obscure schoolteacher lodged. That was back in 1870—and the impecunious instructor was a Frenchman named Georges Clemenceau, destined to become one of the dominant figures in French history before, during and after World War I. I often wondered whether this lowly pedagogue had his dreams of future greatness even then, or whether his chief concern was to earn enough money to keep body and soul together.

In those decades when the Village was the citadel of free love, Freudianism, socialism, imagist poetry and cubist art. Noël Coward lived, starved and wrote in a dark basement at 578 West Broadway just south of the Square. There he worked on the first act of *The Vortex,* which was to bring him to the attention of the theatrical world. Some years later, passing by the site, I found that now there was a night spot occupying the basement—the Caravan. A captain of waiters whom I knew said: "Do you know Noël Coward once lived in this building?" and I said: "Yes, I knew."

"Well," he said, "maybe this will interest you. We have a dishwasher here, Nick Napoli—and already he has written two plays and a novel. Say something about them in your column—maybe he'll be your discovery."

So I did write a paragraph about Napoli, the undiscovered playwright and novelist. But as far as I know, he remained undiscovered.

Shuttered for good are such former bawdy cellars of Bacchus, as the Pirate's Den, the Alimony Club, the Black Cat, the Full House—and so many others—but the Village Vanguard like Chumley's still flourishes to remind us of those gayer days when it was the headquarters of the long- and short-haired disciples of Dadaism, Cubism and other isms.

It's been many years since I have invaded the Vanguard. In those earlier nights, I found it a low, sprawling room with bare tables and chairs, an odor of stale beer hanging over it like a pall, a melancholy pianist in one corner, usually improvising on Debussy, and numberless wisps of cigarette smoke clutching the ceiling like so many well-tapered fingers. Of all the places in the city, this one literally shrieked for a Van Gogh to splash its downbeat effects across a canvas. At the time, it had no liquor license, so most of the patrons toted their own libations. The management charged twenty cents for table space and the privilege of observing the goings-on. The Vanguard's entertainment was spasmodic and catch-as-catch-can. Whenever a customer felt the urge, he stepped to the center of the floor and let loose his inhibitions, and the reward might be catcalls or cheers and, occasionally, a sprinkling of nickels and dimes.

During the course of an evening, patrons might be subjected to such fare as Maxwell Bodenheim chanting prose of his own or John Rose Gildea bellowing rhythm lyrics or Vachel Lindsay offering a recitation. One night when I was there, Harry Kemp offered a few observations on twentieth-century philosophic trends. And on another night, Cleon Throckmorton, the scenic designer, yanked a chair to the center of the floor and proceeded to present his conception of Edgar Bergen, using an animated table companion in the role of Charlie McCarthy.

In later years, the Vanguard became more conservative with

entertainment of high caliber by paid professionals. And many young performers were launched there to go on to loftier prestige in the show world. It afforded Mike Nichols and Elaine May their first showcase—Mike to become an outstanding director for the stage and movies and Elaine a successful film actress. And, of course, a little group calling itself the Revuers was also to find its beginnings at the Vanguard, the springboard to future success. Its principal members were Judy Holliday, Adolph Green and Betty Comden.

How were they to know then that all their secret dreams would be realized—Judy to become the great stage and screen star, only to have death nip her career at its height; Adolph and Betty to become major librettists for memorable musicals for the theatre and the movies.

Also starting off on their career at the Vanguard was the Kingston Trio. Harmonica virtuoso Larry Adler, after some of the bombardment against him by critics of his alleged ideology had subsided, used the Vanguard as the base for his first concert in the States after his self-imposed exile from England.

Of course, twenty cents gets you nowhere now at the Vanguard—not even as a tip to the hatcheck girl.

The slaphappy bohemianism of the Village has yielded to the more frantic rebellion of the hippies and the hallucinogenic set —the lads and girls who go for their "pot," proud of their LSD "trips." There was a time when, if we referred to the long-haired, we meant those going in for culture. Now, need I point out, the long-haired cult embraces the beatniks with their hair straggling down to their shoulder blades—to such musical idols as the Beatles, Monkees, Rolling Stones, and other rock 'n' roll howlers.

I suppose there are still some among our literary set who regret there is no longer the unfettered Village bohemianism which they are convinced prodded the blossoming of the talents of Edgar Allan Poe, Walt Whitman, Eugene O'Neill, O. Henry, John Masefield, Noël Coward and others. To them dimly lit, bare garrets, huddles at tables in drab little cafes, semistarvation are essentials for inspired authorship. But it occurs to me, our current crop of writing geniuses does very well in the more plush apartments or country homes and develops well-compensated literary offerings despite occasional get-togethers over festive and costly viands and wines amid the opulent surroundings of swank saloons or hotel dining rooms.

Paradoxically enough, the change in the Village mood has come about as high-rise apartments have replaced the scabrous old brownstones, and noisy discothèques, for the most part have sprung into favor in place of the little haunts that had so much appeal to us in those other years—the Pepper Pot, the Pirate's Den, Romany Marie's, the Black Cat, Mother Bertolotti's, Greenwich Village Inn, El Chico and the various night spots and restaurants into which Barney Gallant moved in as host.

My disillusionment with the Village today is tempered somewhat by the comforting knowledge that some of the gathering places still retain a certain charm: Asti's, where waiters and busboys sing operatic arias along with the professional singers; O. Henry's, dedicated to the memory of the illustrious writer who himself was so loyal to the section; Bon Soir, which has been a showcase for ambitious newcomers who went out to the lusher fields—Barbra Streisand and Phyllis Diller, for instance. Woody Allen, dead-pan Sad Sack comedian, playwright and actor, such a dominant success in the show world these days, used to deliver his laments in the Bitter End, where TV's Bill Cosby also found a springboard to fame.

The off-Broadway theatre has flourished, too, in the Village of today—at the Circle in the Square, at the Theatre DeLys, and the Sheridan Square Playhouse to name a few—to remind us of those earlier days when Eugene O'Neill was afforded his own showcase in the Village for his rebellious offerings.

And, of course, there are still the periodic sidewalk art exhibits featuring the works of eager young and old artists who never abandon the dream of becoming the Picassos, the Matisses and the Van Goghs of the future.

Not too many months ago, I strolled through the Village again reflecting on the many changes, wondering whether current residents and visitors find the section as colorful and as exciting as we did in those earlier days. I finally wandered up Christopher Street for another look at the apartment house where my wife and I had resided for so many years. That at least seemed unchanged.

As I walked on, I spotted on the pavement a crayon pastel—a forlorn sea, on the bank a solitary withered tree, in the distance a lonely sail, and in the skies, a full moon. The sidewalk artist had not signed his name—only this revealing scrawl: "Out of work—no money—no hope."

4

On the Old Harlem Express

THROUGHOUT THE SPEAKEASY ERA, and for years after, the pleasure-lovers rarely considered the evening's excitement exhausted unless the night, or rather the early post-midnight hours were topped off with a journey into Harlem. We invaded the so-called Black Belt fearlessly and joyously, and regarded the welcome we received as warm and sincere. No one gave a thought in those earlier years to racial discord, to civil rights, or for that matter, paid too much attention to the difference in color, for we mingled on friendly terms, whites and blacks, in the diversion spots.

The entertainment was peppery and different, whether you dropped into the Cotton Club to hear or dance to the music of Duke Ellington or Cab Calloway, to applaud Ethel Waters, or to watch that dancing fool Snakehips Tucker, or listen to Cora La Redd and her blue hymns over at Connie's Inn. Big, stoutish, mannish Gladys Bentley offered her ribald chants at the Clam House, often with Fats Waller at the piano. There was excitement, too, in evenings at the Ubangi Club or Dickie Wells's place, or at

The Cotton Club revue in action when the colorful night spot was among the chief lures in Harlem, the club where Cab Calloway, Duke Ellington, Ethel Waters and others were afforded their chief showcase. And from where a pretty little girl, just one of the chorus, was later to emerge as a dazzling star, Lena Horne.
Photo by United Press International

Johnny Carey's Ye Olde Nest where your adjoining neighbor might be George Jean Nathan. The atmosphere in these dinky places had something of the lift of a reefer. Harlem was booming, and the proprietors prospered. No curfew was observed for the most part. Of course, there might be an occasional raid, a brawl, a stabbing or two, but rarely any friction between the white and black patrons.

It was after the rowdier younger element began to infest these places that the lure gradually evaporated. Young hoodlums, frowned upon by the owners and civic-minded Negro citizens alike, began to display resentment of the white midtowners whom they considered invaders of their territory, and whom they regarded as patronizing snobs who considered Harlem visits just "slumming." Nor was the situation helped as the professional rabble-rousers began to incite minor riots, and a few years ago a major riot.

So gradually fewer and fewer Broadwayites wandered away from their own territory. Harlem was considered out of bounds, and the cold truth is that the great talents among the Negroes no longer need or even want Harlem for their showcase—and without Negro performers, most of the appeal of the uptown area is gone. The star Negro performers now find themselves in demand in the nation's major night spots, theatres and movies, not excepting the once aloof elegant supper rooms of the hotels. Stars like Sammy Davis, Sidney Poitier, Johnny Mathis, Nipsey Russell, Lena Horne, Diahann Carroll, Ella Fitzgerald, Eartha Kitt, Cab Calloway, Pearl Bailey, Sarah Vaughn, Harry Belafonte, Duke Ellington and Leslie Uggams are top attractions, potent lures and command salaries as high, if not higher, than some of their white contemporaries.

One night, during the pre-Repeal days, I escorted Helen Morgan on a tour of Harlem. It was an evening during which we dropped into a number of the rowdier, colorful little saloons—among them Ye Olde Nest, the Clam House, the Lenox and the Artists' Box, and the sultry singer was treated like visiting royalty wherever we went, especially at the Clam House where we listened to Fats Waller as his talented pudgy fingers hammered out syncopations on the battered little upright piano and fat Gladys Bentley delivered her robust salacious songs. Miss Morgan, inspired by this "concert," rose and insisted on singing a few songs herself—mostly her familiar torch ballads. Gladys Bentley was equally inspired, apparently, for she came over to our table later and whispered, "I'm getting married and you're invited." I asked who the lucky man was to be and she giggled: "Man? Why boy you're crazy. I'm marryin'"—and she named a girl—another singer!

Dawn came smiling out of the skies as we left the last of the speakeasies—and as we walked along Lenox Avenue, Helen observed an elderly Negro woman seated on the steps leading to a dreary old brownstone house.

"What are you doing up at this hour?" she asked the woman. "Heavens, the sun's hardly up." The woman mumbled, "I'm goin' to work, ma'am." Helen turned to me, asked how much money I had on me. I fished out my bankroll—about fifty-five dollars.

"Let me have fifty," she demanded, and before I could ask why, I handed it to her. She dug into her own purse, took out all the bills in it, and together with the money she had taken from me, dropped it all in the woman's lap. Then she pulled me away.

"Oh, lady," shrieked the old woman. "Bless you. God bless you. I wish you live a t'ousand years. Bless you."

A few days later, I received a check for the fifty dollars with this note: "I want to keep those blessings all for myself. You do understand, don't you?"

There was another night in the Clam House when the glamorous Lilyan Tashman of the movies had been drinking steadily. Over the protests of her escort, she staggered toward Gladys Bentley, who was singing out one of her naughty ballads, pulled her away from the piano and attempted to force her to dance with her in what was something of a cross between a cooch squirm and the Charleston. Gladys broke loose—the Tashman girl danced by herself a few seconds, and then fell flat on her face. On another occasion, as I mention elsewhere, Jean Harlow had the same dancing urge at the Breakfast Club.

Let me report on one typical opening night of the Cotton Club in March of 1934. The score for the revue was by Harold Arlen and Ted Koehler. One of their numbers, "Ill Wind," was sung by Adelaide Hall. There was a dramatic bit with a voodoo scene in which Juano Hernandez (later to be featured in so many movies) turned in a stirring quiver of dramatic emotionalism. The young Nicholas brothers presented their furious dance. There were other featured numbers and of course the lively chorus routines.

But I merely want to convey some idea of how powerful was the allure of Harlem in those days, especially Cotton Club shows. From my records, I find that among the folks who were present that evening were Irving and Ellin Berlin, and with them film producer Samuel Goldwyn and his wife; playwright Sam Behrman, Gregory Ratoff, Paul Whiteman and Margaret Livingstone; producer George White; man-about-town Jules Glaenzer; harmonica maestro Borrah Minevitch; Cobina Wright; Marilyn Miller, Lillian Roth, Lee Shubert, Miriam Hopkins, Jo Frisco, Ted Husing and Eddy Duchin.

The Cotton Club shifted uptown in September of 1936 into the site formerly occupied by the Palais Royal (and now lodging the Latin Quarter). The opening show had Bill Robinson and Cab Calloway among the starring attractions. It was at this time that a new dance was introduced by the lad and gals in the show, the Susi-Q.

Most of Harlem's hot spots which boiled with bawdy nocturnal acrobatics—crimson poppies of the dry era—wilted at the whiff of legalization; among them, Ye Olde Nest, Dickie Wells' Club Alabam', Ubangi Club, Cave of the Fallen Angel, Hot Feet, Drool Inn, the Hyena. I remember particularly one with an equally provocative label—not with any special affection however—the Death House, where only straight liquor was served—no fancy cocktails. Many of us were ready to swear the chief potables consisted of a blend of turpentine, benzine and carbolic. The Death House, if I recall, lived for three short weeks, not because of the lethal effect of the booze but because a burly waiter was thoughtless enough to slash the throat of the proprietor—quite fatally.

A dancing star and a singing star, Fred Astaire and Harry Belafonte, appear to be far happier than the writing man between them. Twelve years have passed since this picture was taken, and Astaire has eased up somewhat, but Belafonte goes right on delivering his chants and piling up a fortune against a rainy day.
Photo by Hale Haberman

5

"The Great Quench"

IN 1929, AS I TOOK TO MY new rounds, the Prohibition era was at its rowdy, law-defying height. Although I began to refer to the period as the "Big Parch" or the "Great Drought," it actually became the descriptive I later conferred upon it, the "Great Quench." Never had contraband liquor flowed so freely or been consumed in such tremendous quantities. Former teetotalers or occasional imbibers in rebellion took to reckless drinking. The speakeasy bars flourished, and women began settling at the bars along with the men.

Sedate mansions were converted into illicit night haunts. Landlords raised the rents five and tenfold on drab little stores sought out by citizens eager to join the liquid gold rush. And the top hierarchy was the hoodlum set which, if it didn't own the speakeasies outright, preempted silent "partnerships" by the simplest methods. The "boys" would walk into a new operation and without much gentle preamble declare themselves "in" as part owners. A protest, as many learned in the earlier days of the speaks, only enticed a brutal beating, and in some instances, a violent death.

New York could not claim credit, if that's the word, for the introduction of the speakeasy. Wherever there had been legal interference with the free flow of liquor in the U.S.A., there had resulted wide violation of the law. Back in 1821, when Maine attempted to restrict drinking by imposing almost prohibitive license fees, hotels and stores began selling surreptitiously. These oases were usually referred to as "whistling-shops." The label even crossed to Great Britain, and Charles Dickens used it in his *Pickwick Papers.* The terms, "speakeasy" and "bootlegger" originated in the dry South—long before national Prohibition. In the Carolinas, the forbidden saloons were called "blind pigs," and in them you were warned to "speak easy" to avoid attracting attention of the constables.

Manhattan's first illicit drinking place came into existence a day after Prohibition became the law of the land—that is to say, on January 16, 1920. On that day a group of dominant Broadwayites organized the 50-50 Club, with John Steinberg as caterer, and moved into quarters over a garage at 129 West Fiftieth Street. Only fifty members were admitted—with an initiation fee of one hundred dollars each--to go toward furnishing the place. It was strictly a cooperative club—there was no bar but each member had a locker. Noted illustrator Harris Fisher was elected president of the group.

Steinberg made the first important purchase of contraband liquor in New York—a hundred cases of rye from a headwaiter, Jack Kennedy, who later became the proprietor of a prospering chophouse. Next day Steinberg—and this information I gathered from him personally, years ago—bought a large consignment of Scotch. For many months the 50-50 club members drank only Scotch and rye.

The club ran along as the lone reserve into which a gentleman could go without running into thugs and bums. Hundreds of other drinking places had sprung up, but they were dives, drab little hideaways, holes-in-the-wall, and for the most part gyp joints. Some of the proprietors of these places eventually rose to become underworld emirs.

It took two years for the forces of violation to get squared away and know where they were going. In that space of time, the blind pigs had demonstrated that the Volstead Act had no teeth, and their attorneys had already cut some of its few claws. By that time, too, Rum Row and the Canada and Florida trade routes had been organized and there was a sufficient supply of liquor. The great Prohibition Thirst was beginning to develop. Everybody began to get into the racket—headwaiters, ex-saloonkeepers, ex-restaurateurs and others whose business had been ruined by Prohibition police officials, the revenue sleuths.

Then in 1922, a chap named Perkins set up what is believed to have been the first actual speakeasy bar—as distinguished from the 50-50 operation which actually was a private membership club. Until this momentous occasion, even the better places were still pouring it straight out of the bottles. In case of interference, they'd drop the bottles into the overcoat pockets of the customers and claimed they were only serving setups. This was in the now almost forgotten age of the pocket flask.

Perkins took over a brownstone house on Fortieth Street, east of Fifth Avenue, installed a bar and began rattling the first speakeasy cocktail shaker. The house that Perkins leased belonged to a wealthy playboy who used it only occasionally as a temporary residence. The owner went on a long trip abroad and lent the house to a pal. The friend, a bit short on cash, rented it to Perkins. When the owner returned unexpectedly, he found to his dismay that he couldn't get into his own house! The attendant pulling the little shutter from the peephole shooed him away. He didn't recognize him as a patron and certainly not as the landlord.

It was Perkins who set the pattern for what was to follow. Soon restaurants were added to the bars, and the age of the speakeasy really began. This development came just in time to save New York from a tearoom diet—and for a curious reason. In the contracts of the French chefs before the Dry Blight was usually the proviso of a daily bottle of wine as fringe pay. After Prohibition, the law-abiding hotels and restaurants naturally were unable to furnish the chefs with wine. The cooks stuck it out for a year or so but were beginning to migrate in droves back to France, Switzerland and Italy. They were lured back, many of them, by the speaks with the promise of the free bottle of wine each day.

Most of the early haunts opened as chartered clubs, following the lead of the 50-50 club. They kept their charters handy and flashed them on the Feds during raids. This device worked for a while, but gradually the Prohibition agents began to doubt the *bona fides* of the membership lists. A few, like the Artists & Writers Club, the Stork and the Embassy, kept up the pleasantry to the end as an excellent barrier against undesirables.

Few of Manhattan's famed pre-Prohibition restaurants were able to abide by the law and survive. Ancient Lüchow's on Fourteenth Street kept going, adhering strictly to the rules, though under protest, serving nothing stronger than legal near beer while the law was in force. It is a fact, though, that unknown to the bosses, the waiters managed to keep a supply of real beer or an effective needled substitute in an adjacent cellar, and some even managed to sneak harder liquor from their caches to prized customers. Eventually these few were caught in the act and fired.

The speakeasies began to issue cards to patrons. Some even had passwords. For instance, the shibboleth gaining entry to one oasis on Fifty-eighth Street near Park Avenue was "Mrs. Boole" after Ella Boole, the lady who so vigorously had prodded the crusade for a dry America!

From the single-floor arrangements of bar and restaurant, the next step in the speakeasy's progress was to rent entire houses—usually at first, of the shabby brownstone variety in districts dominated by boarding houses. Then came the invasion of better neighborhoods, until finally residences of society families, industrial magnates and merchant princes were being leased. In time, the home of Henry Clews, Wall Street banker, housed the colorful speak known as the Mansion. Another illustrious residence converted for the "cause" was the Donahue home owned by one of the Woolworth heirs. That became the Napoleon, and the operators even bought the original painting that hung on the walls. It was said that when the decorators were putting in bars, dance floors and lighting effects that young Woolworth Donahue who had leased it to the speakeasy lads used to come and look on approvingly.

By the time I became an authorized Broadway recorder, it had become definitely chic to be illegal, and one could be illegal in the embrace of luxury such as New York had never encountered before. Broadway itself degenerated into a street of cafeterias, electric shoeshine stands, soft drink and hamburger kiosks, physical culture demonstrators and street corner demagogues, ten-cents-a-dance halls—while the gates to an invisible paradise in the Fifties suckered away the silk-hat and ermine crowd.

The speakeasy, indeed, had traveled quite a distance in those intervening years when you contrast the first bars—a few planks across a pair of sawhorses—with the silver-and-chromium masterpiece at the Park Avenue Club, for instance, which the enforcement wreckers chopped up one day and carted off to the government warehouse. That bar cost $10,000. After the raid, George LeMaze, the managing director, replaced it with something less expensive in mere rosewood. Incidentally, the decor and the confiscated silver bar were designed by famed decorator Joseph Urban.

In this luxurious setup, host LeMaze served dinners that put old man Lucullus back into the automat class. The feet of his chickens and guinea hens had never touched the ground; his baby lamb came from a special farm in Ohio; every morning the express brought from Florida thirty pounds of pompano *bonne femme,* served with a mustard sauce that only his chef knew how to mix. Every night he donated to the help any pompanos left over.

This interior view of the Park Avenue Club conveys some idea of why it was considered the most sumptuous speakeasy during the Prohibition era. The decor was the achievement of one of the outstanding scenic designers of the era, Joseph Urban, and its Lucullan cuisine was the nightly achievement of George LeMaze. The owners, for the most part, were the emirs of the hoodlum hierarchy.
Photo by United Press International

His lobster LeMaze brought them galloping from Sutton Place—and even in from Southampton. LeMaze went in for such specialties as Burgundy snails and wild boar from the Vosges. He served everything with a baronial flourish—oysters chilling in a half bushel of crushed ice, roasts, sautés and ragouts brought in whole in their pans, pots and skillets. Instead of handing you the menu card, your waiter held up a blackboard on which were chalked the day's groceries.

And moan as you consider the prices. One dollar—repeat, one dollar—for lunch, two-fifty for dinner, table d'hôte! Of course, this piddling sum didn't cover the cost of the raw materials. It was the bar that made the place pay. Drinks were assessed from a dollar up.

The Park Avenue actually was only one of dozens of speakeasies de luxe that New York boasted by the end of the twenties. The elite of New York—of America—judges, senators, state and national executives, generals, admirals, poets, artists, authors, musicians, college professors, stage and screen stars, explorers and Broadway columnists—walked to their furtive doors and either flashed their cards or gave the countersign.

Below these resplendent places were thousands of middle-class speakeasies sustained by businessmen and suburbanites. Still further down the scale we had thousands of bars, dives, shock houses, clip joints, all of them in a nether world invisible to the eye, expressive of the revolt of the citizenry against coercion.

As time went on, new hosts came into prominence and even acceptability, despite the fact that they were operating against the law. Thus we had Sherman Billingsley at the Stork, Jack Kriendler and Charles Berns at "21," John Perona at El Morocco, Barney Gallant at Gallant's in Washington Square, Leon Enken and singing lad Eddie Davis at Leon & Eddie's, John Steinberg at the Five O'Clock Club, Big Jim Moriarty at the Marlborough House —so many more, perhaps too many to catalogue.

And of course, there was the incomparable Texas Guinan and her rowdy night-spot—and her chief rival for a time, Belle Livingstone.

Texas was the undisputed queen of the speakeasy era and ironically enough, her career and her life came to an abrupt end as Prohibition was chanting its death song, too.

She was christened Mary Louise Cecilia Guinan, and she was the supreme mistress of the wisecracks. No one surpassed her in the ability to subdue unruly patrons in her nightclubs. Whether they were murderous mobsters or arrogant stage stars or just run-of-the-mill voluble souses, Texas subdued them not by threats but by sharp, witty and sardonic barbs that prodded hecklers into instant silence.

Her early schooling was in a modest convent in Waco, Texas, where a schoolmate was Mabel Willebrandt, who during the Prohibition days was to be her most consistent adversary, sponsoring raids on her clubs, openly assailing her for violating the dry law. It was Miss Willebrandt who pushed the government's prosecution of Texas at one period, but the Guinan girl through her quick wit and sense of humor emerged triumphant. It cost the government $60,000, which Texas thought was quite a joke. Believe it or not, she actually convinced the court she didn't know how liquor tasted since she had never taken a drop in her life.

Though Mayor James Walker often dropped into her night spot, she conducted constant warfare with his police commissioner, Grover A. Whalen. She originated the salute, "Hello, sucker" and made patrons like it. She also referred to her wealthier customers as "butter-and-egg men"—something that appealed to Playwright George S. Kaufman whose play *The Butter and Egg Man* was to prove a rousing hit.

To repeat, she was a teetotaler. She watched over the beautiful girls in her ensembles with the zeal of a stern housemother. She mingled on equal terms with gangsters like Al Capone, but some of her best friends were leading clergymen. She was the darling of the columnists of the era—feeding them choice gossipy tidbits, donating little gags and quick quips. Guinan-isms which survived for years and were laced frequently into dialog in plays and musicals included: "Never give a sucker an even break"; "Give the lil' girl a great big hand"; "Her brain is as good as new"; "A guy who would cheat on his wife would cheat at cards"; "I'm a country girl who came to Broadway to make enough money to go back and live in the country"; "It's having the same man around the house all the time that ruins matrimony."

One night when Al Capone, surrounded by henchmen, invaded her club and got a bit nasty because he wanted a girl in the line to sit with him, Texas cowed him into grinning meekly and admitting defeat by snapping: "I never asked one of your bloody bodyguards to come and sit with me."

Texas was married three times, each marriage ending in

divorce. Her first husband was a newspaperman, Jack Moynihan, then working in Denver and later city editor of a Chicago newspaper. Her second husband was Julian Johnson, who became a screenwriter for Twentieth Century-Fox. She met her third husband, David Townsend, aboard a ship while en route to Europe, but parted from him shortly after.

At one time, forming a partnership with Harry Pilcer, former dancing partner of Gaby Deslys, she arived in France with her showgirls only to find herself barred on charges of being an undesirable. She insisted on being officially deported—herself and the company—and thereby saved herself some $15,000 in fares, she explained gleefully later.

She once wrote a "Down Memory Lane" column for this reporter in which she discussed her early career. Starting as a bronco buster in a small circus, she was billed as Texas Guinan thereafter. Then she appeared in silent movies, chiefly two-reel Westerns. Publicity-minded even then, she got permission from William S. Hart to bill herself as "The Female Two-Gun Bill Hart." She also worked for the Shuberts in their old Winter Garden revues—salary, she wrote, eighteen dollars a week.

Now for some direct quotes: "During the War [World War I] I went in for overseas service—driving an ambulance and working as an entertainer in spare time. I met Albert, King of Belgium—was saluted and entertained by Clemenceau, did social service work with Queen Marie of Roumania. I toured the trenches along with an all-star cast which included Elsie Janis, Mme Ernestine Schumann-Heink and Elizabeth Brice. Maybe they sang better but I sang louder."

It was Larry Fay, one of Manhattan's underworld characters, who started her off as a night-spot hostess in the LeFay Club, and Texas once told me that she hired Harry Richman, then a comparative unknown, to play the piano. "I fired him the next week," she revealed.

To get back now to her column: "Among those who graduated from my clubs were Ruby Keeler (later to wed Al Jolson), Barbara Stanwyck, Lon Chaney, Irene Delroy, Jack Oakie and Rudolph Valentino." I expressed skepticism about Valentino, but Guinan vowed she would swear on a stack of Bibles he worked for her as a dancing man.

As a fledgling columnist, I first met Texas back in 1929 at her home in the old-fashioned brownstone she owned on West

Eighth Street in Greenwich Village. It was a crazy sort of place—a hodgepodge of assorted furniture and furnishings of all periods from early French Provincial to late Macy's and Gimbel's. I was a bit depressed by a green Chinese drape with dragons crawling all over it—a nightmarish thing that made me cringe a bit inwardly. I should never have murmured a comment, because in her will, Texas bequeathed that drape to me.

She was an avid reader; Mark Twain, whom she claimed she had met once, was her favorite author and Henry Wadsworth Longfellow, her favorite poet.

Here is the Queen of the Speakeasy era, Texas Guinan, hanging crepe on the door of the 300 Club just before prohibition agents slapped on the padlock.
Photo by United Press International

Texas was proud of her bulletproof car, rumored to have belonged once to King Ferdinand. She was rarely threatened—except on one occasion when the word got around she was due for a "snatch." A few of her friends among the mobs learned the identity of the underworld group plotting the kidnapping, lured one of them to a rendezvous and killed him as a warning to his mates.

Although in later life hers was a husky, more or less one-note voice, she showed promise of being a talented singer early in her career, for at the age of fourteen, she won a Marshall Field scholarship for singing. She always yearned for picture stardom, but the closest she got to fulfilling her ambition aside from those earlier days in Western two-reelers was in 1928, when she was featured in one of the pioneer talkies, *Queen of the Night Clubs,* followed by minor roles in a few other films, the final one *Broadway Through a Keyhole.* However she did stage a "comeback" in a two-reeler as a costar. The other star—and you must not giggle—being this reporter. It was in one of his "Down Memory Lane" shorts for Universal.

Death claimed Texas Guinan far from her beloved Broadway, on November 5, 1933, in Vancouver, British Columbia. She had been ill only a few days with an intestinal ailment. Realizing the end was near, and, to repeat, publicity-minded, she made advance arrangements for her funeral. "I've broken box-office records most of my life," she murmured, "Don't let me flop in death." Only two months prior, she had suddenly "got religion" and talked about being an evangelist. A pastor turned over his church to her, but in her confusion she mussed up her notes and was forced to ad lib. She finally broke down and wept openly. "I wouldn't have minded," she said later, "If I could only have saved the situation by thinking up a wisecrack—even one. What a sap the pastor and the congregation must have thought me."

Thousands came to view her remains as she lay in state in Campbell's Funeral Parlor in New York, and it was ironic that a sign placed near the coffin to guide folks read, "Exit to Broadway."

Ironic, too, that the funeral procession passed the Rivoli Theatre where the last picture in which she had appeared, *Broadway Through a Keyhole,* was being featured with her name up there in the marquee lights. There was another grim coincidence—some years later. Texas' boyfriend before her final days was Eddie Baker. The day *Incendiary Blonde,* the film based on her career, opened at the Paramount Theatre, Baker passed away in Montreal of amoebic dysentery—the same ailment which had claimed Texas Guinan's life.

The other colorful woman who moved not too complacently among the operators of the era was the voluble, gregarious Belle Livingstone, who ran the Country Club for a few years on the premises of what later became the Park Avenue Club. Here society and the upper stratum of Broadway assembled, paying five dollars to pass through the sacred portals. Once inside, you could move around the large chamber designed to resemble the garden of Versailles, or you could mount a flight of stairs and perspire over ping-pong or play miniature golf, provided you kept buying drinks at from $1 to $1.75 per copy. It was all very gay, and so were the patrons and so was stocky Belle Livingstone—while it lasted.

It did not last long. Gentlemen in the federal employ descended on the fatal evening of December 5, 1930, and despite the protests of the agonized Belle, slashed a few costly mirrors and some delicately fashioned chairs, sent the patrons packing and fastened a padlock on the doors. Madame Livingstone was quite upset and not without good reason, for only a few months previously, her plush salon (one "o," please) on Park Avenue had been similarly treated. Nor did she fare much better when she shifted her lares and penates to the Reno Club, for again the Feds sought out her intimate little place and closed it.

Belle, who confessed she came from unpretentious antecedents, meanwhile managed to acquire a quartet of husbands in succession, each of whom dowered her with gems and bank accounts. First there was the wealthy Richard Wherry. Succeeding him was the noble-blooded—some even hinted royal—Count Ghiberti Laltazzi. Then came the opulent Edward Mohler and after him the dignified Walter J. Hutchins. La Livingstone, ever the lady, always insisted each was perfection as a spouse but unfortunately not for her.

Once-wealthy and bejeweled Belle, who proudly boasted she mixed with the best, from King Edward VII to Al Capone, died penniless on February 7, 1957, in a Bronx nursing home. She was ninety-two.

Another of the more swanky speaks was Marlborough House on East Sixty-first Street, just off Fifth Avenue. It was operated by big, friendly Jim Moriarty, and after the death of Prohibition, it continued for a time legally. The interior remained as sumptuous as before—the food was suave, the liquor upright—but on the wall now, framed for all to see, was the document licensing the Marlborough House to sell by the glass all malt, vinous and spirituous liquors.

But when legality came in the door, romance flew out of the window. There was glamor in that door in the dry era. It was oaken, awninged, flush with the building line at sidewalk level and as free from sordid proclamation as an exclusive jeweler's windows. Through it passed the elite of the Social Register. The speak itself was an enjoyable place for cocktails before dinner at the Colony Club or Pierre's, and it was always jammed with a tailed and décolleté crowd the night of an Assembly dance.

The flunky under the awning never questioned anyone's identity. Nothing so gauche. This was a class speakeasy—not a dump. The patrons were not the sort who liked to argue on the sidewalk. You might be a Federal snooper, but the doorman would still pass you in.

In—but not "inside." When the street door closed behind you, you found yourself alone in a small vestibule completely sealed in precious woods. Off at one side was another door with a pearl push button; and here at this wicket, away from the vulgar gaze of the street, you presented your credentials.

The first floor, a symphony in scarlet and silver with walls wainscoted in scarlet up to the height of the chair rail, was the dining room. At the street end of the floor was an English type taproom with tables and a long bar behind which paraded and pyramided a greater variety of ardent waters than most high-class saloons displayed before Prohibition—all unimpeachable and smuggled at great cost from Scotland and other ends of the earth.

On the second floor was the cabaret room, done in royal blue, copper and mirrors, with doors and leather upholstery in blue. The walls were completely mirrored. The orchestral dais occupied a recess at the head of the stairs midway of the room, and the band occasionally broadcast its syncopations over national networks. The entertainment wasn't anything to stir the pulses too much —an Egyptian magician perhaps, a torch singer or a foreign dance team.

Jim Moriarty was prepared when repeal stepped in. He was able to boast a country estate, a string of polo ponies and acceptance by the social set. His little excursion into the illicit had tugged neat dividends. Later he was to become host of a colorful and quite legal restaurant, the Barberry Room, where often a quartet of men-about-town would assemble for light libations and viands—a foursome consisting of critic George Jean Nathan, radio sportscaster Ted Husing, literary agent Mark Hanna and this reporter. It is melancholy to reflect that they have all passed on—Moriarty, Nathan, Husing and Hanna—with only this writer remaining with his memories.

West Fifty-second Street between Sixth and Fifth avenues became a thoroughfare for speakeasies, and gayest among them was Leon & Eddie's. Corpulent Leon Enken welcomed each patron at the door like a boniface of the olden days, and his tall, lean partner, Eddie Davis, took care of the entertainment which consisted chiefly of risqué parodies and chatter. It was Leon & Eddie's which pioneered in the development of speakeasy art as distinguished from what had greeted citizens in saloons of another era. Instead of heroic-sized female nudes on canvas, ponderously framed and hung on stout hooks behind the bars, Leon & Eddie's featured spoofing murals executed by the Michelangelo of the era, Zito.

For instance, at one end of the room there were giant caricatures of Leon and Eddie thumbing noses at each other across a series of Rabelaisian panels. Over the entrance doors was painted a paraphrase of Earl Carroll's celebrated toast: THROUGH THESE PORTALS THE MOST BEAUTIFUL GIRLS IN THE WORLD PASS OUT! And over the swinging doors to the kitchen was another version: THROUGH THESE PORTALS PASS THE MOST BEAUTIFUL WAITERS IN THE WORLD—a gibe at the growing invasion of Broadway effeminate lads.

Incidentally, among others of the speaks that featured the lighter art was Julius' bar in Greenwich Village. Here the walls were dominated by scenes from the gaslit period stressing old-time Gotham in its cups. Inebriated citizens in toppers and Inverness capes propped up lampposts; shawled darlings sang "Father, Dear Father, Come Home to Me Now" under the swinging doors of the pubs. There were other offerings, all kidding Dat Ol' Demon Rum.

Getting back to Leon & Eddie's—after repeal, when it had shifted its action to new and larger quarters across the street, patrons continued to flock in, remaining loyal to the former illicit haunt. Its Sunday night guest star sessions became a showcase for young performers who went on to join the loftier echelons of show business. Jerry Lewis and Dean Martin, for instance, after they became partners, Jackie Gleason, Joey Adams and others.

There was a night I took novelist Jim Tully to the place. It was after Eddie Davis had finished his final show for the evening, and Tully was visibly disappointed. I told Eddie that Tully was annoyed with me for not having brought him in earlier to hear him sing. So the ever obliging minstrel man sat down at our table and sang without piano accompaniment. For more than an hour, he delivered his chants—ranging from some sweet numbers like "Stardust" and "Melancholy Baby" to his ribald assortment, including, "She Came Rolling Down the Mountain" and "Virgin Sturgeon." Tully told Davis he was ready made for a book and that he was going to write it: *Saloon Caruso*. He never did, of course.

The speaks crowding one another on West Fifty-second Street were later to be succeeded by Dixieland jazz night spots featuring little bands—at which time it became known as "Swing Lane." In still later years, they in turn were succeeded by dives featuring ladies of the ecdysiast set—and I claim dubious credit for then furnishing the district with a new appellation: "Stripty Second Street."

Other oases nestling near Leon & Eddie's included famed Tony's which became a popular hangout for magazine editors, illustrators and writers as well as literary luminaries, perhaps because owner Tony Soma was a fairly literate chap himself, and perhaps, too, because he was so zealous in trying to proselytize the members of the intelligentsia to his devotion to Yoga.

Then there was the sumptuous Town Casino Club, noted for the electric fountains behind its bar. The bar itself was of sanded glass illuminated by sea-green lights. In the corner behind it was a fountain—a sort of shrine with a canopy and side panels worked out in inlaid woods in combination with blue neon light tubes. On a pedestal stood a futuristic nude statue of a girl. Thin jets of water shot up from the basin as high as the statue's waist, played upon by hidden spotlights.

Like so many others of the speaks, the Town Casino Club refused to die when it became a legal gathering place. It kept in operation for a few years and began offering entertainment as well as food and drinks. One night, making the rounds of the town, with George Jean Nathan and Mark Hanna as my companions, we invaded the club which was featuring comedian Billy Vine, and a newcomer, as far as I was concerned, a beautiful slim singing girl, billed as Peggy Marlowe. Since beautiful slim singing girls were par for the Broadway course as far as I was concerned, I don't remember giving her a thought afterwards—not even having dutifully recorded a Triple-A endorsement in my column for both the quips of Vine and her song offerings. How was I to know that she would enter my life years later—as Mrs. Louis Sobol!

The most famous and the snootiest of the forbidden refreshment places on West Fifty-second Street was Jack & Charlie's at No. 21, referred to almost at the start of its career on the street as "21." I wish I could say I was a frequent dropper-in, but the sad truth is that I never passed the doors in those early years for hosts Jack Kriendler and Charlie Berns had laid down a ukase that no Broadway columnists were to be admitted.

When "21" became a respectable, law-abiding restaurant after

Prohibition, Jack Kriendler revealed why it was practically the only place during the Speakeasy era that barred Winchell, Hellinger, Sullivan and myself. "Suppose something happened," he explained—"like someone starting a fight or some prominent married customer out with a girl or someone else's wife? There was always the danger one of you fellows would have it in the column, and that certainly would not do us any good. Besides, Charlie and I thought it was a mistake to have any publicity at the time—we always thought the owners were out of their minds to let you fellows in and write about their places."

"21" was one of the few operations that defied the mobs. On several occasions they tried to muscle in, but to no avail, and threats failed to coerce the stalwart partners. Indeed, on one occasion two henchmen of a notorious gangster proved menacing—and there was a bloody beating. But the victims were the two hoodlums.

Too, it was just as difficult for a Prohibition agent to crash as for a bum to get into the Morgan Library. Once, though, and once only, was the place raided. The bell rang, and out in the area were the battalions of morality.

"Ladies and gentlemen," announced Charlie, "please drink up quickly whatever's in front of you—the house is pinched."

The front door clicked open and at the same time there was a subterranean crash like Woolworth's glassware department falling off the Empire State. The custodians of temperance stomped in and couldn't find enough evidence in the whole place to fill an eyedropper. In the basement they discovered a pile of broken bottles and a strong smell of whiskey, but you cannot carry a smell away for analysis.

After the discomforted revenooers had flounced out, liquor reappeared from the various caches, and there was a round of drinks on the house. Then the customers were let in on the secret. A touch of a button under the bar and all the bottles had plunged down a chute. In the basement below there was a pile of stones to break the bottles as they descended and below the stones a sand pit to soak up the hooch!

The late Robert Benchley is said to have discovered Jack & Charlie's when it was running on West Forty-ninth Street as the Puncheon Club. In 1929, when it moved to West Fifty-second Street, Benchley moved along with it, and so did most of his gang, many of them from the famous group that used to congregate at the Algonquin's Round Table—Dorothy Parker, Heywood Broun,

A glimpse of the "21" Club during its speakeasy era. The famed bar was so contrived that a push of a button would drop all liquor into the basement, leaving nothing but shattered bottles and perhaps a suspicious aroma to greet the revenue men.

Edna Ferber, Alec Woollcott, Katherine Brush, James Thurber. Other consistent patrons were Ernest Hemingway when he was in town, Paul de Kruif, Laurence Stallings, Michael Arlen, Ben Hecht and Charles MacArthur, E. Phillips Oppenheim, George Jean Nathan, to say nothing of members of the society set.

Another favorite drinking hole was the Stork Club on West Fifty-eighth Street although the term "hole" for this plush oasis probably isn't a fitting term. True, it was not particularly pretentious in its decor, but from its very inception it drew the patronage of the cream of the society and theatrical worlds. And Sherman Billingsley, its watchful host, became for a time one of the wealthier of the speakeasy proprietors. Billingsley it was, always seeking new gimmicks, who hit upon the preprandial bowl of olives, little onions, celery, etc., for gratuitous nibbling, who began gifting women patrons with perfume, men customers with ties (of course, always with an idea for promotion, these bore the Stork Club emblem). Champagne in a bucket of ice was delivered at the table of the regulars—all this, mind you, on the house.

The Stork Club's final lodging place after repeal was on East Fifty-third Street. Before that it occupied a brownstone on East Fifty-first Street, where Billingsley introduced his "singing bar" in the upstairs room, a girl or occasionally a man singer delivering the songs from behind the bar. When I first came to know Sherman, though, he was operating from the site on West Fifty-eighth Street.

The Stork, like "21," was fussy about its patronage, and perhaps, because so many were refused entry, it became a must spot for the night imbibers, that is, those for whom the open sesame sign was flashed. Any night might find among the assemblage the biggies in all fields—a Vanderbilt or a Rockefeller, a Charles Boyer or a Helen Hayes, the Mayor or the Tammany boss, visiting senators, governors, sons of Presidents, or, after the war, the might of our military—and of course, before Prohibition and after, news folks—among them Lucius Beebe, Walter Winchell (in fact, this was practically his office away from his office), Mark Hellinger, Bill Corum, members of the Hearst family, and fellow restaurateurs.

Harold Ross, editor of *The New Yorker,* was a frequent patron until he was barred by Billingsley because of an unfavorable profile in his magazine about Sherman's close pal, Winchell. Toots Shor was barred because Billingsley thought he was taking over one night. Humphrey Bogart and Milton Berle had the "no-admittance" sign put up for them, as did others who brought host Billingsley's displeasure down upon them.

Steadfast customers and close friends remained, besides Winchell (save for one brief period when he barred himself after a misunderstanding)—Morton Downey, Steve Hannagan and Arthur Godfrey, and were for a time associated with Billingsley in his perfume distributorship.

It was Sherman, too, who inaugurated balloon nights—lucky patrons capturing one loosened from a net attached to the ceiling, might find themselves winners of an automobile, a pedigreed puppy, a case of champagne, a dinner for six or eight, a gift certificate for a suit by a fashionable tailor, etc. These gift nights started after Billingsley had moved to East Fifty-third Street.

In later years, patronage began to dwindle until finally a heartbroken Billingsley decided it was useless to continue. He must have cherished memories of the club's more glorious era—of the night, for instance, that Grace Kelly and Prince Rainier dining at the Stork revealed they were to wed—of the celebrities who were favored by being seated at the prize corner Table 50. But these were only memories, and in October, 1965, he shuttered the place. A year later, on October 4, 1966, death took him away from it all.

A popular gathering place was the Five O'Clock Club, though

its reign was comparatively brief. Flo Ziegfeld used to arrive almost nightly just before midnight, usually accompanied by a group of his famed Follies beauties. And occasionally there arrived producers George White and Earl Carroll, usually with some of the beauties from their respective shows—the *Scandals* in White's case, the *Vanities* in Carroll's corner. There was no love lost among the three producers of the girly shows, and this often created an embarrassing situation for Messrs. John Steinberg and John Cristo, for there was the problem of allotting choice tables without displaying what might be called favoritism.

Also there was the musical problem. It was the practice for the band to sound out the melodies identified with any show business personality entering. "Mammy," for instance, if Al Jolson came in; "My Mother's Eyes" to greet Georgie Jessel; "If You Knew Susie" for Eddie Cantor. When Ziegfeld, Carroll and White congregated in the room, it was a dilemma for the bandleader but he solved it by arranging a medley of the hit songs from the production of each.

Then there was the Napoleon Club, with its plethora of illustrious customers like illustrator James Montgomery Flagg, Bob "Believe-It-Or-Not" Ripley, Sir Hubert Wilkins, Floyd Gibbons and others. One late afternoon James Quirk, then editor of a movie magazine, Hal Phyfe, the ace photographer, and I stood at the bar. Quirk turned to Phyfe. "Hal," he said, as he ordered up another Scotch and soda, "I've made a lot of money in my magazine. You open a speak like this—a nice and respectable one—and I'll back you—if you promise not to cut the liquor." Phyfe grinned. "Sounds reasonable to me." If Quirk was serious, he never had an opportunity to prove it. Word of his death on the Coast arrived a few days later.

There was the night at the Mansion when a talent agent asked host Lou Schwartz if he'd permit a pretty girl, a new client, to sing a few songs for the customers. He was granted the permission. The girl delivered her songs and was greeted with some enthusiasm. Her name was Dorothy Lamour. She had been the winner of a beauty contest and had even, for a spell, worked as an elevator girl in a Chicago department store. This was Dorothy's first New York airing. Later, further if minor impetus to her career was accorded by Billingsley who decided she might be an entertainment attraction in the Stork Club. After that, the story of Dorothy Lamour and her meteoric career as a movie star needs little further exposure at this point.

Lou Schwartz also hosted the Club Richman (named after its chief star, Harry Richman) and also King's Terrace, both of which lasted through what the French humorously termed the *Régime Sec*. The luxurious and supposedly impregnable Mansion was raided into oblivion by some thick-skulled axman who had misread his assignment. The Club Richman later changed its label to Club Richelou—this time after Richman and Lou Schwartz. King's Terrace had two notable features—a ceiling over the dance floor beveled with mirrors on all four sides and a dummy bar on the stage behind the orchestra. The working bar was upstairs; the one below was just a prop.

Another luxurious haunt was the Simplon Club, operated by Nick Prounis and John Johnidis on West Fifty-third Street. They had leased the Henry W. Shoemaker mansion for $18,000 a year and engaged Sloane, the Fifth Avenue furniture store, to decorate it at a cost of some $75,000. Among entertainers who appeared frequently in return engagements were Helen Morgan and also the Yacht Club Boys who, while not exactly the forerunners of the Beatles and the Monkees of today, nevertheless enjoyed tremend-

Prohibition agents were notoriously indifferent to the wails of the sensitive operators of speakeasies. Here is how Helen Morgan's nightclub looked after the revenue men got through wrecking it. Later Helen was to have an even more opulent place named after her—one which escaped devastation. *Photo by United Press International*

ous popularity with their voice blendings of popular songs and parodies. The Simplon Club continued to operate for a time after Prohibition had vanished. Later Prounis joined up with Arnold Rossfeld, who had been headwaiter at Barney Gallant's, and opened the plush Versailles restaurant, which for years was one of the more prosperous night-spots in town.

While criminals and public enemies were operating the speakeasies or trying to muscle in on the holdouts, Roger Wolfe Kahn, musician son of multimillionaire banker Otto Kahn, opened a nightclub—only to have it raided before it had got off its wet feet. (Roger was to wed singing girl Hannah Williams, who later became Mrs. Jack Dempsey.) And this independent heir to millions, after having his fling leading an orchestra, turned to another field—he became one of the more daring test pilots for Grumman.

Another unlikely night-spot owner was Harold Meltzer, son of Charles Henry Meltzer, the one-time drama critic for the *New York Herald.* He opened the Artists Club in Greenwich Village, assigning famed designer Cleon Throckmorton to paint the murals for him. As hostess for a time was Yvonne Shelton, who had been romantically linked with Mayor Jimmy Walker. Later Meltzer, who had appeared in several Shakespearean roles, partnered with James Riley in the Greenwich Village Inn, where Barney Gallant, a dominant and colorful personality of the era, had started his nightclub career as manager. Here at one time a promising young comedian—fellow by the name of Jackie Gleason —was featured.

It must be obvious that I am offering only a surface picture of the speakeasy reign. There were hundreds of other places, each with a bit of history. However, it would be neglectful of me to ignore two characters of the era—Barney Gallant and Larry Fay.

Barney, a confirmed bachelor, had been a newspaperman and at one time paid drumbeater for Mexico's General Carranza during the Pancho Villa days. Arriving in Greenwich Village, he had shared a room with a glum writing chap—Eugene O'Neill. Later, by this time running a speak, Club Gallant, he had had the dubious distinction, as he himself once told me, of discouraging another young writer who had written some skits he thought Barney might be able to use as part of the club's entertainment.

"Well, I read them," Barney recalled, "and I thought they were pretty awful, and I told the young fellow that. I even asked him to sit down and have a meal—he looked as if he needed one badly. Well, this young fellow just glared at me, snatched the skits from my hand and walked out. Know who it was? Noël Coward—that's the fellow I tried to discourage. We got to know each other real well afterwards."

Among Barney's close friends were Mayor Jimmy Walker, columnists Mark Hellinger, Walter Winchell and Heywood Broun, cartoonist Peter Arno, to name a few. Indeed, Walker not only was a consistent patron of the various places Gallant hosted but often dropped into his apartment for a chat and a nightcap.

Incidentally, Barney always pointed out with pride that he had the distinction of being the first speakeasy operator to be pinched and jugged for violation of the Volstead Act—and what an outcry there was, even editorials and protests by notables in all walks of life. But Barney served his thirty days and emerged something of a hero. He finally retired to Miami Beach to write his memoirs. He was still laboring away on them when death claimed him in March of 1968.

As for Larry Fay, he was the Beau Brummell of the lads on the fringe of the hoodlum set, though the gendarmes had him down as quite a hood, himself—indeed had listed him as New York's Public Enemy No. 3.

It was Larry who opened Les Ambassadeurs, which brought a young stenographer to Manhattan's attention as a lass who had potentials as a singing gal—Ethel Merman—and it so happened that I was to award her her first press notice, and afterward she always maintained she was my "discovery." Clayton, Jackson and Durante were the starring attractions and it was Jimmy Durante who pulled me aside and chirped: "There's a nice young girl getting a sorta tryout tonight—I think she's got sumpin'. Give her a write-up, like a good fellow." Actually, when Ethel stormed out with the powerful unforgettable voice of hers, I felt, like Jimmy, that she really had "sumpin'" and wrote so accordingly in my column.

Getting back to Fay, if indirectly responsible for offering La Merman her first showcase, he also was credited with introducing Texas Guinan in New York and backing her in her initial venture. But unlike other members of the mob, Fay's fortunes began to slide down. In 1932 he was running the Casa Blanca. But business was on the downgrade. Fay wasn't even making expenses and was beginning to owe back wages to the help. His doorman, Edward Maloney, was among those to whom he owed money—about one hundred dollars. Maloney, on New Year's Day, 1933, brooding over this debt, went on a binge. That evening he staggered into Fay's office brandishing a gun, and during the argument that arose—the gun roared—and on the carpet the so-called Public Enemy No. 3 was supine, his black tie sodden with blood.

Thus Larry Fay, such a power during the height of the Speakeasy era, came to his gory end, broke, mourned only by a few who remembered him as not such a bad chap—as one always available for a touch. There wasn't even the elaborate funeral usually associated with deceased members of the mob hierarchy.

It was quite an assortment of diverse personalities that was to be encountered in this era of the illegal—desperadoes and statesmen, patriots and rats, demimondaines and society leaders, fanatics and sages, crooks and crusaders—all participating in this modern Whiskey Rebellion. Why go to far-off times and places for excitement when this thrilling contemporary melodrama was exploding all about you!

The speakeasy went to its death on April 5, 1933. A complete outlaw, it had won the overwhelming support of the law-abiding public. Its name suggested everything criminal and underhanded, but mothers trusted their children to it as they never did to the legal saloon, and God-fearing aunts and grandmamas from the suburbs doted on visiting it when in town. It brought, to repeat, decent women up to the bars for the first time.

The era was shot through with graft and entangled with the most bloodthirsty bands that had ranged the earth since the Middle Ages, yet many of its customers were the pick of society, business and the professions. Though technically a fugitive from justice, it sought and obtained police protection from its underworld enemies. Accused of being a hellhole of drunkenness, the speak actually discouraged excessive imbibing through fear of being condemned as a nuisance.

It kept alive the lawful art of good living in America through close to fourteen years. Without legal existence at all, the speakeasy cashed no checks, extended no credit, but it maintained an army on its payroll during the years after 1920.

Actually, New York bade the speakeasy farewell without a tear. The town rushed blithely to the licensed hotels and restaurants for a lungful of the fresh air of legality. But who knows—perhaps someday the speakeasy will shine on the pages of history, niched in honor beside the Boston Tea Party, John Brown's Raid and other outlawries applauded by subsequent opinion in the name of liberty.

6

Bandits—Twentieth-Century Style

The mob lads continue to gather in their fair share of headlines and the general public has become acquainted with the label Cosa Nostra as well as the earlier term Mafia. They are, for the most part, less obtrusive these days as they thrust rapacious paws into industry, unions and finance. In the twenties and thirties, they were dominant figures of our nightlife, not only being as we have recorded, behind-the-scenes owners of many of the nightclubs and restaurants, but also showing up with their entourage of henchmen and sweethearts as paying patrons at the gathering places.

Headwaiters, captains and busboys, as well as the official hosts, genuflected, showering them with attention. Currently, if you notice this flurry of attention, you may be assured that the person thus honored is a movie star, a prominent sports or political figure, or a free-spending tycoon.

The bad boys of this era are undoubtedly just as ruthless but for the most part less exhibitionistic. And if among them there are any as murderous and erratic as, let us say, were Louis "Pretty"

Amberg, Jack "Legs" Diamond or Vincent Coll of those bygone years, at least their sadistic activities only rarely come to general attention.

"Pretty" Amberg, for instance, would slap chorus girls around in restaurants, as he did attractive Cackles O'Neal in Dave's Blue Room because she spurned his advances. He punched bandleader Louis Prima at the Famous Door because he wouldn't oblige with a favorite tune. He threatened a jockey, after a race at Aqueduct, shouting like a madman because the horse on which he had wagered didn't have the good sense to win.

Amberg was labeled "Pretty" because he had ugly features to scare little girls and inoffensive citizens, and it is a fact he never went out of his way to be pretty in his manners, especially to reporters. He snarled at them and paid them no more respect than he did his associates, or, for that matter, the overlords. He was a complete intransigent. When his hatchet-hacked body, garroted, burned almost to a crisp, was discovered in the smoldering remains of an auto which had been set afire, there were few tears along Broadway, not even the feeblest of encomiums as had been the case in the bloody elimination of, let's say, dapper Benjamin "Bugsy" Siegel who was cut down by a hail of machine-gun bullets while he sat with his back to a window in Virginia Hill's luxurious home in Beverly Hills back in 1947.

It is true that there is still an occasional report of a snatch of a hoodlum at the orders of a rival mob leader but somehow it doesn't generate the excitement to match the kidnapping of big Frenchy DeMange by Vincent Coll those many years back, or the buzz that went from headwaiters to captains down the line to customers as the flash came in that a notorious gangster had been done in with ice pick or bullet, by garroting or more ingenious devices.

Coll, it may be recalled, met his end the hard way on the night of February 8, 1932, when he was shot down while making a phone call in a drugstore booth on West Twenty-third Street. Owney Madden and "Dutch" Schultz and their respective underlings were suspected but there was no definite proof, and later the authorities concluded the killers might have been out-of-town hired assassins. Years after, a Schultz aide, George Weinberg, insisted that it was actually the Dutchman who had commissioned the murder.

Schultz himself (his real name was Arthur Flegenheimer) was chopped down by gunfire in a Newark saloon in 1935 along with two of his bodyguards. A gunman named Charles "Bugs" Workman was convicted of the slaying and sentenced to a long prison term. Workman had refused to confess, contenting himself with a plea of no defense. He was released on probation March 10, 1964 —twenty-one years after the shooting.

The list of mobsters who met death as violent as those they had dished out or had ordered is a long one. Louis "Lepke" Buchalter died in the electric chair, Albert Anastasia was shot down while being shaved in a hotel barbershop. Frankie Marlow, who had interests in many of the night spots of the twenties, including the Silver Slipper which used to feature Clayton, Jackson and Durante in their earlier careers, was taken for a final ride. Frankie Yale, who had been Brooklyn's Number One hoodlum and who had among his coterie of subordinates the young Al Capone, was riding in his brand-new car when another car came alongside and through an open window machine-gun bullets blazed leaving Frankie a very dead man indeed. Thrust out from the body was a hand on one of the fingers of which was a ring which had been the gift of Capone.

Early in 1966, a man and a woman, each shot through the back of the head, were found in a car in East Elmhurst. They were identified as Little Augie Pisano, one of the mob emirs who had reigned through the dry years and long after, and Mrs. Alan Drake, estranged wife of a well-known comedian.

Then there was the untimely death late in 1935 of Charles "Chink" Sherman, whose body was found, eaten away by quicklime, in a shallow grave in a barn in the Catskills. It was evident, according to police reports, that he had been hatcheted to death by "parties unknown." Some years previously Sherman and the rival hoodlum chief "Dutch" Schultz had engaged in a bloody set-to at the Club Abbey during which Sherman was drilled with a bullet or two and also stabbed, and Schultz dodged bullets but was also stabbed.

I had my own experience with Sherman. One night, entering Club Abbey, after having indulged somewhat intemperately in brandy, I spotted a party of three young patrons and without invitation approached their table, and addressing myself to one of them, exploded: "Chum, you look like a tough guy—but I don't think you're so tough. You're nothing." Nothing happened in the way of an immediate annihilation of a loud-mouth columnist. Instead, the little man said quietly: "Sit down, Louis—have a drink."

I said: "Okay, I'll have a drink with you but I still don't think you're so tough." I gulped down the brandy—and that was one too many. When I awoke, I was in my own bed, partially undressed, with only a dim recollection of what had happened. The following night, I checked with the elevator man.

"I was really worried about you, Mr. Sobol," he said. "These three tough-looking characters carried you in and they wanted me to open the door to the apartment. I said I didn't have the key and one of them said: 'He must have the key in his pocket,' and I guess they found it and opened the door. They were laughing like crazy when they came back to the elevator."

A few nights later, at the Abbey again, I spotted the same three. Inquiring of the bartender, I learned that the smallest of the trio, the lad I had insulted, was the formidable Charlie "Chink" Sherman, suspected of many crimes, and that the other two were his vassals. I went over rather sheepishly, muttered something to the effect: "I guess I talked a lot out of turn the other night—but thanks for taking care of me."

Sherman said: "Forget it, you don't know how funny you were. You and I got one great pal—Hellinger—but you don't drink so good."

Some years later, at the Paradise, of which Sherman was the behind-the-scenes major owner, I sat with him. He was in a glum mood. "You got a nice life," he said. "A nice wife, a daughter—you get around with nice folks. I come from a good family—and I'm a bum. I never know when a slug's gonna get me when I ain't lookin'. That's a great life, hey? Know what I'm going to do? I'm going to get away for a while, up in the mountains. Get around with decent folks, breathe some good air, not this stinkin' nightclub air. I'm gonna do some fishin' and some thinkin'."

He never came back alive.

A recapitulation in detail of the gory exploits of our twentieth-century banditti is beyond the scope of a single chapter, and repetitious, for it has all been written before in any number of books, to say nothing of dozens of feature articles, past and present in newspapers and magazines. I am simply endeavoring to dwell on the hoods whom I met personally and who figured in episodes in which I found myself involved.

For instance, I used to drop into the Cotton Club after it had shifted activities to West Forty-eighth Street from its former Harlem site, and engage in pinochle duels with Big Frenchy De-

Mange, one of the formidable chieftains of gangdom. They were serious battles, and Frenchy would get apoplectic when he lost, though the stakes were minimal. But once the session was over, he became a good-natured host, and it was difficult to conceive that this big, burly man had been on the Public Enemy roster.

My first actual meeting with Waxey Gordon (who was always booked under his real name, Irving Wexler) was, oddly enough, at a soiree at the penthouse—once the home of Ivar Kreuger, the Swedish match tycoon and international swindler who committed suicide—of the famed otologist Dr. Julius Lempert. Gordon, a stoutish chap with porcine features, dropped into a discussion of opera with me, evidencing far more knowledge and displaying such acute analysis of the offerings of Verdi, Puccini, et al., as to shame me with my limited sense of appreciation.

I thought to myself, Surely this can't be the gross, ruthless beer baron with a long record of arrests and convictions for crimes ranging from picking pockets and tax evasion to assault, robbery and larceny—and charged and convicted of heading a narcotics ring.

We even got around to a discussion of some books of the day, and it was evident he had read them through. Not being the aggressive reporter who asks blunt questions that might be embarrassing, I didn't inquire whether his taste for culture and his apparent desire to mingle with "nice people" didn't make him reflect that his own nefarious activities were something he might like to abandon. Nor did I attempt to preach a sermon about the thorny path of the malefactor. You just didn't do that in those days when the chap you were talking to had the reputation for being a ruthless hombre.

Perhaps, though, when he was the tired old man in a prison cell for life, convicted as a fourth offender—this time for heading a narcotics ring—he did think back on some of those more peaceful nights when he was among "nice people" at musicales either at his own home or at some respectable citizen's place—when he could sit down and discuss opera or a book or two.

Death was more merciful to this scoundrelly old man than the law, for he died in Alcatraz on June 25, 1952, some six months after he began serving his final sentence.

The occasion of my first meeting with one of the more murderous of the hoodlums of the era, Jack "Legs" Diamond, was in Dave's Blue Room. One of the Ziegfeld beauties, Marion

"Kiki" Roberts, brought over a slim, sullen-looking chap, and said: "Jack, I want you to meet one of my very good friends, Louis Sobol. He's a real darling man, Jack."

Diamond scowled, glared and muttered: "He's a no-good newsboy. He's a fink," and stalked away. Not long after, he was shot to death in a lodging house in Albany, New York—this thug, who had been riddled with bullets time and again, only to survive. A year and a half later, his widow, Alice Diamond, met a similar fate in her Brooklyn apartment.

Big Frenchy DeMange, Owney Madden, Waxey Gordon—other czars of hoodlumism—lived on to die natural deaths. And a few, like Frank Costello, are still around, having endeavored to invade legitimate fields.

I recall an opening night of a new show at the Paradise when no amount of influence or newspaper status could get you nearer to the floorside then the second or third row of tables. The "boys" had decided that they and their lady friends were entitled to the front tables—and there they were—and the gats that could have been plucked from their pockets and hidden holsters would have armed a brigade.

Some of the mob leaders hosting big tables kept themselves righteously aloof from the beauties surrounding them. These were the faithful swains who had seen to it in advance that their lady-loves were up there in the chorus line. It was such fun, too, in case some unaware citizen, slightly wolfishly inclined, began ogling one of these ladies or trying to arrange a date with her. However, most of the hoodlums were the souls of discretion—they would drag the offending lad out to the street before gouging out an eye or breaking an arm.

Another of the mob emirs who died a natural death was Charles "Lucky" Luciano. I chatted with him a few months before his death. This was at a sidewalk table at the California Cafe in Naples, Italy. He sat in the rear alone, wearing dark sunglasses. His gray hair was ruffled, he looked somewhat haggard and harassed. I walked over to his table and said: "Hello, Charley—I'm Louis Sobol. Haven't seen you since before the war."

Lucky rose, shook hands cordially and exclaimed: "Yes, yes—a long time. What are you doing here?" I explained that my wife and I and another couple were motoring to Ravello. Would he like to come over and meet them? Lucky said, yes, he would. I introduced him to Peggy and author Mike Stern and his Estelle.

The author toasted by a few friends. *Left to right:* Rome correspondent and author Mike Stern; editor of *Variety* Abel Green; and basketball czar Walter Kennedy.
Photo by Bill Mark

He shook hands all around, and then did a double take as he studied the grinning Stern. He dropped his hand as if it were a hot coal.

"You, I know," he exploded. He turned to me: "You're not keeping good company," he said. "He's not a nice man. I'd like to talk to you but not in front of him."

We walked back to his table. "That fellow Stern—he twisted everything I said," he complained. "He's like a lot of the guys—anything for sensation but no truth. No truth at all." (Stern had written a magazine piece about him, recounting his bloody exploits, the rumors that he still headed a narcotics ring from his Naples headquarters.)

To start the conversation rolling, I asked how the plans for the reported filming of his stormy career were progressing. "There are so many versions I've read and heard. Like you're demanding complete script approval, and also $500,000 for the rights and a share of the profits."

Lucky grunted. "You want to do me a favor? You just write there won't be no picture. Not while I'm alive. I don't want no picture about me. I just want to be left alone. You know what they'd do to me if they made a picture—I don't have to tell you." (As this is being written, however, I understand the picture project is finally under way.)

"Charley," I said. "I read somewhere you're planning to get married. I've forgotten the name of the girl."

Lucky shrugged his shoulders. "There is no girl. Not now, there ain't. I didn't get married up to now—you think at my age

I'm going to get myself hooked? No marriage."

"How does life go on for you here?"

"How should it go on?" he said moodily. "Dull. I don't go in for no night life—it don't mean a thing to me. You know I got to take it easy anyway. I was laid up for two months, pretty sick. My ticker. So I'm not doing much running around."

"Do the authorities let you get out of town?" I asked the notorious deportee.

"Sure," said Lucky. "They don't stop me. I can go anywhere in Italy except Rome. They don't let me into Rome—but maybe some day. . . ."

"Have you run into Joe Adonis [another deportee] since he came over?"

"Oh, sure. I see him several times when I go north. Right now he's pretty busy. His family came over to see him, and he's busy with them. He's always been a great family man."

Lucky never smiled once during our conversation. He spoke almost in a whisper. His eagerness to hear about small matters in New York indicated a great homesickness.

I didn't ask about the stories of his heading a big narcotics combine or refer to other illegal activities of which he had been accused. Every newspaperman who had ever spoken with him had asked these questions, and received the same indignant denials.

As we shook hands in farewell, an aging and sad-looking Lucky said: "Don't make me out to be a monster. I'm just a guy trying to make the best of things without bothering anyone—and wanting they shouldn't bother me." Several months later, he was dead. I had been the last newspaperman to interview him.

The lives of our underworld shahs were not without their romantic sidelights. Take the case of Phil Kastel, whose fiancée a beautiful former showgirl, waited patiently and loyally until he had served a prison term. Upon his release, they were quietly married and took up residence on a beautiful estate outside of Stamford, Connecticut, where I once visited them and was duly impressed as Kastel escorted me around the grounds, pointing with pride to the shrubbery and flowers, the private pond, the lavishly equipped playroom, etc.

The pair lived quite happily and contented until Kastel was indicted along with his partner, Frank Costello, in New Orleans. With the case about to come up, and the charges damaging, Kastel had a heart-to-heart talk with his young wife. He urged her to go to Reno and divorce him. According to intimates he told her she must do this. "I may go up for ten years," he said. "I wouldn't want this on my conscience--you having to wait all that time. I want my mind to be clear."

The case was delayed time and again for more than a year, and finally and ironically, both Kastel and Costello were acquitted. Ironically, because meanwhile Mrs. Kastel had obtained her divorce and married a scion of a socially prominent family.

Kastel took it philosophically. To a close friend he said: "Look, just like Humphrey Bogart in this picture, I could have whistled and she would have come back. But what would she get with me? Let's face it—front pages. With him, society pages."

In later years Kastel helped found the Sahara Hotel in Las Vegas, and his new wife masterminded the decor, but Nevada authorities refused to permit the former racket chief to operate because of his past record.

I am indebted to Coleman Jacoby for this story which might be entitled "The Press Agent and the Gangster." Jacoby, one of the better-known writers for television (he is credited with having created several of the characters Jackie Gleason assumes on his shows), recalls that when he was a struggling publicity man, one of the clubs he handled in the Village was controlled by an illiterate racketeer, notoriously brutal in his dealings with employees. Coleman, however, got along well with him—in fact, had won his respect chiefly because the hoodlum was impressed with his educational background and fluency with the English language.

The mob lad had fallen deeply in love with a beautiful showgirl. When the show went on the road, he decided he would have to conduct a correspondence with the girl to retain his romantic franchise. So meekly he asked Jacoby to write her a letter —"y'know, kid, pour on the love stuff." The first letter to the girl made a deep impression, judging from the reply. Also it was evident from her letter that she possessed more than average showgirl intelligence. The correspondence continued until Coleman decided he would have to do even better. So he began sending her ardent love poems, all purporting to have been written by the racket lad. She never knew—and, of course, the pleased boss never found out either—but the inspired poems were right out of Shelley, Keats, Byron, *et al.,* word for word!

The appropriate postscript would be that the mobster and the showgirl finally were married and he reformed. But unfortunately, he was one of the casualties of gangster vengeance.

I recall a night in the early thirties when Sidney Solomon, who operated the plush Central Park Casino, stared coldly as three couples entered, the men immaculate in dinner suits, the girls, all blondes, in evening gowns right out of Paris. It was an opening night for a couple of attractive ballroom dancers—George and Julie Murphy—the same George who was to give up his dancing shoes in later years to become a movie star, and still later to become a dignified United States Senator representing the great state of California.

Solomon didn't think these couples seeking admission were his type of people, and when his headwaiter demurred at his command to order them to leave, he stalked over himself, and addressing himself to the obvious leader of the group, said: "Sorry, there isn't a table left in the place—we're sold out."

And though the girls pouted and two of the men glowered, the chap to whom Solomon had made his address merely smirked and without any further protest led the little company out. It was absolutely unbelievable to some of us who watched and had overheard, and I saw a potential Page One story leave with them. For the leader of the unwelcome group was the ruthless murderer and mob chief "Dutch" Schultz!

It is a fact that most of the bloodthirsty hoodlums who dominated the speakeasy and post-speakeasy eras gradually tried to assume a polish and pose as gentle characters when they mingled with polite society in the saloons of the days. They sent over champagne to Blue Book matrons and their escorts—and orders for twenty-and thirty-dollar hats to prominent businessmen and judges and stage and screen stars. As they grew more prosperous and more powerful, they discarded their flamboyant raiment and dressed conservatively. They tried to check the flow of their double negatives. They sent their offspring to the best schools. They exercised great restraint, rarely slapping their womenfolk in public.

They were an unwholesome lot, but I must concede with something of shame that the Broadway chroniclers usually recorded their activities as if they were shining knights in armor. It took a bold, relentless prosecutor like Tom Dewey to chase them into their holes—and Bill O'Dwyer, when he was later prosecutor, to throw a net over the Murder, Inc., assassins in Brooklyn.

And now we have a former schoolmate of mine, District Attorney Frank Hogan, just as vigorous in ferreting out and gaining convictions of the new but less colorful school of gang boys.

This newer breed of racketeers and assassins endeavors to be more aloof, shunning the exhibitionism of their predecessors. The lads seem more concerned with income taxes, golf handicaps, their investments in so-called legitimate enterprises. Only a few, envious of the excitement enjoyed by the biggies those decades ago, have tried to revert to type. But these Johnny-Come-Latelies are pale carbon copies.

7

Tombs of Broadway

By the scores, once-popular dining and drinking places have disappeared from the scene, their sites, in many instances, preempted by modern edifices, formal and businesslike, which convey none of the excitement, promised adventures, even bizarre charm of the rowdy libation and diversion spots that have passed into limbo. To a Broadway historian, these buildings are merely tombs of the once-turbulent haunts.

I am making no attempt to offer a complete list of the departed but a mention of some of them will prod memories, pleasant or otherwise, for diversion-seeking citizens who sought some measure of escape in these places. The Stork Club, for instance, the Paradise and Hollywood restaurants, pioneer cabarets, as well as the Casa Mañana, the International Casino and the French Casino. Leon & Eddie's, the Eden Roc, the Harwyn, the Hurricane, the Zanzibar, Billy LaHiff's Tavern, the King's Terrace join the melancholy parade as do Texas Guinan's Argonaut, the Club Abbey, the Lido, the Merry-Go-Round and Les Ambassadeurs. Gone, too, are the Casa Blanca, the Monte Carlo, the

Napoleon, the Mansion, and the Simplon as well as the Five O'Clock Club, the Cotton Club, Connie's Inn, the Palais Royal, the 18 Club—and its about time to call a halt.

Take the Lido Club. For years it was a snobbish gathering place where you were barred admittance if the sheen of your tuxedo lapel lacked the proper gloss or if there was dust on the windowpanes of your lorgnette. The *couvert* was gauged to pace along with the monthly upkeep of your Isotta-Fraschini, and while the ginger ale and soda and the booze that went with them were not the best, the tariff was something to make you gasp. Here you sat around and pretended not to be bored because your neighbors were certain, for the most part, to be paid-up members of the Social Register. When it became later than the bosses thought, the Lido went democratic, installed a honky-tonk revue and discarded the *couvert,* to no avail and it perished.

I've made reference to Les Ambassadeurs. Most of us liked this Club—it was jolly going there with Messrs. Clayton, Jackson and Durante kicking the goose high where the goose ought to be kicked. The cash customers and the chiselers poured in by the droves and a good time was had by all. Here it was I met for the first time the lovely Norma Talmadge and her sleek glossy-haired escort Gilbert Roland. But Norma was to be the big love of George Jessel as well as his wife, and Roland was to wed Constance Bennett. I have mentioned previously that it was here one night that I first became aware of a then slim girl, Ethel Merman, with a big voice giving an imitation of Libby Holman singing "Moanin' Low"—also a singing impression of Lupe Velez. Libby was to have more than her share of personal tragedy, and as for Lupe, she was eventually to take her own life. Les Ambassadeurs faded out of the Broadway scene one night.

Something new in the way of nightclub entertainment smacked Broadway when the Club Abbey opened. A stoutish baby-faced lad who lisped and pressed his fingers into his thighs became an overnight rage. That was Jean Malin. With him was another lisping lad who wore frocks and sat on the piano and warbled in the Helen Morgan fashion. Francis Dunn. The girls of the revue wore a handful of beads, most of which were missing. Broadway and Park Avenue surged toward the spot. The nightly list of patrons read like a Who's Who of Grifters' Groove and Snooty Row. Rubbing shoulders you'd find Harry Richman and the Vanderbilts, "Dutch" Schultz and Beatrice Lillie, the Harold Lloyds and one of the Woolworths. And of course the "aristocracy" of the mobster set—suspicious bulges in their hip pockets and under their armpits.

One morning about two o'clock, I left the Abbey to go over to Texas Guinan's Club Argonaut. It was shortly after that "Dutch" Schultz and the rival mobster, Charles "Chink" Sherman had their bloody duel (to which I have referred in the preceding chapter), and Schultz according to the late word had been left to die. He didn't—not then, but the club did eventually. And come to think of it, Jean Malin did, too, some years later when the waters that lick the Pacific Coast sucked him to his death when he drove his car accidentally off a pier just outside the Venice Ship Club in Santa Monica, California, in the early-morning hours of August 9, 1933. Comedienne Patsy Kelly, riding with him, miraculously escaped with minor injuries. Ironically enough, the electric lights over the club read: LAST NIGHT OF JEAN MALIN!

The 300 Club rose phoenix-like out of the ashes of the Abbey and made its brave bid for a place in the midnight sun. The girls of the ensemble were the nudist in town. It featured some bright-talking effeminate lads. But the patrons stayed away and it came to its quick end.

A plush spot, the Belleau, faded out and was succeeded by the new Lido Club, where Helen Morgan sat on the piano and wept her torchants, while a well-known man-about-town, Peppy De Albrew, a pet white mouse clinging to his lapel, acted as host and moved around from table to table, fastening his soft dark eyes on the ladies as the waiters kept bringing more setups and cracked ice.

Far be it from me to upset the serenity of night owls who are content with things as they are, but perhaps one or two may sigh, recalling those other boisterous years when anything might happen in a diversion spot. Like the night Jack "Legs" Diamond, the recalcitrant citizen of the era, walked into the Hotsy Totsy club with some aides and left sundry individuals as dead as Diamond himself was to be some years later. Shortly after the bloodbath, driving along with his girl friend of the time (this was before he took up with Ziegfeld beauty, Kiki Roberts), Legs told her all witnesses were dead—no one could point a finger at him. Whereupon the girl is supposed to have murmured: "But Jack, darling, I saw what happened—you wouldn't, darling, kill me, too!" And Diamond, so the legend goes, said: "I'm afraid I'll have to." And he did!

There was a time when gentlemen like Jack Kriendler of

"21" and John Perona of El Morocco decided to become country squires after a fashion, each opening a plush branch of his respective establishment in Westchester in the early thirties during Prohibition. The "21" oasis in Armonk was labeled the Westchester Embassy and flourished for almost four years. Perona's place in Larchmont was called the Larchmont Bath Club and survived two years. Kriendler once explained why he and his partner Charles Berns had gone ahead with their project. "We just thought for a change our customers, if the urge came upon them, could wander from the bar out into the night air and toss bottles at little sleeping birds and listen to the sweet song of the rustling branches of the trees."

A picture remains clear and unforgettable of a pasty-faced gray-haired man, accompanied by two flamboyant bleached blondes, settling at a table close to mine at the old Chateau Madrid (not to be confused with the current Latin-American club bearing the label). Dan Healy was master of ceremonies; Arthur Brown, the starring singer; and Joe E. Lewis headlining as the comic. (This was Joe's first Manhattan appearance—his comeback after months of hovering between life and death following a vicious knifing by Machine Gun McGurn and several of his henchmen in Chicago.) On this night, the patrons were laughing happily in appreciation of Joe's lugubrious lament, "Sam, You Made the Pants Too Long," but the new arrival remained stony-faced, sullen, as he kept yelling for a waiter. One irate customer yelled: "You must be a nut—you belong in a nuthouse." The man displayed the first signs of emotion. He glared at his heckler, his face crimsoned, and for a few seconds I was certain there was to be a brawl.

But Dan Healy, a captain and several waiters rushed to the elderly patron's table and showered him with attention. The excitement died down and comic Lewis continued his routine.

Later Healy settled down at my table, and then I asked: "Who was that noisy old guy with the two blondes?" He said: "Don't you recognize him? That's Harry K. Thaw. He's not as screwy as you might think. Everytime he orders a bottle of champagne, he sticks a pin into his lapel, and when the bill comes, he checks the number of pins to make sure he's not being cheated."

I understood Thaw's emotional reaction when the word "nut" was hurled at him, for this was the eccentric man of wealth who back in 1906 had shot and killed famed architect Stanford White on the roof of the old Madison Square Garden. It is a twice- and thrice-told tale—Thaw's mad fit of jealousy when his showgirl bride, Evelyn Nesbit, had confessed that White had seduced her some years earlier, the subsequent sensational trial following the killing, Thaw's acquittal on a plea of insanity and his escape from the insane asylum to which he was committed. No, Thaw didn't like to be called a "nut."

His behavior was always slightly erratic when I encountered him in other night spots, but he tipped well and usually subsided when rebuked by a favorite headwaiter. The whole messy case was revived in the newspapers when he died in 1947 at the age of seventy-six. But the original Chateau Madrid had died long before that.

The Ha-Ha Club folded its slightly soiled wings early in May of 1934 and gasped its last. It was a place to go to after three o'clock in the morning just as the Abbey, which had shuttered in earlier years, was a place to go to in those predawn hours.

The show was never elaborate at the Ha-Ha. There was that black-haired smoothy Dan Healy, formerly of the Chateau Madrid, who tossed a wicked hoof when he wasn't too tired and a wicked set of eulogistic adjectives; there was a thinnish, sad-faced glib-tongued clown named Jack White with an offbeat sense of comedy values; there was a slim-legged, still pretty if not too youthful pixie, one Lillian Fitzgerald. They were the mainstays of the nightly entertainment, although from time to time other performers were added.

Here assembled the name personalities in town, and from my own records, I find among those I encountered were folks from such contrasting fields of endeavor as Rear Admiral Byrd and Marlene Dietrich, that spellbinding lawyer Dudley Field Malone and Maurice Chevalier, Norma Talmadge and Ernst Lubitsch, Jack Dempsey and Mary Pickford. The list is endless, but they all giggled and guffawed at the goofy patter and the banter and the general insanities.

I sat one night with a beautiful creature who only a few months previously had permitted herself to become fat and untidy. Now slim and lovely again, true queen of the world's beauties, she was on the eve of a journey to Hollywood where a movie contract awaited—and hopefully perhaps, too, the man of her heart, Russ Columbo. Dorothy Dell was to perish, meeting a violent death in an auto crash, just as the crooning man, Columbo, was to have an equally violent death in an accidental shooting.

The Ha-Ha Club was prospering when banks were closing,

ruined investors were leaping out of windows, a crazy man named Hitler ran amok and took over control in Germany, the United States recognized the Soviet Union, J. P. Morgan sat a midget on his knee, prohibition was swept out, the NRA was beginning to intrude into our daily lives, Tammany was defeated—but we kept drifting into this asylum of buffoonery and forgot the world's woes. To repeat, it finally ran its course, and joined others that had expired because its day was finally over.

A popular night spot for a time was Dario's La Martinique on West Fifty-seventh Street. Here Danny Thomas had his first Manhattan showing—and Danny Kaye, too, his first club engagement. The saddest story connected with this place had famed Mistinguette, the one-time queen of the Paris nightclubs as its chief and humiliated protagonist back in April of 1951. Mistinguette, who once had her famous legs insured for 3 million dollars and who had been linked romantically in bygone days with Maurice Chevalier and Georges Carpentier, was canceled after her engagement had lasted a few days. The lady, who was close to eighty at the time, was a complete flop as a drawing attraction—so the management insisted.

The doors were locked in her face when she arrived for her usual nine-o'clock appearance, and Mistinguette, after vainly banging away at the portals, harangued the gathering crowd of curiosity seekers, crying out her lament: "Nevair anywhere in the world—nevair has thees theeng happen to me." Her parting remark as she left the U.S.A. was something to the effect that she knew she would never return. She never did. Nor did the Martinique after it closed its doors for good some years later.

Gone, though more recently, is a place that seemed as solidly entrenched as the Rock of Gibraltar—with a tiny handkerchief patch of a park now occupying the site—not as a monument to the notable host Sherman Billingsley and the glamorous Stork Club he operated with such pride, but a sentimental tribute by Columbia Broadcasting's top executive, William S. Paley in memory of his father.

There were those nights in the Five O'Clock Club when I would come upon George Raft so absorbed in Molly O'Day, with her sister, Sally O'Neil of the movies, making up an occasional threesome. One evening Raft hailed me and pointing to Molly, exclaimed: "Isn't she something to look at? My gal, Molly—gonna get married someday—watch us. Just as soon as I have five bucks

Danny Thomas and the author after a reminiscent session during which both recall Danny's Manhattan debut as a night-spot performer in the old Martinique—where previously Danny Kaye and Betty Hutton had been afforded similar exposure. Danny used to cry poverty in those days, but when this picture was taken he was already a millionaire, dominant in television both as star and producer and head of his company. He seemed to look well fed, too, in contrast with those earlier days.
Photo by Hale Haberman

of my own." Raft went on to Hollywood and got his five bucks, but he never married Molly, for the truth was, he was still married to his first and the only wife he ever had, and Molly went on to wed comedian Jack Durant. Raft is still around but the Five O'Clock Club has long since disappeared from the Broadway scene.

The once-colorful night spot La Vien and the equally colorful restaurant the Beachcomber are no longer with us. Both enterprises were headed in their heyday by Monte Proser. Monte's has been a rather depressing history, as he so glumly admits. He estimates that he has run through several fortunes even though most of his projects prospered for a time. For instance, he founded the Copacabana, bringing in Jules Podell as his partner. As Proser's debts soared after a few ill-fated ventures, including a theatrical offering, he sold out his interests to Podell. Then, after he had opened one or two night spots in Hollywood which didn't fare too well, he became associated with several of the hotels in Las Vegas as producer of the shows. He also had a run as a television producer with Eddie Fisher as his star, but, as he continues to lament, he never could conquer his free-spending urge. In all, he insists, he has earned and squandered close to 6 million dollars.

"My only asset," he told me recently, "has been my wife Jane. She's been loyal, uncomplaining. And I have five sons." One of them, in the army, asked him to send him a few pictures of stars and pinup girls to prove to his mates that all he had boasted about Monte having been a dominant figure in nightclub and show business was true. Monte sent him the pictures but didn't think of including that of the boy's mother, Jane Ball, beautiful former Fox starlet, whom he married after his divorce from former showgirl, Julie Jenner.

It was his production of *Spring in Brazil* starring Milton Berle that proved one of his major disasters—a $250,000 loss. Also, back in 1941 he decided that Madison Square Garden was made to order for a mammoth dance hall. So he leased it, starring top bands, Benny Goodman, Charlie Barnett, Larry Clinton to provide music for continuous dancing. "The trouble was," he reflects ruefully, "that folks wanted hockey and basketball and fights more than getting on the floor and dancing." The venture collapsed quickly.

Monte confesses that occasionally he writhes in agony as the Copa which he founded continues to be one of the more prospering night spots in the country as it brings in such outstanding stars as Joe E. Lewis, Sammy Davis, Jr., Tony Bennett, Bobby Darin. In earlier years, Frank Sinatra, Jimmy Durante, Phil Silvers, Dean Martin and Jerry Lewis, the late Nat "King" Cole, and Lena Horne were among its potent lures. Incidentally, although primarily an entertainment rendezvous, the Copa is noted for its excellent cuisine. This dedication to fine food has been almost an obsession with the current owner, Jules Podell, who has had long experience in Manhattan's restaurants and night spots. For years, he hosted one of the livelier haunts in town, the Kit Kat Club, and built up its reputation. Its menu ranked high along with those offered in the more exclusive eating places. The Kit Kat, too, is no more.

For a time, the Monte Carlo was a must on the agenda of night lifers. Its host, Felix Ferry, affectionately addressed usually as Fefe, was a suave boniface whose continental manners impressed the patrons of both sexes. It prospered for a time and so did Fefe in his moonlighting projects—namely, assembling outstanding beauties as units for nightclubs in London and in the real Monte Carlo in Monaco. But the Manhattan club, though it lured high society and cafe society, was too generous in the credit it extended, and when bankruptcy proceedings did the club in, it was revealed that some of our best people had dined and wined but had just neglected to pay when the monthly bills were due.

However, the Monte Carlo continued to survive. It was taken over by real estate tycoon William Zeckendorf and his company —some $200,000 was spent in new decor and equipment, a smart restaurateur, Sam Salvin, placed in charge and the place boomed anew for a time. But its popularity finally waned, and it went out of existence.

Gone is the Club Richman built around the singing star Harry Richman, the entertainer whose personal draw at the time was exceeded by few performers. At one time, the lights outside emblazoned the names of not only Richman, but as fellow performers in the club, Irene Bordoni, bandleader Abe Lyman, Norma Terris. And underneath all, just barely squeezed in, Morton Downey—the Downey name getting bottom billing because at the time he had not become a national radio star.

Joan Bennett would come in with her sister, Barbara, who was to become Mrs. Morton Downey, and Joan would then confine herself to paying attention to and being paid attention to by John Considine, Jr., of the theatrical dynasty. That flaming redhead Clara Bow would usually settle herself in the balcony, her eyes on none but her Harry Richman, who, the gossipers insisted, was ready to marry her. And when that romance fizzled, it was Frances Williams who occupied Richman's attentions. She was on the bill at the time, and she and Harry would clown around while Alan Jones, leading the orchestra, smiled a fixed smile that didn't come from the heart because he hoped Miss Williams would become Mrs. Jones. And then one day Frances eloped with a Lester Clarke and as abruptly left him not too long after.

As for West Fifty-second Street, which came to be known as Swing Lane because of the little night spots dedicated to jazz (and later to striptease joints), few of the clubs boasted the loyalty of regular patrons. Gone is the Famous Door where Louis Prima had his first Manhattan showcase and engaged in nightly duets on the horn with Pee Wee Russell. Eddie Condon, too, was a dominant feature. Gone are Jimmy Ryan's, the Onyx, the Three Deuces, as well as more elaborate places which featured songmen, comics and dancers—Leon & Eddie's, of course, the 18 Club, the Royal Box, the Moulin Rouge, the Town Casino.

In February, 1942, a popular eating place, Monetta's on

Mulberry Street, folded as it was marking its silver anniversary. Not for lack of patronage but because "Papa" Monetta, as he was affectionately known, had decided he was tired and that he and Mama Monetta had earned a rest. Monetta's was a gathering place for the gourmets—"Papa" always reminding people that his tutor in the culinary arts had been none other than the great chef Escoffier. Among distinguished patrons who kept frequenting the restaurant were Arturo Toscanini, H. L. Mencken, "Diamond" Jim Brady and Lillian Russell, Mary Pickford—and any number of judges and political figures.

The Simplon Club prospered for a time and there is a memory again of Helen Morgan sitting on the piano, delivering her melancholy love hymns while her bridegroom Buddy Masche sat, somewhat impatiently, waiting for her to complete her chores so they could be together. Helen confided later, "We're on a budget. Even going to budget our love so it'll last a long, long time." But it didn't last, and the divorce court parted them. Nick Prounis and his partner John Johnaidis parted, too, the Simplon folded, and Nick, to repeat, partnered with Barney Gallant's former popular maître d', Arnold Rossfield, to operate a night spot which thrived happily for many years—the Versailles. It was here that George White, once the rival of Ziegfeld with his *Scandals* came in with his little revue in a comeback try—White who once had amassed 4 million dollars only to squander it. It was only fitting, of course, that among the first stars to open at the Versailles should be Helen Morgan, but this time Buddy Masche was not among those present. The Versailles perished to be replaced by the Roundtable, which features belly dancers. And in the upper chamber is a lively little night spot, The Rat Fink Room, where one of our brightest young comics, Jackie Kannon, spouts his satiric thrusts at famous personalities and foibles of the day.

The truly elaborate cabarets began finding favor on Broadway when an enterprising entrepreneur, Joe Moss, decided folks were resentful of the cover charges in most of the night spots. He felt encouraged by the success of several Harlem cabarets, notably the Cotton Club and Connie's Inn, and decided that Broadway needed just such havens for the entertainment seekers. So he opened the Hollywood Restaurant with a policy of name bands and spectacular revues and announced boldly: "No *Couvert,* Any Time."

Broadway's big brains shook their heads and conceded reluctantly that perhaps the plan might draw crowds but how

Three highly rated entertainers, teamed for an appearance at the Riviera, clown it up for the paying customers. *Left to right:* Joe E. Lewis, Harry Richman and Sophie Tucker.

could it possibly yield a profit with the terrific overhead. They were correct in one surmise—the public flocked to the place and filled it to overflow, night after night. It was wrong in its second surmise, for the Hollywood was an immediate financial success.

Then Nicky Blair and Nils T. Granlund and a few of the mob lads behind the scenes opened the Paradise Restaurant, almost directly across the street, importing a dozen film beauties from the Coast who had been in a Samuel Goldwyn picture musical to decorate the ensemble. Abe Lyman and his orchestra were installed. No cover charge and a minimum charge of only two dollars per person. The idea was you had to spend at least that much for drinks and food. Of course, the average check came to far beyond that figure. The Paradise caught on.

Just before repeal, another group ripped out the seats of a large theatre on West Fifty-fourth Street, installed tables on the orchestra and mezzanine floors, installed Billy Rose as the host and producer—and the Casino de Paree was born. Now in addition to a colorful revue, the customer was awarded an added bonus—star vaudeville and musical comedy acts. If I recall, heavyweight champion Max Baer was in that first show with a line of prepared chatter. Among the little gimmicks added were a haughty-looking young woman wearing a black mask who sat down at your table to read your palm, a gentleman in a beret sketched your features; and downstairs, a girl wearing scarcely more than a smile was in a fishbowl waving at you. By the magic of inventive genius, the girl was apparently no larger than a toy doll, some six inches tall

An assembly of show business notables dominant in 1938. The scene is the stage of Ben Marden's Riviera, perched on a cliff of the Jersey Palisades. The occasion was a benefit for the Actors' Fund honoring Producer Daniel Frohman. *Left to right,* we see the former "Fun Mayor" Jimmy Walker and then Harry Richman, Constance Collier, Monty Woolley, Sophie Tucker, Alan Dinehart, John Charles Thomas (leading the all-star chorus in "God Bless America"), Bill Robinson, Martha Raye, Milton Berle, Terry Lawlor, Bert Lahr, Al Trahan, the dance team of Beatrice and Capello, Joe E. Lewis, Milton Berle's mother, ballerina Vera Zorina, Henny Youngman.
Photo by courtesy of Carl Erbe

—while the curious tried to puzzle out whether it was all done with mirrors. The Casino de Paree was jammed almost every night.

In quick succession there sprang up other theatre-cabarets, the French Casino, the Casa Mañana, the International Casino, the Zanzibar, the Hurricane, and, of course, on the Jersey shore there was Ben Marden's opulent Riviera, which boasted an added attraction—the gaming room upstairs where the little balls in the roulette tables clicked noisily and patrons crowded around the dice tables.

Marden previously had renovated the Palais Royal on Forty-eighth off Seventh Avenue, and opened with a highbrow show in which the ladies of the line struck classical poses while Emil Coleman guided his orchestra through something that sounded like bees buzzing. Jean Aubert was the singing star, the Yacht Club Boys roared out their wild chants, and the Boswell Sisters blended their happy voices. Fred Keating made his canary birds disappear. There wasn't a table to be had on opening night but thereafter even if you didn't have a nodding acquaintance with the headwaiter, there was no difficulty obtaining a floorside table. The crowds stayed away.

Marden decided maybe it was a mistake not following the trend of the other cabarets, so he removed the cover charge. That didn't help much. It was then he summoned songwriters Jimmy McHugh and Dorothy Fields and dance director Bob Alton, and they produced a lively show, more in keeping with the spirit of the rival clubs. After that, the books began to show a walloping profit.

They're all memories—these places—and all we have remaining are the Latin Quarter (on the site of the old Palais Royal), and Jules Podell's Copacabana situated in the cave on East Sixtieth Street where once was the Villa Vallee with Rudy Vallee pouring out his torch ballads through a megaphone while a blue spotlight played on the cone.

Real old-timers perhaps look back to gay midnights atop the New Amsterdam Roof when Flo Ziegfeld's "Frolics" attracted the *bon vivants* and their fair ladies for caviar and champagne and lively diversion. In all honesty I must confess that as far as the New Amsterdam Roof activities were concerned, I had to gather my impressions secondhand from among my older Broadway friends, for it also had been laid to rest by the time I began covering the night beat. As had notable *estaminets*—Rector's and Jack's, Churchill's and Shanley's, the original Delmonico's and Reisenweber's.

By the dozens, the little and big taprooms have vanished from the scene, including most of those which boomed along during the Prohibition era. And a few of us, perhaps, still shed tears over their biers—at least, those of us who chronicled the high and low lights of Manhattan, for they furnished so much of our material.

Two colorful personalities in a tête-á-tête at the Riviera night spot in New Jersey in the thirties, the late cartoonist Peter Arno and the first highly publicized glamour girl, Brenda Frazier.

8

With a Song in Their Hearts

SOMEDAY SOME DEDICATED AUTHOR will come along to turn out an updated story of Tin Pan Alley and its fabulous characters, past and present. It will be humorous and fantastic, sentimental and, in many instances, almost preposterous. It should be the required companion volume, perhaps, to an interesting offering back some thirty years ago by Isadore Witmark and Isaac Goldberg entitled *From Ragtime to Swingtime.*

The new history will discuss in detail the composers and the lyricists, the publishers and the now moribund clan of song sluggers—the arrogantly successful, the wistful failures. There will be stories about the tragic Stephen Foster and the gentle Carrie Jacobs Bond, the ill-fated George Gershwin and the inspired Vincent Youmans, the prolific Cole Porter and Irving Berlin, Oscar winners Jule Styne, Sammy Cahn and Jimmy Van Heusen.

The pages will be studded with names like Con Conrad, the team of De Sylva, Brown and Henderson, Harry Akst, Benny Davis ("I was the first white man to say 'hey, hey' on the stage.") . There will be a chapter devoted to George M. Cohan and his potent flag-wavers—and brimming paragraphs embracing Jerome Kern, Sigmund Romberg, Victor Herbert, Richard Rodgers and Larry Hart, Rodgers and Oscar Hammerstein II, as well as Dorothy and Herbert Fields, F. Wolfe Gilbert, Jimmy McHugh, Harold Arlen, Mitchell Parish, Hoagy Carmichael, Mack Gordon and Harry Revel, Vernon Duke.

There would be a fat chapter devoted, too, to Frank Loesser, prolific composer and librettist who contributed scores for dozens of films and stage musicals (*How to Succeed in Business Without Really Trying, Guys and Dolls, Most Happy Fella, Where's Charley*), who gave us such memorable songs as "Praise the Lord and Pass the Ammunition," "Once in Love with Amy," "Luck Be a Lady," "I Believe in You," so many others.

Nor can Alan Lerner and Fritz Loewe who gave us the delightful score for *My Fair Lady* be ignored—any more than

This picture is something of a collector's item. I cannot identify the first man, upper left, but next to him in order are: the famed composer Kurt Weill; Meyer Weisgal who was to become head, years later, of the Weizmann Institute of Science in Israel; humorist Harry Hershfield.
Lower lineup, *left to right:* the author, composer Sigmund Romberg; next to him, two former radio bossmen, Alfred McCoskar and Donald Flamm; movie and stage director Max Reinhardt; publisher Ritter; drama critic Robert Garland; and theatrical producer Sam Forrest. This picture was taken some thirty years or more ago, and only a few of the group are still among the living.

Johnny Mercer can be dismissed lightly. Among the newcomers who have earned the right to be included will be Jerry Herman who, if for nothing else, turned out those rousing international hits "Hello Dolly!" and "Mame."

The list is endless, and the names with the stories about them would read from Howard Dietz and Arthur Schwartz to Jule Styne and Betty Comden and Adolph Green, from Jerome Robbins and Stephen Sondheim (*West Side Story*) to Richard Adler *(Pajama Game)*, Burt Bacharach, Jim Webb, as well as Jerry Bock and Sheldon Harnick *(Fiorello!, She Loves Me, Fiddler on the Roof, et al.)*.

Some basically amateur songwriters might provide juicy paragraphs—Jimmy Walker ("Will You Love Me in December as You Did in May?")—and another citizen who became mayor of New York, John Purroy Mitchell, a lover of the dance, who having invented a step called "The Twinkle" collaborated on a song by that title. John Golden wrote songs before he became an outstanding producer—notably "Poor Butterfly"—and then of course there was the late Vice-President Charles G. Dawes with his "Melody in F."

There is a long roster of other "one-timers," lads who had a single smash hit to their credit and no others. Among them were Frank Silver and Irving Conn who came out with a dizzy song entitled "Yes, We Have No Bananas," which was a riotous success in the mid-twenties, and popularized originally by Eddie Cantor; Mrs. Harvey Firestone's "If I Could Tell You," which became the theme song of the *Firestone Hour* over the networks, and Jack Hope's (the brother of Bob) "Son of Paleface," a collaboration with Bob Hope's stand-in, Lyle Morton.

Song pluggers used to be an important adjunct to the industry, singing songs from autos cruising the streets, or at the music counters in department stores, Woolworth's or music shops. But they have disappeared from the scene. Radio and television performers and the disc jockeys function so adequately now.

There was one song plugger who used to be a favorite of mine: Dave Franklin, who once solemnly revealed to some cronies a dream he insisted he had had. "I dreamed I was in Heaven and I saw Tschaikowsky. He was writing music and I looked over his shoulder to see what it was. And what do you think? He was lifting a tune from Irving Berlin to use in a new symphony! Word of honor!"

Franklin was following up a story that one noted songwriter

had lifted his tune from Chopin's *Fantasie Impromptu Opus 66.* It is a fact that other songwriters, some even to this day, have been accused of plagiarism from Bach, Beethoven, Mendelssohn, Schubert and Mozart, but only rarely does that happen these days.

Actually we have no Tin Pan Alley in the true sense of the word—not any more. The song-publishing firms are scattered, but time was when the Brill Building on Broadway was the Pentagon of the music business, and most of the industry has lingered in the vicinity. Even the cops spoke the lingo of song biz, like "Okay, fella, finish the rest of the chorus around the corner," or "Look, ain't they told you they're not buying ballads this year," or "Awright, awright. Now move on or you'll wind up on my Hit Parade."

To repeat, the musical factories are scattered, and the homely, intimate atmosphere is gone. Now your feet sink into the lush softness of imported rugs, the booths are streamlined, executives sit in front of huge, expensive desks, smoking fat cigars. It's really not the same. These fellows are making too much money.

Composer and newspaperman Monroe H. Rosenfeld gets the credit for the Tin Pan Alley label. He was in Harry von Tilzer's office when Tilzer, playing the piano, was achieving a bizarre effect by weaving strips of paper through the strings. Rosenfeld had just completed an article on the music business and was scratching about for a suitable title. When Von Tilzer finished, he exclaimed: "I've got it. That sounds like a tin pan. I'll call this place Tin Pan Alley."

The Alley was first located on West Twenty-eighth Street between Fifth and Sixth avenues with such reputable musical publishers as Witmark & Sons, Broder E. Schram, Charles K. Harris and Leo Feist having their offices there. Later, one by one, the music publishers moved uptown.

You don't always have to sit down to a piano or at a desk to tap out a song. A fellow named Eddie White wrote "At a Sidewalk Penny Arcade" while posing for his crayon portrait in the arcade at West Fifty-second Street and Broadway—then played it on a ten-cent toy fife for a publisher who bought it.

Speaking of unknowns and how difficult it is for them to invade the field, there is on record the case where the situation was reversed. An obscure young woman wrote a song in 1905 as a valentine and approached E. B. Marks with the request that he print some copies for her so she could send them out to close friends. Marks, after hearing the song, suggested she permit his firm to publish it. At first she demurred, but finally, with much reluctance, consented. The song was "Dearie" and the composer-lyricist was Clare Kummer. Probably the only case on record where a publisher had to beg an unknown for permission to handle her song. Clare Kummer was no Joanie-One-Note. She was to be identified with other songs through her career—"Garden of Dreams," "Other Eyes," "Lover of Mine," as well as authoring the librettos for several operettas.

The history will include, of course, the story of how the American Society of Composers, Authors and Publishers (ASCAP) was born. Two men initiated the move toward establishing an organization or guild which would ensure that men of the song industry would not end up penniless at death as did Stephen Foster back in 1864 in a Bowery flophouse. The two men were Nathan Burke, a famed lawyer who represented many prominent people in the field, and George Maxwell, who represented a publishing firm.

To spearhead the move, they enlisted the interest of the great composer Victor Herbert, who had achieved fame with such operettas as *Naughty Marietta, Babes in Toyland, The Red Mill* and others of equal prestige, and he gathered a few composers and lyricists and a publisher or two for a meeting in Lüchow's. That was back in October, 1913. Another session was held in February, 1914, this time at the Hotel Claridge, and ASCAP was officially launched. Irving Berlin was one of the original members of the Board of Directors.

Since then, this has become a multimillion-dollar project. Its hundreds of members have lifetime annuities, many high in the five-figure range, some in lofty six figures. The sums they receive depend on how often their songs are played or sung in nightclubs, hotel rooms, over radio or television, anywhere and anytime. Furthermore, the payments continue to the heirs after the member's death.

Back in 1940, working on the theory that ASCAP had become a monopoly, a rival organization was formed—Broadcast Music Incorporated, known in the trade as BMI. The broadcasting firms behind the new set-up insisted that the fees ASCAP demanded were too high. An impasse was reached, and for months all we heard over the air were tunes like "Jeannie with the Light Brown Hair" and other Stephen Foster favorites as well as imported tunes from South America and other points abroad.

At the time, I took my stand with ASCAP and quote myself at this point.

> I have no doubt that BMI is a right smart, affable organization, and that its members, chiefly newcomers, are boys and girls of considerable talent. But I have come to know personally and appreciate the ladies and gentlemen of ASCAP and I am willing to break down and confess that much of radio will lose its appeal for me if I cannot hear an Irving Berlin tune, like "God Bless America," let's say, or a Hoagy Carmichael–Mitchell Parish special like "Stardust." I am even going to feel resentful if I am told that no matter how I push buttons or turn gadgets no memorable melodies by Victor Herbert, by Sigmund Romberg, by Jerome Kern or Cole Porter, by George Gershwin or Harold Arlen are to come out of the sound box.
>
> My favorite tunes are "Melancholy Baby," "Who," "April in Paris," "I Can't Give You Anything But Love," "Night and Day." The radio networks advise that starting with the New Year (1941) these are songs among others that will not "taint" the airwaves. Instead they are going to try to convince me and millions of other listeners that we love tunes by other composers who no doubt were or are kind to their mothers and willing to serve under the country's flag in an emergency.
>
> But can I help it if I've developed a great yearn for a tender ballad entitled "And the Angels Sing"—which my radio set will no longer offer to soothe me.
>
> BMI under the sponsorship of the big networks will come through with swing, lullabies, rhumbas and waltzes by some talented newcomers, I am promised, but I'm the kind of fellow who rocks a bit and lets out with hands and a whoop and kicks up a foot when they play W. C. Handy's "St. Louis Blues."
>
> There is still the remote possibility that some sort of compromise may be reached by zero hour. The true friends of ASCAP and of radio hope so. If not, they may have to relabel it Tin Can Alley.

As was to be expected the paragraphs drew dozens of letters, most of them in agreement, but many wondering why I should not also stand up for the newcomers who hadn't been able at that point to join the ASCAP clan. And from an executive of BMI came this consoling note:

> Not all the favorites will go off the air when BMI replaces ASCAP. For instance: "When the Bells in the Lighthouse Ring," "Down South," "Glow Worm," "Mother Was a Lady," "Peanut

> Vendor," "My Gal, Sal," "Love's Old Sweet Song," "My Little Dream Girl," "Parade of the Wooden Soldiers"—are only a few of the family songs in the E. B. Marks catalogue—and E. B. Marks has signed with BMI.

While the ban lasted, people suddenly became aware again of Stephen Foster whose previously mentioned song, "Jeannie with the Light Brown Hair" became the Number One melody, but announcers neglected to mention that Foster had been forced to sell most of his beautiful tunes for petty cash, or that he died penniless.

There are any number of stories of how some popular songs came to be written, but I am contenting myself with revealing the inspiration for a few of them as told to me by the songwriters, themselves, so I had to take their solemn word that these were not apocryphal tales.

The late Walter Donaldson, early in his career, fell desperately in love with a girl he had met in Chicago. After a whirlwind wooing, they had reached the point where they were discussing plans for the wedding. Donaldson had to return to Manhattan for a consultation with his publishers. Each day he put in a long-distance call to his fiancée, but there was no response. He cut short his stay in New York and hastened back to Chicago and started phoning frantically but futilely.

In a melancholy mood, he dropped into a restaurant, and there a few tables away was his ladylove dining with a handsome young man. He was dismayed to observe how cozy the pair seemed, how absorbed with each other. His perturbation mounted when at one point the girl leaned over and kissed the young man.

Finally, Donaldson strode over, hoping against hope this might be a brother or a cousin. But her violent blushes as he approached the table, her embarrassment as she stammered out an introduction to her companion, told all there need have been what the situation was. The songwriter stalked out of the restaurant.

Hours later, the girl phoned him at his hotel.

"I'm sorry, Walter," she cried. "So awfully, awfully sorry."

"Sorry?" roared Donaldson. "What good does it do to tell me you're sorry!"

"But what can I say, dear, after I say I'm sorry?" pleaded the girl.

There was a brief pause and then Walter shouted: "Well,

The harmonizing quartette tugged no bookings, though the picture was taken years before the Beatles roared upon the scene. *L. to r.,* Arthur "Dagwood" Lake, singer-actress Monica Lewis, one-note minstrel man Sobol and operatic star Robert Merrill.
Photo by Hale Haberman

Bandleader Guy Lombardo drops his baton in amazement and amusement—unaware that the author prides himself on being the road company Fred Astaire among newsmen. That's Peggy Sobol in a tolerant mood as her husband guides her about the dance floor.
Photo by Bill Mark

baby, it's not a total loss at that," and he hung up on her. Then he sat down at the piano and wrote one of the great song hits of his career "What Can I Say, Dear, After I Say I'm Sorry."

Songwriter Lew Brown ran into his pal publicist Monte Proser at a dismal period in Proser's life, for his pretty showgirl wife, Julie Jenner, had left him, and all Broadway knew the press agent was carrying the torch. Brown inquired solicitously: "Seen Julie lately?"

Monte sighed: "Yeah—I saw her last night and got that old feeling."

That night, at one sitting, Brown scrawled out the lyrics

of the song: "I Saw You Last Night and Got That Old Feeling," a song which was to pour in heavy royalties.

Mack Gordon and Harry Revel, who often got together with me either in Lindy's or at Grossinger's in the Catskills, explained how some of their songs came to be written. One I recall particularly.

A pretty girl had approached Gordon with a request that he sign her autograph book. Mack pondered and pondered, trying to think of something bright and original, but nothing sparkling emerged, so he scribbled simply: "Stay as sweet as you are."

"Oh, that's beautiful," purred the girl, "really beautiful."

"Beautiful?" repeated Gordon, and then slapped his hands. "Say, you've got something there—and thank you, miss."

Without so much as a good-bye, he hurried off, sought out Revel, and the following day, the song bearing the title was completed "Stay As Sweet As You Are." And quite a hit it was.

On another occasion, according to Gordon, he spotted a stunning girl tripping past Lindy's Restaurant. He dashed out for another look. Some five nights later, sitting at Reuben's, he saw the girl again just as she was leaving the place. Leaping from his table, he rushed after her. But she was gone.

Then weeks later, as he stood in front of the Palace Theatre, he saw her strolling toward him—this vision of loveliness. But now there was no boldness in him. He just watched as she came on, watched her as she walked by and out of his life. He never saw her again and never did learn who she was, but weeks after that final glimpse of her, the whole country was humming or whistling a song he and Revel had written: "Did You Ever See a Dream Walking?"

I have many vivid memories of Falstaffian extrovert Mack Gordon and the more retiring Harry Revel, a great song collaborating team. Gordon, obese and waddling, looked for all the world like a prosperous butcher. Yet from his imaginative recesses, he lured lovely song poems that never failed to infect the nation with their word swing. And Revel, sleepy-eyed, timid mannered, concocted contagious tunes to embrace them. When the inspired lyrics of Gordon were fitted into the musical frames by Revel, song publishers and motion picture producers chanted hosannas.

I recall in the earlier years when Gordon in evil-fitting habiliments and Revel, thinnish and looking half-starved, hung around theatre lobbies at opening nights, pleading with the lads of the newspapers to devote a line or two to a song of theirs—"Underneath the Harlem Moon." As the years marched by, they had no need to make their plaintive appeals as they turned out such memorable songs as "Love Thy Neighbor," "Meet the Beat of My Heart" and as I have mentioned, "Stay As Sweet As You Are" and "Did You Ever See a Dream Walking?" and dozens and dozens of others, to say nothing of the scores they contributed for movies.

I remember Revel once insisting in an interview I had with the boys: "Mack Gordon—he's a poet. His lyrics are nothing short of heavenly," and Gordon maintaining stoutly: "That Revel—his music is like classics from Chopin. He sits down to a piano and right away the angels come floating on soft velvety wings from the keys."

They were a great team.

One night at Dr. Leo Michel's apartment, songwriter Arthur Swanstrom introduced me to Mortimer Weinberg, an insurance agent, and told me this story while Weinberg kept chuckling and nodding his head. Seems the insurance man had been needling Swanstrom about songwriters and their so-called "profession," insisting "anyone who took the time could sit down and turn out a song."

"Oh, yeah?" challenged Arthur. "So go ahead, chum—you do it."

"Okay, I will."

Two days later, Weinberg phoned. "Well, I've written a song. Want to hear it?"

"Nope," snapped Swanstrom. "Wait until you sell a copy, then call me."

Weinberg went out and bought a failing music-publishing company and printed the song himself. He cajoled orchestra leaders and singers to play and sing the number. Many of them were clients of his and did it to humor him.

Some months elapsed, and Weinberg phoned Swanstrom again.

"Arthur," he said. "I have sold a copy of my song. In fact, the song has sold thousands and thousands of copies. In fact, Arthur, it's a juicy big hit. Now can I tell you about it, chum?"

"Sure," yawned Swanstrom. "Tell me about it. What's the song?"

The insurance man purred: "Where-a-You Work-a-John?" One of the truly runaway song smashes of the year.

So many singing girls must be grateful to composer Harold Arlen for the songs he provided for them and with which they became identified. Ethel Waters, for instance, for whom he wrote "Stormy Weather," and what a storm the patrons raised at the Cotton Club when she first sang it. Another memorable tune for Ethel contributed by Arlen was "Happiness Is Just a Thing Called Joe." Similarly, Judy Garland rarely can get off stage in any of her personal appearances without responding to the demand for Arlen's "Over the Rainbow," which she first introduced in the film, *The Wizard of Oz.* Which may explain why she interrupted her performance at the Palace Theatre in August of 1967 to toss a kiss at Arlen seated in an aisle seat in the third row. Billy Daniels is another forever grateful to Arlen for the big song in his routine—"Black Magic."

But the little story I wanted to tell was about a lass whom Arlen didn't even know in those earlier years, certainly not when he wrote "Stormy Weather." This was just one of the pretty girls in the Cotton Club chorus, and after hours in the dressing room, she would give out with her own impersonation of Ethel Waters singing the song. One night, Ethel in her own dressing room heard the girl entertaining her dressing-room mates and walked in much to the embarrassment of the lass who mumbled: "Oh, Miss Waters, it was all just in fun."

"In fun, girl?" exploded the star, "that's fine singin', girl. You get busy and don't let anybody stop you from singin' from now on."

And indeed, the girl didn't. And when they came to make the picture, *Stormy Weather,* it was just like a chapter from the fairy tales, for the star of the film was the former chorus girl Lena Horne.

Years ago, humorist Arthur "Bugs" Baer was enroute by train to Florida and while seated in the lounge he saw someone he was certain he knew, but to be sure, he waited for a nod of recognition. It came in the form of a salute, "Hello, John." Bugs knew that once again, as on previous occasions, he had been mistaken for then sports columnist of *The New York Times,* John Kieran.

Before he could identify himself, the man hastened over and apologized. "Stupid of me—you're Bugs Baer."

The humorist reassured him he wasn't miffed and then to ease the situation, said: "I get mixed up, too, Cole. There's that other songwriter—what's his name? You know, wrote 'Great Day,' 'Tea for Two'—uh—"

"You mean Vincent Youmans?"

"Oh, yes, that's right."

"I," said the chap who Baer was certain was Cole Porter, "am Vincent Youmans."

Some songwriters seize upon a current event for inspiration—"I Didn't Raise My Boy to Be a Soldier" by Alfred Bryant and Al Piantadosi is an outstanding example. That one clicked big, but few others did that I can recall. For instance, there was a couple rushed out when Floyd Collins was trapped in that cave-in: one a lachrymose ode labeled, "The Death of Floyd Collins," and another, "Floyd, America's Heart Is with You."

When Rudolph Valentino, the pomaded idol of the femme population died, Tin Pan Alley rushed bravely to the front with, "There's a New Star in Heaven Tonight." A rival publishing firm shortly after pushed out a heart-wringer entitled, "We'll Never Forget You," and to make certain, the cover bore a picture of the crowds milling around Campbell's Funeral Parlor! Others soon joined the parade of musical bouquets, among them, just as forgotten: "Rudy Isn't Gone" and "Valentino's in Valhalla."

It doesn't take much to set the lyric lads going. They gave us one, and it wasn't too bad, about Joe DiMaggio and his thumping bat, but they also gave us a dilly when Enrico Caruso died. The great tenor had scarcely been laid to rest when one publisher was out with the still damp copies of an item entitled: "They Needed a Songbird in Heaven so God Took Caruso Away."

Sometimes there are specialty numbers written exclusively for a performer. Example "Kaltenborn Blues" and "Poor Little February (only 28 days)," which Joe E. Lewis included in his repertoire for many years.

When the fuss between Daddy and Peaches Browning was at its name-calling stage, there was a brace of lulus thrown at us: "I'm All Alone in My Palace of Stone" and "All Is Not Peaches with Daddy."

As a rule, our more established songwriters rarely violate the code of decency and good taste, but there is one instance when one of them, Irving Berlin, was himself the victim of a stinker.

It was shortly after he had married socialite Ellin Mackay that we were afflicted with a number "The Kid from the East Side." The unabashed lyrics described Berlin's East Side background as contrasted with Ellin's silver-spoon-in-her-mouth breeding. I don't think many copies were sold—unless Berlin himself bought them up to get them out of circulation.

Charles A. Lindbergh got the full treatment. Tin Pan Alley greeted his return from that epochal flight with: "Charlie Boy, We Love You," "O, You Lucky Lindy," "Lindy, You Came Through" and "Just a Typical American Boy." Charles Levine's flight inspired only one wail: "Levine in His Flying Machine."

As for Gertrude Ederle, after her backbreaking span of the English Channel, the best she could inspire was: "Gert, You're Our Girl for Cert," which so incensed Ring Lardner he wrote a series of sardonic pieces blasting Song Row and what he termed its "messy opportunism."

Of course, the hillbilly songwriters were building their composition around personalities and events long, long ago. A historic example is the classic of pre-Civil War days: "John Brown's Body Lies a-Moulderin'," etc., etc.

Songs have been a prolific source for titles of books. John Steinbeck's *Grapes of Wrath* came from "The Battle Hymn of the Republic" ("He is trampling out the vintage where the grapes of wrath are stored"). Major George Fielding Eliot's *The Ramparts We Watch* was from our national anthem. John Weld's *Don't You Cry for Me* is from Stephen Foster's "O, Suzanna" ("O, Suzanna, don't you cry for me," etc.). Frances Gaither's *Follow the Drinking Gourd* was from the old slavery chant: "When the sun comes back, when the first quail calls, then the time is come—follow the drinking gourd." Cedric Belfrage's *Let My People Go* was from the Negro spiritual, "Go Down, Moses."

Among our prolific songwriters was Gus Kahn, who turned out the memorable lyrics for such outstanding hits of the past as "Little White Lies," "Carolina in the Morning," "It Had to Be You," "I'll See You in My Dreams" (which became the title of the movie based on his career), "Toot, Tootsie, Goodbye" and hundreds of others.

But at home, Gus was sometimes a pain in the neck to his ever loyal wife, Grace, chiefly because of his addiction to pianos and organs. He had no less than five pianos and three organs lodged in the house, and Mrs. Kahn often complained there was no room for other furniture. One day, in desperation and in rebellion, figuring Gus would never know, she sold one of the pianos to a dealer and donated one of the organs to a church society. The following day, a truck pulled up to the house. Out of it men carried in what was probably the largest grand piano in America and two fair-sized organs.

Gus, arriving home shortly after, blandly explained: "I couldn't help it, darling. I got all three at auction for only $900. By the way, dear, what did you get for the piano you sold?"

Johnny Mercer, a foremost lyricist—some of his memorable lively poetry was hugged by such melodies as "Lazy Bones," "Jeepers-Creepers," "I'm an Old Cow Hand," "Goody-Goody," "Blues in the Night," "That Old Black Magic," "One for my Baby," "Days of Wine and Roses"—wrote scores of others too numerous to mention with his composer-collaborators including such distinguished melodeers as Hoagy Carmichael, Harold Arlen, Jerome Kern, Arthur Schwartz, Henry Mancini—and some years back he was featured over the air with Benny Goodman's band. One day, while in Savannah, Georgia, he visited with his aged papa.

"Pa," he said, "Have you been listening to me on the air? What do you think?"

"Yes, Johnny," said Pa Mercer, sadly, "I listen in. It's the only way I can tell whether you're taking care of yourself, whether you've got a cold or something."

Mercer told me later: "I got the message. I started writing to Pa twice a week without fail."

Sigmund Romberg and his wife, Lillian, and Peggy and I became close friends shortly after Peggy and I were married in 1950. I had struck up an acquaintanceship with the composer as far back as 1931, when I persuaded him to write some highlights of his career for my "Down Memory Lane" column, but it wasn't until 1950 that we became intimate friends.

The Rombergs hosted a party for Peggy and myself at their Beverly Hills home, and among the guests I recall were songwriter Harry Ruby and his wife, playwright Joe Fields and his wife, Marion—and a portly lad whom I had asked the Rombergs to invite.

Romberg sat down at the piano and delivered a medley of

melodies from some of his better-known operettas: *New Moon, Student Prince, Blossom Time, The Desert Song,* and others. Ruby, a facile raconteur, also obliged with some of his own songs, among them, "Three Little Words," "I Wanna Be Loved" and "Who's Sorry Now?"

But the lad I wanted to be among us at the party never uttered a word. He sat there awestricken, he didn't even volunteer a laugh or a chuckle when Ruby told some amusing stories. Later, I said to my friend: "You certainly clammed up tonight. What was the matter?"

Said Jackie Gleason, for that's who it was, "What would a lowbrow like me be putting in my two cents with a guy like Sigmund Romberg? He is a genius. He's king. Don't you know that what I always wanted to be was someone who wrote that kind of music?"

Gleason, in part, fulfilled that ambition, for he is credited with having composed instrumental melodies like "Melancholy Serenade," "Lovers' Rhapsody" and others along those lines.

Getting back to that night at the Rombergs, the composer recalled that back in 1943 he had appeared with his concert orchestra in Buffalo, and among other numbers had offered Mendelssohn's "Wedding March," announcing it as "the most popular march in the world." After the concert a man came backstage, introduced himself as Robert Mendelssohn and expressed his opinion that it was quite a compliment to his illustrious forebear to label the famed melody as the most popular march, especially since it was wartime when the martial type was dominating.

This festive group includes, *from left to right:* Adam Gimbel, department store tycoon; Dorothy Fields, musical comedy librettist and songwriter; Sigmund Romberg, who gave us the scores of so many memorable operettas; Peggy Sobol; and Joseph Fields, famed playwright. Romberg and Fields died some years after this picture was taken.

"I told him," said Romberg, "there really was no competition, since they both had to do with arms, but Mendelssohn's concerns itself with the softer and sweeter type."

In the "Down Memory Lane" piece for me, Romberg wrote of meeting Victor Herbert and thereafter holding him and his memory in reverence, for Herbert had taken it upon himself to guide him through pitfalls that beset every young upcoming composer.

"And of course," he continued, "there was Franz Lehár. When I returned to Vienna for a visit, Lehár invited me to the Johann Strauss Theatre. He directed personally, in my honor, the score of *Friederike*. After the theatre, we had a little supper at Sacher's. We talked of art and life. Then he played the piano for me until three or four in the morning. I've never forgotten that night."

Romberg also recalled his thrill when the "Shubert offices called me up and told me that I had established a record for a living composer—four revivals of my operettas were playing in one season—*Maytime, Blossom Time, Student Prince* and *My Maryland*.

A little more than a year after the party, on November 9, 1951, Sigmund Romberg died suddenly, victim of a stroke, in his New York apartment in the Ritz Towers. This great composer with a record of seventy-eight musicals and more than two thousand songs to his credit, was only sixty-four.

That amazing old songman, Joe Howard, passed out of this life as he hoped he would—still performing. Death mowed him down on the stage of the Civic Opera House in Chicago at the reported age of ninety-two.

I used to sit with this energetic veteran in Bill's Gay Nineties where he was one of the featured acts. He was in his seventies then, and he airily insisted he was going to live to be a hundred and ten —"and I'll be singing right until the breath leaves my body." I recall, it was about the time he and his sixth—or perhaps it was his seventh—wife had parted. (The widow he left behind at the time of his death was his ninth!)

The remarkable thing about Howard was that in his seventies and even eighties, his voice had lost none of the vigor and quality that had distinguished it in his earlier vaudeville days. He needed no microphone to sing out robustly the songs he himself had written: tunes like "I Wonder Who's Kissing Her Now," "What's the Use of Dreaming?", "Goodbye, My Lady Love," "Hello, My Baby"—all of which were high on whatever passed for the Hit Parade in the long ago when they first came to the attention of the public.

Joe Howard had the distinction of having a movie based on his life: *I Wonder Who's Kissing Her Now,* after the title of his song. I don't know how much money Joe received for the film rights, but I do know that he always claimed he was broke. He would snicker when I asked him why, at his advanced age, he did not retire. "If you put all the dough I have," he said, "it would be two feet short of from here to the piano there" (a distance of some five feet). "In one dollar bills," he added.

One night back in 1944, I asked Robert Benchley what he thought of Irving Berlin's musical, *This Is the Army,* and he said he hadn't seen it but wanted to very much if for nothing else than to hear Irving Berlin sing his "K.P." song again as he did that night on the huge Century stage some twenty-five years before when, as Alec Woollcott had written, "left alone there with his scrubbing pail. Berlin's thin, shy, plaintive voice was raised in this refrain:

> 'Poor little me
> I'm a K.P.
> I scrub the mess hall
> On my bended knee.
> Against my wishes
> I wash the dishes
> To make this wide world safe for democracy.'"*

I told Benchley that no, Berlin did not sing the "K.P." song this time, that his voice was thinner and more plaintive than ever, but he did sing "Oh, How I Hate to Get Up in the Morning."

Benchley said: "Say, that Berlin—isn't he about the most wonderful fellow in the world?"—sounded almost like Saroyan, Benchley did, for "wonderful" was Saroyan's favorite descriptive.

*From "Kitchen Police" by Irving Berlin.

I couldn't and wouldn't argue with Benchley for I thought, and still do, that Irving Berlin is wonderful. Most of us recall the silly rumor spread years ago that a little colored boy actually wrote most of his songs, preposterous as it sounds. One popular story has it that when Berlin had arrived back in New York after holidaying in Palm Beach, songwriter Harry Ruby, studying his deeply tanned face, shouted: "Ah—there's the little colored boy who writes Berlin's songs."

Now it's ridiculous for me to attempt in a few paragraphs to cover the life and career of little Izzy Baline, the onetime singing waiter at Nigger Mike's who became Irving Berlin and married the attractive society girl Ellin Mackay. I simply want to ramble on in full appreciation of a supertalented gentleman who hasn't changed too much in all the years I've known him except, perhaps, for the better. He seems to have become kindlier and more thoughtful and more gracious and more willing to do a favor with each succeeding year—which for some mysterious reason, until recently, tucked no gray among his jet-black locks, but now the gray has appeared and is quite becoming, too, to this eighty-year-old, still active composer.

It may be a purely personal opinion but to me Berlin is and has been for many years America's Number One songman, and I am confident there are many others, including some fellow composers, who will agree with me about this skinny fellow with the most unmusical voice—a chap who can scarcely carry a tune and who has to thump out his melodies with a single finger of his right hand. Berlin has none of that phony modesty that sickens you. He is willing to admit he has the knack for writing salable tunes, and when he says, as he did once to me, "I'm the kind of guy who can think of only one song at a time—the song the other fellow wrote which I wish I had written," you needn't take him too seriously because he is convinced he can write just the kind of songs he wants to write and the public wants him to write.

Berlin, who holds one of the highest ratings with ASCAP, pulls in reportedly from $500,000 to $1,000,000 annually in royalties, in the dual role of songwriter and publisher. Once, for a brief spell, he was a member of the New York *Journal* staff. This was back in 1909. He and George Whiting were strolling along Broadway when George remarked casually, "My wife's gone to the country."

Berlin murmured: "Hooray"—and then added, "Hey, that's

a good title for a song." The two marched back to their office and there they tapped out the melody and the lyrics. The song caught on immediately and became a national rage. Berlin was asked by the *Journal* if he could continue to write new choruses for the song—and thereafter, for many months, a three-column feature (180 variations in all) was contributed by the songwriter.

The legend prevails that Berlin, seated in Lindy's Restaurant one evening, spotted through the window a familiar and slightly kooky character of the era whom we all knew as "Broadway Rose." She was usually bedraggled, and on this occasion she was wearing one of her grotesque bonnets burdened down with carrots, frayed artificial roses, a fern or two and some dangling shoelaces. Berlin mused, "You're in your Easter bonnet, hey girl?"—and that did it. According to the legend that was the genesis of "Easter Parade."

But I knew better—and I should—for I had created the little fairy tale. There is more to the story than that.

Actually, the tune had been composed by Berlin as far back as 1917 and was entitled, "Smile and Show Your Dimple." It was not an outstanding hit. Years later, the composer resurrected the melody and wrote the "Easter Parade" lyrics for it, planning it for the musical, *As Thousands Cheer.*

Berlin played it for Moss Hart. Moss heard no more about it, and a week or so later, he demanded, "Irving, that song—what about it?"

"Oh, I've thrown it away," confessed Berlin. "Didn't care for it."

Hart did a little storming about until the composer went hurrying over to a clutter on a shelf and finally dug it up, and into the show it went and became the Number One hit of the year.

Back in the late thirties, there was a bit of a controversy over who first sang Berlin's "Alexander's Ragtime Band," with some half dozen singing lads and gals claiming the distinction. When I asked Irving to settle the matter for me—it might make for a line or two in the column—he confessed ruefully he couldn't help out. "I really don't know," he said. So I offered his comment, hoping to tug some letters that might spur on the argument. And I was rewarded with a note, among others, from John W. Rumsey, then president of the American Play Company, which apparently cleared up the case.

"The song," he wrote, "was not written until late in 1910

and was first tried out before an audience in Chicago in the same year by Emma Carus. But in spite of that lady's gifted talents, her rendition of the song was not a success. It was not heard again until after it had been published on March 18, 1911, and its so-called official presentation took place on Sunday evening, May 28.

"The place was the New Amsterdam, the occasion, the Friars' Frolic. It was none other than Irving Berlin himself—and how can he forget it—sharing with Jean 'Bedelia' Schwartz in the Piano Bugs number who walked down to the footlights, and, accompanied by Harry Williams, sang the now famous song—and put it over with a bang. In thirteen consecutive days, Irving sang it in fourteen of the largest cities. After that, it was in."

Nobody knows actually how many hundreds of songs Irving Berlin has turned out, not even the composer himself. "I'm a songwriter—not a mathematician," he tells you, but the industry figures close to 2,000 would not be exaggerating the truth and Berlin doesn't dispute the figure. "You'd be surprised," he comments, "how many of them weren't too good, but who wants to talk about that?"

How does one pick favorites among all those notable songs? My own selection include: "When I Lost You," "A Pretty Girl Is Like a Melody," "Blue Skies," "White Christmas," "Always" and "Russian Lullaby"—and having thus written, I now find there are dozens of others I want to include.

Berlin is fond of Chinese food, preferring to find his dishes in the little joints on Pell Street in Chinatown, and he's quite proud of his deftness with chopsticks. He directs them so rapidly, with just the proper flip, that they look like miniature propellers. Until recently, he used to be a chain gum-chewer and usually, when his dinner arrived at one or another of the restaurants, he deposited a package of chewing gum in front of him.

One of his favorite yarns revolves about the time he took Ellin with him to visit his old Bowery haunts. They boarded a sightseeing bus and were amused by the barker's spiel. It was so fantastically cockeyed. The man credited Berlin with having written, "Chinatown, My Chinatown" (actually the collaboration of composer Jean Schwartz and lyricist William Jerome) and then, standing in front of an old mission, he described solemnly how Berlin had written his first song there. While the Berlins stood among the crowd, listening in amusement, an old Bowery loiterer who had known the composer from the ancient days, sauntered over and from the side of his mouth, so that Ellin wouldn't hear—whispered: "A lot of baloney, hey, Irving?"

"And do you know?" said Berlin, "I suddenly realized that's what it was. It was an awful letdown."

Berlin, these days, prefers to spend a major portion of his time at his sprawling estate in Livingston Manor in the Catskills where he fishes for trout in his well-stocked stream. It is his delight to broil the fish in the open for his guests, or prepare them from his own special recipes. And often he will dispatch a batch of the trout by bus, cab or his car to New York, where they are picked up by one of the employees of his music-publishing company and taken to some special friends.

The sad truth, though, is that he has few close friends these days for so many of his intimates are gone: Cole Porter, Wilson Mizner, Joe Schenck, Herbert Bayard Swope, Moss Hart, E. Ray Goetz, Robert Sherwood, to name a few. Now he feels closer to about four or five—among them, cartoonist and former columnist Irving Hoffman, theatrical lawyer A. L. Berman and composer Harold Arlen.

He is still turning out occasional songs. For the revival of *Annie Get Your Gun* back in 1966, he intruded a new rollicking number "Old-Fashioned Wedding," with which Ethel Merman stormed out and brought the house down. Berlin's major "moonlight" interest and chief hobby is painting. And many galleries, impressed with their merit, have wanted to have them for exhibits. But Berlin shies away from these offers, not convinced that his paintings have the professional touch—not yet.

Once he painted a portrait of his pal Harold Arlen seated at the piano, whereupon Arlen, also devoting himself to painting as a hobby, called upon him to make a deal. "I'll buy that portrait from you. Just name your price." Berlin snickered, "It's not for sale," he said. "But I'll make a trade. You give me that portrait you did of me and I'll give you this one." And the barter was made.

On another occasion, in 1966, a leading advertising agency approached Berlin and proffered a sum of money for the reproduction rights to one of his art offerings to be used in advertisements of one of their major clients. Berlin hung up on the man. He confessed he was shocked, actually shocked, that anyone would think he would lend himself to such a commercialization of his name, for he was certain it was not the painting that was considered so essential as the Irving Berlin tag.

The veteran songwriter welcomed his eightieth birthday on May 11, 1968. It was not an event to go unnoticed. On the Sunday previous, Ed Sullivan extended his usual one-hour television session by a half hour, and celebrities by the scores turned up, including outstanding fellow composers—many onstage to participate in the ceremonies, others in the audience to applaud. Among the performers were Ethel Merman, for whom he had written so many of her memorable songs, The Supremes, Bob Hope, Fred Waring, Robert Goulet, and, by remote control on video tape, Bing Crosby, who sang "White Christmas." President Johnson was heard and seen offering his praise in a video-taped message from the White House. The finale had Berlin himself leading hundreds of Boy Scouts and Girl Scouts in chanting his "God Bless America" —and nobody thought Irving's thin little voice was anything but glorious on this occasion. And on his birth date itself, some thousand or more Girl Scouts assembled in Central Park with others to salute the composer and chorus out the song again.

The late Cole Porter was not a gregarious soul. He extended his grudging friendship to a select few, Irving Berlin, for instance, (remember the line in one of his famous songs: "You're the top, You're a Berlin ballad"?) Others of his intimates were Elsa Maxwell, Ethel Merman, who introduced so many of his numbers, Monty Woolley from as far back as their Yale days, and perhaps three or four others. He mingled rarely with fellow songwriters, cared little for Broadway. He was disdainful of small talk and could never lend himself to it. He directed many of his songs toward the social sophisticates but he found just as many fans who "dug" him among stenographers, housewives, prostitutes and young women of the nightclub ensembles.

Assigned to turn out a magazine profile, I spent considerable time with Porter in his luxurious apartment in the Waldorf Towers, but I found it difficult to entice revealing personal sidelights. He'd say: "Oh, so-and-so did a piece on me last January—why don't you get it and read it?" or "I think everything was pretty well covered in Howard Taubman's piece in *The New York Times* magazine section."

Nor could I get any particularly favorable comment about fellow songwriters except, of course, Irving Berlin. He was unrestrained in his appreciation of Berlin's talent. He was not popular with the composers and lyricists who congregated at Lindy's or at Dinty Moore's. "You have a feeling," explained one

ASCAP member, "that you and he don't belong in the same set. You know—he's Shakespeare and you're Laura Jean Libby, sorta. He doesn't give out."

A perfectionist, who studied his rhyming dictionary zealously to lure just the right word, Porter's collegiate background cried out in horror at such makeshifts as "June" and "boom." He told me he was still pained at the memory of one rhyme in the historic explosion "You're the Top." In it there appeared among the lines dedicated to Waldorf salad and the aforementioned Berlin ballad, as well as old Dutch masters and Mrs. Astor, this couplet: "You're the steppes of Russia, You're the pants of a Roxy usher." Porter lamented: "It would have been so simple, now that I think of it. I could have written 'Sing Sing crusher' to rhyme with 'usher.'"

Porter recalled that the close friendship with Edgar Montillion Woolley, better known then and later as Monty Woolley, had its inception at the annual *Yale News* banquet when the heads of all the college organizations were invited to take part in the induction of the new staff. Monty, then beardless and not a man who could afford to come to dinner too often unless someone else paid for it, was the popular president of the Dramat (Yale University Dramatic Association) and cheerleader. Porter at the time was a lowly freshman—the only one present at the dinner, and invited because he had written "Bingo."

After the formal festivities, he was urged to sing a few tunes for the boys. He played the piano and sang half a dozen of the current hit songs, and then as a finale and a flag-waver, thundered out his own fighting hymn as the upperclassmen joined in, "Fight, fight, with all your might," etc., etc.

Woolley, the junior, discovered at that precise moment that he disliked the upstart freshman very much. When the shouting had subsided, he cornered him and said curtly: "Son, you're great stuff, you think, huh? Don't let it go to your head."

Cole, awed in the presence of the magnificent king of Dramat, twitched nervously and mumbled in great humility: "Mr. Woolley, I know. If I broke this little pink finger and couldn't play, nobody here would give me a tumble."

Woolley said nothing for a few seconds, then put an arm around the lad and murmured: "Son, give me time. I may yet get to like you."

As Cole told me the story, he permitted a slight grin to caress his lips. "I hate to toss a cliché at you," he said, "but it was the beginning of a beautiful friendship."

Incidentally, that friendship led to Woolley's first entry into Broadway theatre, not as an actor as he became later, but as a director when he staged Porter's *Fifty Million Frenchmen*—on Cole's insistence to producer E. Ray Goetz.

On April 28, 1968, the Lambs Club honored Richard Rodgers. I was asked to contribute a piece for inclusion with other articles in the little journal gotten up for the occasion. My tribute, entitled "Some Enchanting Guy" ran as follows:

> How and where does one begin in saluting the musical genius who goes by the name of Richard Rodgers?
>
> The man has composed more than two thousand melodies—the bulk of them ever memorable, and no one has come forth to accuse him of thefting a bar or two, voluntarily or involuntarily, from any of the ancient masters. Indeed, the truth is, from time to time we have had tunes thrust upon us that are reminiscent instead of Rodgers originals.
>
> Dick was already climbing to the heights when this reporter was just a fledgling Broadway historian and that was forty years ago. Years before that, in 1925, to be exact, he and his collaborator Lorenz Hart had zoomed into powerful attention with their frolicsome, tuneful *Garrick Gaieties* and the critics, both drama and musical, were shouting their hosannas and crystal-balling, so correctly, that much good, entertainment-wise, would emanate from the youthful combine.
>
> Since there will be, no doubt, considerable all-embracing biographical data submitted in this *Lambs Journal* covering Rodgers' career as one of the world's most prolific producers of hit melodies, I'm not indulging myself in a listing of the imposing array of his songs and musicals—songs which remain classics around the world, and will be played and sung long after this writer has become a dim memory, or for that matter, if you'll pardon the melancholy thought, all you who read this piece.
>
> The man himself has remained unspoiled by the international acclaim that has hailed him through the years—glowing appraisal of his genius that amounts close to adulation on the part of many. Yet he is not an awesome personality. I mean he is easily approachable and endowed with a sincere modesty. I don't recall that he has ever manifested resentment of the occasional and so very rare disparagement offered by a dyspeptic critic now and then, or stooped to dash off an indignant note or wire to a supercritical newsman.
>
> He is the type who might easily be lost in a crowd—unidentified, because he is not the flamboyant, exhibitionistic gentleman

of super talent who takes himself too seriously. His melodic offerings—oh, yes, those he does take seriously for he is a perfectionist, as a true craftsman must be. What I am getting at, though, is that he is the neighbor next door concerning himself as do most of us with the unimportant facets of living as well as with whatever distresses all of us in the conduct of national and world affairs. But he doesn't set himself up as a know-it-all prophet nor have I ever heard him express disdain for the output of fellow composers. In fact, he is the first to bestow high praise on the offerings of his contemporaries.

The truth is, in my opinion, that if Dick had been projected into some other field of endeavor,. God forbid, he would still be the high-grade gentleman who would be tapped for honors—such as this occasion offered by the Lambs in affectionate salute.

Believe me, folks, Richard Rodgers is truly One Enchanting Guy. The world has been richer—our generation particularly—for having him among us.

For the theatrical group assembled at the affair, it was unnecessary to record Rodgers' memorable melodies and the musicals to which he and his collaborators had contributed the great scores. Who can think of Rodgers without associating him promptly with *South Pacific, Sound of Music, No Strings, The King and I, Oklahoma!, Carousel,* et cetera, et cetera, et cetera? Or some of his contagious tunes—"Some Enchanted Evening," "Ten Cents a Dance," "Mountain Greenery," "With a Song in My Heart," "My Funny Valentine"? Just a few of the thousands of Richard Rodgers melodies.

The stormiest songwriter in the profession—an erratic but on the whole, warmhearted genius—was the late Lew Brown whose lyrics included besides "That Old Feeling" (the genesis of which I referred to earlier in this chapter), such others as "I'd Climb the Highest Mountain," "The Varsity Drag," "Life Is Just a Bowl of Cherries," "Beer Barrel Polka," "You're the Cream in My Coffee" and dozens and dozens of others equally notable, as well as lively scores for stage and film musicals.

Brown, a highly sensitive soul, was always ready to give battle when offended but equally quick to forgive. He once sued me for $100,000 for alleged libel, only to call the suit off a few weeks later when he barged into a party in my honor, publicly announcing all was forgiven and forgotten as he kissed me on both cheeks.

When he viewed Ernest Borgnine's portrayal of him in the film *The Best Things in Life Are Free,* he was resentful and he

Composer Richard Rodgers seems genuinely interested in the remarks of the author, but Peggy Sobol is apparently more concerned with the contents of her purse.
Photo by Wide World Photos

insisted it wasn't a true or flattering takeoff. He phoned me to express his anger. Either he met Borgnine later or was impressed with the glowing reviews, for he phoned again to say he took it all back. "Maybe I should be flattered after all," he conceded—"and you can quote me—I am. But I was never that tough."

He was quite absentminded. Once, driving up to a theatre with his first wife, Sylvia, he stepped out of the cab, tipped his hat and murmured politely: "It was nice meeting you," and started to walk off. On one occasion he phoned me urging me to meet him at once at the old Billy LaHiff's Tavern to discuss a matter of vital importance. When I arrived, he stormed that I had written a dangerous article about a well-known racket king, Phil Kastel, and his advice was to get out of town immediately for a few weeks until the man's rage subsided. A week later, I ran into Kastel at Dinty Moore's and approached his table, somewhat diffidently I must confess, and asked him meekly was he still incensed.

Kastel stared at me in visible puzzlement. "Mad at you? Why should I be mad at you?" he demanded. "Look, I never get mad at reporters. I'm not that dumb."

It isn't always the glory road for songwriters. Take Jimmy Campbell, the British lad who wrote such winners (occasionally in collaboration with other tunesmiths) as "If I Had You," "Goodnight, Sweetheart," "Try a Little Tenderness" and others equally notable. Riding high in the late twenties and thirties, he had squandered his royalties by the forties, was bankrupt and an alcoholic. He was even jailed for fraud in connection with bad checks, and at one point in his career, he sought a cure in a hospital's alcoholic ward. But it did seem that the sun was shining down brightly again when in 1951 his song "Down at the Ferry-boat" became quite a hit.

The story is that after a long siege of despondency and a continued battle with his thirst, some happier days came along when Sinatra, Tony Bennett and others began singing his well-known songs again, especially on their long-playing record offerings.

Campbell moved to Tangiers in Morocco in 1967 and had scarcely lodged himself there when he broke a leg. He was flown to London for hospitalization and died there on August 19, 1967.

Then there is the melancholy story of songwriter Roger Graham, who authored the lyrics for "I Ain't Got Nobody" as well as the words for some 125 songs, including a big hit, "Shim-Me-Sham-Wabble," which proved so popular with dancers who trotted around to the tune in an early version of the Big Apple.

Graham died in Chicago in October of 1938 penniless, alone, forgotten, in a charity ward in the Cook County Hospital. No one claimed his body and it was taken to the county morgue. They might well have sung out his song as a dirge: "I ain't got nobody —and nobody cares for me."

Graham, for some reason, was not a member of ASCAP, but the organization, learning that the body might be deposited in a pauper's grave, forwarded funds for a more suitable burial.

Successful songwriter though he was, Fred Fisher found the final days of his life burdensome as he fought off his incurable illness. Composer, lyricist and publisher, he had few financial worries. He wrote the lyrics for one of the top sellers, "Dardanella," and composed or wrote the lyrics for countless other hit songs, among them "Peg o' My Heart," "Ireland Must Be Heaven," "Ma, He's Making Eyes at Me," "Oui, Oui, Marie" and hundreds of others.

Getting back to "Dardanella," the tune was originally composed by Johnny Black under the title of "Turkish Tom-Tom" and later it was submitted to Fisher, who by that time also had his own publishing house. Fisher decided to write new lyrics for the melody, renamed it, and it became the greatest selling phonograph recording of all time—6,500,000 platters—as well as selling close to

2,000,000 copies of the sheet music. (Black, incidentally, was killed in 1936 during a roadhouse brawl in a dispute over the trifling sum of 25 cents.)

On January 14, 1942, Fisher, despondent over his illness, hanged himself in the bedroom of his luxurious penthouse. He was sixty-five.

Songs these days rarely linger on in favor to the extent that they did in earlier eras before radio and television. Now, if a tune catches on, it is played or sung so continuously that the public tires of it, although it is quite true that a decade or so from now, it may be resurrected and gain a new lease on life. Which reminds me that on one occasion, after Kate Smith had sung Irving Berlin's "God Bless America" for a sequence in the picture *This Is the Army,* Berlin commented that the song had been sung and played so much over radio that it was threatened with extinction because of overplugging. He recalled what Georgie Jessel had said to him about this overexposure. "Irving, Francis Scott Key was much smarter than you. He made 'The Star-Spangled Banner' hard to sing."

I have never been able to join the apostles of rock 'n' roll, and indeed, to indicate how much of a square I am, must confess that I react only lukewarmly to Le Jazz Hot, though the Dixieland type has a certain appeal. The truth is, I am partial to the sweet in melody: pop, operetta and the corny offerings, too.

But I do admit that the careers of the lads of the past and present fascinate me—from Bix Beiderbecke, Frank Teschemacher, Leon Rappolo, Red Norvo to Louis Armstrong, Louis Prima, Duke Ellington, Lionel Hampton, Pee Wee Russell and others. I like to hear about the dedication to jazz of the old-timers who were willing to starve for their love and who, whether or not there was enough booze around to lift the spirits, kept at it—playing until sunup and then repairing to squalid flops or hideaways to continue to ignite cornet cadenzas, tail-gate trombone glissandos and clarinet trills. The pioneers of the hot and noisy were unpredictable personalities, stuffed with genius, naïve when it came to material things and strong only in the big urge—to express themselves on the horn or the keyboard or even the violin.

Sarah Vaughn once offered her definition of jazz. "It's like I'm singing with a choir. We all have our music in front of us—

and we're singing from the sheets. That's classical. Suddenly the lights go out. It's so dark, nobody can read the music. But I'm still singing. Well, that's jazz."

During the years, I naturally found myself becoming a fan of certain singers. In the beginning, my favorite troubadours included Tommy Lyman, Harry Richman, Maurice Chevalier, Tony Martin, Bing Crosby, Russ Columbo, Benny Fields and Rudy Vallee. Later, I added to my list Perry Como, Frank Sinatra, Dean Martin, Enzo Stuarti, Nat "King" Cole, Bobby Darin, Robert Goulet, Vic Damone, Mel Torme—perhaps a few others, including that delightful team of Tony Sandler and Ralph Young.

The distaff contingent found me rooting for Nora Bayes, Ruth Etting, Belle Baker, Helen Morgan, Sophie Tucker, Ethel Waters, Ethel Merman, Libby Holman, Judy Garland, Lena Horne, Dinah Shore, Julie Wilson, Gertrude Niesen, Ella Logan, Jane Froman, Edith Piaf, Blossom Seeley—and more recently Barbra Streisand, Pearl Bailey, Diahann Carroll, Petula Clark, Kaye Stevens and Leslie Uggams.

Singing styles changed, and we finally reached the era of Elvis Presley followed by the onslaught of the Beatles and other rock 'n' roll groups. But I remain a square at heart—still preferring, as I have mentioned earlier, the sweet and soft in melody.

Do I have to identify this smiling youth with the author's hand resting on his shoulder? He was a hopeful singing lad with his future ahead of him then—also Ava Gardner and Mia Farrow, plus a multimillion-dollar empire.

9

Nights to Remember— and a Few Afternoons, Too

BROADWAY, WHICH USED TO BOIL along with activity until sunup, suddenly found itself trapped by a midnight curfew ruling during World War II, and much of the spirit of night life evaporated, even though, as Toots Shor philosophized, "A guy who can't get loaded by twelve o'clock ain't half trying." It's true some of the more daring bistros occasionally defied the curfew, but the law stepped in quickly.

Then, in May of 1945, the ban was lifted. I went out into the streets expecting something of the revelry and excitement that had sizzled in the wild joy over VE-day but this first dividend on the European Victory, the lifting of the curfew, elicited little of the hell-raising. It's true I found Broadway and its thinnish arteries crowded and the little saloons of the Skid Row type jammed with shouting, drinking customers, but this bibulous gaity and gregariousness had been the Manhattan mood for months except that it was usually quenched at midnight. The chief difference now was there was no mass exodus at the witching hour. Customers lingered on in both the larger and smaller groggeries. But no cheering, no lachrymose emotionalism.

Only the nightclub and restaurant hosts, especially those operating the larger cabarets—Lou Walters of the Latin Quarter, Billy Rose of the Diamond Horseshoe, Carl Erbe and Joe Howard of the Zanzibar, Nick Prounis and Arnold Rossfield of the Versailles, Monte Proser and Jules Podell of the Copacabana—greeted the end of the restrictions with enthusiasm.

"Now," said Erbe, "we have a couple more hours to beat the nut. Our places have big shows—chorus girls, highly paid performers, costly bands. We were drawing big crowds, but they couldn't drink fast enough to cover the expenses."

Broadway itself, of course, presented a dazzling spectacle as the millions of lights exploded into the refulgence so characteristic of prewar days, and the throbbing, boisterous thoroughfare and pedestrians bathed joyously in the warm brilliance. The fact that Broadway's lights after the dismal blackout years were on again did more to lift drooping spirits than abandonment of the curfew or the news that horse racing had now been granted the green signal.

The restoration of racing did make a happy conversation piece in the night spots. Especially did it bring happiness to certain gentry, immaculate, smooth-shaven, puffing on Havana cigars, as they tugged at their expensive Charvet or Sulka ties and discussed soberly and not too loudly their plans for corralling customers again. These were the bookmakers who had suffered silently through the long dreary shutdown months. Some had even gone to work, and they shuddered as they described their horrendous experiences.

It was actually the lights-on, rather than the suspension of the curfew, that enticed thousands of strollers to Fifth Avenue for the delight of window-shopping at night. In fact, even at 2:00 A.M. there were still throngs of our worthy burghers strolling that luxury thoroughfare which had usually been deserted after midnight during the blackout.

I found Tallulah Bankhead at the Stork Club, seated with theatrical publicist Richard Maney, the perambulant thesaurus who was to become her biographer. Tallulah, in her usual machine-gun staccato, declared that it was wonderful, this business of being able to stay around in a saloon until almost dawn-break, because the curfew, she insisted, was a form of regimentation.

Jack Kriendler of "21" was less enthusiastic than other hosts, pointing out that the plush dining place had usually preferred at all times to have its customers out of the place by 1:00 A.M. even prior to the curfew.

The theatres, both legitimate and cinema, benefited mightily, and receipts tilted noticeably upward. Most of the movie houses promptly made arrangements for the return of the midnight showings. The nightclubs with entertainment resumed the old schedule—three shows a night, to the dismay of most of the performers. Parenthetically, the stars began balking over the third show, so accustomed had they been to the leisure provided when only two shows were required. You may attribute it to the curfew that to these days performers usually contract for only two shows nightly, except on Saturdays, and in some of the hotel supper-clubs, the more dominant stars insist on only a single show a night.

I remember as I left the Stork Club that I asked the veteran, white-haired, usually smiling little Greek, Jimmy Coulis, guardian of the rope that barred entry or was lifted for the favored, whether he was pleased the curfew days were over.

"I tell you, Mist' Somb'," said Jimmy quietly. "I no t'ink much about how it is. My boy—las' mont'—he was killed in the war."

By way of contrast, how does usually frivolous, self-centered Broadway react when the nation's chief is embraced by death? From the news story I wrote for the *Journal-American* on Friday, April 13, 1945, you may get some idea of the reaction to the news of Franklin D. Roosevelt's death.

> Broadway fumbled about in an emotional fog last night as it endeavored to show how sincere was its grief over the passing of the All Right Guy who had been President.
>
> Like the rest of the nation, Broadway was stunned at the unexpected news—and for an hour or two wondered just how it should show its respect and genuine sorrow.
>
> Then one by one the nightclubs stopped the music, called off the entertainment. El Morocco closed the bars. Others shuttered for the night, among them the Zanzibar, Jack Dempsey's, Leon & Eddie's.
>
> There was no weeping in the streets. Folks in the restaurants and in the saloons were singularly limited in their verbal expression of grief.
>
> It was "Gee, at least he should have lived a few more days now we've got the Nazis licked" or "What a tough break! Right

when it's almost over, he has to die" or "So many heels in the world—and it has to be a good guy like Roosevelt."

Broadway—and it is to be presumed the rest of the nation—couldn't understand why it had no prior inkling that the President was so gravely ill, although it was admitted he didn't look so well in those late newsreel shots. Why hadn't his doctor, Vice Admiral Ross T. McIntyre been with him at Warm Springs? How come they let him wear himself out posing for a picture? And so on and so on.

Boisterous Toots Shor, subdued and suspiciously red-eyed, telephoned to his friend Robert Hannegan, the Democratic party's Mr. Big. Hannegan, choked with grief, said he had spoken to the President only a day previously.

"We've lost a great fellow—a great, great fellow," he said. Incidentally, Shor told me that only a few days before, he had received a note from then Vice-President Truman requesting a bill for the pair of tickets the restaurant man had obtained for him for *The Barretts of Wimpole Street.*

Broadway confessed it rather liked Harry Truman, the new President. It had gotten to know him within the past few weeks. He had visited several restaurants, had been to the fights at Madison Square Garden and to the theatre. He revealed a liking for music, and Broadway knew him to be tolerant of the lighter things of life to which the Big Artery is so partial—and so on the whole it wished him well from the bottom of its heart.

There were some who seemed more deeply moved than others by Roosevelt's death. Frank Sinatra, followed like a Pied Piper by a procession of sober-faced disciples, unshouting and undemonstrative for a change, hurried to St. Patrick's Cathedral to offer his prayers.

I heard the news as John the Barber was shaving me over at "21." John, only a few months ago, lost his pilot son, killed in action in Burma.

"That's bad—bad. I feel like I want to sit down and cry," he said.

At the theatres where comedies were featured, the audiences remained apathetic. In many cases, people walked out after the first act and didn't return. There were hundreds of cancellations of ticket reservations. The majority of New York's citizens, regardless of political affiliations, was in no mood for frivolity.

Somehow I had to contrast that night's prevailing attitude with the reaction around Broadway when another President died. That was in August of 1923. I was then assistant city editor of the *Waterbury Republican,* and I welcomed the errand which afforded an opportunity to stay overnight in New York.

When I woke in the dinky midtown hotel the following morning, the elevator man was the first to tell me the news—Warren G. Harding had died.

Now it seems a cruel thing to say, but as I mingled around with the crowds on Broadway and listened in on the conversations then, I could detect no expressions of grief, nor much concern as to how the nation would fare with a new President at its head.

In fact by the afternoon, most of the talk had drifted back to the usual channels—baseball, horse races and girls—although, of course, the more serious-minded did discuss Coolidge, the new President.

The night we mourned FDR's death was different. From the doormen at nightclubs, colored entertainers in little groups in front of the Fifty-second Street jive joints, cops on their beats, stars in their dressing rooms, little chorus girls, authors, composers to hard-boiled reporters in the city rooms of the metropolitan newspapers—there was a sense of shock, almost incredulity that Death should steal in a lap ahead of the inevitable World War II victory.

The Big Town seemed even more shocked on November 22, 1963, as the news blasted through over radio and television that President John F. Kennedy had been felled by an assassin's bullets. For the city considered JFK one of its own. He had been a frequenter of the restaurants and night spots around town before his elevation to the White House, and of the theatres, too, and even the dignity of his high post failed to dim the impression that he was just a Right Guy whom you might invite to stand up at the bar and have a drink with you.

Practically every nightclub and hotel supper club closed for the evening. Scheduled gala events were canceled, including a Celebrity Register Party at Lüchows. Jan Mitchell, Cleveland Amory and Earl Blackwell sent wires to more than six hundred invited guests calling the affair off and expressing grief over the national tragedy.

Canceled, too, was the dinner of the Academy of Television Arts and Sciences which was to honor Jackie Gleason, and canceled were the annual Newspaper Women's ball at the Astor and the Concert Opera Association's affair at the Plaza.

Restaurants that featured music remained opened but dismissed the bands. Most of the legitimate theatres as well as movie houses closed shop. Toots Shor was one restaurant man so grieved over the tragedy that he closed the doors of his eating place that night. The sad news was delivered to Mrs. George Skakel, sister-in-law of the Robert Kennedys, while she was at lunch at "21." She broke into tears, left the lunch untouched and rushed hurriedly from the place.

The Plaza's Persian Room shut the room down. Ethel Merman, starring that week, commented, "It's just as well. How could I have possibly sung a single note after this terrible, terrible thing. I would have done nothing but cried."

Arturo Miratelli, who operated La Scala restaurant, had planned to keep his place open as some other restaurants had decided but on the way to his place he ran into author Ben Hecht. Hecht, in a deeply depressed mood said: "I think this murder is the worst shock I have had in my entire life—the worst." Miratelli thereupon gave orders to shut down for the night.

In the places that did keep open I heard Republicans and Democrats alike expressing what seemed genuine grief—some commenting on the string of tragedies that had afflicted the Kennedy family. At Danny's Hideaway, for instance, Attorney General Louis Lefkowitz, staunch Republican, said: "It's unbelievable—simply unbelievable that anything so shocking could happen in these so-called enlightened days. I'm simply stunned and I grieve with all my heart for and with the family. This was a fine young man."

The Jolly Madhouse

New Year's Eve in 1939 found me far from the bluster of Broadway, miles away at retired comedian Joe Cook's country estate up Lake Hopatcong way where all should have been quiet and restful. Cook had named his place Sleepless Hollow, and I was shortly to discover why. Indeed, at evening's end, I made up my mind that next time I sought peace and quiet I'd hie off to a nice sedate insane asylum.

I can't recall all who were among the fellow victims, but I do remember editor Harold Ross of *The New Yorker,* cartoonist Rube Goldberg and his wife, Irma, singing comedienne Helen Ford, a handsome young Britisher who was introduced as Lord Ruthven, which may or may not have been his name, grocery tycoon William Seeman and his then wife, Phyllis Haver, graduate of Mack Sennett's bathing beauties, theatre critic John Chapman and his wife, film producer Lew Gensler and some dozen others who popped in and popped out and then popped in again in various costumes.

James, the gentleman who served as butler—in brown shoes, baggy threadbare pants and a voluminous braided and epauleted crimson British general's swallowtail, was someone who must have understudied the late Lon Chaney. We put on our coats and galoshes and earmuffs at Cook's command to journey over to "Schultz's Tavern," and arriving there, we found that the Teutonic-looking Mr. Schultz was suspiciously resemblant to the solicitous butler. Also that Schultz's actually was merely two flights down in the main house. Shortly after, we were ordered to go over to "Kelly's" and the affable, Gallic-looking Mr. Kelly, I could have taken an oath, was a brother of the Teutonic-looking Mr. Schultz, who was the dead image of the British butler, James.

At midnight, a cannon boomed, and we left Kelly's to pile into the snow and there, fifty yards ahead on an elevation, blue, red and white flares illuminated into a giant "1776," and suddenly the entire vicinity was alight with blue fire and on the mound appeared the symbolic trinity of the American Revolution—the fifer, the drummer and the flag carrier. Somehow, the flag carrier looked like Kelly who looked like Schultz who looked like James the butler.

In Mr. Cook's elaborate private theatre, a special show had been arranged in which Mortimer Gaxton (yes, he looked like Messrs. Schultz, Kelly and James) was the master of ceremonies, and the cast consisted of Mr. Cook's sleepy-eyed hound who nibbled on a dog biscuit and then slumped into a quiet slumber as the curtain fell.

We were herded off now to play pool—but not too long, because everytime the ball went into the pocket that was the end of it. It simply disappeared. I sat on a soft chair to inspect Mr. Cook's personally collected stereopticon views, and suddenly the chair bounced me up and down, electric needles prodded my legs, and from nowhere water squirted into my ears.

The ceiling in "Schultz's Tavern" was littered with tiny gadgets—from ten dollar gold pieces to thimbles. The idea was that almost everything that could be held in a hand would be found on that ceiling. The mantelpieces were decorated with agates ranging from the ordinary-sized marble to some as large as footballs. Mr. Cook explained that: When he was a boy, he could only afford those little clay miggles, and he envied the more opulent lads with the glossy agates. So when he came into the money he began collecting the finest assortment of aggies he could locate.

Kelly's was cluttered with drinking mugs. They hung from the ceilings. They smothered the walls, they bulged from the windows and leaped out at you at the tables. Some were centuries old, and comedian Cook was confident that with the possible exception of Robert Ripley's this was the most complete collection in the world. When he was a youngster, he told us, he had his first drink of beer out of a mug which dropped from his hands and shattered into little fragments. He said that first drink gave him a feeling of exaltation he had never experienced before. He couldn't pay for the broken mug so he put in a day's work in the kitchen of the saloon for compensation. For some reason that gave him the inspiration to collect drinking urns.

We also played golf on a rare course on which no matter how or where you hit the ball, somehow it drifted onto the green (which had been cleared of snow) into the aperture that rewarded you with a hole-in-one. Nor must I ignore the ping-pong table which had the chronic staggers. Incidentally, at five o'clock in the morning, when most of us started to take our departure, the chambermaid blew a saxophone in a farewell sendoff. The tune? "Three O'Clock in the Morning"—perhaps a gentle hint that we had overstayed out visit.

A rare practical joker was this comedian who had graduated from vaudeville into musicals—with Raymond Hitchcock in *Hitchy Koo,* in Earl Carroll's *Vanities,* in *Rain and Shine* and *Fine and Dandy.* His zany offerings included his famed hilarious imitation of for Hawaiian ukelele players. His stooge was a chap named Dave Chasen—the same Dave Chasen who went on to become a dominant restaurateur in Hollywood, with some of his financial backing coming originally from *The New Yorker*'s Harold Ross.

Joe Cook prided himself on his culinary artistry, especially in the barbecuing of spareribs and preparing of chile con carne. The story is told that at one of his Sleepless Hollow gatherings playwright-actor Marc Connelly was among the guests and deeply appreciative of the chile. Three years later, he attended the opening of *Fine and Dandy.* After the final curtain he barged into Cook's dressing room. As they shook hands, the comedian awaited

Connelly's criticism. "What did you think of it?" he asked.

"Best chile con carne I ever ate—the very best," said the playwright.

Cook snapped: "The show—I'm asking you about the show."

Connelly answered calmly: "You must give me the recipe for that chile" and walked out leaving the performer staring at his retreating back, unhappy and puzzled.

About six months after my experience at Cook's estate, I received a note from auctioneer Joseph P. Day wondering whether I would be interested in purchasing "Sleepless Hollow" as a country home for the Sobol clan. The price he quoted was eminently reasonable, $42,000, but unfortunately Mr. Day did not suggest where the amount might be obtained by an improvident newsman. It was finally sold to a real estate firm for a sum undisclosed.

Joe Cook ended up his final days suffering from Parkinson's disease. He died on May 17, 1959.

With Some Old-Timers

Ordinarily, a chap in the business of writing daily pieces for his newspaper regards an invitation to a cocktail brawl staged by a picture company about as inviting as a bid to read a rival's press clippings.

Anyone with an even distribution of his gray matter senses that when a movie company's publicity department goes to the trouble of hiring a hall, bringing in one or more of its glamor girls or male stars and handing out the drinks and free hors d'oeuvres, it is not because of a great philanthropic gesture of hospitality.

However there was something in the wording of the message arriving at my office on March 7, 1944, pleading my attendance at a rally of veteran performers at the musty but colorful old Murray Hill Hotel that appealed to my zest for nostalgia. I realized fully the motive behind the party—it was a none-too-subtle rup-a-dup-dup of the ballyhoo drums for a picture coming into town, *Shine on Harvest Moon* which purported to be the story of and about Nora Bayes. Nevertheless, I decided to attend. It was a happy decision.

First of all, the moment I entered the dignified, spacious

lobby of the ancient edifice, I drifted back to another era—to hansom cabs and bustles and peekaboo shirtwaists and rococo decor. Any second I expected some florid-faced old dandy in a silk top hat and a swirling cape and twirling a gold-topped cane to strut by me.

Joe Laurie, Jr., a vaudevillian and later a historian of vaudeville, was the emcee. The late diminutive Mr. Laurie affected that Jr. after his name, but intimates whispered and foes shouted that actually he was one of the college gentlemen who sent Abe Lincoln a book to read by his cabin fireside. I knew this to be a malicious canard.

At any rate, I realized I was in for happy moments as soon as I entered the big ballroom where the party was in full swing, because the first two people I spied were those veteran character actors Fred Stone and J. C. Nugent in a huddle at a center table. A second later, there was a great deal of noise when Jimmy Durante began breaking up the furniture and climbing on the chandeliers while Eddie Jackson did a strut. Ethel Levey, the ex-Mrs. George M. Cohan brushed by, commenting she couldn't understand why she was at the affair at all, since it was a party sponsored by Warner Brothers and she was in the midst of suing Warners' for something or other connected with the picture about the late Yankee Doodle Dandy.

On my way to the bar for a preprandial libation of aqua needled with lemon juice, Pat Rooney, the dancing man, stopped me to introduce his brand-new bride. A few seconds later he was up front with his sister Kate, dancing away as the two of them did in other days and other years, away back when there were older Rooneys in command and these two were the baby newcomers in the act.

The exchange of chatter revolved, of course, about Nora Bayes herself—the tempestuous, temperamental, glorious personality who had been laid to rest some sixteen years previously. Bobby Clark recalled a night he had danced with her until she begged off, and critic Kelcey Allen said he still had a note of appreciation from her for the glowing review he had written of her act. Gitz Rice, who wrote the beautiful World War I ballad "Dear Old Pal of Mine," Eddie Darling, who so often had booked Nora into the Palace, the veteran vaudeville team of Smith and Dale, the Duncan Sisters—all drifted into sentimental moods as they remembered their own contacts with the departed star.

In a tribute to Nora, eighty-nine-year-old Lucius Henderson, who was a vaudeville star when vaudeville was in its infancy, offered fragments of his old routine and was followed by seventy-two-year-old Hal Ford, who had been a musical comedy favorite forty years before this party. Ford sang a few old-time songs which he insisted had been favorites of Miss Bayes.

So many of those who were at this memorable get-together are gone—as is the Murray Hill Hotel, itself.

Desert Song

I go back to a night in February of 1939 at the B-Bar-H ranch in Palm Springs, California. It may be balmy during the day, but darkness comes early in the desert cup, as the sun glides swiftly down behind the mountains—and with darkness comes the nip of wintry cold. So it was that we had slipped into sweaters and jackets despite a blazing fire in the open fireplace, and as we sat there waiting for dinnertime, Harpo Marx suggested that if Eddie Cantor would carry the tenor and Moss Hart the baritone, he himself would lead in the melodies and thrust in, he was certain, a satisfactory bass as well.

So the three of them blended voices in a few tunes and during a pause, Cantor recalled another impromptu singfest some months previously when Al Jolson had invited him, Harpo and Lou Holtz on a yachting trip. Four miles from shore on a roughing sea, Jolson gathered his shipmates and proposed they join him in a little harmony. Those of the yacht's help who were not occupied were commanded by Jolson to stand by and listen.

For two hours the timbers rang under the harmony of "Old

An anniversary party being celebrated by Eddie Cantor and his Ida, initiated by a quintet of singing Western Union lads when the "Singing Telegram" was the fad in the late thirties and early forties.

Black Joe," "Sweet Adeline," "Three O'Clock in the Morning," "I Want a Girl, Just Like the Girl" and so on. "He really dug them up," said Cantor, as he pursued with the story.

"Well," he went on, "Here was Jolie, about the greatest entertainer we have, and Harpo and Lou Holtz are no slouches and in the big money, and I guess maybe I shouldn't complain how I stand in show business. Well, our business is to entertain—and we don't get paid off in nickels and dimes—but here we were on a holiday and, like a bunch of barbershop hangers-on, giving out for free for the sake of a few ship's help."

Cantor confessed he tired first. Then Holtz's voice gave out and Harpo's bass fell flat. This left Jolson to carry on single-o, and for a few bright moments he did sing out lustily. Then he looked appealingly at his friends. Each shook his head. Jolson pleaded, just one more sweet song. The boys said "No."

Then like Caesar in his tent, the great Jolson started sulking. He walked away from the group, sat by himself, hummed a little, got up and walked toward the bow of the ship. All during the evening mess he sat silent, refusing to talk to the others. It was an excellent dinner, and the wine was good. When the second cup of coffee had been passed, Cantor rose and sang out softly, "I had a Gal, I had a Pal." Harpo broke in with his bass, Holtz with his quavery alto. The Jolson face relaxed. A grin spread slowly from ear to ear. Then the Jolson voice boomed in, his hands gestured, and the four set their arms about each other affectionately, and for three hours thereafter there was more quartette harmony.

"That's not the end of the story," said Cantor. "About a week later I received a long-distance phone call. Would I make a week's appearance in Chicago—just sing a couple of songs, tell a few jokes, salary, unbelievable, $15,000 for the week. Well, just as unbelievable, I said I was sorry, that was a lot of singing, five times a day. I couldn't do it. 'Why,' I said over the phone, 'don't you try Jolson?'

"I got my answer. 'We talked with him.' I was told. 'He said he wouldn't do that much singing—not even for $25,000 a week!' "

The lads at B-Bar-H now broke into a final tune and the call came for dinner. Among us at the time were Moss Hart, Beatrice Kaufman, Howard and Peggy Cullman, Jack Kriendler of "21," Metro's Si Seadler, Irene Hervey (her husband, singing man Alan Jones, was to arrive the following day) and a few others whose names elude me at this time.

After the meal, somehow the conversation drifted to the Ziegfeld era, and many of us insisted that never again would there be as glamorous or as tradition-steeped an institution as the original Ziegfeld Follies and the Ziegfeld operettas. The talk swirled about some of the personalities associated with the showman—of Will Rogers and, of course, Eddie Cantor, of Mary Eaton and Anna Held, of the Astaires and Jack Donahue, of Fanny Brice and Marilyn Miller.

It was when Marilyn Miller's name came up that Moss Hart took over. "Irving Berlin and I were in Bermuda," he recalled, "just finishing *As Thousands Cheer*. They were insisting we ought to use Marilyn Miller but Irving and I were doubtful. The parade had passed we thought, for Marilyn. We wanted someone refreshing, vibrant, youthful. Well, I got back to New York and was at a party and next to me sat, of all persons, Marilyn. She was beautiful —I cannot remember when she was more beautiful—and all the thrill of the days I used to sneak up to the balcony of the New Amsterdam and watch this lovely dream girl on the stage below came back to me. I think I was very much in love with her, and very much in awe, too, at the time.

"Well, she was gay. She seemed the most alive person in the place. She talked about many things. Her eyes danced, and I fell in love with her all over again. I thought maybe I should wire Berlin—perhaps we were making a mistake in not considering her. Then she began telling me about something that had happened some few days back. Seems she was on Forty-second Street, and passing the New Amsterdam she had the impulse to drop in. There was only an old doorman, and she had quite a time before he would let her wander backstage.

"She told me she went into her old dressing room and sat there and recalled when she had been the star and the room had been crowded with flowers and gifts from admirers. Then she went out on the stage.

"It was empty, of course. There was just a little pilot light throwing down a blueness. She walked down front and looked out on the empty house and fancied for a few seconds that the seats were occupied with the gay, well-dressed audience of those Ziegfeld years, and now she was one of the stars again and these people were waiting to cheer her.

"So she danced a few little steps, and then realized this was just an empty house and never again would there be for her those thrilling moments of opening-night triumphs.

"Well, as she told it to me, she stared out at those dusty, empty seats and the tears began to come. On that fine old stage of the New Amsterdam, Marilyn Miller, alone, in the path of a faint blue light, slumped down and sobbed. Then, she said, she ran out, hailed a cab, went to her apartment and cried for the rest of the night.

"We were at this party—come to think of it, it was at Charlie Lederer's, and she was telling me all this. I knew what she was getting at. This was the great Marilyn Miller, and she was through. Still in her early thirties—beautiful, wealthy, and she was through. The magic of her name lingered, but as far as the theatre was concerned, Marilyn Miller was a has-been.

"I'll tell you something. I didn't wait to wire Berlin. I long-distanced him. I said over the phone, 'Irving, maybe I'm wrong, but Marilyn Miller is our lady for the role.' It wasn't the most important role in the show, but it was a powerful part. Berlin said, 'Maybe, you're right.' That's how Marilyn Miller got into our show, and I know how she felt the opening night when they cheered her to the rafters, because I went into her dressing room, and there she was crying."

At this point, Beatrice Kaufman, whose husband, George S. Kaufman, had been Moss Hart's collaborator on *Once in a Lifetime,* the play that skyrocketed the then newcomer, Hart, into fame, told us a few stories about Kaufman's eighty-year-old mother whom George never seemed able to impress with his achievements. The aged Mrs. Kaufman was always in a deprecatory mood, said Bea. For instance, she would call up George and say: "Did you read what the critics said about Eugene O'Neill's new play? My, how they praised it!" This in a tone of reproach, as if it were George's fault, as if he should have had the foresight to have done something about it.

"There was the night, too," Bea recalled, "Mama Kaufman was watching a dress rehearsal of one of George and Moss's plays. 'Mama,' asked George, 'What do you think of this one? Like it, yes?' Mom shrugged her shoulders. 'Seems to me,' she mumbled, 'your producers might have spent a little more money on it. Seems pretty cheap.'

"'Cheap? Why Mama, this is an expensive production. Didn't you notice—three sets?'

"'Yes, yes,' she agreed impatiently, 'but all in the same house.'

"On one occasion George Gershwin's mother met Mama

Kaufman in Atlantic City and said: 'How are you, Mrs. Kaufman? I am Mrs. Gershwin—my son wrote something in music with your son.'

"Mama Kaufman said stiffly: 'Maybe. My son writes with lots of people'—and walked off."

The elder Mrs. Kaufman, according to her daughter-in-law, would never concede an admiring tribute to her son's plays—not to him, at any rate. *You Can't Take It with You* elicited only a disapproving grunt. "People like that should be in the crazy house," she insisted. *Once in a Lifetime* she stamped as an exaggeration. *Dulcy* was too talky.

But let a play open that was the work of another author—Bernard Shaw or Clifford Odets, Eugene O'Neill or Ferenc Molnár—and she would be on the phone promptly when the reviews were glowing, caustically reminding her son that it might have been his play if only he had set his mind to it.

George would say gently: "But, Mama, other people have to write plays. Can I help it if they're good—and hits?"

"They're friends with the critics," complained Mrs. Kaufman. "You should be more sociable."

Now again Eddie Cantor wanted to get into the storytelling act.

He was reminded of the time Georgie Jessel was scheduled to appear at a benefit at the Ziegfeld Theatre, and he dropped in on Cantor, who was stopping at the Warwick Hotel, and asked him to come along with him. In the distance from the hotel to the theatre, they began fashioning a quick little act.

It went over big at the benefit. "Georgie," said Eddie as they walked off the stage, "This is too good to waste. I thought up some new little gags. Maybe there's another benefit."

There was. At the Mecca Temple. Cantor and Jessel walked on, unsolicited, and did their act—only this time it had been expanded from six minutes to about twelve. The audience laughed and cheered. They walked out of the Temple elated, and this time it was Jessel who said: "We can't waste this. There must be a benefit somewhere." They did find another, and then went on the quest for still another. Learning there was some affair in the Imperial Theatre, they dashed over, only to discover the benefit was over.

Crestfallen, ready to call it a night finally, they spotted the doorman. "Well, you may or may not believe it," said Cantor, "but we two hams sat that old fellow down in his chair in the little waiting room at the stage entrance and for fourteen minutes—just like he was maybe an audience of thousands of people—we did our act, with all the gestures. We paused for laughs and we waited for applause. 'How'd you like it?' we asked the man.

"It was okay," he said.

"Well, I thought for a second or two, and then I asked: 'Maybe, you got some friend's house we can go to?' "

A Night with a Newsman

Among the more colorful newspapermen of our times—although he deserted the business to become a highly successful author—was Gene Fowler, one-time managing editor of the New York *American*. He was more or less an idol to many of the newcomers, and of course his friendship with his old Denver confrere, Damon Runyon, was something of a legend in newspaper circles. My own intimacy with him came about through my gratitude for a glowing letter of praise he sent me for a column I had written—a valentine I still cherish among my souvenirs. Many years later, he deposited another valentine when he wrote the foreword to my book of hometown reminiscences, *Some Days Were Happy*.

Of the many times I encountered him in Manhattan, I recall one particularly back in 1941. The big, good-looking, gray-haired fellow came toward me as I was ordering up at the "21" bar, and I remember he wore a white sweater under his jacket, though this was midsummer.

"Did you get that autographed copy of *The Jervis Bay Goes Down*?" he asked, and I said: "Yes, I did and thanks. It's a swell poem—swell."

Fowler said: "Sobol, don't get cocky with me. I'm a columnist now myself—beginning three weeks from my last drink tonight. Say 'sir' to me, mister. Would you like to read a letter W. C. Fields sent me? I always call him W.C. to friends instead of Bill, because I always like to think of Bill as W. C. Fields."

"I certainly would like to see what W. C. Fields wrote to you," I said. Fowler handed me the letter and urged: "Read it slow, will you? So I'll have time to go upstairs and bring that hermit Ben Hecht down here with the peasants. Read it twice and give me time. Do that much for a fellow who soon will be a columnist himself, will you?"

I read the letter from W. C. Fields slowly but aloud to Emil, Nick and the other bartenders. Since I recorded the night in my column, I am able to offer the contents intact:

> I have received your note on Hotel Delmonico stationery telling me you are down with the flu—I imagine an abbreviation. Writers of your ilk do not stop at the Hotel Delmonico—this I have read many times in movie magazines. A—— and myself have been dancing every night at Chasen's cafe and I took the check off my income tax as entertainment. Was I justified? Incidentally, now that the University of Chicago scientists who have looked into more than one hundred chronic alcoholics' stomachs (Nosey Parkers) and found that proper diet, vitamins and general nutritions build up an immunity to all intakes, there is nothing further for me to worry about—but I am not too certain about you.

Novelist John O'Hara came to the bar and ordered a glass of champagne with a lump of ice in it—his usual afternoon pick-me-up. I read the letter out loud to him, and he seemed bored. As he yawned, Gene Fowler returned with Ben Hecht and as if there were some prearranged signal for the curtain to go up, there entered: (1) producer Morris Gest and his black flowing tie; (2) accordionist-comedian Phil Baker; (3) Sid Silvers, Baker's stooge-in-the-box.

Fowler said: "My reading man Sobol here is tired, and he don't read so good anyway, or I'd have him read W. C. Fields' letter to you. You wouldn't understand it anyway."

Ben Hecht said: "Y'know I never see Morris Gest, I don't think of the time Percy Hammond reviewed his show, *Mecca,* and wrote he had heard Gest had paid $200 apiece for those cushions on the stage and later when he ran into Gest, he said: 'Morris, you must be crazy to put cushions costing $200 on the stage. Nobody in the audience can tell whether those cushions cost $200 or twenty-five cents. Seems to me nobody can afford such crazy extravagance.' Gest answered mildly: 'Mr. Hammond, I can.' Morris, I always like you for that."

Gest smiled, said simply: "Thank you, Ben."

Gene Fowler was paying little attention to Hecht's story. He tapped on the bar. "O'Hara," he said, "that hero of yours in *Pal Joey* is a heel. You want to know something—he's 180 percent dipped-in-pickle-brine heel, and because he's a heel I love him. I love your Pal Joey because he's a heel."

O'Hara ordered another drink and murmured, "Thank you."

Now Fowler looked down from his towering height and said: "Sobol, I'm fifty and a grandfather. Remember, that, a grandfather and about to become a columnist three times a week—interesting people and the like. Think I'll write about Chaplin. Nobody thinks of Chaplin as anything but a genius—comedian, tragedian. Why doesn't someone think of him as a great dancer? Remember that great dance in *The Dictator*? I'm giving you an idea for nothing. I'm going to write about it myself. Sobol, sometimes—and quite often—you are the finest writer of all the column boys. But you want to know something, Sobol? Sometimes—and quite often—you are not the finest. You are the stinkiest! Take your choice, Sobol—you make it one or the other—don't keep swaying between the two. You know I love you."

I said: "Thank you, Gene, I love you too."

Bartender Emil placed another old-fashioned in front of me. Fowler said: "You must learn to love your fellowmen. Especially your fellowmen who are columnists. I stand in front of you now, a fellowman about to become a columnist. Once again after these many years a newspaperman. Let's drink to all of us—O'Hara, Fowler, Sobol, Hecht, Silvers, Baker and even Morris Gest—newspapermen, each and every one of us. If not all of us in fact—every one of us in heart, in deed, in spirit."

Everyone drank, and Fowler reached for the check.

Much later that night, wandering over to Bleeck's on West Forty-ninth Street, a popular hangout for the news lads of the *Tribune*—and the *Times,* too—I ran into Fowler again huddled with Stanley Walker, another of the colorful newspapermen of the era. As I sat with them, Fowler recalled that several decades previously, as a young reporter for the New York *American,* he and Walker, then a newcomer to the *Herald,* had been assigned to cover a hoboes' convention in Chatham Square. The boys thereupon rented high silk hats, flowing opera capes and were driven down to the meeting in a hansom cab. The hoboes were all for electing Fowler and Walker Honorary Kings until someone pointed out their ineligibility—they had regular jobs.

By 2:30 ayem, Fowler and Walker were in a mellow and nostalgic mood. The rest of the story I got from Gene the following day. They left Bleeck's and rode down to what remained of Park Row. Here they got out, stood silent before the old *World* building, bared their heads in reverence, put their hats back on their heads and exchanged stories of illustrious typewriter punchers and pencil pushers—Don Clark, Martin Green, George Buchanan Fife, Irvin Cobb, Joseph Jefferson O'Neill. Then the boys went down to South Street, saluted the *Journal-American* building, after which they toured the Bowery, wandered through Chinatown, had a few more drinks, this time in a dinky little gin mill, and ended up in a Bowery lunchroom eating hamburgers smothered in onions. At 5:00 A.M. they returned to the old *World* building, got out of their cab and again stood bareheaded in reverence.

"Well," Fowler told me, "While we were riding back uptown, I got the blues, and Walker noticed it. He wanted to know what was the matter, and I told him the sad truth.

"Just occurred to me," I said, "I never worked on the old *World*."

The postscript is a melancholy one. Of the principals who figured in the get-togethers on that night back in 1941, gone are Fowler, Walker, Baker, Gest, Hecht and the letter writer W. C. Fields.

I Meet a Legend

On an auto trip to the Coast back in January of 1939, I stopped over at an opulent hostelry, the Samarkand in Santa Barbara, and encountered a Living Legend. As a matter of fact, there were three fascinating and completely divergent personalities gathered at the place this particular afternoon: Alma de Brettville Spreckels, at that time considered one of the five wealthiest women in the world; Brother Philip of the nearby Santa Barbara Mission, who had no use for riches or material comforts, and the Legend, Maude Adams.

I was en route to San Francisco, and Mrs. Spreckels, who flattered me by advising she read my offerings in the *San Francisco Examiner,* insisted that when I arrived in San Francisco, I must not go to the hotel as I had planned but dwell in marble halls as her guest—in brief, her fantastic mansion, the size of a small cathedral. (I never did take advantage of that invitation.) Brother Philip offered me nothing but a personally guided tour of the mission, and that invitation I did accept. Maude Adams merely smiled meekly, and I remained awed in her presence.

Mrs. Spreckels, an energetic, portly, voluble woman, who for some reason reminded me of the late Marie Dressler, told me she had concentrated considerable of her wealth in the operation of Samarkand—"Heart's Desire," if you are up in your Persian—and said the place provided her with her greatest thrill.

To make a patron feel as if he were in his own humble apartment sitting around in his socks. Mrs. Spreckels had hung rare tapestries on the walls, some worth in excess of $100,000, paintings by past and present masters, costly statuary in various nooks and priceless rugs. The only thing missing was a Rodin or two.

I commented on that because it was known that she had collected the largest group of original Rodins in the world. "Didn't you know," she commented, "I have donated them all to the San Francisco Legion of Honor? I had to pawn most of my jewels to buy them." This wasn't quite clear to me because it was my impression she still had a few costly baubles left—some of which blinded me in that hot afternoon California sun.

I knew that, in addition, this amiable, slightly eccentric lady of wealth had also donated an entire golf course for the use of the city folk who couldn't afford a private club, and a collection of Will Sparks's murals to the missions. (Sparks was the odd chap who had been a pupil of Henri Harpignies and Jean Charles Cazin and anatomical artist for Louis Pasteur.) Mrs. Spreckels revealed that he had written her a touching letter before his death, expressing his appreciation of her great loyalty to his art in his obscure days.

I felt I wanted to talk to Maude Adams, but her attitude was discouraging. She was practically a recluse even then, of course, but I thought I might draw her out by commenting on her memorable role, the one which had rewarded her with worldwide fame, Peter Pan.

I recalled reading that the Sir James Barrie play, which had premiered in 1905, had been opened against the producer's better judgment and only because Miss Adams had insisted. Also that on that momentous night when she stepped forward to the footlights and asked the audience wistfully, did it believe in fairies, the assembly rose as one man and let loose with a thundering "yes."

"What a thrill that must have been!" I said.

Miss Adams smiled gently. "Yes," she said.

I said: "I didn't catch you as Portia in *The Merchant of Venice,* but I read it was quite a tour de force."

Miss Adams was a bit more communicative about this. "It is a foolproof part for any actress. I enjoyed the role—yes, very much."

"Weren't some of your other roles as rewarding?" I asked,

hoping against hope to warm her up into conversation.

"I hope you'll excuse me," she said, and smiled shyly. "I do think I must go to my room. I need a rest."

It was the last I saw of the Living Legend who, when she died in Tannersville, New York, in July of 1953, was considered important enough in the American scene to be accorded a full two-column obituary in *The New York Times.*

"You mustn't feel too badly," commented Mrs. Spreckels, detecting my disappointment as I watched Miss Adams walking slowly away. "She is very shy—introspective, you might say. She never has much to say."

I departed with Brother Philip for a tour of his mission. As he guided me through the stone-walled labyrinths of the ancient structure, the ascetic, thinnish-faced, slightly toothy friar revealed an intimate acquaintanceship with present and past art, history and horticulture, and above all, a droll humor that startled at times, coming from one attired in the somber habiliments of a monk.

In the collection of oddities he pointed out to me were coins dating back two thousand years, ancient musical instruments, odd-shaped skulls, Indian relics. He led me to the crypts in the chapel, with the names of those buried etched in marble slabs on the floor, the fountain built a century and a half ago, and the trough at which Indian women used to wash clothes. There were a thousand and one objects of interest, and Brother Philip carried on with fascinating, knowledgeable, explanatory comment.

I paused at his urging before the small tomb in which lie the remains of the beautiful daughter of the De la Guerra de Ors—she whom Dana named as the bridesmaid in his *Two Years Before the Mast.* Above the tomb doors was engraved this tender message: *"Quiero descansar con los que Tanti ami,"* which Brother Philip translated for me—"I wish to rest with those whom I loved so much."

The good friar then pointed to the olive tree planted by the King of Belgium when he was Crown Prince, calling my attention to the four tenderly entwined cypress trees over the shrine, also to one tree especially, from which the white-petaled angel's trumpets drooped, Brother Philip said: "They say at night she wanders out among this peace and quiet and there is song in the air. Pretty legend, isn't it?"

I returned to the Samarkand to bid Mrs. Spreckels farewell, hoping against hope that perhaps I might get another glimpse of Maude Adams—a futile hope, as I have commented earlier.

A Flight with Marlene

Of the many flights through the air I have taken, none is quite so memorable as the one originating from Los Angeles, December 12, 1965. We took off on schedule at 10:00 A.M. for what should have been a routine journey landing us at Kennedy Airport some five hours later—or by New York time, 5:00 P.M. But because of foul weather and a stacking up of planes, we circled for a couple of hours and finally landed in Pittsburgh for refueling. Then we proceeded on the last lap, an hour's journey at most, but again were forced to keep circling.

Some passengers evidenced signs of the jitters as we continued to circle. It was then that comic Jerry Lewis decided to relieve the tension, and the tedium too. And so did Marlene Dietrich and Jayne Meadows, otherwise known as Mrs. Steve Allen. Mr. Lewis, who was traveling with three of his younger sons and his wife, started to dispense little jokes. Not big ones especially, but they drew laughs and seemed to quiet a few of the more nervous travelers. Then he began clowning with the beautiful Miss Dietrich, who responded, to the astonishment of many awed by being so close to the glamorous lady, by clowning back with Mr. Lewis.

Mrs. Steve Allen made a few attempts at some pleasantries but subsided soon because, as she confessed ruefully, she was going to be late in arriving, and the hour she had spent on the plane fixing her makeup would go for naught. She was scheduled to be a panel member of TV's *What's My Line?* that night. "If I had

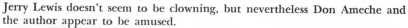

Jerry Lewis doesn't seem to be clowning, but nevertheless Don Ameche and the author appear to be amused.

taken that earlier plane with Steve," she moaned, "I'd have arrived in time. But Steve and I never travel on the same plane, you know, because of the children."

Mr. Lewis made a little face, and Jayne smiled and then giggled. "Know why I made a face?" chirped Jerry. "Because up to now, of course, I couldn't say anything. But who do you think was to have been the Mystery Guest on *What's My Line?* Hmmmm? Ya betcha—the li'l ol' funmaker—me!"

Mr. Lewis invaded the tiny kitchen, drew the drapes, then poked his head out. "Wake me," he roared, "When we get to Pittsburgh." Miss Dietrich laughed fit to kill. Mr. Lewis hugged her. "I have a thing for you," he confided. "You know why?" Miss Dietrich suggested rather meekly: "Because I am charming, yes?"

Mr. Lewis shook his head, went into a crouch, straightened up and said: "Nope. Because you laugh at my jokes. I didn't know you ever laughed, and you're laughing at my jokes."

"Hey, folks!" he shouted, "Marlene Dietrich is laughing, laughing at my jokes!"

Miss Dietrich said: "You are a funny man. Know something? My oldest grandchild is as tall as you. I've got four of them, you know."

Mrs. Lewis for the first time had something to say. "Give me time and with my six sons, someday I'll even up the score with you."

Now, for a few seconds, Miss Dietrich was solemn. "I just flew in from Australia, and tonight I was to catch the seven o'clock plane to Paris and then to Israel. Will they wait, I wonder?"

I suggested that if she remained on the plane, it would at least carry her to Frankfurt, Germany (it was to continue on to that destination) from where she could make the rest of the flight in easy stages.

Miss Dietrich tossed her lovely and famous head from which she had shortly before removed the bobby pins so that her hair flowed loose. "I don't care if I never see Germany again," she said, "but maybe my plane will wait." But it didn't.

There were only three passengers who did not laugh at Mr. Lewis' mild little jokes and his antics, nor did they even ogle Miss Dietrich or Mrs. Steve Allen, for that matter. Jerry's three youngsters were much too absorbed in their electrical games. They looked up only when their father, between jokes, went around snapping pictures of everyone and everything, including the "Fasten Seat Belt" signs, and commanded the lads to pose. We did hear one utterance from one of the boys.

"Don't forget, you promised to take us up the Empire State Building."

"We're circling it right now," barked Mr. Lewis. "What more could you ask?"

To repeat, it was a long, long trip—but by no means dull.

Vagabonds Abroad

One afternoon in mid-June of 1958, little lines of comment were crawling out of my typewriter in my office on South Street like spring worms, and the following afternoon Peggy and I were being carted in a creaky old bus up the picturesque highway snaking its path along the Mediterranean from Nice to Monte Carlo.

That night we joined a dressy group for the world premiere of *Kings Go Forth,* starring Frank Sinatra and Tony Curtis, and then mingled with the others at the midnight gala at the spacious Sporting Club, where Princess Grace seemed the gayest in the assembly and Prince Rainier seemed somewhat bewildered.

Noël Coward was the master of ceremonies, first addressing us in his best French, accent and all, in bringing Sinatra onstage, and then offering an English version. I complimented him later. He grinned and said: "That's fine—fine—but if you honestly analyze what I said, there were no precious little pearls—just an ordinary emcee job I would say."

"You're much too modest," insisted a gentleman standing next to him, and now I turned to that gentleman and murmured: "Years ago, when we chatted at the Stork Club, I told you then how long I had been one of your admirers and avid readers, and nothing you have written since has changed my loyalty." Somerset Maugham permitted himself a weak little smile. "I didn't catch your name," he said, "but I will confess something to you anyway. I am always susceptible to flattery, and credit it to the fullest."

At this point, there was a bit of a buzz when Aristotle Onassis entered and was ushered to the Rainiers' table, and seated next to Sinatra. The report had been current that the Greek millionaire shipowner wasn't in his Highness' best graces, but apparently, for the time being anyway, there had been a resumption, sincere or not, of amiable relations.

Missing, though, was that peripatetic friend of the Rainiers —Elsa Maxwell—and missing, too, though no one commented on it, was that well-known foursome, the Gabors—Mama Jolie and her three daughters.

But ex-King Peter of Yugoslavia, Michael Wilding, film star Joan Caulfield, the Peter Lawfords (seeming so blissfully happy then), playwright George Axelrod who authored the *Seven Year Itch,* novelist Irwin Shaw and their wives were among us, and so were Lex Barker, Howard Keel, Betty Furness, Curt Jurgens.

The following morning, during the postmidnight hours in the Monte Carlo Casino, the roulette wheels were silent, the *chemin de fer* tables blanketed, for it was past the curfew hour—1:00 A.M.—yet in the little barroom folks sat or stood around, drinking, laughing, refusing to go to bed. Ludwig Bemelmans, artist and author, expounded on the virtues of confirmed alcoholics as he sipped some champagne. "Disregarding everything," he insisted, "the fact is I have never known a genuine alcoholic who wasn't also a brilliant man. Maybe it's their escape because they can't tolerate the rest of their more conservative fellowmen who aren't brilliant."

Bemelmans then proceeded to name half a dozen outstanding figures who had been alcoholics or still were. He lost interest in me, however, when I said meekly: "I limit myself to two drinks on any given day." "I was mistaken about you—badly mistaken," he said in apparent disgust.

Earlier that day I had patched up a misunderstanding with Sinatra that had existed for some months following a paragraph to which he took exception—but precipitated myself into another misunderstanding with someone else. Sitting on the porch of the Hôtel de Paris, I spotted the Harry S. Trumans and with them their close friends and traveling companions, the Samuel Rosenmans. I saluted Truman with a cordial "Glad to see you, Mr. President"—even an ex-chief of state doesn't mind that form of address—and then hailed Rosenman with a "Hi, Mr. Rosenblatt." Since the former legal adviser to Presidents and the late Sol Rosenblatt, society's legal adviser, did not resemble each other in the least, Mr. Rosenman greeted me with an icy stare. It was then that Mr. Truman grinned, and assured me he would "straighten it all out."

And apparently, he did, for in later years at the periodic get-togethers at the home of fashion coordinator Tobe Davis, Rosenman by his cordiality seemed to have forgiven and, perhaps, have forgotten.

Some Nights Were Happy

My literate but temperamental literary agent, the late Mark Hanna, in a melancholy mood because he had just turned forty, implored me on the night of October 30, 1938, to take him on a round of the town to cheer him up. "But let's make it different this night," he pleaded.

We dined at Leone's. "This," commented Mr. Hanna, "is different because we are at an Italian restaurant and I am going to order roast beef, American style, Scotch and soda—no wine, but apple pie and coffee." Mr. Hanna paid the check and I sensed immediately that indeed, this was to be a different evening.

"Shall we," I suggested, "go to the cinema or to a play or the pool parlor?"

"I should like," said Mr. Hanna, firmly, "to visit the Metropolitan Opera House and inspect the Ballet Russe."

We entered the sacred old barn and watched the pretty young ballerinas toss themselves to the ceiling, and handsome and shapely young men pirouetting and occasionally embracing the pretty young ballerinas.

"This," said Mr. Hanna, rubbing his hands, gleefully, "is different, don't you think?"

At intermission, we invaded the tradition-steeped bar, where Mr. Hanna ordered a Scotch and soda and I, a brandy—neither steeped in tradition. Mr. Hanna paid the check.

"Now," said Mr. Hanna, "to be different, and because I am now forty, let us not return for the second act but wander these streets of gay New York." We walked down Forty-second Street, and there in front of the tradition-steeped Eltinge Theatre was young Mr. Rudnick looking very forlorn indeed. "Would you," he asked sadly, "like to come backstage and watch our polite burlesque show from the wings?"

We accepted the invitation. Here again there were pretty young ladies who were less zealous about tossing themselves ceilingward but seemed intent upon shedding as many garments as possible within a set period, to the accompaniment of slow music and a peculiar strut in which the hands flung themselves gracefully outward, between unloosening of snaps and straps. We spoke to several of these ambitious young women, and I, for one, was pleased to hear from their own lips that if they had time, they should like very much to devote themselves to literature and such. Mr. Rudnick, uncertain of the effect these ambitious young students would have on two Broadway wanderers, led us gently into his managerial office, where he summoned Raymond the Great, who was the stage doorman.

Raymond was an elderly but emotional sort with a bulbous nose and gentle eyes which could pop on occasion. Without much preliminary fuss, at the prodding of Mr. Rudnick, he gave us his impression of kindly Dr. Jekyll's transformation into the baleful Mr. Hyde. It was really fascinating the way Raymond's cheeks puffed out—and his eyes, too. His neck reddened until it was the color of a ripe tomato. Raymond then obliged with an impression of George M. Cohan and ended up in a blaze of glory with his interpretation of a young man-about-town betting on a horse at the race track—a horse apparently with no chance to be in the money, but which, just before the finish line, nosed out a sensational victory.

"This," insisted Mr. Hanna, "is the most different thing I have ever seen or heard."

We went back to the Metropolitan and sat there on edge as Massine and Danilova and half a hundred pretty young ladies and gentlemen pranced about in something exciting called *Gaieté Parisienne,* in which a naughty but tasty French cancan was the feature—and well worth the price of admission.

The difference continued with a visit with Colonel Nicky Blair at the Paradise, thence to John Perona's El Morocco, where Miss Lili Damita waved in most friendly fashion, and decorator Vernon MacFarlane admitted he had gained fifteen pounds, chiefly by eating well. Then we went to the Stork Club where Mr. Sherman Billingsley, being informed by Mr. Hanna that we were celebrating his birthday, sent over a bottle of champagne which we declined—Mr. Hanna preferring Scotch and soda, and I remaining loyal to brandy. We decided to end up at "21" but the famous iron gate was locked.

Suddenly, Mr. Hanna shrieked, "Look—up there. In the sky."

"Pie?" I inquired politely.

"No," screamed Hanna, "a queer light. A light in the sky."

I realized then that this was evidently the first time Mr. Hanna had ever seen the sun come up.

I ask to be forgiven for this tongue-in-cheek account of an actual evening I spent with Mark Hanna. I present it in tribute to the memory of a witty companion who numbered among his friends Marie and Averell Harriman, *Variety* editor Abel Green, publisher Bennett Cerf, broadcaster Ted Husing—to name a few. He was my agent for many years—indeed, was able to convince Warner Brothers to pay out a handsome sum for an original screen script coauthored by Ernest Lehman and myself and to wrest advance fees for my several books.

Peggy and I were in Rome in August of 1958 when the shocking news arrived that Mark had died suddenly. He had been, before we left on holiday, in such vigorous good health.

You Meet Such Interesting Folks

In August of 1956, while at the Eden Roc at Cap d'Antibes in the south of France, I wandered over to where a furious tennis match was in progress—a duel between Mel Ferrer and banker Gilbert Kahn, and watched with interest as the ball boy scurried back and forth across the courts to retrieve the ball, for it wasn't a ball "boy" at all but a beautiful, long-legged, slim girl, Audrey Hepburn. In between her chores, she'd come over to remark that while this was an unpaid labor of love, she was beingly amply rewarded by keeping in trim without suffering in the monotony of calisthenics.

She told me she was starting a picture in Paris later in the week with Gary Cooper, *Love in the Afternoon.* "I think it'll be great fun. I adore that man, he's such a darling."

Later that evening, Cooper expressed similar enthusiasm. "About one of the few times in twenty years," he said, "I'll be playing a white-collar chap."

Who was to suspect that this vigorous, rugged, handsome star would be dead a short five years later? Or that a dozen years after that tennis match, Audrey Hepburn and Mel Ferrer, cherished by so many as the ideal couple, would come to a final parting of the ways?

That night, dropping into the Cannes Casino, I watched as film producer Otto Preminger made a killing in baccarat and chatted with Kurt Frings, who was gloomy because his clients,

Audrey Hepburn and Mel Ferrer were among the happiest of married couples at their villa in Italy when they posed for this picture and sent it on to the author and his wife. They were recently divorced.

Elizabeth Taylor and Michael Wilding, had called quits in their marriage. "Wilding is here," he said, "and I want to tell you, he may be carrying it off like he doesn't care, but he does, believe me he does."

Aly Khan was at the Casino that night, too. He had escorted both Joan Fontaine and his girl friend, Bettina, to the gala at Monte Carlo. Aly won handsomely, too, that evening, at least during the short period during which I kibbitzed. I moved over to the roulette table where Mrs. Woolworth Donahue in all her jeweled glory was also trying to swell her fortune, but it seemed to me she was only swelling the coffers of the Casino management. Later I learned that she usually preferred to do her gambling at the Casino in Monte Carlo and only rarely patronized the Cannes haunt.

The following day, Peggy and I drove over to the beautiful and ancient estate in Auribeau where Elsa Maxwell was summering with her close friend Dorothy Fellowes-Gordon. At the time, Elsa told me she was completing two books, one on the art of entertaining, the other a revealing tome (as indeed it turned out to be) entitled *Confidentially Yours.*

"One Paris newspaper wrote that I was ruthless and relentless in treating people about whom I write," she said. "Well, now, let me tell you—actually I'm soft and tolerant, but in this book, maybe I can live up to the reputation they've given me. I'm going to mention names, even that very charming person the Duchess of Windsor"—placing a peculiar accent on "charming." It was at a time when Elsa and the Duchess were not on the friendliest terms. Miss Maxwell is gone, too, but the Duchess remains very active and still a source of comment for society chroniclers.

A Fourth of July Hoedown

It was at a party at Romanoff's in Hollywood on July 4, 1958, that gradually I found myself flanked by three Gabors, all hurling their accented remarks in different directions. This was Mike Romanoff's "Citizenship" bash to celebrate his final acquisition of the precious papers, and most of Hollywood had gathered at this invitation.

Mama Jolie Gabor's voice dominated. "Look at my darleenks—so beootiful—Zsa Zsa, Eva—I vish only Magda vass here. Charmink, brains, but hoppiness, no. Vy? Vy can't they find hoppiness? Me, I find it. I am not telling you my age, but I find my hoppiness because I have got a good man. That is hoppiness. A good man for a hossbund. A good hossbund—that's all a girl should haff she should be hoppy. It is neffer too late. Maybe Zsa Zsa and Eva—so young yet, so beootiful—they will take hexomple from their momma. I vurry over them."

We noticed others around who hadn't quite found their "hoppiness." Frank Sinatra, for instance, sitting only a few tables away from his ex-wife Nancy, who was seated with her closest friend, Barbara Stanwyck, who couldn't have been too happy either since, quite by accident apparently, her ex, Robert Taylor, and his bride, Ursula Thiess, had settled down at the adjoining table.

Only a few days previously, we had itemed how unhappy the widowed Elizabeth Taylor was over having her name linked by the gossip columnists with young Arthur Loew, but here she was at the party with Loew for all the world to see. Judy Garland and Sid Luft seemed among the happier pairs, too, exhibiting togetherness. Judy and Ethel Merman combined in a sister act to duet "My Country, 'Tis of Thee," dedicating it to Mike Romanoff and his recently won citizenship.

"To think," Mike said to me at one point during the evening, "I spent seven years on and off Ellis Island because I was stateless.

Bing Crosby and Bob Hope have just cast a negative vote against the author's plea to permit him to costar with them in a "Road" picture—which explains the crestfallen look on author's face.

This is the second happiest day in my life. The other was when Gloria said she'd marry me, and actually did."

Perhaps the greatest tribute to Mike was the fact that The Groaner, Bing Crosby, a party shunner and a crowd avoider, showed up with his bride Kathy Grant, who was then pregnant. She chatted for a few seconds with another expectant mother, Janet Leigh, who was then married to Tony Curtis.

Producer Fred Brisson settled down at our table. "I want you to take notice," he said, "in spite of what you once wrote, I do stay in Hollywood once in a while—and I am with my wife, that very charming Waterburian of yours, Roz Russell. So spread it around—the Brissons were seen together and quite happy."

As Peggy and I left shortly after three o'clock in the morning, the floor was still crowded with dancing couples, with a promising young chap singing out the refrains over the mike—chap by the name of Dean Martin.

The sad postscript is that Zsa Zsa tried to find "hoppiness" twice more after that night, but with two marriages that faltered. Eva Gabor was more successful, wedding a Wall Street broker,

Dick Brown, who since has turned writer. Janet Leigh and Tony Curtis parted a few years later, both to wed others. Ethel Merman, who had been married twice previously, was to divorce airlines tycoon Bob Six (he went on to marry Audrey Meadows) shortly after and then to marry screen star Ernest Borgnine in June of 1964—a marriage that lasted only a week or so. Judy Garland and Sid Luft parted, and Judy contracted another marriage, a brief one with Mark Herron. Liz Taylor and Arthur Loew called off their brief romance, if it was that, and she went on to wed Eddie Fisher, and after their divorce became Mrs. Richard Burton. Frank Sinatra, despite recurrent rumors that he might rewed either Nancy or Ava Gardner, remained single until the youthful Mia Farrow came along, and the world at large knows how brief was the run of that marriage. Nancy Sinatra and Barbara Stanwyck have never remarried. On the other hand, Bing and Kathy Crosby and Fred Brisson and Rosalind Russell still hold on to their "hoppiness"—and for that matter, so do Mike Romanoff and his Gloria.

Night at a Movie

We were at a preview of *The Jolson Story,* this night in September of 1946, and now we were at the portion of the movie where the slim energetic star in blackface, was running, jigging, swaying and singing on a runway, the first runway, an idea of his own we were led to believe, and the man sitting to the left of us in the small crowded theatre said: "That's really him. That's Jolson himself—not Larry Parks." And I said, "Waddaya know? 'S that a fact?" and I lost myself in the tender nostalgia evoked by the scenes and the songs.

This was a picture for us who loved Broadway—this film about the Mammy Man—and some of us sang softly along with the Jolson voice as it boomed out in that still magnificent baritone: "April Showers," "Rock-a-bye Your Baby," "California, Here I Come" —and a dozen or more others.

The man sitting to the left of me said: "You'll love this scene. Wait 'til the old man takes another sip of wine. Say, it makes me cry everytime I see it." The old man was Jolson's papa, the cantor, and the scene was of the wedding anniversary when Papa Jolson starts humming, "yum, yumpty, yum, yumpty, y-yum" and looks appealingly to his son—and Al (Larry Parks in the picture) finally joins in—the "Anniversary Song."

The man to the left of us was right, because when the old couple went dancing around and around on the spacious patio, and Larry Parks was singing that song with Al Jolson's voice, there were folks all around, including my wife, Lee, who dabbed at their eyes and blew their noses.

I could understand Lee weeping a bit, perhaps because she had known this fine old gentleman who had fathered the Mammy Singer. She had known him because he had been her favorite uncle, and she had loved him for his wit and his gentility and thoughtfulness. She had remembered the days when occasionally he had held her on a knee and sung rousing melodies to her, and she had memories, too, when, like his father, the son, Cousin Al, had sung to her and her sister a few favorites from the Lew Dockstader's Minstrels, with which group he was the white-haired-boy-in-blackface.

The man to the left of me said, "If Poppa was only alive now, how he would love this. He should have lived to see this." I agreed, but I was thinking back to the first time I had heard or seen Jolson. It was a Sunday night at the Winter Garden before World War I, and I sat in the balcony and thought, This is the most wonderful city in the world and this the most magnificent theatre, next to the Hippodrome. Someday I am going to live in New York where I can mingle with and see some of the amazing people of the show world, like Jolson and Flo Ziegfeld, Nora Bayes and Sophie Tucker, Irvin Cobb and Don Marquis. At the time, Jolson was a big star, and I was only a young fellow who had to go back to my job in Waterbury the next morning because I had just enough money for the one night's splurge.

The next time I got to see Jolson was when, having become engaged that afternoon to Lee Cantor of Yonkers, we walked up Forty-second Street and turned up Broadway until we came to the Winter Garden—and there in huge lights was emblazed Jolson's name over the title of the show, *Bombo*. It was a sell-out, for which I felt relieved, because if I had been compelled to shell out for two tickets I would have had no train fare back to Connecticut. Lee seemed disappointed, so I suggested brightly, "Why don't we go backstage and ask your cousin Al to get us in?" The girl shook her head. She wouldn't think of any such thing, and I felt powerfully ashamed and wished I hadn't made the brash suggestion.

So we went to a movie, and late that night, again passing the Winter Garden, out came Al Jolson himself with half a dozen other men. Lee said: "Come on, I'll introduce you." This time I said: "Oh, no, don't let's do that." I was too awed, and I was even worried he might say something that would inspire the girl to give me back my little engagement ring and call it all off.

All this went through my mind as I sat and hugged memories and thrilled over the warm sequence in the film, though Lee later told me that much of it was fictional—and why hadn't they brought in Al's older brother Harry who had gone part of the way with him in show business—or why didn't they point out that it wasn't really Al's mother in the picture but his stepmother?

When the lights went up in the little theatre, folks turned and the man to the left of me got up and said: "I feel like I have been through a workout. I feel pooped." The people came over to shake his hand and comment enthusiastically on the warmth and beauty of the picture. Some asked for autographs. Lee said: "I loved it, Al. I cried." And Al Jolson kissed her and said: "Know somethin', honey—I cried, too. I wished Poppa had lived to see it." Then we three dropped over to Reuben's, where patrons rose from their tables to make a fuss over him, and I wondered whether, like in the picture, Jolson would give out with a few songs. But he didn't.

Lee Sobol passed away in mid-January of 1948. On July 28, 1950, Peggy and I were married, and a few days later, I took her over to visit with the Jolsons. Al, by this time, was happily wed to lovely Erle Galbraithe, and they lived quitely enough on the big estate which he had bought back from his ex-wife, Ruby Keeler. Joley asked us to watch as he swam the length of the pool,

The author poses with two friends in Hollywood: Bobby Connolly, who had made his mark as a dance director in musical films, and one of the great performers of all time, Al Jolson.

back and forth, a dozen times. "You do that when you get to be my age," he shouted. "Cut out those cigarettes and live like Joley —the good clean life."

Two months later, on October 23, 1950, a fatal heart attack felled one of the era's great and most dynamic performers, Jolson, who on one knee, brought an entire world to its feet, who made every performance seem as fresh as the first and every listener feel like the only one, who was the first real "heavyweight" to regain his World's Championship, who was so great that imitations of him became a basic industry.

By way of postscript, of his close to a 4½-million-dollar estate, he not only bequeathed $1,000,000 in trust for his widow Erle but also set up a $100,000 trust fund for Ethel Delmar, the second of the four women he had married.

And for another postscript, his widow some years later married playwright Norman Krasna, who had been my secondstring aide when I held the post of drama critic for the *Evening Graphic.*

Parties Can Be Fun

It was in June of 1946 that there was quite a get-together for a noisy ex-shave boy with a sandpaper voice. A thinnish little soft-eyed fellow with shoe-black hair named Irving Berlin at one point during the evening said, "This could make you feel sad—just remembering," but I couldn't understand why Berlin should ever feel sad, considering how Lady Luck scattered her rose petals all over him every time he made a move. Earl Carroll, who was sitting at my table, said, "I guess only on Broadway do folks get so soft about someone they like."

At any rate, this was quite a night in tribute to a beloved clown, Jimmy Durante, and some persons near me became almost weepy when Eddie Jackson, grayer and heavier than in the earlier days, joined Jimmy in singing a song and then out trotted the aging Lou Clayton to plunge into a quick-step jig. For this night at least, the team of Clayton, Jackson and Durante was reunited. Broadway citizens were in the little cellar dive which had been revived for the one night as Club Durante and which had previously been the old Silver Slipper where the mob kings and vassals of the speakeasy era used to mingle with Broadway and Park Avenue nabobs at a time when you never could tell whether the fellow who was asking you to come and have a drink on him might not be found a few hours or a few days later with holes drilled through his head.

It was the kind of night when Sherman Billingsley shook hands with Big Jack Entratter and Copa's Monte Proser, despite their long-standing feud. For Sherman had fired Jack, who then moved on to the Copa, eventually to become millionaire president of the Sands Hotel in Las Vegas until a much richer millionaire named Howard Hughes bought the place. Nor did I think it odd that Leon Enken, a bossman of Leon & Eddie's, should be acting as headwaiter on this occasion. Nor that Ethel Merman should rise to blast out half a dozen songs, and that for once Billy Rose had brought along his own package of cigarettes. Billy was always swearing off smoking in those days but kept on cadging them from the nearest available victim. Billy said: "That Durante—that's really Mister Broadway, and I'm sorry Hollywood's got him. Some day I'd like to build a play around him—I mean without an elephant," and then he went mute, perhaps enjoying a little bit of traveling with himself down Memory Lane to the night his musical *Jumbo* opened.

"Inka dinka doo," roared Durante, and over the bedlam I could hear Earl Carroll trying to convince the attractive, shapely cigarette girl, Wilma Allen, that he was leveling when he offered her a job with him on the Coast as of the following day. She giggled and then she shot a semiscornful stare at him and walked away. A few minutes later she was back. "You *are* Earl Carroll, aren't you?" she said, quite subdued, but I never did follow up to learn whether she accepted Carroll's bid.

"Evva have a feelin' dat ya wanna ta go?" sang Jimmy. "Evva have da feelin' dat ya wanna ta stay?" Eddie Jackson shoved a battered old silk topper atilt on his head and shuffled and strutted. Now comedians began to pour in, their own labors complete—Milton Berle, Jerry Lester, Jack Waldron, Georgie Jessel. They stood along the wall paying respectful attention. Jimmy was making a speech. "Say, I rememba I am in a show wid Eddel Merman an' Bob Hope an' da show closes. I don't know what become o' dem but I went right on ta bigga t'ings. W'are's dat valett o'mine, Umbriago?"

The night rolled on boisterously. The cellar room that was once the Silver Slipper was hot, and the smoke of cigarettes and cigars drove little needles into your eyes. As I left in the early morning hours, Ethel Merman and the funnymen, adorned with

Jimmy's prop flappy hats, were joining him in a reprise of "Inka dinka doo," and trying to shake their heads and imitate his strut.

A Date with a Star

I never realized what a gracious chap I was until one day in May of 1946, when a publicity man named Newt Thompson phoned and pleaded with me to be a good fellow and have cocktails with a nice person from Hollywood. He said her name was Ingrid Bergman, and hastened to assure me that though she was in pictures, she was quite a personable young woman and would not bore me. Also—and Thompson was quite apologetic—would I mind if Miss Bergman and I were alone, just the two of us?

"You mean," I demanded, "Bergman and Sobol, by themselves, and not another soul around? What kind of deal are you trying to get me into, Thompson? You mean I can't bring my wife along, or suppose my boss wants to join us?"

It was pitiful the way that Thompson fellow cringed over the phone, but I will say this for him—he was firm on this one point. It was Ingrid and I alone together—tête-à-tête or cheek-to-cheek—but no outsiders.

I sat with Miss Bergman at a corner table in the Drake Room. Softly the pianist played "Liebestraum." A waiter placed a short Tom Collins with two awning-striped straws in front of her and smiled wistfully. Then he scowled at me and shoved over a Scotch mist—with straws.

"Cheers!" I said brightly, holding up my glass.

"Cheers!" said Miss Bergman agreeably.

I studied her soft, fine-spun, light brown hair but gave no thought to Jeannie. I decided her eyes were light blue threatening to be green. I thought if I were anyone else but a hard-working, serious-minded, unromantic and very much married reporter, it might be very easy to fall in love with this wholesome-looking young woman who was then among the foremost screen actresses of the period.

My reverie was disturbed by something Miss Bergman was saying. It was about those pesky autograph pests. They had made life miserable for her during her stay in New York. Some of them actually had gotten up to the door of her hotel suite and had hammered away to force her to come out and see them. Others had piled into a cab and followed her down to the Village. On one

The Sobols, while in London, drop in on a pair of friends during a lull between takes of a film. *Extreme left:* Akim Tamiroff; *extreme right:* Ingrid Bergman; the picture: *Anastasia.*

occasion, she had been terrified when almost a hundred of them had crowded around her cab and practically pulled her to pieces.

Miss Bergman said she knew all the clichés about "Don't worry over autograph seekers until they stop wanting yours," but that just the same it would be nice if these moronic kids who hang around in groups outside of theatres and nightclubs and hotels would have a heart and let her go around unmolested.

I said: "Ingrid" (naturally, this was after my third Scotch mist), "you are beautiful."

Miss Bergman smiled, but discouraged my advances by telling me she had been to see *The Glass Menagerie* twice and expected to view it again. "I went backstage," she said, "and I told Laurette Taylor: 'I am coming back again and again, to watch you. You are wonderful.' I told her, 'I want to learn all your little tricks,' and I do."

I said: "Most of us love you because you are so natural, so unaffected on the screen. Why do you want to learn little tricks?"

Miss Bergman said well maybe "little tricks" wasn't what she really meant, but those wonderful expressive gestures of Laurette Taylor's had thrilled her.

"I'm coming back in October," she continued, "because I must do a play. Nothing must keep me from going on the stage. I guess I'm a ham, yes? But way back—almost when I first came over to this country—I said in an interview I wanted to play Joan of Arc, and I meant it. I've never changed my mind."

(She did fulfill her wish, appearing on the Broadway stage later that year in Maxwell Anderson's *The Girl from Lorraine.*)

By this time, it must be evident, Ingrid and I were getting on deliciously intimate terms, and there is no telling what might have developed if, like a bolt from the clear, there hadn't come the interrupting baritone voice of man.

"Ingrid, it's seven o'clock. Don't you think you better begin getting ready?"

That fellow Thompson had lied. All the time Ingrid and I had been "alone" together, Joe Steele, her personal press representative, had been at an adjoining table, listening. Naturally I left quickly, leaving it to him to figure up and pay the tab.

A Night with an Author

Jim Tully, the late iconoclastic novelist, arrived in our town in April, 1940, and we made an appointment to invade a few of the drinking holes in Manhattan. Hatless, coatless and tieless, his shirt open to reveal a large V-expanse of brawny, hairy chest, he strutted into "21" some fifteen minutes late. The immaculate Jack Kriendler shuddered. Men without ties were a painful phenomenon to the meticulously correct Mr. Kriendler except on those occasions when he guested at the B-Bar-H ranch outside of Palm Springs.

Mr. Tully spurned the suggestion of a preprandial cocktail. "Beer," he thundered, "and keep the gin out of it." He explained his tardiness. "I'm late because I was with Mencken and Nathan. Nathan is quite a guy. He got a letter from a fellow in jail who had six more years to go and wanted out. Nathan wrote back: 'I envy you your isolation.' Wonderful guy. Think of writing that."

Mr. Tully saw a meekish-looking fellow sitting at a table across the room. "I've see that face," he said. "Writes poetry, doesn't he?"

"That's Deems Taylor," I told him. "Buried up to his neck in music—good music."

"All music is good," insisted Tully. "Anything that sings is music, and music is good. So's this beer—great beer."

We traveled on to Bill's Gay Nineties, and Spike Hennessey

sang "I Brought My Harp to the Party." The novelist nodded his head in approval. "There's meat in that song. Porterhouse steak smothered in the savory onions of great understanding. It's a good song." He stood before the faded poster displaying the stalwart figure of William Faversham in *The Squaw Man.*

"I saw him in it," he commented. "Great performance, stinking play."

We wandered into Fefe Ferry's Monte Carlo. Fefe didn't quite catch the name—he insisted upon "Mr. Kelly." Neither did Fefe quite catch the idea of a patron without a tie. He tried not to look too unhappy. Tully peered into the recesses of the ornate, formal room, studied the ornate, formal people in their fancy evening clothes.

"Do you think," he asked, "they're having a good time?" I said, yes, I thought they were.

Mr. Tully had a chuckling idea. "That dame with the big chest—can you get a picture of her, riding the rods? Hey?" The fancy pleased him and he kept chuckling.

We moved on. To Leon & Eddie's. Eddie Davis said as he sat down with us, "We're kind of alike, you and me, Mr. Tully. I used to work the carnivals—'Here y'are, la-a-adies and gen'mum, step up fast and watch your breath. But hurry, hurry, hurry—'" And Davis continued with a typical rapid carnival spiel.

"I was pinched at a carnival show once," recalled Tully. "There were two of us, and we wandered into New Orleans. The kid with me had guts, plenty of guts. Too much, I guess." And he went into a long and detailed story of their adventures.

We left Leon & Eddie's and dropped into the Stork Club, where Sherman Billingsley introduced us to Wilbur Shaw, then auto-racing champion of the world and twice winner of the Indianapolis 500-mile race.

Tully said: "Floyd Roberts went to his death. A burning awful death in last year's race, and you won."

"Yes," said Shaw, quietly. "I won. I passed his burning car, and I kept on. There were thirty others and we were all friends —and we all kept on. Do you understand that, Tully?"

The novelist said, "No, I don't."

Shaw said: "Do you understand that all the crying which goes on in the heart can't keep you from pushing on. Only when the race is over. That's when you really cry."

Tully said: "No, I can't understand it."

Shaw said: "Become an auto racer or an airplane racer or a racer of any kind. Say you were a jockey and your friend was a fellow jockey and his horse fell upon him, would you stop during the race?"

Tully insisted stubbornly: "I would."

Shaw shook his head, stared at the writer out of pained eyes, and then left the table. As he did: Tully whispered: "That Shaw lad's a fine fellow. I like his answers. I hope he knows I'm only ribbing him. Someone ought to tip him off what a great story he has there: 'What does a racer think when he sees a fellow racer burning to death in an overturned car and has to keep on, and he does keep on and he wins the race?' It's a great document—a document with guts. Shaw ought to write it."

Billingsley now settled down with us—poker-faced as he noticed for the first time that Tully wore no tie and had his shirt open. He beckoned to a captain who returned shortly with a tie bearing the Stork Club emblem and presented it to the novelist. Tully said: "Thanks," but made no attempt to put it on.

Billingsley, still evincing no displeasure, said: "Seventh week now—not a drink—not a cigarette." Whereupon Tully chirped: "Bring me a beer. Now in my opinion, Jack Dempsey was the greatest fighter of all time. But more than that, he had and has the touch—the great touch of humanness."

Billingsley said quietly: "Tunny beat him twice. Twice."

This was more than Mr. Tully could bear. Leaving the tie on the table, he signaled for us to leave, and we went out in the crispness of the three o'clock morning air.

"This town of yours," he said, "Is full of characters, some good, some very dull. Very dull. Let's catch up with each other again."

When Characters Get Together

I stood in the wings backstage of the Strand Theatre one night in March of 1945 waiting for the oozy-eyed Peter Lorre to finish his act. As he joined me he droned sepulchrally: "I'm glad I am in this big, lovely city with the curfew on. At midnight New York is dead—deaddd—deaddd. It is won-derr-ful."

We walked up to his dressing room and for some reason he whispered, "Don't fence me in," as the door bearing the cabalistic symbols "O-H-I-O" (to this day I don't know what it meant) closed upon us. Lorre changed into a dark-blue suit, adjusted a bow tie decorated with what must have been a significant motif —a green ant chasing an orange python. He murmured: "I am restless tonight. What's cooking?"

We drifted over to the atelier of cartoonist Irving Hoffman above The Tavern. Before he had an opportunity to offer us a refreshing libation, in trooped a group of characters, reading, from front to rear, Jack Tirman, Eli Lloyd Hoffman, Eddie Jaffe and Sid Heller, all impetuous young citizens who lured a living out of press agentry. It was the worst thing that could have happened for us in our restless and melancholy mood, for each was an amateur Groucho Marx, spilling out their punny, if not always funny, quips.

Eli Lloyd Hoffman immediately blurted out: "See where we've taken the Saar—yes, Saar, tha's my babee! So Saary, dear!"

"Peter Lorre—meet the characters," I offered.

"I know, I know," acknowledged Tirman. "Lorre, the best dread man of 1945. You're a friend of Xavier Cugat. Did you know he's writing a book, *Forever Zamba*? Reminds me Henny Youngman met Milton Berle, and Berle said he'd been to the dentist again and is now calling him the great American Yank, and Youngman said, 'I stopped going to him. His magazines are too old.' Berle said: 'Well, I told this dentist you think you've got some pull, you great big jerk,' and he looks me in the mouth and says: 'One more cavity—and they'll be able to play miniature golf in your mouth.'"

Lorre shook his head in dismay—he looked at me appealingly in a mute suggestion that we leave, but Eli Lloyd Hoffman grabbed his arm and said: "Mr. Lorre, I'm writing a book full of old jokes. Would you mind if I called it *G.I. Joe Miller*?"

Host Irving Hoffman, who had been perturbed, too, decided something drastic must be done. He dropped a platter on the phonograph and out came the thinnish voice of the Duke of Windsor in his poignant abdication speech of 1936. Lorre muttered: "Crazy, crazy. Let's leave these creeps," and Host Hoffman said: "I'd like to leave with you, and I think I will."

We ended up in Lindy's, where Lorre shook his head from time to time and sighed: "Crazy, just crazy. Tell me, Irving, is this an act those nuts are rehearsing?"

Hoffman said: "Everything you heard tonight, you'll be able to read in the columns, only they'll credit their clients with it."

She Had a Crush on Words

They dragged me away from my Coke at the bar in the Stork Club, and the first thing I knew there I was sitting by the side of a Beautiful Girl, and the cameraman from *Cosmopolitan* was snapping pictures of us just when I forgot to present my better side.

I would have left at this point to return to my Coke, but the Girl was saying something. She was saying: "I just love the word 'empathic.' Have you ever used it?"

I said: "No, I have never used it. Words are my business, but I have never used 'empathic.'"

The Beautiful Girl said: "I love words. I love new ones. There are some words that just caress the eyes when you see them in print. They excite you, but they aren't words you want to use in speech."

"For instance?" I wanted to know.

"Well, like 'cacophonous.' It's just beautiful in print. I could look at it for hours, but it jars me to say it in speech."

The cameraman was back to us again, and again he caught my worst side—of which I have three, if you include the front view.

This was in December of 1949, and the party was for illustrator Jon Whitcomb, and photogenic darlings were drifting all over the place.

"What is your name?" I asked the Beautiful Girl who loved words. "Debby Reynolds," she told me. "Debby for Deborah."

"Are you one of Whitcomb's models?"

Debby said: "Yes, he's a darling. I pose for some of the other artists, too."

I said: "I am always amazed by little girls who leave their homes and come to New York and become successful. I can see by just looking at you—you're so self-assured and at ease—that you are a success. Was it a long struggle?"

"Heavens, no," said the Beautiful Girl. "It was no struggle at all, and I didn't leave my home and come to New York. I stayed right at home, and the first thing I knew there I was posing for the big artists. I live in Westport and have never left it. It just happens a lot of the big artists live there and work there, too, and that's how it happened. Just stayed at home and the jobs came to me."

"Amazing," I repeated, but Miss Reynolds was back being profound instead of personal.

"Tell me," she pressed, "are you satisfied with the writing our authors here in America are turning out? Do you think they compare with what we get from Europe? Have we a Gide or a Maugham or somebody comparable here in our country?"

I said: "Well, I'm just a fellow who skirts close to the pavement, just missing the gutter in the kind of work I do, but if my opinion is worth anything, I think we're taking the lead in literature. I'll match Faulkner and Steinbeck and Hemingway and some of the other lads with any of the overseas crowd."

The Beautiful Girl who had never left her hometown in Connecticut said: "I'm glad you feel that way. I think maybe we're reaching a Golden Era in letters right here in America. And I think our playwrights are leading the field. And our artists. Yes, and our composers, too."

I was beginning to feel uncomfortable. Surely, I thought, here is a girl who poses for artists, and why couldn't she come down to my level and talk about Betty Grable's legs and Sherman Billingsley's perfumes and the slow and welcome death of bebop instead of throwing cumbersome words at me, spoken or printed —and the trend of culture.

"Debby," I inquired, "would you call yourself the Average American Girl?" She looked at me a bit puzzled and then replied: "Why, certainly not. Who wants to be average? I don't know what being the Average American Girl is, anyway. I just want to know everything there is to know and keep learning new things and reading everything worthwhile. I like meeting new people and I like to keep busy. I like to talk to old people—they've been around and have learned so much."

"Old people. Like me, for instance?" I mumbled.

"Yes, yes," she replied sweetly.

"Tell me," I asked of this Beautiful Girl who at the time had become one of America's outstanding artists' models—there was a picture of her in the issue of the *Saturday Evening Post* that very week—"just how old are you?"

"Twenty," she said.

Slowly I rose and tried to straighten up on my aged, rheumatic limbs. As I hobbled feebly away, my top-heavy years crowding against me, I was halted by an ancient crone—an old bag of easily twenty-five or twenty-six.

"I loved what you wrote about Jimmy Durante," she said. "Just loved it. He's my favorite."

I felt better right off.

I have often wondered what became of the Beautiful Girl who bore a name similar to that of the movie star of these days, Eddie Fisher's ex-wife.

Show Folks Jamboree

One Sunday night in April, 1934, clings to the memory, and a study of a report I made a few days later brings the event into full focus. It was an evening at the Astor Hotel when the Jewish Theatrical Guild was honoring George M. Cohan and Sam H. Harris—Cohan, the song-and-dance man who had partnered for theatrical projects with Harris, ex-manager of prizefighters as far back as 1904, and who, when the partnership had been dissolved, remained bosom friends.

They got up on the stage and sang and danced together. Then Eddie Cantor appeared in an organdy frock and solemnly offered a ballet dance, Lew Brown, the producer and songwriter, affected a public reconciliation with producer George White after they had been hissing each other for months. Mr. Brown also placed his arm about producer-songwriter Buddy DeSylva and announced, with almost a suspicion of a sob in his voice, that he and Buddy were again to resume their partnership.

Georgie Jessel was the toastmaster, but one of the wittiest speeches came from the usually reticent and certainly rarely voluble Sam Harris—something about his recent venture into gold mining on the Coast and the subsequent misadventures following the news that the mine had burned down. Most of us were convinced that the talk had been authored by some of Mr. Harris' brilliant young playwrights, headed by George S. Kaufman and Moss Hart.

Getting back to some of the stage action. It was Jack Benny attired in the height of the mauve decade fashion with pantaloons tied to the shoes, who escorted the frocked Eddie Cantor out to face his critics. As an introduction, Irving Berlin chanted his "Alexander's Ragtime Band"—sang it out with all his heart and soul and emotions but none too well or too strongly. Ethel Waters fared better with her offering of "Otchi Tchorniya," and Sophie Tucker in a dress in which no color of the rainbow was omitted also brought down the house.

Then something unusual happened. Harry Hershfield told

half a dozen stories which were quite funny, too, but not a single one in which a Jewish gentleman was mentioned.

Scanning my report, I find that among the dominant folks of the thirties who graced the dais, besides the guests of honor, were such personalities as veteran producer Daniel Frohman, comedian Joe Weber, comedians Willie and Eugene Howard, actor Walter Huston, composer George Gershwin, comedian Jack Pearl, radio tycoon David Sarnoff, Postmaster General James A. Farley, Colonel Theodore Roosevelt, crooner Rudy Vallee, radio executive M. H. Aylesworth, actor Otis Skinner, songwriter Gene Buck, Attorney Ferdinand Pecora (later to become an eminent judge), Major Edward Bowes and a few others—including, of course, those who had entertained.

Following the affair, Lew Brown insisted on escorting me to the Paradise Restaurant, along with George White. As we sat at the cabaret, Brown insisted that all feuds were silly. He was happy he had ended the feud with me, he insisted. In fact, he was going publicly again to kiss and make up with George White. He strode to the floor, grabbed the microphone, invited White to join him. White did. He did more than that. He danced while Mr. Brown sang a song he had once written for him and which Rudy Vallee had popularized, a song entitled "Life Is Just a Bowl of Cherries." Mr. Brown, who had a one-note voice, sang several more songs—his latest from his recently completed picture, *Stand Up and Cheer*. It was at this point I noticed that Paul Gallico, then a sportswriter, arose and left the place, not to return. His own form of criticism!

Gus Edwards now got up on the floor and played and sang some of the songs he had written—and when he came to "School Days," comedian Lou Holtz, who was at our table, sang out lustily, almost tearfully and it occurred to me that he was the only young gentleman of distinction in show business who had not been a member of the famed Gus Edwards troupe.

By this time, the milk of human kindness was flooding the veins of Lew Brown. He dragged me over to where George White was, urged that I shake hands with him to signify we were no longer feuding, even though there had been no quarrel of any sort between White and myself. Then he had the three of us pose in a most affectionate embrace for the cameraman. Mr. Brown promised faithfully to send me a copy of the photo, but he never did.

When Nostalgia Reigned

According to my records, it was on the night of March 21, 1941, that, having dined with the temporarily teetotaling sports scribe Will Corum at Toots Shor's Inn and having duly commiserated with the ever reticent young newsman Jimmy Cannon, who was to enter the army at any given hour as a buck private and not as captain, I bade the conventional adieus, slipped a shawl around my frail shoulders and set off with a brave heart, humming an ASCAP melody.

A northerly gale slashed at me with dirks of freeze. A sullen moon glowered down. A taxi driver bawled me out for not looking where I was going. I pushed on through Broadway's thicket of aftertheatre mobs. I knew whither I was drifting.

In my pocket was a personal telegram from Billy Rose, the Little Genius who specialized in Colossal Heart Throbs, Nostalgia and Glamor on Land and on Sea. In more than ten words he hinted that once again he was flinging open the seasonal shutters to permit another glimpse into the colorful and tender past. There was a wistful appeal in the invitation to inspect the Silver Screen —1906–1941, at the Diamond Horseshoe.

In keeping with the courtly mood of Cecil B. De Mille days, host William Dillingham Rose stood at the doorway, greeting his guests. Pretty girls in fragmentary frocks which barely reached below the waistline helped incomers off with coats and hats and volunteered to furnish cigarettes or cigars—any contribution over a quarter of a dollar welcomed.

I found myself seated next to an unusual family group consisting of Ben Bernie, the musician, his first wife from whom he has been divorced for several years, and their son Jason, who was to enter the army the following day.

Behind me was an animated chattery goldenhead of the footlights, Miss Betty Hutton, with a youthful Mr. Millionbucks known to society of Register and Café as Huntington Hartford, Jr.

Suddenly there was a blast of chords, the curtains parted above the bar, and the screen idol of other days when I was trying to pass my geometry exams stepped forward, a silver-haired, cameo-profiled gentleman of the cinema of the era in the matter of looks and poise, and when I remembered how the girls in our high school used to swoon maiden-like in the corridors and on the streets whenever the name of Carlyle Blackwell was even mentioned—well!

Betty Hutton, who was very young, leaned over and whispered, "What kind of act did that man used to do?" Made me feel mightily and uncomfortably old, a feeling which didn't leave me the rest of the night.

Carlyle Blackwell sighed out loud about the screen sirens of other days like Betty Blythe and Barbara LaMarr and Louise Glaum, and then after a respectful two seconds of silence to lend emphasis to what he was about to announce, he offered the magic name of Nita Naldi. And out stepped this sumptuously voluptuous woman with the Oriental eyes and thick ropes of black hair wrapped around that magnificent head. Just as in other days. And in her low, seductive tones she sang out the immortal lines: "A fool there was, and he said a prayer—even as you and I," etc., etc. I want to tell you it sent a shiver or something down the spine and made a fellow feel almost contemptuous of upstarts like Hedy Lamarr, Dorothy Lamour and Paulette Goddard, among the then current sex symbols.

Miss Betty Hutton who, to repeat, was very young, whispered in awe: "Oh, boy, I'll bet men went daffy about her." Mr. Huntington Hartford, Jr., looked uncomfortable, and Mr. Ben Bernie tugged at his big cigar furiously.

The lovely litheness that was dark-eyed and sweet-faced and called herself Lila Lee took over and introduced Gilda Gray, who had lost none of her great charm. Gilda sang and weaved through her immortal dance. The house thundered its applause around and in front of her and forced her into several encores.

Lila Lee then brought out the original Glamour Girl, the beautiful lady with the hair of spun gold, the One and Only Mae Murray, as Lila herself put it in just those words, and when Mae danced the Merry Widow waltz with Georges Fontana—well, I want to tell you some of us got up on our chairs and yelled and cheered and wondered what these puny newcomers like Ginger Rogers and Eleanor Powell and the like had that our girls of other years didn't have, doubled in spades.

It was just too much when Joe Howard, who was either seventy-five or seventy-eight at the time, sang his own songs, "I Wonder Who's Kissing Her Now" and "Goodbye, My Lady Love," and finally strutted into a cakewalk and encored with something that was a cross between the Suzy-Q and the Viennese waltz with a little of Truckin' added—much too much.

While the folks were tearing down the gables and stamping big holes into the floor in their enthusiasm, Miss Betty Hutton, who was very young, exclaimed earnestly: "I bet that Mae Murray must have been the Betty Hutton of her day!"

Tête-à-Tête with a Star

I go back to a night in October of 1960 when I settled down for a spell with a glamorous personality who had been one of my secret crushes years ago. She looked as thrillingly beautiful as she had when I first viewed her from a distance. We were at the Bourbon Ball in the Grand Ballroom of the Astor Hotel. The affair was being held to honor soldiers, sailors and marines, and every so often one of them would come over for an autograph. Even while we were chatting, one tall marine approached and asked timidly would she honor him by dancing with him. She consented promptly, and I am sure it has remained a conversation piece with him since.

During our talk, Gloria Swanson said: "I don't understand women's reluctance to reveal their ages. I'm sixty-one, and I never felt better, happier or younger. It's because I'm never bored. I keep working. I'd rot away if I didn't have some activity going for me. I've got seven grandchildren—seven [by this time, the number may have increased]—and I've got a wonderful mother who is eighty-one and scampers up ladders and gets around as if she were a kid of twelve. She keeps busy all the time, too. Would you believe it, she took up tailoring a year ago. Tailoring! How about that? Just for a new interest."

I said: "Gloria, everyone in show business is writing an autobiography, or having one written. You ever thought of getting busy on your story?"

Miss Swanson said: "Don't think I haven't been approached. But not me—at least, not yet. Why should I tell the world all that I should really keep to myself. I don't go for this exposing yourself, telling everything just to stir up a public's curiosity.

"By the way, speaking of my grandchildren, do you know I was the first to break through the old Hollywood taboo of not letting the public know you were going to have a baby? When I was having my first, I wanted it to be no secret. The studio bosses almost blew their tops. They thought it meant the end of my career. They thought I'd lose face with the fans. Silly. Didn't hurt my standing at all. After that, all the others went ahead and had their babies without trying to hide what came naturally. Do people think a star isn't a woman just like other women, subject to marriage and children and the happiness that comes with them?"

"Do you miss the excitement of picture making?" I asked.

Gloria Swanson puffed furiously at her cigarette, pondered for a second or two and then said: "I never look back. I always look ahead. I never regret. I have excitement every waking minute, and I don't sleep much, so there are a lot of minutes to enjoy all the excitement of right now."

At this point, man-about-town Harry Evans, who as editor had built the magazine *Family Circle* into the widely circulated publication it still is, claimed her for a dance, so I remembered I had a wife at another table who might have a few statements to make to me, too.

But We Couldn't Swim

We had promised to weekend at the exciting estate of Mike and Marajen Chinigo, who publish the Champagne (Illinois) *News-Gazette*. The beautiful villa and extensive grounds are located in the spur of the Apennines in Ravello, and if you look up some four or five hundred feet you get an excellent view of the hilltop villa once occupied by Greta Garbo and Leopold Stokowski during their brief reported romance.

Italian industrialist Gofredo Manfredi pointed out it was foolish for us to get up so early to catch the boat from Capri for Amalfi, from which point we were to motor to the Chinigos' place. No indeed, it would be more comfortable if we went with him in his brand-new speedboat. We agreed with Manfredi, so we piled in, accompanied by Princess Marcella Borghese and Rosemary Knobloch, wife of the then air attaché to the American Embassy in Rome.

We were out—far out—when suddenly we detected smoke curling from the rear of us. And then flame. Manfredi shut off the motor. Peggy and I, who can't swim, tried to appear calm. Mrs. Knobloch, who was in her swimming suit, remarked placidly: "The water looks lovely. I'm going for a swim." Princess Borghese who was in a swimsuit, said: "Ah, yes—me, too." She also dived into the water and began swimming around with evident enjoyment.

Manfredi adjusted a skin diver's helmet—he was in swimming trunks—and then plunged in. He looked around under the boat, came up shaking his head, took off the helmet, tossed it into the boat, and calmly joined the ladies in their swim.

Peggy and Louis Sobol, who, to repeat, cannot swim, sat in the boat, which bobbed up and down, tilted left and right, looked at each other and wondered who was going to get seasick first, or whether it mattered at all—since the boat was going up in flames or would explode anyway.

As we sat trembling, the swimmers gradually drifted back. The smoke and flame had subsided. "Maybe," said Manfredi, "we try to make Amalfi on one motor, yes? Maybe, we make it, who knows?"

To Meet the Bride

There is every reason for me to remember the night of July 27, 1950, and the day following. Betty Hutton had invited some two hundred folks from the film colony for a gala premarriage party for Peggy and me at the Beverly Hills Hotel. I must explain. Originally, it was to have been a bash in my honor, a "sort of gratitude" affair as Betty explained, for having been so helpful to her in the early days of her career. But a few nights before the scheduled get-together, I had proposed to Peggy at Romanoff's, received the gratifying "yes" just as Louella Parsons settled down at our table. She broke the story in her syndicated column the following day, so Betty hastily sent out new wires announcing that another honor guest had been added.

The reason, aside from the personal relationship involved, that this was to be a night to remember was that there were two masters of ceremonies, Georgie Jessel and Bob Hope, and when has there ever been an engagement party with masters of ceremonies? But then anything is plausible in Hollywood.

They all trooped in: movie stars, directors, producers, writers, —among them the Danny Kayes, the Jack Bennys, the Rouben Mamoulians, the Lee Bowmans, Humphrey Bogart and Lauren Bacall, Nancy Sinatra, Tony Martin and Cyd Charisse, playwright Norman Krasna, Claudette Colbert, Milton Berle, composer Johnny Green and his wife, Bunny Waters, the Alan Ladds, the Jerry Walds, Maureen O'Sullivan, Sonja Henie and her then husband, Winthrop Gardiner, Dinah Shore and George Montgomery (so happily married at the time), Don Loper, Errol Flynn and Nora Eddington, then man and wife—too many others to mention.

Agent Johnny Hyde came in with a shy little girl, and I never did catch her name. Nor did I even give her a thought until I read years later Maurice Zolotow's excellent biography, *Marilyn Monroe* and came across a photo of the two with a caption revealing that she was the "shy little girl" at our party.

The following day, Peggy and I were married in Santa Barbara by the same Justice of the Peace who had united Tony Martin and Cyd Charisse, and later Tony and Cyd hosted the bridal luncheon at the Biltmore Hotel in Santa Barbara, ordering the same menu that had been featured at their bridal luncheon in the same dining room.

Among the small party witnessing the ceremony and joining us at the luncheon were film actress Audrey Totter, the late novelist Lionel (*Sealed Verdict*) Shapiro, Abel and Grace Green of *Variety,* the Eugene B. Rodneys (he produced TV's *Father Knows Best*), department-store heir Lyman G. Bloomingdale, screenwriter Paul Yawitz, and my daughter Natalie and her physician husband, Colonel Ramon J. Spritzler, one of the decorated heroes who had served with General Chennault in the Flying Tigers.

(Natalie was to go to her tragic death in a freak accident some years later when during a heavy downpour she drove over to fetch her son Johnny from school. Parking her car in front of Van Heflin's home, she waited for the boy. A tree undermined by the rains crashed into the car, killing her instantly. She was my only child.)

(opposite)

At the premarriage party in the Beverly Hills Hotel for the author and Peggy, hostess Betty Hutton livens things up in a dancing tête-á-tête with Milton Berle.

At the same party, the same hostess, this time in a merry singing duet with Dinah Shore.

10

"There's No Business Like . . ."

In recent years there has been a tossback to the good old days in the theatre. Audiences have been dressing up for Opening Nights. Even the working press, critics and columnists have been showing up in black tie and dinner suits, although I am not convinced this return to formal attire has been altogether a sincere gesture. Actually, if any credit has been due, attribute it to the growing practice on the part of producers to host gala supper parties after the premieres—with the gentle admonition at the bottom of invitation cards or wires, "Black Tie."

In those earlier years in the late twenties and through the start of the thirties, when I held the franchise of drama critic, some habitual First Nighters would rather have been discovered in their nighties than to appear at an opening in anything less than the evening formals, but the rank and file of us preferred the comfort of our mufti. Only at Ziegfeld, George White, Earl Carroll, Morris Gest and occasionally some outstanding Shubert musical did we of the newspaper set tug out the faithful tux and the black tie.

As a rule, it is all very gay at these gatherings, and the feeling of togetherness dominates until the first editions carrying the reviews are brought in, and read—sometimes aloud—to the assembly. The party becomes even gayer and toasts are drunk to producer, director, star and cast if the notices are glowing. It's when negative reports are turned in that a pall descends upon the scene, and the wingding usually dies out as one guest after another suddenly remembers the lateness of the hour.

The after-theatre or after-movie parties are not exactly a new feature of Manhattan's night life, of course, but it is only in recent years that the tab has been picked up by the producers. In other days, it was usually some well-known host or hostess who issued the invitations, with the affairs taking place at their homes. Among the well-known men-about-town of that bygone era who endeavored to blend the society and theatrical forces into a congenial group were Otto Kahn, Jules Glaenzer and Condé Nast.

However, there were a few producers, too, who didn't think the evening was complete without a fancy blowout following the final curtain, and foremost among these hosts were Gilbert Miller, Flo Ziegfeld and Earl Carroll. Mr. Miller's parties, let me say at this point, were far more sedate and social than those arranged by Messrs. Ziegfeld and Carroll.

In fact, there are some of us old enough to remember when Mr. Carroll once produced a brawl that could, by no stretch of well-chosen wordage, be termed "sedate." On that occasion, as a special diversion for those of his guests who might be facing boredom, he arranged for a shapely young woman named Joyce Hawley to dip her nude body into a tub of champagne. Besides paying the markers for both party and the girl's services, Mr. Carroll, it will be recalled, was asked to pay an even stiffer price. The notoriety that ensued brought action by the city authorities, charges were brought against the showman, and Carroll, having gallantly fibbed about the girl's nudity, was found guilty of perjury and sentenced to a year in prison for perjury.

I won't say that after some forty years of turning out for Opening Nights the excitement evaporated, that I found it only a required chore. Actually, I greeted each rising curtain with happy anticipation, hoping to be in on the birth of an epochal hit or have the happy awareness that a new star was aborning, like Tallulah Bankhead, Ethel Merman, Lilli Palmer, Libby Holman, to mention a few who lent excitement to the footlights' scene in earlier years, just as in more recent times along have come other lasses to stir up our hoorays: Julie Andrews, Angela Lansbury, Barbra Streisand, Carol Channing, Gwen Verdon—not to forget the late Carol Haney and Judy Holliday.

We looked forward eagerly in the earlier period to the arrival of any play by Messrs. George S. Kaufman and Moss Hart or by other collaborating teams, Ben Hecht and Charles MacArthur, Howard Lindsay and Russel Crouse, Bella and Sam Spewack. Equally anticipated were offerings by Maxwell Anderson or Philip Barry, Clifford Odets or Sidney Kingsley, Lillian Hellman or John Van Druten, Robert Sherwood and, of course, Eugene O'Neill. In more recent years, the theatre has been invaded by such playwrights as Tennessee Williams, Arthur Miller, William Inge and Edward Albee, who, like O'Neill before them, spurn happy endings or lighthearted plots, preferring to convey gloomy messages of one sort or other to convince us, no doubt, that this is not the best of all possible worlds.

The earlier musicals had scores or librettos by Sigmund Romberg, Jerome Kern, Cole Porter, George and Ira Gershwin, Dorothy and Herbert Fields and their brother, Joe Fields; also by Irving Berlin, Richard Rodgers and Lorenz Hart—and later Rodgers and Oscar Hammerstein II; and in more recent years the newcomers have included Alan Lerner and Frederick (Fritz) Loewe (*My Fair Lady, Brigadoon*), Jerry Herman (*Hello, Dolly, Mame*), Frank Loesser (*Guys and Dolls, How to Succeed in Business Without Really Trying*), Jerry Bock and Jerry Harnick (*Fiddler on the Roof*), Richard Adler (*Pajama Game, Damn Yankees*), Cy Coleman and Dorothy Fields (*Sweet Charity*)—and again the list is incomplete.

I have commented in a preceding chapter that much of the excitement of premieres centered about the arrival of faithful First Nighters like banker Otto Kahn—it was something to watch as he stepped out of his limousine, regally handed out instructions to his chauffeur and then, with his Inverness cape draped around his shoulders, his silk topper slightly aslant on his head, strode into the theatre. Or Jules Brulatour and Hope Hampton as they walked down the aisle—Hope aglitter with gems, and usually sporting a new fur piece, a fixed smile on her face, flouncing down while Brulatour followed meekly behind. As they settled in their seats—always in the first row—Hope would rise, spot one or more friends, wave gaily or even shout a bit of a greeting.

There was always George Jean Nathan, and on wintry nights he would stand outside during the intermission, enveloped in his cumbersome bearskin coat, a cigarette in a long holder, surrounded by a few—the very few personalities whom he deigned to accord recognition as equals. He was the type of First Nighter and critic, who once he was comfortable in his aisle seat, refused to rise to ease the passageway of others to their seats in the row. It didn't matter whether it was a thin woman or a stout man, you had to climb over George while he glared steadfastly to the front. Invariably his companions were colorful folks who ranged from authors like Sinclair Lewis and William Saroyan to ladies like Lillian Gish or Frances Langford, and in later years, Julie Haydon, who finally became Mrs. Nathan.

And there was tall Herbert Bayard Swope, who was so impressive looking that, even during the intermission melee, fellow First Nighters made way so he could pass by. You could never tell from his expression whether he approved of the evening's offering.

These nights, as this is being written, the regulars among the First Nighters include the Bennett Cerfs, Composer Jule Styne and his Maggie, industrialists Francis Levien and Harry Gould and their wives, Henry Berger and his wife Anita Louise, the former movie star, the Gilbert Millers, Howard and Peggy Cullman and Ira and Rita Katzenberg, the champs among all First Nighters—for they were in evidence even those forty years back when I first began taking in plays.

Of the hundreds of theatrical premieres I have attended, I am offering for attention the turnout for just one, *Seven Lively Arts,* which Billy Rose presented in the Ziegfeld Theatre on the night of December 7, 1944. This one was truly a dressy assembly, and among those we recorded as having been present that night were: Elsa Maxwell, Cole Porter, the Robert Sherwoods, Lucius Beebe, the Adam Gimbels, the Gilbert Millers, the Alfred Hitchcocks, the James A. Farleys, the Herbert Bayard Swopes, Moss Hart, George S. Kaufman, Oscar Hammerstein II—and of course Billy Rose, himself, with his wife of the time, Eleanor Holm.

When I came upon the scene, among our dominant producers were Lee and Jake Shubert, Charles Dillingham, Flo Ziegfeld, George White, Earl Carroll, Al Woods, Max Gordon, David Belasco, Brock Pemberton, Guthrie McClintic, Jed Harris, Gilbert Miller, John Golden, Eddie Dowling, William A. Brady, Vinton

Freedley, Daniel Frohman, Herman Shumlin, Dwight Deere Wiman—but I am not going to attempt to present the entire roster. They were, for the most part, a colorful and venturesome lot. There are a few among the present breed equally as colorful: David Merrick, Hal Prince and Alex Cohen, to name a trio.

Merrick, for instance, is as flamboyant in many respects as were Mike Todd, David Belasco, Billy Rose and Jed Harris before him, and he manages to stir up more than his share of controversial attention—his feuds with critics, for instance, or his abrupt closing of Truman Capote's *Breakfast at Tiffany's* on the eve of its scheduled premiere. He had a running hassle with critic Walter Kerr of *The New York Times.* Back in 1963, he sent out a special valentine, entitled: "Elegy Written in Shubert Alley" (with apologies to Thomas Gray). Its opening lines went like this: "The Kerr-few tolls the knell of parting play, The Weeping Actors pitiful to see, the Playwright homeward plods his weary way, and leaves the street to darkness and to me." The concluding lines were: "He gives the Theater all he has, a sneer, when what the Theater merits is a Friend."

Despite the Angry Young Producer's beef against the critics, it is a fact that he has lured more than his fair share of high praise from the lads in the aisle seats for many of his offerings, stemming back to one of his earlier successes, *Fanny* in 1954 and *The Matchmaker* the following year. Merrick's personal Hit Parade since then has included *The World of Susie Wong, La Plume de Ma Tante, Becket, Irma La Douce,* as well as *I Can Get It for You Wholesale* (which launched Barbra Streisand's meteoric career), *Hello, Dolly* (the latter gained new impetus when Merrick converted it into an all-Negro musical, thrusting Pearl Bailey into the role originated by Carol Channing), *Cactus Flower* (which brought Lauren Bacall back to the Broadway stage), *Marat/Sade, Don't Drink the Water, I Do! I Do!,* the award-winning *Rosencrantz and Guildenstern Are Dead, The Happy Time*—and who knows what else by the time this book is read. These have for the most part lured the hurrahs of the critics as well as keeping the box office cash registers ringing out their happy tunes.

I'm beginning to believe Mr. Merrick is running out of beefs against critics or anybody else and will have only his successes and bank balances to fall back upon for comfort. I hope not, as I still am hungry to read about new exploitation gimmicks he may originate. Such as, for example, when during the run of *Look Back in Anger* he arranged for a woman in the audience to leap onstage

If I seem happier than usual, who wouldn't be with an arm around Lauren Bacall? She's one of the girls I could always claim "I knew her when"—as indeed I did when she was a magazine cover model who used to ask me to point out celebrities in "21." And then Humphrey Bogart came into her life—and film stardom, as well. After that, folks pointed to *her* as a celebrity.
Photo by Hale Haberman

and pummel the leading man, Kenneth Haig, while screaming out her apathy to and hatred of all members of the male sex. The cops finally arrived and took her away—to the relief of Haig who, it seems, wasn't in on the stunt at all. Merrick, I am told, had a tough time convincing the police that it had all been prearranged.

On another occasion, when he was displeased with the notices accorded *Subways Are for Sleeping,* Merrick ran huge newspaper ads with laudatory quotes attributed to individuals bearing the names of Walter Kerr, Richard Watts, John McClain, Whitney Bolton and others of the Critics Clan, but if you studied the accompanying pictures, you became aware they were other persons than the critics. Merrick had rounded up citizens who bore similar names and had invited them to the musical, after first treating them to dinner. Then he had solicited their opinions—all favorable, as it turned out—and followed up with the ads. The publicity that ensued paid off handsomely for a time. Critic John McClain, commenting later, reported: "The only reaction that affected me strenuously was a letter I got from somebody saying: 'I just saw your picture in the advertisement for *Subways* and then I looked at your picture in the paper and I like the one in the advertisement better.'"

With only three major newspapers remaining in New York, thus endowing their critics with the increased power to help or destroy a play's chances for survival, the radio and television reviewers have assumed great importance. But not with Merrick, who insisted, "I loathe each and every one of them. They insult our business with their one-minute reviews." He barred Edwin Newman, aisle occupant for Channel 4, from the premiere of *We Have Always Lived in the Castle,* because of Newman's adverse report on a previous Merrick offering, *The Loves of Cass McGuire.*

Not quite the extrovert, but eminently successful, is young Harold Smith Prince, better known as Hal Prince. Eager for publicity for his shows, he insists he cares not at all for any drumbeating about himself, and it is to be presumed he is sincere. He has quite a record. I need mention only *Damn Yankees, West Side Story, A Funny Thing Happened on the Way to the Forum, Fiddler on the Roof* and *Cabaret.* This young man was born to wealth, and during his college days at the University of Pennsylvania, wrote and even directed some of the shows. He still finds it all happy going.

The third member of the dominant triumvirate, Alexander Cohen, was persuasive enough when other producers had failed, to lure Marlene Dietrich to the Broadway stage for a one-woman show in October of 1967, and with Marlene turned in a performance that can only be described by the well-worn phrase "tour de force."

Merrick, Prince and Cohen are the champion after-premiere party-givers, with Cohen's midnight galas probably the most lavish and costly. He has no peer in the field except that energetic movie producer Joseph E. Levine, who is the closest rival we have today to the late Mike Todd.

There are, of course, a slew of anecdotes that come to the memory as we consider the big favorites among the stage stars, but there is a limit to how much we can devote to them in a book of this type. I'd like to offer two concerning the acknowledged queen of our theatre, Helen Hayes. One testifies to her persistent and unquenchable ambition in the earlier stages of her glorious career. The story came to me from playwright Marc Connelly.

When he, George S. Kaufman and producer George Tyler were looking for a leading woman for their still unwritten play, *To the Ladies,* they finally decided upon Miss Hayes and approached her. "Of course," queried Connelly, "you play the piano?"

"Why, certainly," replied Miss Hayes serenely.

"Good," said Connelly. "We have an idea for one of the acts —and it will help immeasurably if you play the piano."

The act was written and Miss Hayes played the piano as she said she could and would. It was months later before Connelly learned that she had bought a piano and started taking lessons for the first time in her life less than twenty-four hours after she had left him.

The other story was relayed to me by Helen's husband, the late playwright Charles MacArthur. Back in the days when she was touring with *Victoria Regina,* Miss Hayes canceled arrangements made in advance to house her in the swank Roosevelt Hotel in New Orleans, insisting that she wanted to live in the quaint Latin Quarter. She herself selected the inn, and when MacArthur arrived, naturally that's where he found himself stopping, too. Then he began to notice that whenever Miss Hayes was being interviewed and she mentioned among other things that she was residing in the "lovely old hotel" in the Latin Quarter, eyebrows would go up and amazement fill the eyes of the reporters and others who listened in. MacArthur finally discovered why. Naïve Helen had selected as her "quaint" New Orleans abode a glorified bordello!

Incidentally, as an indication of how important Helen Hayes has been as a theatrical personage, she is, as far as I can ascertain, the only show-business star who was ever accorded a record eight lengthy installments of her life story, written by her mother, Catherine Hayes Brown, in the *Saturday Evening Post.* To say nothing, of a perpetual monument—the handsome theatre now bearing her name.

Another queen of the theatre, though she has been less active in recent years, is Tallulah (The Voice) Bankhead. I am going to offer a few excerpts from a "Down Memory Lane" she wrote for me in the issue of the *Graphic* of May 2, 1931.

> New York—very broke. I was willing to work for enough to eat and then Producer Selwyn offered me $500 a week, knowing how hard pressed I was. [But Tallulah neglected to mention whether she went into a play for Selwyn.]
>
> The friendliness of Charles B. Cochran when he "sold" me to Gerald du Maurier for a show in London. Being almost signed —and then turned down. Wondering what was to follow when the soothsayer Evangeline Adams advised strongly for me to go

> abroad by all means. Without my father's knowledge, I borrowed fare from an old friend of the family, General Dupont, and left in great pomp in the form of a farewell luncheon attended by General Pershing, among others.
>
> My first night in London in the play, *The Dancers.* The final curtain. Then wild shrieks that shook the rafters. I had heard much of London audiences and their booing but I didn't know they could be so unanimous. I fainted. It took me days to realize they were not booing but rather doing just the opposite.

Tallulah proceeded to record her experiences, most of them dismal, in other plays in London, and finally her decision to forsake England and the stage and return to her home in Alabama.

> I was making ready to leave when Noël Coward called to say he wanted me to take the lead in *Fallen Angels.* It was to open in four days. There were 150 pages to learn in that time. I did it, and the play proved the gateway to the hearts of the London audiences. There really must be something in astrology, for after that the planets sent me such plays as *The Green Hat, They Knew What They Wanted, Her Cardboard Lover, Let Us Be Gay* and *Camille.* It was during my run in *Camille* that Ethel Barrymore came backstage one night and showed me a damp spot on the top of her head. She told me it was caused by the tears of a young girl in the balcony.

Tallulah, having been the rage of London for several seasons, finally returned to America in 1931 to star in her first picture, *Tarnished Lady.* At its premiere at the Rivoli Theatre, I first met the star, in the executive office on the balcony floor. She was pulling her stockings up tightly over her shapely legs. Her first words were (although she didn't even know who I was, intruding on her this way), "I can't bear to watch it—I just can't. I wish I could stop them. I should have stayed in London." It was the first and only time I ever noticed her lacking confidence in herself or her talent.

As time went by, I found it was not difficult to interview the lady. You merely started off by saying meekly: "Now tell me, Tallulah—" and having gotten that far, you settled back and hoped only that your pencil would travel as rapidly as the speech which flowed out of her at a machine-gun pace. It was futile to try to interrupt. Miss Bankhead talked on and on, and every sentence full of punch—just bucketsful of sparkling-word Burgundy covering every subject, from stage, politics, the then New

York Giants, to her talking myna bird who perched on her shoulder and kept asking querulously, "Who are you?" No wonder, Howard Dietz once observed with an air of resignation, "A day without Tallulah Bankhead is like a month in the country."

I remain her most devoted admirer.

Back in May of 1936, I dropped into the Trocadero in Hollywood and came away impressed with a thinnish, sad-faced girl who sang out a few operetta arias in a magnificent voice. I devoted a few lines to her in the column, and in my enthusiasm, suggested the musical comedy field was missing a great bet in this young woman. Then in November of 1938, turning out for the new musical *Leave It to Me* starring William Gaxton, Victor Moore and Sophie Tucker, I shared the general excitement when an attractive girl oozing great salable personality sang out "My Heart Belongs to Daddy," as she slowly divested herself of her costume in a genteel strip. And then I recognized her and studied my program to make certain. It was the same Mary Martin whose act I had caught at the Trocadero.

What happened to Miss Martin after that is theatrical history —as we remember her in *South Pacific, Peter Pan, Sound of Music,* up through the more recent *I Do! I Do!*

Which reminds me, Billy Rose hosted a gala New Year's Eve party as 1949 drew to its close. He transformed the large room atop the Ziegfeld Theatre into a nightclub for the occasion and labeled it "Chez Eleanor" in honor of Eleanor Holm. Billy himself acted as emcee, and in introducing Mary Martin revealed that when he was auditioning for talent for the Fair in Fort Worth, Mary, dressed in high silk topper and full dress suit, had approached him and asked for a place in the show. She assured him she could dance and she could sing. He asked her to sing, and she sang "Gloomy Sunday."

"Can't you sing anything else?" he inquired. Meekly, she informed him that was the only number she had learned, because it was the only one she liked. So Rose, having been told she was married and had a child, advised her to forget show business, go home and take care of the dishes and diapers. "I forgot all about her after that," he confessed ruefully.

Miss Martin then rose, and before singing her first number for our assembled group, announced that everything Rose had said was quite true, adding: "And now, I would like to introduce 'diapers' in person. There he is!" Up stood a shy, handsome lad of about sixteen—her son, almost six feet tall, Larry Hagman, who in more recent years has had his fling in the theatre, too.

Incidentally, it was at this party that Harry Armstrong, composer of "Sweet Adeline," had the unique satisfaction of leading a community sing of distinguished voices, among them, Lily Pons and Andre Kostelanetz, Ray Bolger, composers Frank Loesser and Arthur Schwartz, critic George Jean Nathan, author Paul Gallico, and many others, including Ezio Pinza and Miss Martin, Milton Berle and Abe Burrows, Irwin Shaw and Clifford Odets, Henry Fonda and Sidney Kingsley, Oscar Levant and Deems Taylor.

There was a night back in November of 1961 when, seated at the Friars Club with a veteran performer, I listened as he expounded on the virtuosity of past and present-day stars of the stage. Listened, I might say, with something of amazement, for this was a performer from whom I expected little gags or dialectic stories—or at best some anecdote about nightclub or vaudeville clowns. It was a comedian who was doing the talking—Lou Holtz, who by this time was in semiretirement.

Holtz lamented the dearth of high-caliber stars comparable to those of other years, and among the names he tossed about were the Barrymores—Ethel, John, and Lionel—William Faversham, Maude Adams, Otis Skinner, E. H. Sothern, Walter Hampden and Jane Cowl.

"You don't get dedicated people of the stage like that anymore," he complained, "And you know why? Because we don't have training schools for them. I mean the old-fashioned stock companies where actors would be going through a play one week, matinee and evening every day, with maybe Sundays off—while rehearsing for a different play for the following week. Don't ask me how they found the time to do it, but, boy, what a schooling that was!

"Nowadays, these summer stock companies want an established name. It could be someone who's a flash on TV or has come out with a hit record or maybe drew a lot of publicity for some freak role in a picture."

I threw in a few names of performers I thought would stand up fairly well in any estimate: Helen Hayes, Sir Laurence Olivier, Sir John Gielgud, Lynn Fontanne and Alfred Lunt, and Holtz conceded they had his vote, as did Shirley Booth, Tallulah Bankhead, Judith Anderson, Paul Muni and Katharine Cornell, but added: "They belong to the old-time bunch who got thorough training. They didn't know from radio and television and couldn't care less about the movies when they were training for the stage. But who's coming up to take their places?"

This conversation, as I have pointed out, rambled along back in 1961, so I brought up the names of the younger set who were eligible at the time, to my way of thinking, for admission to the sacred circle: Julie Harris, Geraldine Page, Sidney Poitier, Robert Morse, Tony Perkins—and added the name of Paul Scofield, who had been turning in that magnificent performance in *A Man for All Seasons*. There was a bit of grudging assent by Holtz.

Grudging, because, looking through the binoculars at the colorful bygone eras, memory endows the stars who have departed or retired with a halo of glory and glamor, and those who snuggle up cozily to the warm past are loath to accord recognition to the very alive competitors of the present. To these diehards it is almost a sacrilege to equate the performance of, let's say, Julie Harris with the great Maude Adams, of a Paul Scofield with a William Faversham, or to maintain that perhaps David Merrick is as colorful a producer as was David Belasco.

In the early fifties, the theatre found new outlets in what was termed off-Broadway. In the beginning, production costs were minimal, and box office prices were satisfactorily low in contrast with the soaring tariffs uptown. Memorable are the long runs achieved by *Fantasticks*, now in its eighth year of continuous run, *Threepenny Opera* and *Man of La Mancha*. But the trend has changed. Production costs have mounted for the off-Broadway projects, and so have the admission prices, though they still remain under those of the offerings in the theatrical area proper.

The Two-A-Day

For years I was branded as the assassin of Big Time Vaudeville.

The accusation was based on the undeniable fact that, following my engagement at the Palace Theatre during the week starting July 9, 1932, the big house abandoned its long time two-a-day policy for a grind of four-a-day, featuring full-length movies and minor acts. Then the live show was eliminated and the Palace devoted itself to the showing of films exclusively.

Some nineteen years later, in October of 1951, Sol Schwartz, who had become president of RKO theatres, brought the Palace

The author has his name in lights. The famed Palace Theatre was unable to withstand the shock, and this show ended so-called Big Time vaudeville.

temporarily back into so-called Big Time, opening with Judy Garland in a "comeback." She remained on for some five months, five prosperous months for both the star and the theatre. After that, other luminaries of show business had their names up in the marquee lights, among them Danny Kaye and Betty Hutton.

Then the Palace reverted back to the picture policy until the new owners, David T. Nederlander and his sons, brought in a musical, *Sweet Charity,* starring Gwen Verdon, and when its run was over, back came Judy Garland with an assortment of acts in support, among them John Bubbles, in July of 1967 for another epochal run to be followed by Buddy Hackett and Eddie Fisher.

For the records, the bill I headed consisted of such troupers as Jay Seiler and Frances Wills in a bit of slapstick, Fred Keating the magician (the lad who used to make canaries disappear), the Diamond Brothers, Leon Janney, graduate of the movies, Ross Wyse, Jr., and his parents, the 18 Ingenues, Richy Craig, Jr., one of the clever comedians of the era, and finally Pepito, the clown, followed by a newsreel.

Without this newsman as the alleged star, perhaps this diverting bill might have sufficed to keep Big Time alive for a time, but the critics were not too impressed with my contribution.

Joe Schoenfeld, then of *Billboard,* turned in this report:

> Louis Sobol was introduced by Craig but remained glued behind the desk and mike, neglecting to remove his hat thruout. When he did later and the spot caught his bald pate and glasses, you couldn't outline his face until he turned to a profile view. His act consists of reading a specially prepared column, a duplicate of his radio work, giving the audience the lowdown on several celebs intermixed with jokes. . . . As a freak act Sobol delivers as well if not better than expected, but his drawing power is questioned.

Bige in *Variety* had this to say in part:

> How he felt behind the mike wasn't known, because he couldn't be seen, but his voice never faltered. When he stepped out into "one" at the finish, he permitted Craig to do all the talking. Sobol is a columnist at all times and an actor at no time—even while attempting to act.

But no one could suspect that my big thrill was not appearing as a headliner on the stage of the famed vaudeville house—I had no illusions about my allure. The excitement that was mine daily was in occupying the dressing room backstage where Sarah Bernhardt and Ethel Barrymore, Lillian Russell, Nora Bayes and Eva Tanguay, Jimmy Hussey and Joe Frisco and so many others of the illustrious queens and kings had sat, adjusting their makeup, getting ready to go on.

I had always been a fan of vaudeville, and even as a young newsman in Connecticut with a meager salary, had managed occasionally to train into New York for the delight of standing in front of the Palace and trying to identify show business personalities—before entering to get to my seat in the high balcony, there to drool over such female stars as Valeska Suratt, Rae Samuels, Irene Franklin, Olga Petrova, Sophie Tucker, Elsie Janis, Nazimova, Gertrude Hoffmann and her dancers in their flimsy drapery, Annette Kellerman—and of course a few of the ladies mentioned previously.

I wasn't around in the era that Lillian Russell walked out on the stage, aglitter with diamonds—real ones. I've been told, large ones. Nor did I ever catch the original Rooneys, old Pat dressed in a cutaway coat with tight sleeves, fancy waistcoat, pants with large plaid checks, a plug hat, and whiskers. This Pat could practically jig up the side of a wall as he sang out "Biddie, the Ballet Girl" or "Owen Riley," but I did come to know Pat Rooney, Jr., who told me about the glories of earlier vaudeville days and stories about his pop and mom, and indeed, this second Pat kicked up a spry foot right into his seventies.

I got around to my gallery seats about the time Nora Bayes was having it out with almost everyone else, including Sophie Tucker, but what a song that Nora delivered, especially "Shine On, Shine On Harvest Moon," and I did catch Eva Tanguay's act—mad, uninhibited Eva who could and did make many demands of the bookers because she was the top-money draw of them all for a long spell.

When I played the Palace, it was my impression that the dressing room I occupied had also been the star quarters for Sir Harry Lauder on his periodic farewell tours, but an artists' agent, William McCaffrey, wagered me Lauder had never played the Palace, and checking, I discovered he was right and I was in error. My research revealed that the Palace had balked at paying what it considered Lauder's "demanding wage," so his appearances were elsewhere in Manhattan, at the New York Theatre (it later became the Criterion) and at the Casino, to name another. The nearest Lauder came to playing the Palace was in 1914, when the theatre offered a short in which he was shown singing his numbers, a synchronization with his recordings. (This may have been the first "talkie.") Three sheets in front of the theatre had Lauder's name in letters over four feet high, and in tiny print, the legend "Singing Picture," so that folks passing by were convinced that at last Lauder was playing the Palace in person.

I used to laugh myself fit to kill listening to Georgie Jessel delivering his "Momma" routine over the telephone, and I relished the exchanges between Mr. Gallagher and Mr. Shean. The four Marx Brothers had me in stitches, and so did that trick comedian cyclist, Joe Jackson. I was even fortunate enough to be among those at the Palace that night after World War I when skinny little Irving Berlin wearing his olive drabs sang out in that thin cracked voice of his, "Oh, How I Hate to Get Up in the Morning"—and stampeded the big house. Also the night a young comedian—Bob Hope—couldn't seem to get his message over to the audience.

I remember the fuss the trade papers made over the pulling

power of Kate Smith, who was held over for the unprecedented period of ten weeks in 1931, a record at that time. Later, others were potent enough box-office lures to be held on beyond the usual one- or two-week limit—Eddie Cantor teamed up with Georgie Jessel, William Gaxton combining with Victor Moore, Lou Holtz and several others. And, of course, Judy Garland many years later established, as indicated earlier, the all-time record.

But if I almost ruined the appeal of vaudeville as we knew it at the Palace, someone up there in the Loew's headquarters decided that if one columnist named Ed Sullivan could bring a group of attractive entertainers into the Loew's State, so could another. So in September of 1935, I found myself back on the vaudeville stage, and was to alternate with Sullivan thereafter twice or three times a year for several years.

The lineup of my first unit for Loew's State was headed by the three Ritz Brothers. We had a ballroom dance team, Reed and Mele. Billy Reed, that was—the same lad who was to become one of the top restaurant and night-spot owners in our town, starting with the Little Club, where Doris Day was to make her Manhattan debut. Jack Waldron, a popular nightclub comic, was on the roster, and because he thought he'd like to have a femme stooge, I brought in a little singing comedienne who, I was convinced, was headed for loftier status in the show world. Girl by the name of Martha Raye.

On the subject of Martha Raye, it was a few years later, while in Hollywood, that John Steinberg, who was managing Billy Wilkerson's night spot, the Trocadero, and Joe E. Lewis, who was emceeing the Sunday night guest sessions, came to me and asked whether I could persuade Martha to be one of the guests the following Sunday. Steinberg said they had invited her, but had been turned down. Martha was appearing in one of the nightclubs on the Strip at the time. I settled down with her between shows and asked her why she had spurned the bid.

"Oh, I didn't come to Hollywood to do benefits," she said. "I'm working too hard as it is."

I explained it was no benefit and that the Trocadero was one of the best showcases for unrecognized talent. I pointed out that it was after appearing at one of the Sunday night sessions that Deanna Durbin had been tapped for her first movie role. I finally convinced Martha to go on. She was a riotous success, and the following day was signed by Paramount Pictures. She phoned me and asked: "Hey, you wanna be my manager?"

Martha Raye and I have just finished reminiscing of the days when I lured her into her first vaudeville engagement in my unit at Loew's State, and of the time I practically bullied her into making a guest appearance at the Trocadero in Hollywood—as a result of which she was signed for her picture contract with Paramount. We skipped one subject, however—her several unsuccessful marriages. *Photo by Hale Haberman*

Getting back to my first show at Loew's State, a pretty lass, Edna Sedgewick, and a favorite singing team, Chic Endor and Charlie Farrell, rounded out the bill. It was a sturdy enough setup, even without a columnist as master of ceremonies, but unknown to me, my manager, ex-vaudevillian Paul Small, had phoned dozens of show folks and invited them to have some fun on stage at their pleasure and leisure, and so it was that at every one of the four shows daily, celebrities would flock onto the stage and take part in the action.

Among those who dropped in during that first engagement were Jack Dempsey, Gus Edwards, Joe E. Lewis, Jay C. Flippen, Harry Hershfield, Hal LeRoy, Pat Rooney, Sr., Bob Hope, Sheila Barrett, William Gaxton, Joe Frisco, Cliff Edwards, Bert Wheeler and scores of others. And almost every night, Georgie Jessel would walk on and take over, to the delight of the audience.

This time, the critics were kinder. Sid Harris in *Billboard* insisted:

> With the booking of Louis Sobol, the *Evening Journal*'s columnist, Loew's built a unit, *Broadway on Parade,* surrounding Sobol with a sock array of talent, a group which would be a setup for the biggest of night clubs. . . . Runs a little under an hour with the audience working overtime on applause throughout and finally tearing down the house with the performance of the three

> Ritz Brothers. Sobol, a quiet chap, but at the same time radiating a lovable [*sic!*] personality, heads the show effectively. He works as m.c., introducing the turns in a businesslike way and in a clear voice [etc., etc.].

Scho in *Variety* (the same Scho who under his full name, Joe Schoenfeld, in *Billboard* years earlier had found me so dismal as an attraction) had this comment:

> Sobol makes no claim of being an actor. The ex-New Haven mug unostentatiously makes his entrance after a screened intro, goes right into Edna Sedgewick's toe dance—and from there on Waldron does everything but take Sobol's check. From Sobol's entrance starts a whale of a show: an entertainment holding almost everything but Sobol's and Waldron's missing hair. . . . The columnist will do a big business this week—they were standing all over the house Friday night. [And then added as an afterthought] But there was also Garbo in the picture *Anna Karenina*.

Thereafter, twice or three times a year, I was easily persuaded to return to the State, especially since that first salary of $1,500 a week was raised until I reached, to me, the staggering fee of $2,500 for the seven days' ordeal. So it came to pass that I was billed over veteran performers like Joe E. Lewis, Cross and Dunn, Ben Blue and others too numerous to mention.

And at the end of each week, as I sat in the dinky star's dressing room, the treasurer would come in and hand me that nice fat check, but I didn't trust his smile. Behind it I detected a sneer and could almost hear echoes from the walls: "Sobol—someday they'll get you for grand larceny." Nor did I care for Georgie Jessel's remark one night as he came onstage to interrupt the act and shout to the audience: "One more appearance of Sobol, and Billy Rose will take over this house and fill it with water."

The bosses at the *Journal* office didn't seem too impressed with the reviews or the planted publicity pointing to my amazing attributes as a vaudeville star. They greeted me with coolness, and I became aware that memos were coming in unusual profusion from the editor's desk, implying that I had been hired originally as a Broadway columnist to chronicle the events of the day, to deliver perky observations—in brief, to write a readable column. One final memo hinted, in fact, that if the *Journal* had wanted a

Big Name theatrical star as a feature, it would have approached John Barrymore or Helen Hayes.

I got the message. My vaudeville career came to an abrupt end.

Loew's, too, finally was to abandon vaudeville in December of 1947, yielding to the more potent draw of first-run major films. This time, however, I was not to blame.

Vaudeville has shifted from the stage to the television studios —with Ed Sullivan pioneering. It was followed in time by a flock of others until the home screens poured the variety acts into millions of households on the shows of Jackie Gleason, Merv Griffin, Jack Paar, Johnny Carson, Mike Douglas, Hollywood Palace, Joey Bishop and others. Television, which threw a fright into the movie industry in earlier years, proved to be a paper tiger as far as filmdom was concerned. Indeed, it turned out to be a prime benefactor of the industry, as its demand for motion pictures grew more and more ravenous. But it did kill off vaudeville, despite the occasional one-star shows at the Palace, even when the star sometimes is surrounded by a few other acts.

Just one little anecdote before we leave the vaudeville scene.

Some years back, when *Variety*'s editor Abel Green and Joe Laurie, Jr., combined to bring out a fascinating book, *Show Biz,* I urged Rosie Dolly Natcher to read it by all means. This brought on a reminiscence from Rosie back to the years when she and her sister, Jennie Dolly, were playing the vaudeville circuit.

Every time they appeared in New York, the late Sime Silver-

Johnny Carson at the microphone is tossing a few barbs in Sobol's direction while managing editor Paul Schoenstein seems to be enjoying the needling. This was at Toots Shor's when the New York Press Agents' Club was honoring the author on the occasion of his twenty-fifth year as a columnist.

man, founder and publisher of the theatrical publication, or one of his staff, would write a review of the act, labeling it mediocre or worse. Even when the Dolly Sisters were headlining at the Palace at $5,000 a week, a top figure for those days, Sime wouldn't change his attitude. However, when he encountered the sisters, he would assure them that he was quite fond of them personally.

One day, Rosie phoned him and invited him to be their guest at dinner, a dinner they were preparing themselves. Sime accepted, and the girls put on a sumptuous spread for him, from caviar to soufflés and champagne.

At dinner's end, Sime kissed Rosie and he kissed Jennie and said affectionately: "You two are darlings. I love you both and always will." A few days later, *Variety* came out with a review of their act at the Palace, written by Sime, himself. He wrote that never in all his experience on Broadway had there been a worse act than the one the Dolly Sisters were inflicting upon the public!

Burlesque

Back in 1964, Ann Corio, still a dedicated ecdysiast, boldly invaded our town with her starring offering *This Was Burlesque,* bringing with it memories of the rowdy form of show business that used to delight many of us who refused to be prudish. This show purported to be a spoof of old-time burlycue, but the strippers came out in full force and there were the usual naughty *double-entendre* blackouts.

I must confess I was quite partial to burlesque, and so were, believe it or not, that scornful critic George Jean Nathan and his pal H. L. Mencken. In fact, on several occasions, they invited me to accompany them over to the Jersey shores after burlesque had been stifled in Manhattan during the reign of Mayor Fiorello La Guardia and to enjoy there the corny and ribald proceedings still permitted across the river.

I still recall, even somewhat wistfully, jolly moments in the dinky theatres on West Forty-second Street in those earlier years when the Minskys were the burleycue monarchs in our town, offering frolicsome, impertinent, bawdy hilarities in which tramp Hebrew, Irish and Dutch comics spewed out their slapstick humor, tripped up straight men, leered at and flirted with the shapely soubrettes. The blackouts were scampishly indecorous, but these days they would be like prayer meetings compared with the brazen and even obscene scenes in our legitimate theatre and in the movies.

In fact, it wasn't until the fading days of burlesque that the strippers became bolder and nudity began to prevail. In the early era, we were excited enough when the leading lady emerged in her white or pink spangled tights. Some of our womenfolk today walk around the city streets in more daring leotards, and in minute mini- and microskirts that are far more revealing.

The memories hover over the Hurtig and Seamon frivolities, the Columbia wheel, Jean Bedini's *Puss, Puss Co.* and *Billy Watson's Beef Trust*—as well as notable performers who were poured out of the faucets of this scorned relative of show business: Fanny Brice, Jim Barton, Bert Lahr, Leon Errol, Jack Pearl, Gypsy Rose Lee, Clark and McCullough, Phil Silvers, Red Buttons, Abbott and Costello, "Rags" Ragland and dozens of others.

It was after the death of burlesque that the drab little night spots on West Fifty-second Street began flourishing as strip joints, so for quite a few years, the uninhibited little ladies who wanted to show all kept on earning a handsome living wage.

I'm trying to recall the names of some of the belles of burlesque who dominated—I am able to come up with, in addition to Ann Corio and Gypsy Rose Lee, the well-stacked Georgia Sothern, Rose La Rose, the witty Margie Hart, a lass billed simply as Hinda —and I'll let it go at that.

There have been a few other attempts to bring back burlesque in New York, but apparently the allure has disappeared. To repeat, the offerings seem too tame compared with what the movies offer in nudity and in sex sequences. Girls practically naked strut around in some of our cabarets from Coast to Coast—and of course you may be served in some night spots by girls stripped to the waist. As for bawdy blackouts—they can't compare with the brazen scenes in some of the plays on the legitimate stage or sequences in the movies.

Moonlighting

My vaudeville ventures were not the only "moonlighting" excursions to which I must confess a feeling of guilt. Earlier I had been starred in a series of film shorts entitled: *Louis Sobol's Down Memory Lane,* and had appeared in minor roles in several pictures: *Copacabana,* which starred Groucho Marx and Carmen

Miranda, and featured, besides myself, Columnist Earl Wilson and *Variety* editor Abel Green; *College Confidential,* a tawdry offering despite a cast which included Steve Allen and Jayne Meadows, Mamie Van Doren and Walter Winchell; and finally, another shoddy little film, *Kiss Me, Stupid.*

In addition to me, columnists Phyllis Battelle, Bert Bacharach and Bill Slocum and several other newsfolks had been imported for *Stupid,* a picture starring Dean Martin and Kim Novak, but the entire affair lived up to the title, for all the producers wanted for the camera were the backs of our heads. And for this, money was shelled out for the expensive plane trips, hotel accommodations, etc.

My only consoling memory of this one is the time when we gathered on the set between takes and listened to Ira Gershwin singing out in his foggy voice songs he and George Gershwin had fashioned and put away in the "trunk." One of them, into which he put real feeling, was a number "Oh, Sophie, Be Mine," singing it to Kim Novak who lounged over his shoulder as he sat at the piano, with Dean Martin humming along.

Later, as I chatted with Dean, he scoffed at the drunken image with which he was associated. "Actually," he said, "I don't think I take more than three—well, maybe, at most, four drinks through the day. But they built up this image of me boozing, and I go along with it, and I really put it on strong in my nightclub act. What's the difference?"

One other film venture—one that, by way of contrast, was accorded a favorable reception after its initial showing at the Capitol Theatre. Its theme is best conveyed by how *Time* magazine in its issue of March 21, 1932, evaluated it.

> For their best shots, newsreels are dependent upon accidentally suitable events like the Lindbergh kidnapping. Otherwise they are too often forced to use clichés like battleship launchings, cherry blossom time in Japan, baby parades, Mussolini, sporting events and animals that can dance or court. A new type of newsreel called Louis Sobol's Newsreel Scoops made its appearance last week. It showed what in newssheets would be feature stories—shots of Harry K. Thaw and Evelyn Nesbit as they looked when Harry K. Thaw shot Stanford White and as they look at present; various ladies who have been friends with or married Rudy Vallee; three Broadway playboys playing cards in a penthouse; the man who makes Mayor James J. Walker's

> shoes and Mayor Walker in a jolly mood, strumming one of his own tunes on a piano.
>
> In effect much like the chipper colyum of Broadway gossip which Louis Sobol writes for the *New York Evening Journal,* the Sobol newsreel seems ingenious and potentially popular, depending almost entirely on the intimacy of the revelations made. Observers wondered where Sobol had procured his material. He had borrowed old shots of Thaw and Nesbit from old newsreel libraries, had new ones made to order. Guy Loomis, an oil stock promotor who found his land really contained an oil well; William (Billy) B. Mishkin who expects to inherit a fortune in a few years; and a Manhattan sport named John Walker were readily persuaded to be revealed as Metropolitan spendthrifts.
>
> Mayor Walker is not at all averse to posing at the piano as a postlude to the portrait of his cobbler. Other items in the first Sobol newsreel were: a survey of careers open to Follies girls, with three examples; a short of the interior of a speakeasy, deleted by the censors after one showing.

What *Time* did not mention was also a shot of a nudist camp, and that, too, I recall, was ordered deleted after one showing. The speakeasy mentioned was the Mansion. It was a good idea—this newsreel—and to this day I think it might have prospered, but the producers ran out of cash, and the project died after that one week's showing.

And then there were my radio assignments, starting with my shows on WOR for a furniture company, Ludwig Baumann; then succeeding Winchell on the Lucky Strike Hour over WEAF; then in later years on the Borden Show over WOR. Finally, I conducted daily broadcasts over the American Broadcasting network for close to a year, starting off with Ethel Merman and Jimmy Durante for the initial session. My lineup during the months that followed found me interviewing Audrey Hepburn and Mel Ferrer, Charles Laughton, Eli Wallach and Burgess Meredith, Gilbert Miller and Basil Rathbone, Sammy Davis, Jr., Eddie Cantor, Milton Berle, Fannie Hurst, Johnnie Ray, Ted Lewis, Joe E. Brown, Cornelia Otis Skinner, composer Jule Styne, lawyer Roy Cohn, Ella Logan, Sam Levenson, Beatrice Lillie, Richard Rodgers and Oscar Hammerstein, Pearl Buck, Robert Ruark, Robert Merrill, Harry Belafonte, Paul Whiteman, Sophie Tucker and Dan Dailey, William Saroyan and his children, Senator Jacob Javits, Liberace, novelist Faith Baldwin and Dorothy Thompson, Ben Hecht, Lou Holtz, Billy Rose, Bob Hope, novelist Stuart

The amiable "King of Jazz" was in semiretirement when this picture was taken, although shortly after he was back in action with his orchestra, fulfilling a month's engagement in Las Vegas. During my interview with Paul Whiteman, I asked for his frank opinion of rock 'n' roll. His answer was something to the effect that he was partial to any type of music that prodded folks into dancing or even "just stomping your feet." I recall he also said he never deserved the title of "King of Jazz"—rather, he'd bestow the crown on Duke Ellington or Benny Goodman. Ironically enough, as I was fashioning this caption, word came over the radio that the lovable maestro was dead—just two days before 1967 expired.
Photo by Hale Haberman

Jackie Robinson, athlete supreme, business executive and occasional politician, had just named the men he considers the greatest of our ballplayers, past and present, including among them, I recall, Christy Mathewson, whom he never saw in action he confessed, Joe DiMaggio and Mickey Mantle, Stan Musial and Ted Williams.
Photo by Hale Haberman

Cloete, Joey Adams, Crown Prince Bernadotte, biographer Alden Hatch, Jackie Robinson and many others.

I felt considerable regret when this series was concluded, for it had enabled me to probe into the thoughts and reactions of notable personalities and to wrest from them some hitherto unrevealed incidents in their respective careers.

11

"... and Cabbages and Kings ..."

I RESERVE A SPECIAL VALENTINE for as interesting a group of people as we have in our midst—Show Folks. My burning crush on the men and women of the entertainment world has never abated. They are warmhearted and generous, happy go-lucky and always great fun. Some of them remain children at heart to the day they die. Others are adult from the cradle. They are rarely dull.

No class of our citizenry has contributed as much. Without their aid in the way of personal appearances, many of our great charities would flounder. They have brought cheer to the fighting men on all fronts, often at great personal danger. They are clannish. They will envy one another's successes, but will be the first to come to a rival's defense when the chips are down.

They are the softest touches. The late Fred Allen had a private pension list, and George M. Cohan's lavish distribution of funds to down-and-outers of the profession was no secret. Comedian Joe E. Lewis can't say "no" to any request for a loan, and the late Sophie Tucker's charities were a byword. Who ranks with

Georgie Jessel in the time he has given to fly to banquets and funerals and public affairs—so often at his own expense—to deliver eulogies over departed friends, to praise others, to pour out generously of his wit at dinners honoring notables?

Jack Benny, who presents professionally the phony image of penuriousness, has his purse open at all times for needy causes. For that matter, the list is a long one of performers who, having fallen on dismal days, penniless and ill, have been kept going with no fanfare of trumpets by fellow show folks. I can name you several dozen entertainers of the past who would have become public charges had it not been for the generosity of more fortunate actors who kept donating out of their pay—sans publicity. And, of course, the various organizations of the show world, American Guild of Variety Artists (AGVA), American Federation of Television and Radio Artists (AFTRA), Equity, Friars, and Lambs have seen to it that their own should be kept from want.

I love them for their little acts of thoughtfulness. When comic Rags Ragland died on the eve of his scheduled opening as costar with Phil Silvers at the Copa some years ago, it was Frank Sinatra who flew in from the Coast to help Silvers through the

This is part of a group the author had assembled for one of the shows for wounded soldiers at Mitchell Field during World War II. Among them you may recognize Jay C. Flippen, Betty Hutton, Lucille Ball, Lawrence Tibbett and his wife, and Leon Leonidoff, who stages the Radio City Music Hall shows.

heartbreaking night, filling in as a willing stooge. Similarly, singer Vivian Blaine and comedian Jan Murray rushed to fill in at the Palace Theatre, without pay, when Judy Garland collapsed. There have been dozens of instances where performers have come to the rescue when, for one reason or another, the scheduled entertainer has been unable to keep the commitment for the night or for several nights. When I was presenting shows weekly at Mitchell Field for our wounded G.I.'s during World War II, Betty Hutton canceled a flight to Europe to answer my appeal to be one of the stars.

They are funful companions, and I don't know of any group of people I'd rather sit around with and just listen. Ninety percent of their conversation is shop talk, but is there anything more fascinating than the light banter that swirls about show business? Their exchanges may be right out of Joe Miller, but I giggle and guffaw. They are quick at the thrust and the counter-thrust, and an hour with these lads and lasses is the most effective therapy for the dread affliction known as the "yawns."

They are wholesome hosts and diverting guests, and man for man or woman for woman, I'll match their decorum against that of the aloofish entries in the *Social Register*. Ask the average citizen if he had his choice with whom would he prefer to walk down the block—the president of a bank or Bob Hope, the head of the D.A.R. or Elizabeth Taylor?

It was at a Friar's dinner for Jack Benny that the venerable Bernard Baruch remarked that if the enslaved people of the Iron Curtain countries could be treated to a healthy dose of the wit and comedy which had come over the dais from Fred Allen, Georgie Jessel, George Burns and others, they might be more eager to mingle with and become part of a peace-minded world.

Be that as it may, you may count me as one who would consider this an empty existence if it weren't for our show folks. If you'll pardon the expression, I'm crazy for them.

Show World Hierarchy

Definitely there is a hierarchy of performers in our entertainment world. Of course, there is no recognized Social Register for the bluebloods of show business, although there have been occasions when a personality with a stage, screen or television background has had his or her name included in the official *Social*

Peggy Sobol tells a funny which evidently amuses George Burns and Carol Channing, the original *Hello Dolly!* doll.
Photo by David Workman

Register through marriage. Nevertheless, the citizens of the show world have themselves through the years come to regard with awe and respect certain members of their set—awe and respect many of the snooty entries in the *Register* do not command from their equals.

Unlike the aristocrats of Society with the capital "S," the performing patricians do not boast unimpeachable social background with imposing family trees. It is through sheer talent and personality—that certain something that no one quite successfully defines —that they have attained stature that perhaps has given them the nod of their fellow performers. Furthermore, there is no race or color barrier.

If Helen Hayes has indisputably earned her right to her place in Showdom's High Society, then so has Sidney Poitier, and so had the late Paul Muni, even though each might have tilted a respective eyebrow at the "aristocrat" tag and exclaimed, "Who, me?" Certainly, composers Richard Rodgers, Irving Berlin and Harold Arlen to name a few, rate inclusion, and cinema offers Cary Grant, Sir Laurence Olivier, Bette Davis, Ingrid Bergman, Deborah Kerr, Sir John Gielgud, Maurice Evans— well, it's fruitless to go on with the complete roster.

Every field of show business, of course, has its candidates. We can in offhand fashion name Zero Mostel, Johnny Carson, Barbra Streisand, Alan King, Sammy Davis, Jr., Judy Garland, Merv

Griffin, Frank Sinatra, Tallulah Bankhead, Paul Scofield, Anthony Newley, Mike Douglas, Lucille Ball—so many others—and not only performers, but writers, directors, producers and singers who pop in and out of the news and the columns with frequency but, let's face it, many in the field do not command respect among their equals, though in some instances, they are more successful as far as earnings and influence with the general public.

The truth is, the show world has its own code, too. It understands the value of publicity but frowns on notoriety. It forgives personal weaknesses, but it is as straitlaced and unyielding as any other class of society when it comes to those flaunting the accepted social standards. It never confuses natural eccentricities, which often lend colorful flavor to a personality, with deliberate flamboyance, arrogance, bad taste and conceit.

There is another classification among show folks, traits that would rate high in popularity polls among their own kind as distinguished from the fans at large. They are beloved in their own entertainment set because of their warmth, their generosity or in some cases, their personal modesty—for instance, Perry Como, Bing Crosby, Jimmy Durante, Joe E. Lewis, Bob Hope and Jack Benny.

And there are those, let's point out unhappily, who, though eminently successful as outstanding box office lures, or commanding high ratings when seen on television, all boasting swollen bankbooks, rate almost zero with their show business contemporaries. You'd be amazed what Big Names I have in mind, but when fellow performers get together, these are the stars nominated to head the All-American Obnoxious Team.

Shelley Winters is apparently startled by the flash of the cameraman's bulb, but Jack Benny remains calm under fire—always the imperturbable. In the background, former vaudevillian Jesse Block, now a Wall Streeter, Peggy Sobol and her husband.

We should offer a salute to show world patricians of the past, and certainly among them, regardless of what we have come to learn of their personal failings, are the Barrymores, George M. Cohan, Fred Stone, Edwin Booth, Victor Herbert, Jerome Kern, Maude Adams—to name a few.

I feel certain no one will go to the trouble of compiling a Performers' Social Register, but now there seems to be hope that a pet project that I have been advocating for close to a quarter of a century is about to be realized—that is, a Hall of Fame for the biggies, past and present, of show business. Certainly, if baseball can have its select circle honored, why not the folks who contribute so much to our pleasure?

Salute to the Fun-Lads

I must confess, too, that I am particularly partial to the funnymen of our nation. Perhaps I am so appreciative of the sterling worth of our harlequins and of the gifts they spread so lavishly because of my own woeful deficiencies as the teller of comical stories or as the creator of original gems of humor. I admire the quick and pungent retort because I am what is known as a "taxicab wit," that is, a dunce who thinks up something smart he might have said hours after the occasion.

How we rock and roar and beat our chests and cackle and snort and hold our sides and yelp and whistle and dry our eyes as Joe E. Lewis delivers his zany stories and hilarious parodies, though so much of the routine may be familiar to us *aficionados*. And we wait eagerly for that fit of coughing, fully aware that he will mutter, "I must get a room tonight."

Danny Thomas and his lugubrious laments, especially his pessimistic wail regarding the auto jack lacking in his time of need, and his woeful anticipation of what the garage man will charge him—we all know the story, but we want to hear it again and laugh anew. In other days, we realized that a meeting between Mr. Lapidus and the Maharajah would have been a dignified business of state, but not when Lou Holtz flicked an imaginary speck of dust from his neatly creased trousers, waved his cane, and solemnly recounted what actually took place.

Marty Allen and Steve Rossi in their peppery "Hello, dere," offerings, satirizing the events and the personalities of the day;

Jimmy Durante tolerating one fly on the schnoz but rising in anger when the fly's playmates join it and screaming: "Jes' f'dat, ya all get off!" Milton Berle's quickies, Jack E. Leonard's staccato stabs, Georgie Jessel's droll tales, and for that matter, the little and big jokes of any of the funnymen, new gags or old, are therapeutic to those of us fighting off the melancholy. Parenthetically, I feel saddened by the recent split-up of the Allen-Rossi team.

Uncle Sam has recognized the value of the laugh, for in our major wars comedians were in demand at the fighting front to cheer our soldiers just as today, a top morale builder, Bob Hope, brings laughs to our G.I.'s in Vietnam, often disregarding personal danger. I can well believe he deserves the highest civilian honor in the power of the President to bestow. In fact, I'd rather be in Hope's company, and in the company of so many other comics and comedians, than make a night of it with a highly decorated general.

We come to a matter of semantics. I love the entire tribe, but there are lines of distinction to be drawn among comics, comedians and humorists, monologists, clowns. Some years ago, critic John Chapman defined a comic as "generally a man who sucks a microphone like a lollipop and hires somebody smarter than he is to write his funny lines." I put it into different wordage a decade or so ago when I insisted that "A comic lives by the sweat of his gag writer's brow." Through the years I have tried to distinguish among the breeds, though I have never intended to denigrate comics or claim that comedians or humorists belong to a more elegant clan.

The fact is, you can give one performer a snappy line to offer, and it may come out a dud. Give the same line to experts like Milton Berle, Jan Murray, Henny Youngman, Johnny Carson, Alan Gale, Marty Allen, Joe E. Lewis, Joey Adams, Joey Bishop, Buddy Hackett, Nipsey Russell, Jackie Kannon, Jack Carter and a dozen others I should name, and it will tug a howl.

Comics whip away with quips. Comedians, on the other hand, are primarily deft actors who do not depend upon snappy lines or contrived ad libs, but rather a situation monologue. A comedian, by the tilt of the eyebrows, a twist of the lips, a shrug of the shoulders, can stir the titters or even the belly laugh. The late Bert Lahr was both comedian and clown, as is Sid Caesar. In this classification I would include Red Skelton, and when they were active, Charles Chaplin, Jack Pearl, Jack Haley, Harold Lloyd, and the late W. C. Fields. Jack Benny, Jimmy Durante, Joey Bishop, Jack

The late great comedian-clown Bert Lahr in a casual get-together. This outstanding funnyman was an inhibited personality offstage, rarely was amusing and never tried to come through with a quip. He was a good listener, but unlike Groucho Marx, Milton Berle or Bob Hope, he contributed little to the evening's fun. But once onstage, a metamorphosis took place, and he became a supreme clown.

Red Buttons salutes the author with jeering remarks during the New York Press Agents' dinner in 1954 honoring Sobol for his twenty-five years as columnist. The comedian's first television break came when he was tapped to portray Joe E. Lewis in a home screen version of Lewis' career based on a profile written by Sobol.

Carter, Red Buttons, Jack Lemmon, Tony Randall are primarily comedians. As for Bob Hope, he becomes the comedian in films, the monologist and comic in public appearances.

Nor must they be confused with humorists, although some possess a blend of the talents. Whether you like their style or their message or even their ideology, it must be conceded that fellows like Mort Sahl, Nipsey Russell, Morty Gunty, Jack Douglas, Johnny Carson, Shelley Berman, Harry Hershfield, Woody Allen, Bob Newhart, Alan King, Myron Cohen, Georgie Jessel, Pat Cooker are basically humorists. Their offerings would be as giggle-provoking in print.

Ed Wynn personally preferred to be known as a comedian rather than a comic, though he often resorted to comics' gimmicks. He is quoted as having insisted that a "comedian is not a man who says funny things. A comedian is one who says things funny. For instance, a comedian is not a man who opens a funny door; a comedian is one who opens a door in a funny way."

Time recalled that in the role of a waiter in a musical, *Manhattan Mary,* in the late twenties, Wynn was asked by a gangster patron for a suggestion as to what to eat. The comedian thought he might like a jelly roll or perhaps ladyfingers.

"Ladyfingers!" exploded the mobster, "I'm so hungry I could eat a horse!" Whereupon Wynn ran offstage and returned leading a swaybacked horse! And as he brought the animal near the table, he asked quietly: "Will you have mustard or catsup?"

Groucho Marx is both comic and humorist. Fred Allen was both comedian and humorist. Danny Kaye, Jonathan Winters, Danny Thomas, Joey Bishop, to me are comedians. Whereas Jerry Lewis is strictly a comic of the slapstick variety. So is Soupy Sales.

The same definitions may apply to the distaff members of show business. Lucille Ball is certainly a comedienne, and so are Martha Raye, Carol Burnett, Imogene Coco and Carol Channing. Phyllis Diller, on the other hand, is all comic and so is buxom Totie Fields.

Jackie Gleason has graduated from the comic status to become a situation comedian, and, for that matter, Red Buttons, who started out as a burlesque comic, has not only gained comedian stature, but has proved himself capable of purely dramatic performances, as he did in his Oscar-winning role in *Sayonara.*

In the profession, there are comics and comedians and humorists who have no greater applauders than fellow performers.

It is no secret that George Burns can push Jack Benny into convulsions by merely scratching his chin or reciting the weather report. Similarly, comic Jan Murray doubles up in what might be termed laughing anguish over comic Harry Ritz's zany quips or buffoonery.

At this point, I want to comment on a new trend that has developed these later years—whether commendable or not depends upon the attitude of the night-spot patron. Replacing the comics and comedians who depend on good-natured quips, parodies, solid gags or humorous storytelling, there have sprung up the "insulters"—Don Rickles, Jack E. Leonard, Billy Gray, Jackie Kannon, Mort Sahl, and until his death, the uninhibited Lenny Bruce, who, in my book, was a "dirty" humorist, though cleverly spewing out his four-letter smut, as did B. S. Pulley before him.

The approach differs. Sahl, Shelley Berman, Kannon, and occasionally Jack Douglas, when he tries the night-spot circuit, flay away at high dignitaries and at customs of the day, tackle diversified subjects on which to try out their special brand of satire.

Leonard, Rickles and Gray specialize in the studied insult, usually directed at *well knowns* among the assemblies at the nightclubs or at special dinners at which they grace the dais.

Leonard usually directs his barbs only at victims with whom he is on a friendly, even intimate basis, and though he is merciless at times, his victims seem to be enjoying themselves even though the laughs are at their expense.

Rickles, on the other hand, has what seems to be a cruel sense of humor, and though the subjects of his attack seem to take it all in good grace, I have often suspected that many of them smart under the barrage and wonder why they are saps enough to stand up as he usually asks them to, and smile and just take it, unflinching. Rickles thinks nothing of digging the deflating stiletto deep into a star's pride in his or her achievements or physical endowments—or into their peculiarities or background which they would prefer not exposed to the public's sneers.

Billy Gray, who operates chiefly in Hollywood and Miami Beach, comes halfway between Jack E. Leonard and Don Rickles in his approach, but his is such a disarming personality that I cannot recall anyone ever having walked out of his night spots offended. And he does rattle off a string of quips and gags in between his insults that provokes the guffaws. For that matter Jack E. Leonard's quickies are of the highest order, extremely quotable, too, as indeed they are from time to time in the columns. He has this redeeming trait, too—he pokes as much fun at himself as at his victims.

I have maintained this is a new breed—the "insulters"—but I must confess that going back to the nights when the rowdy 18 Club was a potent lure for the midnighters, Jack White and his troupe of amiable associates prodded away at cash customers, and indeed often induced some of them to come up and be made the butt of their jokes.

I recall the night Bing Crosby, who never was too gregarious, stood up and exchanged banter with White and Frankie Hyers and then at White's command: "Sing for your supper, you bum," actually obeyed and chanted a couple of tunes.

Some of the funny lads, by the strangest of coincidences, use almost identical material, the same quips or jokes or wisecracks or swifties. Some are deadpanned when they deliver. Others show all their teeth. The methods vary but the punchline is the same.

For instance, a favorite when an audience doesn't seem to be receptive: The comic cups a hand over his eyes, peers out in semi-bewildered fashion and murmurs: "Folks, I can't see you—but I know you're there. I can hear you breathing." This is always good for a titter and slight applause. Also for a consolatory laugh for the next gag.

Often the comedian will repeat a quip spilled earlier in his monologue. This does not dismay him. There is a standard cover-up employed by such experts as Joe E. Lewis, Milton Berle, Henny Youngman and others: "Oh, I said that—that's where I must have heard it."

When the evening seems to be moving slowly, a Berle or a Jackie Kannon will observe with proper melancholy, though apropos of nothing: "I loved her—she was my true love. She had the face of a saint (*pause*) —of a St. Bernard."

The boys refer to recent hotel accommodations. They speak approvingly of their rooms "with adjoining towels." Completely air-conditioned—"every half hour the bellboy comes and blows through the keyhole."

Other familiars you are doomed to hear over and over again are among the following:

"The last place I worked in they had the ropes up. The owners hanged themselves."

"I'll be back here this winter—I heard the manager say, 'It'll be a cold day when he plays here again.'"

"Let's give a big hand to Mr. and Mrs. Harry Stravasin. They were married at 8:00 o'clock and now it's 12:35 sharp—and they're still here. Yessir, they're still here, ha, ha, ha."

"Don't think it worries me when you start walking out. It's when you start walking toward me."

"Ladies and Gentlemen, I have a pleasant surprise for you tonight. I have just noticed sitting over there at the table near the piano—your favorite personality and mine—Marty Allen. Marty, get up and take a bow—Oh, my mistake, Pardon me, madame!"

(When a patron keeps talking through the act) "Please excuse me—I thought I was doing a single."

I don't know how or why this picture came into my possession—but it's a study of youth worth preserving. *Left to right*—as if you didn't know—Milton Berle, Fred Waring and Harry Richman—when they were so very young at heart—and in age.

(To quelch a heckler) "May I borrow your I.Q.? I've got a date with a moron tonight."

If, to repeat, I am partial to funnymen, I am equally allergic to the breed that tries to tug laugh material out of the sewers. From time to time, I delivered blasts at the smut spreaders and vulgarity displayers, and apparently I was not alone in my displeasure, for hundreds of approving letters would flood in.

Without mentioning her name, there was one comedienne, otherwise talented, who used to brush a handkerchief under her armpits to wipe away imaginary sweat or pat her front or rear bulges and look slyly over to front-pew gigglers as she tossed out lewd comments that couldn't be misconstrued by a five-year-old.

Nor broadminded as I've considered myself and well versed enough in my Krafft-Ebing, Freud, Forel and Havelock Ellis to be tolerant of the lads who want to be ladies and the gals who would like to wear galluses, I draw the line only when they come on in a night spot and project their transvestite eccentricities as entertainment. When they confine their "artistry" to a display of genuine talent, I am among the first to applaud. But when they consider it smart to offer a pollution of verbal slime and nauseating posturings, then I want to leave the room in a hurry—and throw up.

I have certain favorites among the funnymen, and some of them are not above offering purple *double entendres* but at least they don't indulge in obviously salacious gestures or make broad references to certain types of plumbing, gent's room vagaries, anatomical deficiencies or prodigalities.

I sometimes feel like stealing a familiar line from Milton Berle by extending an invitation to offensive comics: "I'd love for you to come to my house some night—and we'll open a gas jet!"

Farewell to a Patient Clan

If the true boulevardier is a species of the past, then, let's face it, so is the stage-door Johnny, that patient, chivalrous, often dudish cavalier. I know he was quite evident and visible in my earlier days on Broadway.

They came in all styles and sizes, the stage-door Johnnies. Some were young, some were old. Some were lean, some were fat. Some were clean-shaven, some affected beards. But most of them had that same adoring, fatuous, hopeful expression on their faces as they waited either just outside the little lane leading from the stage entrance or at the forbidden portal itself. In dinner suit and black tie, in tails and white tie, in toppers atilt on their heads, or, occasionally, in milder weather, held in one hand while the other clung to a floral love offering—they comprised as integral a part waiters were tipped adequately and the headwaiters magnanimously.

The more fortunate were accorded special privileges. They were permitted to enter through that magic little door right past the doorman into the sanctum sanctorum itself—the dressing room of the Lady. That is, of course, when the Lady was the star or one of the featured performers, entitled to her own backstage boudoir.

But for the most part, the stage-door Johnny was content to wait outside until his dream-girl, who might be the second from the left or even the fourth in the rear of the assembly of beauteous creatures who walked regally, never in a hurry, attired in sumptuous gowns or adorned with nothing much more than a fixed smile and a wisp of veiling—until, let me repeat, this Vision of Loveliness was through with her chores and ready to join him.

Before my time, most likely they would be off to Rector's or Delmonico's, to Reisenweber's or to any of the lobster palaces of the era where they would mingle with other fair beauties of the show world and other stage-door Johnnies. They would dance to the seductive strains of Viennese waltzes, they would sip their champagne, they would woo and promise, and often this led to a nobler step, such as marriage. They ate well and drank well—the waiters were tipped adequately and the headwaiters magnanimously.

The stage-door Johnny of that forgotten era took the creature of his dreams out riding in a horse-drawn hack or in his own barouche, and in later years, in his limousine or flashy Stutz Bearcat. Before the Broadway columnist came along, most of this courting passed unnoticed by the general public because no nosey newspaperman made mention thereof. When the snoopers came along with their gossip columns, this anonymity vanished, and soon all Manhattan was aware of the stage-door Johnny's identity, the gifts he showered on his special charmer—the furs, the jewels, and also the occasional brawls in which he participated because of jealousy.

He was still a dominant member of the scene when I began paying some attention. Most of the old lobster palaces were gone, but the speakeasy had intruded satisfactorily as a happy and romantic retreat, and while the champagne now was something out of vinegar and spice and not altogether nice, and was poured usually from pitchers, nevertheless, it sufficed.

But something of the old grand tradition was gradually evaporating. It was to be observed among the Lingering Set that there were lads who eschewed the conventional garb. These rebellious uncouth newcomers actually wore sports suits or ordinary mufti, fedoras and even caps as they waited for the ladies of the chorus. And instead of a gentle posy in their hand, there was a suspicious bulge in their hip or side pockets. Often this was a contraband flask—just as often, a lethal weapon known as a gat or rod.

I am not at all sure in my recollections just when the tribe began to dwindle. As a matter of honest record, even to this day there are still a few gentlemen of the old and honored school who are not above waiting discreetly across the street from the theatre or the cabaret until their darlings emerge, but they are a weakling, pusillanimously craven lot, for they seem to linger in the shadows furtively on the lookout lest someone detect them. The old flair, the overt chivalry, is gone.

Nowadays, when a lady of the chorus or the ballet has a prearranged rendezvous with a man, she usually meets him at a designated place—perhaps "21" or El Morocco, Kippy's or Gallagher's or at the gayer midnight haunts such as the Copacabana or Latin Quarter or one of the discothèques. It is a different era and the customs are bolder. Now a woman walks boldly into a restaurant or night spot without an escort and meets her man there or sometimes, arriving earlier, waits for him. She may even sit at a bar, or stand against it and may openly smoke her cigarette or powder her nose.

And quite often it is the lady who owns the flashy car and drives her beau around in it.

By the time I was beginning to report on the Manhattan action, the famed supper parties of another era were only memories, little undraped beauties no longer rose out of huge pies and tossed silken garters to the gentlemen. Nor were the frail creatures demanding lobster Newburg anymore, although some still were insisting on caviar.

In fact, the glorious Venuses of chorus and showgirl line of cabaret ensembles have become quite independent, and worst of all, many of them, if you're to credit the plaintive wail of our men-about-town, are stricken with the woeful affliction: Ambition. They spend off-hours studying, taking dramatic lessons, moonlighting as models. The result is that when their labors are completed, they are much too weary or too aware of the early rising hour they have scheduled for themselves to be willing to disport at the saloons. A sandwich in a corner drugstore, with one or two fellow coryphées along, is the height of their dissipation.

Under the circumstances, what future is there for a stage-door Johnny? The somber truth is, his day is done. Fini.

"*. . . Is Like a Melody*"

The boulevardier and the stage-door Johnny may have vanished from the scene, but the showgirl remains, though for some reason she no longer stirs up feature-page excitement or causes a rumble of attention as she enters a restaurant or night spot. Outwardly she offers the same enticing facade: the long slender shapely underpinnings, the exciting contours, the provocative strut, but she seems to have lost out in the most important department—what we term "glamor."

She had her big day in the Ziegfeld, White and Carroll era, and when the cabaret extravaganzas were dominant entertainment lures. Those were the days when the typewriters thumped and roared and crammed the feature pages of the columns with word silhouettes of the Gladys Glads, the Mae Murrays, the Jessie Reeds, the "Stuttering Sam" McDowells, the Iris Adrians, the Hazel Forbeses and countless others.

They were well paid and well fed, these lithesome, blithesome ladies, but it wasn't their general good health and their general good looks and their general touching loyalty to their stage activities that kept the populace and the writing lads in a dither. It was what went on after the final curtain rang down, or before the opening curtain rolled up.

Theirs was a life teeming, for the most part, with excitement and frivolity and often tragedy. We pulled out the well-worn descriptives, not the least of which were the "flighty moth" or the "carefree butterfly." Men of means and prestige swarmed about them, and many of them went on to fame in other fields, but many fluttered about unhappily until a sorry end obliterated them from public view, but not from public mind—violent death, alcoholism, poverty.

There were lavish jewels and furs and champagne suppers for these lush lovelies, and always reams of publicity with newspapermen eager to pay their homage in print. These were free-spending eras going into a crescendo of extravagance for years after World War I was over and up to World War II. As they stepped out of the showgirl line, other beauties, eager and ambitious, replaced them, and soon they, too, were tasting the glory of feature page and column attention.

Those were the days of orchids and champagne, of pearl necklaces and sables. Wall Street tycoons, mob leaders and society lads fought to be their escorts. And through it all, the drumbeaters for the lucky producers and night-spot owners grinned happily and rubbed their palms gleefully, for theirs was an easy job. The folks of the newspapers were only too eager to help out and to keep the names of these darling showgirls in print.

These days, it becomes a task to try to name even a half dozen outstanding showgirls. Many of them are just as beautiful, but the times have changed, and the attitude of the girls has changed. Today's crop is ambitious, too, but less extroverted. Their escorts, as a rule, are solid young businessmen who rarely figure in the news or column paragraphs. Many of the breed of the current sixties want out as quickly as possible, either through marriage, a movie contract or a career away from show business.

And it is true, outstanding models have stolen the play from them—recently even a skinny, flat-chested, pouty-lipped lass like Twiggy, for instance.

We Shoulda Stood in Bed

Disillusionment embraces most of us in its melancholy arms, especially when we greet an old friend after many years. The lovely, creamy-complexioned, slender, animated girl who stirred up so many emotions in our youth doesn't seem at all the same lovely creature when we meet her again—now perhaps a grandmother, stout, garrulous, lines of age and harassment etched on her once lovely face. It's that way with some of the plays and pictures that once stirred up to heights of enthusiasm.

Like so many others, I find escape occasionally after the day's chores are over in the Late or Late Late Shows, and oh, how sad and how comical, too, the once so-exciting action and the corny dialog and the hammy performances seem to our currently advanced ears and eyes.

Take those two prized favorites of the past: *Little Caesar* and *The Public Enemy*. How we looked forward to the gory baths as the snarling Rico (Edward G. Robinson) pumped lead into gangster foes or as a grim Tom Powers (Jimmy Cagney) with a sardonic smile ruthlessly mowed down those who opposed his progress. We wanted again to revel in the charms of that dreamboat Jean Harlow.

It was a mistake to catch up with the films again. I should have known better. I should have nursed my illusions. The youthful-looking Robinson was a study in the delivery of corn. He looked as sinister as the mailman delivering a special-delivery letter. Cagney was as tough-looking as a choirboy. Jean Harlow looked fat around the hips and as seductive as Jackie Gleason eating a cream puff. As for giving any evidence of being an inspired actress, I've viewed better performances in amateur high school plays.

Oh, well, poor glamorous Jean is gone, and we should think only kindly of the lady who was the Marilyn Monroe of her day. Robinson and Cagney have proved since that they belong with the elite of the cinema fraternity, and it is not their fault that these gangster classics of the past prove so lacking today in the stuff we consider acceptable melodrama. Far from offering the chills and thrills that had us shuddering in our seats in those other years, I found myself laughing at and talking back to our heroes of the screen.

I must confess other oldies of the tough school do hold up: *Petrified Forest* with Humphrey Bogart for instance, and *The Killers, Asphalt Jungle, High Noon* and *Winterset.* They still convey terror and suspense.

I don't want to risk a letdown by returning to some reading that kept me enthralled in boyhood. I don't mean those perennial favorites, *Robinson Crusoe* or *Treasure Island,* but the Merriwell series, for instance, the *Liberty Boys of '76,* Horatio Alger, or the old Nick Carters.

And I want to retain the glow as I remember old comics, "Happy Hooligan," "Gloomy Gus," "The Hall Room Boys," "Foxy Grandpa," "Lady Bountiful," "Little Nemo"—the entire gallery of heroes and buffoons who contributed to our glee and joy in other days, but I don't want to take the chance of renewing acquaintance with them. I want to hold on to my illusions.

I don't want to press the subject too hard, but I could list dozens of plays of the past that drew the cheers of the critics and audiences alike, but occasionally when they have been revived by stock companies, Oh, how dated they are, how yawnsome. Of course, we don't mean offerings by Shakespeare or Bernard Shaw, or those delightful George Kaufman-Moss Hart satires.

Only songs retain their spell, no matter how far back their origin. The popular tunes of other eras inspire a warm nostalgic feeling, continue in favor and we never tire of them.

Just the same, I wish I had been content with my warm memories of *Little Caesar* and *The Public Enemy.* What a mistake it was to view them again so many years later.

Which brings up that facet of my disillusionment which initiated these melancholy observations. It has happened that during my later columnar years I have found myself seated quite close to Joan Crawford or Marlene Dietrich, to Gloria Swanson or Liz Taylor, to Ingrid Bergman or Deborah Kerr, and my blood pressure has remained firm and steady, and I have gone right on

A glamorous film star, Joan Crawford, who moonlights as a super soft drink exploitation woman, offers some sweets to the author.

sipping my spiked lemonade without any fever racing through my veins. You must not conclude I have been or am immune to the charm of these ladies, but I no longer spend my nights tossing in unrest because I have been within whispering distance.

I can't say I like this change in me. It is not good that I should come into contact with glamor and not feel the surge of hot blood, the ripple of pin punctures up my spine. Why, it seems only the other year I was madly in love with Miss Swanson and alternately in love with Miss Crawford, and the mere mention of Marlene's name set me off into one of those foggy-eyed dazes.

The fact is I was in love with many beautiful women of the screen, especially back in the days of the silents. I had a crush on Bebe Daniels and on Theda Bara, too. I went for Anita Stewart in a big way, and oh, the daydreams I had in which Mary Pickford and her golden curls and big blue eyes dominated. There was a time, too, when I couldn't make up my mind between Shirley Mason or her sister, Viola Dana, and Sally O'Neil could have had me for the asking, or just for the looking.

I watched them in their love scenes on that silent screen, and later in the newfangled talkies, and I substituted myself for the heroes. They were pretty fair hunks of men, those heroes, from William S. Hart to Tom Meighan, Broncho Bill to Wallace Reid, Rudolph Valentino to Jack Holt, Maurice Costello to Francis X. Bushman.

But sadly enough, when these days I get to see an old-time movie, I find myself laughing out loud at the very beautiful ladies whom I adored and the very handsome stalwart gentlemen whom I envied. They look and behave so oddly with their vintage tailoring, their bizarre makeup, their corny overacting. But it's a laugh with a tug at the heart, for the memory still holds the lovely ladies, at least, in fond embrace.

As the years trooped in, I met them one by one, and age had crept upon them as inexorably as it had on me. Some of them were delightful, and others were bloody bores, and only one or two of them still inspired me with a certain amount of the onetime awe. There even came a time when one of them sought me out for counsel—she was so desperately in love with a mutual friend, and he would have none of her anymore.

And I met another, this one the hero of early Westerns. In the pictures he typified everything good and wholesome, fearless and virtuous. I was new to New York when I met him, but my heart pounded as I shook hands with the Great Man. And then young as I was at the time, I realized that a casual remark he made to me was inordinately stupid and vulgar. I learned later he was a dipso, and a year after that there were news stories about him and an unsavory escapade with a minor.

Fortunately William S. Hart had come up by the time this other chap's star had dropped out of fame's skies, and Hart reconfirmed my faith in the men who play Western heroes. In later years, as I mention elsewhere, I was to conduct a happy correspondence with the big silent man who was so quick on the draw.

I got to know Tom Mix, too, and he carried on in the true tradition so that my dismal impressions of Western he-men vanished. For Mix knew the value of illusion. He dressed for the part of the Western glamor hero, and I loved him for it. Gene Autry and Roy Rogers were smart hombres to follow the example he set.

But to get back to the ladies. Just by luck, and by virtue of a byline, I had the opportunity of sitting tête-à-tête occasionally with current queens of the cinemas—such talented girls, such breathless beauties. And what did they discuss? The furnishings of their new homes, their husband's improved golf game, their children, and, of course, their last picture and what was in store for them in their next.

No particular mystery. No excitement. A fellow was better

off just devoting himself to his wife. She at least knew why the big thrill had vanished. She knew his true age!

They Had Their Day of Glory

Unlike old soldiers, old performers do die, but while they live, they never quite fade away. I run into them on Broadway or when I stop in occasionally at the clubrooms of the Friars or the Lambs. Cheerful citizens for the most part, well dressed, sometimes even ostentatiously. Their greetings are warm, and they vie with one another in an exchange of light banter and cackle at a well-pointed quip. Yet I never leave them without a sense of melancholy.

For these are the men who through the years offered a commodity we all need so much—entertainment, in one form or another. These are the comedians, songmen, dramatic actors, vaudeville, stage, movie or radio stars of bygone years—performers who have been dropped out of the grand march because age has stifled their talents or, as Broadway bluntly puts it, they no longer have it.

It is true some have been prudent and have saved their money and are not in danger of being public charges. But many of them lived it up while their names twinkled in headlines or feature stories or in the fan magazines. All they have remaining are memories, some good clothes—and hope, always hope, that far from being out of the running, Lady Luck is going to tap them again for something big. It happens rarely.

The agony is more poignant as they regard the names of contemporaries still in the Big Time—fellow performers, male or female, who still command public esteem: Jimmy Durante, Ted Lewis, Helen Hayes, Georgie Jessel, Jack Benny, Joe E. Lewis, Lynn Fontanne and Alfred Lunt, and until their deaths in recent years, Sophie Tucker, Bert Lahr, Claude Rains, and many others.

Hollywood occasionally softens toward its onetime favorites and tosses them a morsel by awarding them temporary employment in bit parts or as extras. Not too long ago I saw no less than four who were top luminaries in their day, potent box-office lures, assembled as extras in a picture starring an actor who was in knee pants and a girl who was playing with dolls when these extras in their heyday couldn't walk through a street without being mobbed by fans.

Stealing a line from comic Jack E. Leonard, Sophie Tucker, "Last of the Red Hot Mamas," roars, as she poses with the author: "Louie, I've lost more pounds in three weeks than you weigh!"
Photo by Bill Mark

Some have drifted into other fields of endeavor to earn a living, and continue to enjoy a certain modicum of glory in being able to hold fellow employees spellbound (they hope) by recounting their experiences, their association with the Big Names who made up their world, the stars with whom they hobnobbed, the contracts they were offered and the contracts they occasionally spurned.

A few have invested wisely and are wealthy or at least comfortably fixed; yet how eagerly they grasp at an offer to appear occasionally on a television show or even at a benefit or the chance to be seated on a dais when a dinner is being given in honor of some younger star.

You won't hear them ever concede their day is over. They cling to the fiction that they have voluntarily "retired" (Remember when Sarah Bernhardt and Sir Harry Lauder used to "retire" every year?). One lovable oldster was in my office some years ago and spent an hour telling me how much he was enjoying life now that he was in retirement. I thought the old chap was probably lonesome and had come down merely to chat but just as he was leaving he sounded off: "By the way, if you've got the space, you might put in a line in your column suggesting when they do this play [he mentioned a forthcoming production], they might think of me for the father part. I could eat that part up. Who else fits it like me?"

The sad truth is these soldiers of show business would rather die than fade away.

The Gimmick's the Thing

Psychologists, and maybe psychiatrists, too, have some sort of word for the tendency to pair things or events in one's mind. "Association" is one term. Not to be too vague—if someone said quicklike, "Rock and—" most of us would promptly add "roll." In days gone by the oldsters would have said "rye."

Only the strongest-minded can refrain from adding to "ham and—" the completive "eggs." Of course, there are some misguided folks who, when you toss "hot" at them, will immediately blurt, "babe"—but the more conservative among us—especially during the Christmas and New Year's festivities, would respond with "toddy."

Which brings me to the thesis for these few paragraphs—the association of show folks—as well as others, with certain props or songs or expressions or idiosyncrasies.

When you think of Jimmy Durante, you conjure up his De Bergerac nose, his strut, and those slouch hats the Wizard of Schnoz crushes on his head in mock despair. Before Jack Benny helped embalm vaudeville he used to deliver his patter between mournful squeaks of a violin, and to this day you still associate him with his fiddle, as well as his sighing "Wu-ell!"

With Charlie Chaplin, we associate the wobbly old shoes, the battered derby and the cane. Ted Lewis, the Tragedian of Jazz—well, you know it's the slightly askew, shabby old silk topper and of course two melodies: "When My Baby Smiles at Me" and "Me and My Shadow." The legend—and that's all it is—is that Ted won the hat in a dice game from a Negro cabbie.

You can't think of the late Sophie Tucker without her song, "Some of These Days." Just as Bobby Darin is linked with "Mack the Knife." Harry Richman was associated with the gaily banded straw skimmer and the song "Puttin' on the Ritz." And, of course, there is Groucho Marx and his painted moustache, and the late Bobby Clark seemed naked without those goggles painted around his eyes.

George Burns, Groucho Marx, Danny Thomas, Alan King—always with big fat cigars protruding from their mouths—and that was true of the late Joe Frisco. I never think of the late Lee Shubert without envisioning him with those choker collars he affected, and of course if you mention Mae West, you can't help recalling her classic invitation: "Come up and see me sometime." Millionaire Morton Downey doesn't have to sing for his supper anymore, but those of us who were his fans associate him with his theme song when he was Mr. Big over the radio networks, "Carolina Moon." And you are tempted to hum "When the Moon Comes Over the Mountain" if Kate Smith's name is mentioned.

With Helen Morgan there was that piano on which she was perched, and her melancholy chant, "My Bill." Marlene Dietrich, legs—and what legs! Bing Crosby and the inevitable pipe, Perry Como and his alpaca sweaters, Jackie Gleason and his "And away-y we go!", Soupy Sales—pies in the face. Comedian Marty Allen—the bushy hair and his salute, "Hello, dere!"

This could almost be a game as you bring up Dean Martin holding on to a glass of whiskey—Joe E. Lewis, ditto; Van Johnson and his red socks, Arlene Frances and that diamond heart pendant; Bert Lahr and his robust "one-gong-gong"—and so it goes—even as far back as the late Ethel Barrymore and her plaintive: "That's all there is—there isn't any more."

The Unforgiveable!

For a brief period over radio and television I had been dismayed by a trend that threatened to endanger the course of true and pure English—something which had filled many of us with dismay and prodded us into beating our breasts in horror at the ominous thought that the nation's youth might eventually come under the dire influence. Spoken speech like nothing I had ever encountered in real life used to afflict our hearing apparatus—and some shows and pictures—*Guys and Dolls,* for instance, seemed to encourage the trend. But I thought the woeful era was finally over.

But recently the old fears came back as I scraped the beard from my face and listened to gangster drama issue dolefully and occasionally noisily from the portable radio near the shaving stand. For it was a resurrection of the type of patois with which in those other years scriptwriters endowed their characters—writers evidently weaned on Damon Runyon.

One character ended up his lament about a doll this way. "She is strickly a no-good, and I am knowin' this on account I make a mistake once, mister. I marry her."

Now this I can tell you. I have met many of the guys and dolls who inspired Damon Runyon. At times, in the days before he lost the power of speech, I sat with Damon Runyon and one or more of his favorite characters in Lindy's and in Billy LaHiff's Tavern and listened in on their conversation with him. What he managed to do with personalities is by no means a scoop. He set a new pattern in American literature.

But if he were alive today, this great newspaperman would agree with me, I am certain, that no one we knew ever actually spoke the way he had them speak. I knew Cheesecake Ike, Chuck Green, Swifty Morgan, Johnny Broderick and a few others of the colorful set immortalized by Runyon, and though there were richness and originality in their mode of expression, the words never emerged in the bizarre form of sentence that illuminated the fictionist's copy.

Actually, this stilted patter in the present tense is by our modern standards pretty corny stuff and excruciatingly dated. These days we have become accustomed to the type of hipster slang, affected by the beatniks and the reefer set, "make the scene," "gasser," "pads" and other mysterious references. I concede even there is a certain excitement engendered by this more up-to-the-minute assassination of pure English—at least, there's some fun trying to work out a translation.

One night I even brought up the subject in a casual conversation with Runyon and he grinned. "The trouble with you is," he said, "you only hear the words that are spoken." Then he added: "I can tell you something confidentially. I have heard from reliable sources that the folks Bill Shakespeare wrote about never talked the way he had them talk." So I muttered: "So long, Mr. Damon Shakespeare," and he chuckled.

But, oh, if my late confrere had only known then what a dreadful effect his spirited writings were to have on scripters for radio, television, movies and the stage! Perhaps he did—and is still chuckling—wherever he is.

Tub Thumpers

Not the least important fraternity in what we call show business—and certainly a breed that is by no means overmodest or self-effacing—is that of publicity men. I have always been willing to dip my skimmer in appreciation of their efforts to gain gratuitous linage and picture space for their clients.

But, to inject a pessimistic note, I do find myself discouraged these days with the apparent lack of imagination on the part of most drumbeaters. I will not go so far as to assert that the new generation of press agents has so far receded from its strict code of its calling as to be dull by being completely truthful in its mimeographed, typed or telephoned offerings to columnists, feature writers, and city editors, even though the clan continues to attribute precious bon mots to stolid saloonkeepers and emotional bandleaders and endow dance masters with the peppery epigrams of Oscar Wilde or Ambrose Bierce.

What has become of the ballyhoo-hoo man who beat down the hardboiled city editor's defenses with a spicy tale of an actress plunging into Central Park Lake in the nude at midnight; or the press agent, Harry Reichenbach, who had his client dipping into milk-baths, as was the case of Anna Held, or having a star ride a bicycle with a solid gold frame as one imaginative flack had Lillian Russell doing, with its resultant reward in oodles of free space.

In the past, the principals, ignoring their tub-thumpers, applied their own imagination and came up with some honeys. Houdini drove a team of spirited horses through a heavy midtown traffic while blindfolded. P. T. Barnum, we have read, tried to send an elephant through the mails. Texas Guinan, in my own time, rode around boldly in an armored car—a block to a gallon of gas—and never denied that it once belonged to the King of Portugal. And, of course, there was that classic—the lion registered at the Belleclaire Hotel as T. R. Zann—by coincidence just a week before *Tarzan of the Apes* opened.

I can recall how the papers fell—with pictures, too—when Marlene Dietrich was "mobbed" in front of the Cotton Club—the comments by the paragraphers, including this reporter who didn't know at the time it was all a stunt engineered by his own brother, Harry. A frenzied mob was assembled through the simple expedient of tossing one-dollar bills around with the crowd scrambling for them. He told me it required an expenditure of a little more than one hundred dollars, but the free space was worth thousands.

The late Julian Eltinge, most famed of the female impersonators of his era, crashed through for plenty of space, too, by boxing with Jim Corbett. And that master showman, Barnum, had Jenny Lind stand up on the back of a dead whale at the old Castle Garden. Sandow, the Strong Man, heeding the advice of his press agent, had himself harnessed to two fire engine horses, each pulling in opposite directions.

In the late twenties, publicity man Irving Strouse almost got himself into something of a jam when he had his clients, a dance couple, attempt a "double suicide" in the Central Park reservoir. They got wet all over, were arrested and danced happily ever after, but not quite so nakedly. I can't even recall their names now, though there was quite a news coverage at the time.

When the going was tough, Lois DeFee, a six-foot-five-inch Amazon, married a midget, and after the divorce became a prospering stripteaser for a time. The Ziegfeld Girls Club, which has operated so successfully for years, was actually initiated as a one-time promotion stunt by Bernard Sobel for the moving picture *The Great Ziegfeld.* Harry Klemfuss turned Rudolph Valentino's funeral into a circus on behalf of his client, Campbell's Funeral Parlor, drawing the beginning of the huge mob by planting twelve stooges in front of the mortuary and having them stare mournfully into the windows from dawn until midnight.

Enough of that. I am not attempting to denigrate the current fraternity of press agents. They are hard-working young men and women who beat the drums vigorously for their clients, and newsmen and editors have found them invaluable unpaid aides when stories require some inside facts which the p.a.'s are usually able to furnish if the stories concern their clients. For each free break these boys and girls receive in the columns, they usually pay three- and fourfold by contributing news fragments or the latest yarns moving around town.

Still and all, I do wish they would resort to some of the old-fashioned fiction, for it made for such fascinating, if not always trustworthy, reading.

"Climb Tho' the Rocks Be Rugged"

Whoever it was that first, ever so long ago in a sentimental mood, decided Broadway was the Street of Dreams, probably never realized for how many their dream came true. An ungainly girl, chafing because she was so "homely" but tremendously ambitious to become a show business Somebody, was reconciling herself to a drab, uneventful life, especially when she made the rounds of the booking offices and was rebuffed. Then along came a musical, *I Can Get It for You Wholesale,* and someone thought she was just ideal for the role of the secretary. Barbra Streisand practically stole the show with her one big number, "Marmelstein"—and the rest is theatrical history.

Ethel Merman was a stenographer tiring of her typewriting and shorthand chores before she emerged as a dynamic musical comedy luminary. Another stenographer, Billy Rose, became a successful songwriter, then a theatrical producer and finally a financial wizard. A busboy in a Catskill Mountain resort, Grossinger's, became a headline figure, not so much because of his meteoric rise as a singing lad but because of his marriage to glamorous screen beauties: Debbie Reynolds, Elizabeth Taylor and finally Connie Stevens. That was Eddie Fisher, of course.

A secretary to a Broadway columnist, Mark Hellinger, found himself in time a best-selling author, Jim Bishop. A singing waiter, Irving Berlin, in a downtown dive became one of the immortals among our songwriters. A former barber lad discovered singing could pay off far better—Perry Como, just as another former barber boy, Jimmy Durante, became one of the more beloved aces of show business. And how about a onetime stilt walker in Coney Island rising to the eminence of movie stardom—Cary Grant?

There was the case of a successful sports announcer who abandoned the mikes to become a Broadway stage star overnight and then a film star—the late Paul Douglas. A garment center salesman, Myron Cohen, tired of his calling and became one of the top storytellers on the nightclub circuit and over TV. A burly bouncer in restaurants and night spots, Toots Shor, decided there was more future in being the boss, and now is the owner of a nationally famed restaurant situated, coincidentally enough, on the very site of the nightclub, Leon & Eddie's where he was once a lowly wage slave.

Eddie Fisher and Ethel Merman pose with the author at the March of Dimes dinner honoring him as "Man of the Year." Both Miss Merman and Fisher have always credited Sobol with according them their first columnar notices.

A once discontented press agent is now a dominant and controversial producer in television, host also of his own show over the home screens as well as producer of films and plays. I'm referring to David Susskind. A policeman, Sevario Saridis, who had a burning desire to be a singer, finally found himself starring in the Persian Room of the Plaza Hotel, a hotel which was located on the very beat he patrolled. Which brings us to a lad who was trained to become a hotel man who preferred dancing instead, and it paid off—Dan Dailey. A burlesque stripper, Gypsy Rose Lee, became a successful author and even had a musical built around her career. And a onetime showgirl had a secret dream amply fulfilled when she had her first novel, *Valley of the Dolls,* dominating the best seller list for a record-breaking run of months—Jacqueline Susann. And how about that former truck driver who came to rainbow's end as one of the dominant male film stars of our times—Rock Hudson?

The list is endless, the dreams continue, and for so many they haven't been futile.

"How You Gonna Keep 'em Down on the Farm?"

Let no one dispute the general interest in hamlets, towns and the big cities around the country in what goes on in Manhattan, and in Hollywood, too. The reason is simple. For all the general belief that New York and Hollywood represent the ultimate in sophistication, the truth is, many performers dominating our night life and show business originated in various sections of our land—some far, far distant from bustling metropolis of New York and from sprawling Los Angeles.

Perhaps that is why Broadway and Hollywood columnists find a ready market in the newspapers of other cities and why the citizens there are as hip as the average Broadwayite on who frequents Danny's, Sardi's, Shor's, "21," El Morocco, Kippy's, Gallagher's, Barberry Room, Colony, Whyte's and others of our more prominent restaurants in Manhattan—or Chasen's, La Scala, the Bistro, Perino's and like places on the Coast.

Let's consider from where some of our stage, film, nightclub and TV and radio luminaries hail. Mary Martin, for instance, was brought up in obscure Weatherford, Texas. Danny Thomas was born in Deerfield, Michigan. Martha Raye, who knows her way around the champagne route, originated in Butte, Montana.

Perry Como, who delivers those smooth songs in big-city style, hails from Cannonsburg, Pennsylvania. Orson Welles, who keeps himself in self-imposed exile, was born and raised in Kenosha, Wisconsin. One of our fine film actors, Wendell Corey, saw no future in his native small town, shook it early—town of Dracut, Massachusetts. Singer Connie Towers was born and raised in Whitefish, Montana. Harry James, who blows up a storm here and in the capitals of the world, started out in Albany, Georgia, while Betty Grable came from a real sizzling town, St. Louis, which is perhaps why, in view of their parting, James trumpets out "St. Louis Blues" in real melancholy fashion.

Bing Crosby, who has become quite urbane, was a mild-mannered lad when he was growing up in Tacoma, Washington. The late Cole Porter, whose sophisticated songs deal with big city folks, knew more about the simpler things of life as a growing boy in Peru, Indiana. Fred Astaire came out of Omaha, Nebraska, and the divine Cyd Charisse out of Amarillo, Texas. Cary Grant (then Archie Leach) was reared in Bristol, England, and Laurence Harvey was born in Yonishkis, Lithuania. The late Buster Keaton used to confess ruefully that his birthplace was Pique, Kansas.

Fredric March was born in Racine, Wisconsin; Robert Cummings came out of Joplin, Missouri; Jerry Lewis was raised not too far distant from Broadway—Irvington, New York; and Joe E. Lewis emerged right out of our Lower East Side, so perhaps these two don't deserve being listed with the others. On the other hand, Bob Hope hails from London, England, was brought to the States

The late Buster Keaton in his usual deadpanned mood, the ebullient Gypsy Rose Lee and the author, looking somewhat puzzled.
Photo by Hale Haberman

when he was about four and spent his early life in Cleveland. As for Jack Benny, does anyone need to be reminded that Waukegan, Illinois, is his hometown? They even have a school named after him. Soupy Sales—and no one is less Southern in speech and attitude than this master of the slapstick—was born in Wake Forest, North Carolina. Dinah Shore has lost her Southern accent though her early years were spent in her birthplace, Winchester, Tennessee.

The Skeptic

There is one friend of mine who not only is not envious of Broadway and society columnists and the "empty" lives they lead, but actually considers them with something akin to pity mingled with contempt. He's an egghead, of course, but he will deny vehemently that his cerebral superiority dictates his opinion that the futile careers of the lighthearted paragraphers are based on trivia.

He is, of course, a great admirer of men and women of accomplishment. He will discourse for hours on the literary stature of Hemingway, Faulkner and Maugham. He analyzes the offerings of playwrights Tennessee Williams, Edward Albee, William Inge and Arthur Miller, and grudgingly concedes that perhaps eventually they may compare favorably with Eugene O'Neill but never, never with Bernard Shaw.

He is not above attending what he considers a worthwhile play or a musical of distinction and will confess an enormous admiration for Richard Rodgers and the late Oscar Hammerstein II, or Irving Berlin and Cole Porter—and also for Judith Anderson, Katharine Cornell, Fredric March, Helen Hayes and a few others as effective interpreters for our leading dramaturgists.

He rarely attends a movie, but will admit with some reluctance that the cinemas have occasionally offered palatable, even constructive, diversion. Almost shyly, he acknowledges that he has been moved by performances of Olivia de Havilland, Ingrid Bergman, Lee Cobb, but his big favorites back to silent days were Henry B. Walthall and Lillian Gish.

He snorts at television, though being quite honest, he concedes that he did cheer a performance some years ago over the home screens by Sir Laurence Olivier. The only TV comedian he digs is Art Carney. "His," he insists "is comedy of the highest caliber—gentle, whimsical, with a blend of pathos and defeat. In my opinion, he is Chaplin's only rival."

As for citizens like Sinatra, Crosby, Liz Taylor, Jackie Gleason, Milton Berle, these are strangers in the wilderness, pariahs as far as he is concerned, and he'll have no truck with them.

As I listen so often to his denigration of my calling, I come to my own defense as well as that of my fellow workers in the neon-lighted pastures of Broadway.

And where had I met them for the first time? In the very frivolous haunts which he so roundly scorns. Somerset Maugham, for instance, in "21" and later at the Stork Club. Irving Berlin in Lindy's, Ingrid Bergman in the Drake Room, Olivia de Havilland and Sir Laurence Olivier at El Morocco. Judith Anderson in Sardi's, Helen Hayes and Tennessee Williams in "21." Ernest Hemingway at the Stork and the Colony, Eugene O'Neill at the Algonquin, Art Carney at the Eden Roc, William Faulkner at Sardi's.

Continuing my defense I tell him that his greatest idol, Bernard Shaw, was not above dropping into a tiny bistro, Janet of France, whenever he was on his visit to New York many years ago—that I had even chatted with him. But I omitted to tell him how brief and rather pointless the chat was, because Shaw was not too impressed when Janet introduced me as a "great journalist of the Hearst papers." Mildly, he commented that from time to time he had contributed to Mr. Hearst's papers, and then in abrupt dismissal turned his attention to his two companions.

I pressed on, explaining I had talked frequently with Edgar Lee Masters as he sat with H. L. Mencken and George Jean Nathan at Lüchow's; that Richard Rodgers and Cole Porter, too, as well as Noël Coward had often mingled with the frivolous set at El Morocco, "21," Little Club, Sardi's, Colony, Le Pavillon. And since my scornful friend admits to being an admirer of Chief Justice Earl Warren, I advised him that the first time I met him was at Toots Shor's.

And so I rattle off names from time to time—like any name-dropper—of personalities, who, to his way of thinking, were citizens of accomplishments—and relentlessly but truthfully place them in the butterfly gathering places he disdained—people of talent like James Michener, Truman Capote, composer Harold

Arlen, Lily Pons, Thornton Wilder, John Gunther, Sir John Gielgud. I pluck them off my string of the famous like precious pearls, one by one, as offerings to win him over to my side.

He remains, as always, unconvinced.

"People like that," he sneers, "wouldn't be found dead in those sties you and those other fellows write about."

With the Literary Set

About six years ago, I watched as an alert little man walked up to the newsstand at the Waldorf, picked up a copy of Carlos P. Romulo's *I Walked with Heroes,* asked the price, paid it and walked off. The man behind the stand wasn't exactly impressed even though the purchaser was the Philippines' hero and later Ambassador, Colonel Romulo himself.

Actually, it is nothing unusual, for the newsstand at the Waldorf displays books written by eminent patrons who lodge at the inn—either as frequent transients or as permanent residents.

This is true, too, that at "21's" cigar stand, books of customers are prominently displayed and sold, books authored by those who rank high in the literary field. Thus Ernest Hemingway, Robert Ruark and George Jean Nathan, to mention a few, always knew their books would be featured at the stand, as do Bob Considine, John Hersey, James Michener, John Gunther. The list is endless and the writer would feel hurt if his books weren't placed on display and for sale.

Nathan, who was a nightly diner at "21," rarely refused to autograph one of his books when it was bought at the stand, but he stipulated to one of the Kriendlers or Jerry Berns when they brought a volume over to convey a customer's request: "I'll sign it gladly, but on one condition. Don't, under any circumstances, permit this person to come over and thank me. I have written a book he wants to buy and read. That's the extent of my obligation to him." I was always convinced, however, that the late critic, who posed as a disdainful dyspeptic, was inwardly highly flattered at these requests.

I think I boast one distinction. As far as I have been able to determine, I was the only author signally rewarded. Not only was my book *Some Days Were Happy* prominently displayed, but the late Jack Kriendler, in addition to the volumes purchased for sale at the cigar stand, shelled out for one thousand additional copies of the book (I spent long hours autographing each copy), and sent them out as gifts to friends and favored customers throughout the country and even to distant ports around the world.

Another pal of authors, provided they patronized his restaurant, is Danny Stradella of Danny's Hideaway. Danny features their books prominently at the entrance in glass-enclosed cases, although he often confesses he rarely has time to read any of them. Good or bad, the books get their display because the authors are customers.

And, of course, no one was more of a friend to writers than the late Lee Chumley, who, as I have indicated at more length earlier in these rambling memoirs, gave up practically all the wall space in his Greenwich Village restaurant for displays of book covers. And in many instances, Lee was instrumental in originally getting both author and publisher together, for many of his customers were among the dominant book publishers of the day.

The late Leo Lindy, too, early in his restaurant's career, began displaying books of patrons in the windows along with pictures of prominent patrons. And now, cigar stores and drugstores apparently find it profitable to include books, chiefly paperbacks, among the merchandise. Even the so-called "penny arcade," the amusement center on Broadway, devotes an entire window to these paperbacks.

So our authors cannot complain of lack of exposure. On the gloomier side, though, is the less rewarding exposure offered at the secondhand stalls. Some deserve no better fate, but occasionally I have come across a brave book with rare ideas and a fresh treatment moldering with the rest in this Potter's Field of Literature. Filled with compassion for the unknown who has labored long to this unhappy end, I buy the book, dust it off, carry it home tenderly to read it more carefully through to the end. I rarely do, though.

The Waltz—What's That?

A slim dancing man, "Killer" Joe Piro, was chiefly responsible for the genesis of the discothèque in our town. It started at a rowdy little place, the Peppermint Lounge, and soon the cafe society set and some loftier blue bloods as well as show people were assembling, learning the twist as Joe patiently demonstrated —and the rage was on. After that, discothèques sprang up all over town, and indeed, all over the country. Joe and other masters of the dance began introducing new versions—frug, swim, watusi and so on.

Then Sybil Burton, freshly divorced from her Richard, founded Arthur on the premises formerly occupied by the original El Morocco, and since the principal backers included dozens of well-knowns of show business and society, the new place caught the fancy of the public, especially since it became so crowded that hundreds had to mill around outside hoping to get in eventually.

For Sybil and her backers, it was not only a financially successful project, but it also led to romance. In June of 1965 she eloped with young Jordan Christopher, leader of the rock 'n' roll group, The Wild Ones, which she had lured away from the Peppermint Lounge to serve the hot music at her place.

Now there are branches of Arthur in various cities of the country. Other discothèques have proved potent lures—one of the more successful on the Coast, as enterprise with some of Hollywood's leading stars as the financial backers, is The Factory.

It is evident the discothèque is here to stay—the only new note in night life in decades.

A Gloomy Confession

There came a depressing period in my career when I began to believe that my eyes and my ears grazed only over the surface of what they saw or heard, and I concluded that if I were to attain the coveted status of a molder of opinion, I had better damn well do something about readjusting my bifocals and hearing aid. I arrived at this dismal conclusion regarding my critical deficiencies after reading my own reports on plays and pictures and personalities and comparing them with others.

For instance, I might have viewed a spectacular Western, let's say, and blithely depose that in the thrilling canvas, the hero was the bravest, fightingest, shootingest hombre who ever fought his way to a gory victory over some dirty dogs. I might make further comment on his pardner, lauding his clean, vigorous integrity, and sum up by opining that this, indeed, was one whale of an exciting film.

Then I would read the reports of others and discover I had missed the boat. It appeared actually that this was all symbolism—it was Good conquering Evil—Virtue Triumphant. Even the big paid ads would put me to shame for they suggested solemnly that the hero was "a man not like others. A man with something in his guarded eyes that hinted of wildness held checked—of fierce fires low banked. A man capable of things terrible and tender." And stupid me, thinking all the time I was viewing a spirited Western.

It was that way with plays, too. I'd come away sometimes delighted because I had a good time, only to learn in reading the analyses of my more profound and discerning contemporaries that this particular offering was a socially significant document, revealing the frailties of a segment of our population—or the battle of an intellectual force against the disintegration of humanity. Sometimes I would return to the play in question to determine why I had failed to get the message in the first place. Usually I emerged even more baffled than before.

Or, let's say, I met an interesting personality. For instance, my first encounter with the Italian star, Anna Magnani. I wrote that she by no means was my conception of a cover girl—and perhaps it was unchivalrous of me—but I did point out that her disheveled coiffure and her indifference to what we term "good dress" eliminated her as a candidate for either best groomed or best dressed category.

A few days later I picked up a piece by apparently a more perceptive and certainly more articulate observer and read how much I had missed. For instance: "Above this wide, mobile mouth and straight generous nose, the Magnani eyes reflect childlike trust and the stark inscrutability of tenement windows."

Now why didn't I see all that?

On the other hand, I might assume the garb of a cynic. Thus, reading a publicity release to the effect that Ethel Merman had never taken a singing lesson in her life because the late George Gershwin had urged her to "Be yourself at all times," I wrote a scoffing paragraph and suggested that Al Siegel had much to do as a singing coach in developing her voice style.

Came promptly a note of reproach from Miss Merman. Oh, yes, it might be true, she wrote, that Siegel had taught her a few tricks of showmanship, but her powerful voice—that was her own, with no fancy trimmings ever inflicted by a singing teacher. It seems I was wrong again. I brooded for a day or two and then sent off a little note to Ethel, pleading for forgiveness and meekly expressing the hope she would invite me over to the house someday to help her catalogue her accumulation of fat bankbooks.

Then there was the time a new performer was being featured

at the Copacabana and hailed as having a new and quite distinctive approach to comedy. At the time I was turning out a series of brief profiles for the *Saturday Home Magazine,* and the press agent for the comedian pleaded with me to wrap my inspired phrases around his client. I told him that while I did not think the chap was lacking talent, and that indeed he was quite original in an offbeat fashion, these profiles were about people who had already attained success or who showed promise of reaching stardom and becoming newsworthy. As gently as I could, I insisted to the publicity man that his client had a long way to go before gaining genuine recognition—if ever.

Less than a year later, the national magazines were clamoring for articles about this performer. He had blazed meteorically into the top echelon of television stars and had captured the fancy of the entire nation with his zany comedy. Fellow by the name of Sid Caesar!

So you may understand why I entertain skeptical reactions to my impulsive first thoughts on plays, movies and people. Indeed, the late David Selznick was slightly despondent when he learned that I had turned in an enthusiastic report on one of his pictures. The legend is, he moaned: "Oh, no. That could be the kiss of death!"

However, a fellow can't keep striking out forever. The picture which won my full-hearted endorsement was *Gone With the Wind.* I thrived on my successful appraisal of that one for months.

12

Some Unforgettables

OF THE HUNDREDS OF COLORFUL personalities I came to know during my forty-odd years as a Manhattan newsman, there are a handful, living and departed, who remain indelibly impressed on my mind—perhaps, because I never found them boring. Some I have mentioned in preceding chapters. Here are a few more from various walks of life who, if nothing else, furnished me from time to time with bountiful material for my daily columns or occasional feature pieces.

Literary Iconoclast

Let's start with that ebullient, voluble William Saroyan. My first contact with him came back in July, 1938, through a letter received from him from San Francisco. I had made some comment on the apparent mild feud between the comparative newcomer and Ernest Hemingway.

> I've never met Hemingway [wrote Saroyan]. We exchanged some letters after his essay in *Esquire;* they were friendly letters; his remarks about my writing flattered me, irritated my friends and some of his; everybody knows he is one of the most natural of all the naturals of American letters. Like myself, he can't write badly; anything he writes is good even when it's terrible.
>
> I have written some of the worst stories ever to appear in print but there've been good ones, too; over a hundred of my stories are now in books; I wouldn't apologize for any one of them. A writer writes one book; all his books together are one book. If he is natural they are himself and we all know there is no man who is not simultaneously all opposites, good, bad, great, small and so forth and so on. A natural doesn't bluff; an artist has to. A natural makes form; an artist accepts it.
>
> I never did learn the first thing about writing and never will; all I know is how to do it the way I do it; Hemingway is one of the few living writers I admire and enjoy reading; most of them gripe me; I'd rather read a newspaper any day; art got phony and never should have; a man like Hemingway comes along and starts a crusade to stop the nonsense.

My only postscript to this letter at the time was: "I am convinced Mr. Saroyan prefers Mr. Hemingway—also semicolons."

It was almost a year later before I met Saroyan for the first time. I was lodging in the Mark Hopkins Hotel in San Francisco when the phone rang, and I was informed Mr. Saroyan was in the lobby and would like to come up. When this slim, black-haired, handsome young Armenian entered, I was not all disillusioned, for he looked exactly like his pictures, and he had the self-assurance of someone who had arrived. I don't think Saroyan was quite as free from disillusionment when he saw me, for I imagine he had quite a different conception of how a New York syndicated columnist whose writings he followed in the *San Francisco Examiner* should look. He covered up by beginning to talk rapidly, and it was the beginning of a beautiful friendship.

Not too many months afterward, Saroyan came to New York, and as we sat in the boisterous 18 Club, he announced that he planned on the following day to start on a play. Then, quite confidently he said: "I should have it ready in a week or so."

I shrugged my shoulders, stared at him a bit skeptically, but Saroyan wasn't too sensitive. He simply said: "Where do we go from here?"

Where we went was to the Riviera on the Jersey shore—an

elaborate cabaret which had an additional lure, and one Saroyan took to like a chorus girl to a diamond bracelet—the little gambling casino upstairs. Reluctantly I guided him through the portals which were usually barred against any but patrons known to the guardian. I was known, for I had passed through that doorway many times, and usually emerged unhappy and poorer.

But for the record, the exuberant author, after two hours at the dice table, was even more exuberant. He had won something like four hundred dollars. On the ride back to town, he exulted: "New York is a pitcher of rich heavy cream, and I like rich heavy cream."

By this time, I was accustomed to Saroyan's effusive explosions, although I didn't always get the message.

He didn't finish that play in a week, but it was ready for a producer in some three weeks and had a quick sale, for Saroyan came fortified with a nationwide reputation based on his best seller *The Daring Young Man on the Flying Trapeze.* The play, *My Heart's in the Highlands,* had a brief run. The critics were divided about its merits, and some were even violent in their denunciations, but did that depress the Armenian lad from San Francisco? Not at all.

Instead, he boasted he was going to work on another. "I'll have it out in a week," he said. And, he did—in six days, to be exact. This one, produced by the Theatre Guild in association with Eddie Dowling, who also had the role of the drunkard, Joe, was *The Time of Your Life.* It was greeted more joyously by the critics and had a run of some six months. It was tapped for the Pulitzer Prize Committee as the best play of the season and received the Drama Critics' Circle Award.

Now Saroyan acted up. He spurned the Pulitzer Prize money, one thousand dollars, insisting that "wealth shouldn't patronize Art," and, of course, drew reams of publicity which he accepted quite graciously.

One night as we sat in "21," Bill noticed an attractive young woman seated with producer-actor Eddie Dowling. "Migod," he exclaimed, "that is a beautiful girl. She looks all soul. She looks like she ought to be on a boat in a windswept sound and her hair flying loose and a fellow playing accordian."

I said: "Why, Bill, don't you know that lady? That lady is Clare Boothe who just wrote *Margin for Error,* you know, and she also wrote that play *The Women.*"

"Migod," said the author-playwright, "just like I thought. She's clever, too. That's wonderful, wonderful." And he went over to have Dowling introduce them.

Another time, in Sherman Billingsley's Club Room, Peggy Joyce leaned over toward George Jean Nathan at an adjoining table and exclaimed: "Heavens, who is that beautiful, beautiful man with you?"—a query that didn't seem to set too well with her sullen escort. Nathan said: "Why this is William Saroyan."

"Well," sang the Orchidaceous One, "Mr. Sarong, or Strong or Soybean or whatever your name is, you are a beautiful man"—whereupon the Beautiful Man rose, bent over and kissed the lady's hand in the Continental fashion while the room full of patrons beamed over in approval. "You," said Mr. Saroyan, "are undoubtedly someone about whom a play must be written, perhaps by myself—" adding sadly, "something along completely normal lines."

Not all of Saroyan's plays were successful—especially something titled *Across the Board on Tomorrow Morning and Talking to You,* which lingered for eight futile performances. But it was distinguished by marking the acting debut of the eccentric poet-novelist Maxwell Bodenheim. Also in the cast was pretty Carol Marcus, destined shortly after to become Mrs. William Saroyan.

At any rate, for the rehearsals of this play, Saroyan collected a board of "advisers," among them Daniel Boone, an odd character who strutted around the streets of Manhattan in a buckskin outfit like the woodsman after whom he named himself. Besides Bodenheim there was another Village character, Joe Gould, who for almost two decades had been writing *The Contemporary History of the World,* which was never finished because, as Gould pointed out, it never could be finished since history itself keeps changing. At that time, the manuscript had accumulated to such an extent that it filled his tiny lodging, so that Gould slept outside the room in the hallway half the time.

Oona O'Neill was another of the "advisers" although she rarely opened her mouth. She was a close friend of Carol Marcus and was being considered for a minor role in one of the sketches. The stage manager suggested that while Oona was a lovely girl, she didn't have stage experience and that it would be risky to give her a part.

"She is the daughter of Eugene O'Neill," said Saroyan. "Eugene O'Neill is one of the most wonderful men in the world—a genius. His daughter is, therefore, the most wonderful actress in the world. She couldn't be anything else."

Parenthetically, one night when Carol and Oona joined Saroyan, Nathan and myself, Carol confided that she, Oona and Gloria Vanderbilt, who had been close friends from almost childhood, had decided to marry when they were eighteen—and to marry older men of accomplishment. Carol and Oona did follow through—Carol at eighteen wedding Saroyan and Oona at eighteen becoming Mrs. Charles Chaplin. But Gloria, though she kept to the pledge to be married at eighteen, picked a far younger man, Pat DiCicco, a popular figure in cafe society at the time. It was only after their divorce some years later that she became the bride of the man old enough to be her father—the noted musical conductor Leopold Stokowski—but later divorced him, too, and again wed a man closer to her in age—Wyatt Cooper. Only Oona's original marriage to the elderly Chaplin remained intact, and does to this day.

One hot night in July of 1942, Saroyan lured Carol, Nathan and myself down to the Lower East Side to an atmospheric loft cabaret on Allen Street, the Oriental. Here we were treated to a phonograph concert of minor key wails of Arabia, the Sahara, Turkey and Armenia, which conjured up visions of snakes swaying in front of fakirs, Oriental bazaars and cow-eyed women with veils suspended above the bridges of their noses.

Then the orchestra came on. It consisted of three men in shirt sleeves and no ties drawing music from a violin, zimbalim and an oud, which is something like a lute with a watermelon back. The baldish artist performing on this rare instrument was someone named Bagdasar Bogdasarian. "My cousin," announced Saroyan. "A true genius. A lover of life, and a wonderful man."

We left the Oriental, walked a short distance to the Old Roumanian, where a crew of four musicians wore jackets and ties, and where a girl named Roxanne, with a fine voice, sang "Miss You," "Wonderful One" and other chants requested by Messrs. Saroyan and Nathan. I also made a request for two of my favorites, "Melancholy Baby" and "Stardust," but before Roxanne could comply, Nathan insisted he wanted to play "Egern on the Tegren See" on the piano. He started for the tiny platform, but before he could settle at the piano, Saroyan started singing a Japanese lullaby in Armenian-Chinese double-talk, which inspired Nathan to dance a Viennese waltz with Carol Marcus.

As we drove home, Saroyan said: "I am writing a play about George. I'm calling it *The Youngest Man in America.* Naturally, it will be with music." If he was serious about this, the fact is, he never did get around to the project. Another night when I met Bill at "21," I said: "You're always talking about going down to the waterfront to look at the boats nesting in the big dock at night. This is the night we do it, Bill."

Saroyan nodded. "That would be wonderful," he agreed. "But first let's go over to the Stork Club for a quick one." So we went to the Stork and there we found Chinese-American movie actress Anna May Wong with cartoonist Irving Hoffman. Hoffman suggested that perhaps we ought to drop in on the Press Photographers' Ball. Saroyan said: "That would be wonderful."

As we stepped into the taxi, two young Japanese passed by, and Miss Wong hissed very hard. Saroyan said, "You must dislike them very much," and Anna May Wong replied, "They are not friends of the Chinese."

At the Ball, Bill shook hands heartily with William Gaxton and Victor Moore, with Mary Martin and Jimmy Durante, and then in order with Harry Hershfield, Nancy Carroll, Milton Berle and Judy Garland. There was an indescribable expression in the playwright's eyes as he met each of them and shook their hands. "I feel," he said, "as if I had been locked in a cellar and now I am out breathing fine, clean air and plucking daisies." I murmured something to the effect that this puzzled me because only a few weeks prior he had been in the great outdoors of Mexico City.

"Maybe now," I suggested, hesitantly, "those boats—down at the docks, you know." Saroyan said: "Boats on the river at midnight remind me, you know what? Of popcorn in a basin of boiling water. Is there some lively cabaret we can go to first?"

We dropped into Nicky Blair's Paradise and watched as two dozen of the town's prettiest girls danced and also posed in tableux. A boy and a girl and two dogs did an act. A fellow threw an apple into the air, and it came down and split itself on a knife.

Saroyan said: "Maybe you don't see it my way, but all of life that is complex is crowded into these beautiful girls and those people with their trick acts." Just another of Bill's enigmatic outbursts which baffled me a bit.

I said, "No, Bill, I can't honestly say I see it that way at all." He grinned and conceded, "I was only kidding. It's good entertainment, though."

We strolled down to Fifth Avenue in the soft postmidnight hours and we stood on the Saks department store side so we could look across the street and up the length of the great Radio City obelisk. There were lights in many of the windows, and two spotlights threw broad ribbons of bluish-gray.

"I would like to have a slingshot," commented Saroyan, "and just pop away at those windows." We walked on and passed a haberdashery shop. The writer said: "I bought this hat today. The brim's too broad, don't you think so?"

By this time, I knew we weren't going to get down to the waterfront. Instead, we dropped into Jack White's 18 Club. Comedian Pat Harrington said to "Doctor" Lee, the club's elderly waiter and stooge, "Don't let a week's work go to your head," and Saroyan laughed fit to kill. "He says that every night," I whispered, "it's running gag," but Saroyan still laughed. "There's philosophy in that crack," he insisted, "it's good."

The matron from the ladies' powder room came out and blew on a long-handled rubber-cupped plunger while from the band came a trumpet call to arms. "This is wonderful, this is crazy," said Saroyan. "I love it. In fact, there's a play in all this and I'm going to write it before I leave town."

"When are you going to leave town?" I asked.

Saroyan said: "In two weeks." But he lingered in our midst for more than a month.

World War II blazed and Private William Saroyan was called to service. On the day he received word from his publisher that, in addition to a record distribution of 342,000 copies of his book *The Human Comedy* by the Book-of-the-Month Club, advance sales had reached an additional 50,000 copies, he was on KP in Astoria, Long Island. After peeling his quota of spuds, Saroyan telephoned to Carol, suggested that by way of celebration of the epochal sales and royalties they become Mister and Missus. He would come to Manhattan and they'd have the knot tied. Whether she gave her "yes" at the time is not recorded, but half an hour later, Private Saroyan received orders for his temporary transfer to Dayton, Ohio. A few days later, Carol Marcus, eighteen, journeyed to Dayton and married William Saroyan, thirty-four.

A few years later, the Saroyans parted, but Bill wooed Carol anew and they were remarried, only to head for the divorce courts again. Though she vowed she wouldn't wed again until she was forty, a few years later Carol married stage and screen star Walter Matthau.

About a week or so after the marriage of Carol and Saroyan, producer Mike Todd went to Dayton to discuss production plans for Bill's *Get Away, Old Man.* The soldier-playwright invited him to join him and his brand-new bride at a quaint little Hungarian restaurant he had discovered.

"Nothing fancy," he assured Todd (as the producer told me the story later). "Simple food—and simple people. The food is honest like the man who owns it and the girls who serve it. It's the spirit of the nation. It is the American flag in cotton bunting with no fancy trimming. It is 'Oh, Say Can You See' and 'God Bless America.'"

"I'm very fond of goulash," said Todd.

A pert Irish girl waited patiently for them to give their order. Spaghetti and meatballs was the special on a predominantly Italian menu. "I thought," said Todd, "you told me this was a Hungarian place."

"Wait until you see the owner," explained Saroyan. He asked the Irish girl to summon the boss. A few minutes later, a genial, rotund chap came to the table—a Swede! The owner and the playwright discussed baseball, the wine grapes of California and the quality of Dayton's faucet water.

Finally a hungry Todd interrupted. "How's your goulash today?"

"Try the spaghetti and meatballs," suggested the beaming Swedish proprietor of the Hungarian restaurant. "Or maybe you'd like chicken cacciatore, hey?"

"You see what I mean," said Saroyan, when they left, some hours later. "It's 'My Country, 'Tis of Thee.' It's people praying on their knees in the open fields at sundown. If you're here tomorrow, I've got a real little Armenian place you must try. There's a fellow there who plays the Jew's harp like it was a Stradivarius violin."

Todd said, "I took the next train back to New York."

The Melancholy Crooner

He was the crooner's crooner, this thinnish balladeer with the tight-drawn skin, the thin-lipped smile and the eyes that seemed always to look inward. Tommy Lyman was his name, and he was around and in the Big Time when I was making my first timid invasion of Broadway. He was chanting his lullabies when Rudy

Vallee was blowing a sax in New Haven in between boning for his Yale exams, when Bing Crosby was a member of Paul Whiteman's outfit, and when Sinatra, Perry Como, Tony Martin and all that singing crew were playing one o' cat and mumblety-peg.

When melancholy enveloped me I'd take to easing into whatever little saloon was featuring Tommy at the time. I'd sit at a table sipping my seltzer while this thin whip of a man with the weary, dreamy eyes and the nervous manner chanted endlessly and huskily. It was Tommy who first sang "Melancholy Baby" for me and taught me to love it above most other tunes.

He was unbelievable and lovable. He was someone out of a Hollywood movie script. He was ageless and tireless and restless, and there was no one like him to soothe a fellow into a quiet, tender mood when he had the jitters.

You had to be mighty careful about saying nice things to or writing nice things about him. He was so confounded grateful and his appreciation was appallingly embarrassing. Once my wife received roses from him every day for five weeks, and all our appeals to Tommy please to stop were of no avail. So we threatened the florist.

There was a period in the late thirties when every day brought a package to the house, each containing a tie. I can't begin to tell you the measures I had to resort to before I convinced Lyman that he was jeopardizing my reputation and that I didn't want people going around hinting I was being subsidized. That put an end to the ties.

A week later, I received half a dozen shirts from the unsquelchable minstrel man!

Finally I was successful in putting an end to that sort of embarrassing nonsense and was able to sit for hours listening to Tommy softly sob "Montmartre Rose," "Chinatown, My Chinatown," "What's the Use of Dreaming?" or explode mildly into "June Is Bustin' Out All Over" without fretting that a messenger would come pounding on my door the following morning—with perhaps even a Tiffany bracelet for my wife.

He would stand upright, barely whispering song after song—old torchers, new ones—ancient ones right out of the cornfields and up-to-the-minute sobbers—and though he never used a mike, wherever you sat you heard him.

The big treat, and only a favored few were rewarded, was when Tommy settled down, staring vaguely out of those weary, dreamy eyes and, drumming his time-beat on the table, delivered his soft chants. Then, if you had a pretty girl with you, you wouldn't have to waste time handing out your line. The job was done for you after the first song. If your wife had been cross with you, you would just have her sit with you listening to Tommy, and you'd feel the buttery meltiness of her as she reached for your hand. Or if she was the fearless and slightly brazen kind, kissed you smack in front of all the crowd.

Lyman was the original torch singer. It was Damon Runyon who first applied the label when Tommy sang the song he had written, "Gee but It's Tough When the Gang's Gone Home." Runyon called it the "Torch Carrier's Anthem." Tommy also wrote "Montmartre Rose" for Fanny Brice, but he took it over for his own repertoire through the years just as he popularized Ernie Burnett's "Melancholy Baby."

Lyman became something of the sensation of France after Floyd Gibbons, then editor of the *Paris Herald,* began trumpeting his singing appeal. He became the intimate of royalty—both working and castoffs—of social nabobs, international hoodlums, literary biggies and con men. And when in later years, some of them were in Manhattan, they would flock to whatever bistro was featuring him.

Once a night but sometimes not quite that often, the skinny balladeer with the aloofish warped smile would slap on a threadbare cap, pull up his jacket collar, and then you really had something worthwhile coming. It was Tommy sighing Joe Howard's "What's the Use of Dreaming?" with a poisonous light spreading Paris green over his kisser and a cigarette dripping loosely and smokily from the corner of his mouth. It gave you the feeling of something sinister and saturated you with a sense of delicious guilt about something or other.

Maybe that's why Tommy Lyman never required the services of a paid drumbeater. He had most of the writers on his side—Runyon, Winchell, Hellinger, Sullivan, Sobol—those of us who were the pioneer columnists before the newcomers came along who hadn't known Lyman in those brighter earlier years.

Tommy in his final years was harassed by financial woes. Engagements, even in obscure little night haunts, became scarcer and scarcer. He was reduced to selling ties and taking orders for Christmas cards. But he never whimpered, and he never tried to make a touch from his former affluent friends in the show world. In fact, when members of the Friars Club, from time to time, would try to press a few ten-spots or more for an order which came to five or six dollars, Tommy would shrink back, revealing his deep hurt.

When a friend or someone close to a friend passed away, he always lit a candle in the church. Yet—few—so dismally few, attended his funeral in Chicago early in March, 1964.

This brief profile is my own lighted candle to the memory of one of my all-time favorites among singing men.

The Magnificent Imposter

I first met "His Imperial Highness, Prince Michael Alexandrovitch Dmitri Obolensky Romanoff" in the early thirties, after his dismal tilt with the authorities. He had been branded a fraud, an imposter, a passer of bouncing checks, yet he was so completely likeable, so disarming and so articulate, that I warmed toward him immediately.

Thereafter through the years, I felt happy as gradually he progressed to respectability, picking up close and important friends on the upward path, until in his capacity as boniface of a plush eating place in Beverly Hills, he became the arbiter, you might say, of status. That is, you knew you belonged to the esoteric stratum of the elite if His Imperial Highness set aside the proper and coveted seating for you in his restaurant.

One night in December of 1959, he tossed his royal prerogatives aside and in true democratic fashion, befitting his "abdication" to become, as he put it, "a peasant, wresting a sordid living from a public eating house," Mike settled down with me to advise he had almost completed his book.

"I want your opinion," he said. "What do you think of this for a good title, *No Title!?* Rather provocative, old chap, don't you think, in view of my surrender of my royal heritage? Then by way of subtitle, what would you say to this, *My Struggle Toward Mediocrity Through the Throes of Poverty?*"

"Good, good," I agreed. And then inquired, "Who's ghosting it, or collaborating?"

Mike looked at me sadly. "Every word of it is mine," he said. "I would never stoop to having a book bearing my name written by someone else. That is fraud, chicanery, deceit. I couldn't live with myself." As far as I know, the book has yet to be completed.

On another occasion, when he was in town on a brief visit, I huddled with him at "21." "Old chap," he said, "you may correct an erroneous impression that has long prevailed. My name is truly Michael Romanoff and not Harry Gerguson. That is an error, and I am partly at fault in not interposing a correction long ago. However, I now confess to having been in error about the royal blood of the Russian Romanoffs coursing through my veins. I have discovered—not particularly, understand, that I have any regrets—that I am a Romanoff with no connection with the Russian clan. However, I have my consolation. I have my own car, a valet, three months' rent paid in advance, and a checking account like any peasant."

I reminded him of another occasion in the late thirties when he was leaning against the bar at the same "21" Club, one hand grasping a Scotch and soda, the other thrust out in front of me, with precisely seventeen cents in its palm. He was a bit wistful that evening. "Tomorrow," he said, "the most daring and literate of the Romanoffs sheds his title—for all time—and becomes a farmer, eager to woo the soil. From the soil I hope to lure that which sustains and nourishes. Only the soil, Louie, is honest and sincere and without guile. The soil returns twofold for the little it receives. Good-bye—and wish me well."

Three years later, again I found Mike in almost the same position, except that the bar against which he leaned was in Dave Chasen's place in Hollywood. But this time, the other hand was not thrust forward to reveal any coins. Mike was then acting as a greeter and host for Dave. "Prosperity," he confided, "has come to me, entirely unsolicited. Outside I have a drosky—twelve cylinders and expensive. I now have my man, and money in the bank. Life has been good to me here in Hollywood, but tomorrow, perhaps next week, I am giving up all this. I am returning to Virginia, where I have the life use of 240 fertile acres outside of Fredericksburg by courtesy of the Chamber of Commerce, and there I will become a gentleman farmer. I discovered the last time I worked on a farm I was truly a son of the soil. Will you join me in a drink?"

The years marched by. Mike now was host of his own restaurant, thanks to the financial backing of close to a dozen biggies of Hollywood who were fond of him and willing to back up that fondness with cash. We had been on the Coast, but we had never dropped in on Romanoff's. It was my wife who said: "I think it's only but fair and right, for auld lang syne, we should have dinner in the little restaurant of your friend, the Prince. I know he will be so grateful that you have remembered him, and after all, honey, as I always say, every little bit helps. Are his prices right?"

We pulled up in front of what looked like a drab little house —not too promising. My wife whispered: "Say something nice, remember, when you write about him. It may help bring some people in." In the dark of this Hollywood evening, she did not seem to be encouraged by the unimpressive exterior or what we might find once we entered.

No sooner had we passed through the door when someone tapped me on the shoulder—a baldish, grinning chap, Ludwig Bemelmans, writer of offbeat humor and a top-flight caricaturist and illustrator. He seemed more subdued than usual. "She doesn't want to dance with me tonight," he explained, and pointed to his companion, the famed Lady Mendl. She was attired in an ankle-length chinchilla coat, and she was carrying her pooch under her arm. It was the same pup that had been granted the rare privilege by Sherman Billingsley of free entry to the Cub Room of the Stork Club at all times, no questions asked.

Just then the "last of the Romanoffs" greeted us. There would be a slight wait, he announced—perhaps not more than half an hour. In the meantime, would we make ourselves at home at the bar. He hurried off and was back within a few minutes, leading us to a table in the crowded room. "I only said about waiting a half hour," he explained, "because I didn't want the rabble near you to conclude a table was available just for the asking. That is not according to the imperial code."

Sidney Kingsley, the Pulitzer Prize-winning playwright, joined us. He was then working on the screenplay of Sinclair Lewis' *Cass Timberlaine,* and the report around Hollywood was that he was to receive some $80,000 for the ten weeks' assignment.

Now the parade began to pass us by, some entering, some leaving. A few friends stopped at our table to chat, chiefly those a bit homesick for New York or who remembered that once they were happy in New York until Hollywood beckoned with its promise of solid gold. Also some who were quite happy with Hollywood. Among them we recall was Gene Markey, then just recently married to Myrna Loy, and Robert Montgomery, who had starred in my short-lived play, *The High Hatters,* and was now a major film star. Celeste Holm told us she had been preparing to go back to Manhattan, but her plans had been changed because just the day before she had been signed for a new picture. Others who stopped by were Ben Hecht (in a lumberman's shirt), Don Loper, prosperous designer and interior decorator—the same Don

Loper who, with Maxine Barrett, not too many years previously had been featured in my vaudeville unit at Loew's State as a ballroom dancing duo. Herbert Marshall, Guy Bolton and others passed by on the way to their tables, but Spencer Tracy did settle down with us for a few seconds to announce with great joy that he was mighty glad to be back in Hollywood.

"Didn't you have a good time in New York?" I demanded.

"Oh, it was all right, but it's swell to get back to Hollywood," he insisted. "Stay around awhile—you'll get the fever."

Meanwhile, as the crowd waiting impatiently for tables grew to almost menacing proportions, Romanoff sought refuge at our table. "It seems only yesterday," he sighed, "when I worked on that farm—you remember, in Virginia. I wrote you that at last I was happy, and that I had found peace and contentment. . . ."

I looked around at the flourishing, colorful restaurant. Every table was packed with what passed for celebrities. I studied the mob waiting for tables and the customers jammed in at the bar.

The author flanked by Spencer Tracy and Clark Gable on the set of *San Francisco*—two of filmdom's most beloved citizens whom the entire world mourned when death claimed them.

I considered the lofty prices on the menu, and remembered Mike's troubled, harassed days during the penniless years.

"Oh, come now, Mike," I said, "don't tell me you're not happy now."

"In my place," he said glumly, "Would you be?"

At this point, the waiter brought the check, and I suddenly felt glum, too.

A few years later, the original Romanoff's became too small for the ever increasing patronage, and Mike moved his establishment to a more elaborate lodging around the corner from the Beverly Wilshire Hotel. He still kept insisting that his happiness lay in farm life—even as he continued to prosper, to marry a beautiful young girl, his Gloria, and to move into a costly residence. At this writing, he is in semiretirement, and having sold the site, Romanoff's, to the regret of so many, is no longer a part of the Hollywood scene.

There were other encounters with Mike throughout the succeeding years, and I always found him a highly interesting gentleman, impeccable in manners as well as in speech and in attire. He is well read and well acquainted with the works of the masters of literature and philosophy—indeed, can quote from them accurately. He looks back at his imposter days not with any regret but almost with affection, even though he will ruefully concede there were nights when he was flaunting his bogus background that he had to sleep on a bench in Central Park. "Stony broke, you know," he will tell you with a grin.

One thing must be said about Mike. During those starving years when he borrowed fives and tens from friends or issued worthless checks, he kept a record in a little book, and when finally a bit of prosperity came his way, he repaid every one of those loans and made good on the checks, to the astonishment of all concerned.

One brief anecdote. One night, while some New York refugees were sitting around in Romanoff's waxing a bit nostalgic about Manhattan, playwright Freddie Finklehoffe moaned: "Even right now, I can just see the mob piling into Toots Shor's, and I can hear old blubbermouth yelling, 'Go some place else, ya crumbum!' " He turned to Romanoff. "Y'know, Mike, come to think of it, your place is sort of a branch of Shor's."

Mike bristled. "Old chap," he snapped, "there is no comparison. People go to Toots Shor's—only because he is a character!"

The Boffer

On January 17, 1966, in the early hours in a neat farmhouse snuggling among two hundred peaceful sprawling acres in Middletown, New York, Johnny Broderick, hailed as America's toughest cop, met the one adversary he couldn't lick. Death, fisting him as Johnny himself had two-fisted so many hoodlums during his lifetime, dealt the fatal blow ironically enough on the very morning of his seventieth birthday, thereby ending the career of the man before whom thugs had cowered or from whom they had fled in terror.

My own first meeting with "The Boffer," a nickname he cherished, came when a hood and excon, Jerry Sullivan, resenting an item I had printed about his overlord, had threatened me over the phone, ending up with the warning, "If you ain't made your will out, make it out quick, punk!" Late that night I was in Dave's Blue Room, and proprietor Dave Kleckner introduced me to Detective Johnny Broderick.

During our brief conversation, I mentioned the threat. Broderick said: "Pal, you ain't got nuthin' to worry about. I'll take care of it." Two days later there was another call from the gangster. "Hey, kid," he said, "you didn't take me serious, did you? I was kiddin'. Get Broderick off my neck."

Johnny, in his slightly more than twenty-five years on the police force, put the "scare" in the high and mighty and the lowliest of the murderous lads of Broadway—men who killed or ordered killings with as little compunction as swatting a mosquito—mostly with his powerful fists, often with just glaring at them, which sent them scurrying off.

There were hard-shelled citizens among them: "Dutch" Schultz, Pretty Amberg, Vannie Higgins, Waxey Gordon, Jack "Legs" Diamond and others. It was Broderick who, in the dying days of the Prohibition era in 1931, took in the half-mad killer "Two-gun" Crowley in a memorable episode. An army of police had Crowley's ground-floor apartment on upper Broadway surrounded and were pouring gunfire and tear gas fumes in the place. Crowley kept firing back, screaming, "You'll never take me alive."

According to some printed stories of the time, Johnny broke down the door of the apartment where Crowley had barricaded himself, walked in on the snarling killer, ignoring the gun pointed at his belly, took the weapon away and Crowley into custody.

Actually, according to The Boffer's own account of the episode to me, this is what happened. Johnny felt confident he could take the besieged man alive and asked permission to try. Police fire ceased but the gunman kept sniping away. Broderick kept walking ahead, ignoring the fire, knocked at the door, identified himself to Crowley, whom he knew personally. "Pal," he shouted, "you ain't got a chance. Come on out, and I'll see nothing happens to you." Crowley finally opened the door and turned his gun meekly over to the detective.

Then there was that memorable affair at the Tombs back in 1926 when three hardened holdup men, Red McKenna, Hymie Amberg and Bobby Berg, all armed, broke out of the prison, murdered the warden and a keeper and started shooting their way to freedom. Scores of police were rushed to the scene, but the three cons, using a huge coal pile as a barricade, held out against the law's guns and tear gas.

Enter Broderick. Ignoring the crossfire, he got to the coal pile, climbed over—but here the stories vary. All three were dead when the corps of police rushed in. Broderick vowed he had shot them all, but one of the police theories was that the thugs had been so terrorized by the very sight of The Boffer, they had committed suicide. "Aw, that's a pretty story," Johnny commented, years later, as he recalled the event. He grinned. "Sure, it was suicide. They just ran into the slugs from my gun."

That was the year he won his first medal for valor. This was after he had entered a restaurant, found a man menacing patrons with a gun, rushed him and hauled him to the station house.

Broderick was fond of dumping tough guys into garbage cans, headfirst, or, grabbing each by the tie and twisting it, he would push them against buildings. If they still put up a fight, he would use his powerful fists.

He was suspicious of characters who wore derbies and stickpins or who affected fancy vests and smoked big cigars from the corners of their mouths. Once, in front of Lindy's, he spotted just such a character and was convinced he was loitering in the vicinity for no good intent. Ignoring the fellow's three companions, Johnny pushed the chap against the window and roared: "Wotcha doin' here?"

The man, cigar still in his mouth, just stared, seemingly speechless. Broderick stormed: "I asked ya a question, and I expect an answer"—and slapped the cigar in his face.

Finally, one of the group protested timidly, "Hey, Johnny, you crazy? This is Joe Frisco. He's headlining at the Palace."

For once, Broderick turned a bit meek and released the famed stuttering dancing comedian. "Did you apologize, at least?" I asked him. Broderick said: "I brushed the cigar ashes off him."

John McClain, the late drama critic, was once invited by the detective to take a ride with him. As they were cruising along, they passed an uptown pub. "Let's drop in," suggested Johnny. "You look like you could use a belt." (Broderick himself never touched the hard stuff.) They had just about settled at the bar when Johnny suddenly walked away toward a fellow sitting quietly at a corner table. To McClain's dismay, the detective, without apparently any provocation, began slapping the man around; then he frisked him and came up with two guns and a knife. It developed he was wanted for several slayings.

One of the favorite stories—and this is no legend—happened at Reuben's, gathering place in the thirties for show folks and top racketeers. Broderick entered one evening and found a husky lad roaring drunk and raising quite a rumpus. As he strode toward him, someone shouted, "Hey, Johnny, that's S.——, the intercollegiate heavyweight champ." Broderick kept right on walking toward the offender, landed two punches and announced, "You are now looking at the new intercollegiate heavyweight champ."

After one memorable encounter with him, that mad hoodlum "Pretty" Amberg zealously kept out of Broderick's path. A chorus girl was hospitalized in a state of shock after being threatened by Amberg when she spurned his advances. He vowed he would slash up her face if she didn't accompany him to a hotel room. Someone reported the episode to The Boffer who scouted around and learned that Amberg was in one of the speaks of the era, King's Terrace on West Fifty-second. Broderick walked over, ordered the doorman to tell Amberg to come out. The gangster ignored the summons. Broderick stalked in, dragged him out into the street and roared: "Now, get out your knife and try it on me." Amberg ended up in Polyclinic Hospital.

Another of Broadway's badmen, Jack "Legs" Diamond, foolishly began bragging it was time someone "got" Broderick, and that he had decided he was the lad to do it. Broderick caught up with him west of Broadway on Forty-sixth Street one night and walked over to him, ignoring his henchmen and snapped: "Okay, Legs, how about it? I been hearing you wanna take me for a ride."

Diamond backed away. "Oh, come now, Johnny, can't you take a joke?"

"Sometime I don't laugh so easy," bellowed the tough detective and knocked him to the pavement. The mobster sat there, rubbing his chin. Quite a crowd gathered. "Get up, come on get up," taunted Broderick. But Diamond refused to rise. Johnny stared at him disdainfully and walked away. He returned with an ash can, almost full, and emptied it over the gangster's head.

So many legends were built around Broderick through the years that Damon Runyon took advantage of them, incorporating the hard-hitting cop into many of his tales, thinly disguised as Johnny Brannigan. There was even a comic strip, "Mickey Finn," patterned after Broderick. And Dore Schary, then production head of RKO studios, bought the film rights to Johnny's life story, paying him $75,000 and $15,000 additional as a consultant fee. But the picture was never made, for some unknown reason.

Paradoxically enough, off his beat, Johnny was quiet spoken, soft-mannered, neither smoked nor drank, and he detested foul language. He was a devout churchman. His usual salute to women was "Little Lady." Men whom he liked he addressed as "Little Man." Men of importance he hailed as "Chief."

Rarely did anyone address him as "Johnny." It was always, "Hello, John," or "Hi, John." Even Toots Shor, who was so close to him during those years, addressed him as "John." The detective, who was a great one for personal dignity, despite his rough methods, remained awesome enough so that Shor never added his favorite salutation, "crumbum."

I had expressed my admiration for Dore Schary's many talents and achievements—as a movie director and producer, as an author and a playwright (he had just completed his play *Sunrise at Campobello,* destined to be one of the season's hits—and meanwhile was engaged in several crusading projects). Schary beamed his appreciation.

Broderick hated lawbreakers with a fierce intensity. But his loyalty to friends was equally intense, and his purse always open for a touch. Thus, when one of his friends phoned him one day from Saratoga, confessing ruefully he had gone for a bundle and could Johnny wire him $10,000, Broderick drove up to the resort town and handed his pal $10,000 in cash. (This was after he had been enriched by the $90,000 from the sale of the film rights to his life story.)

Broderick used to tell me that one thing he regretted was that he had such little schooling. He had to quit at the age of twelve to support his family. He drove a truck in his teens, was connected with the Teamsters Union in a minor capacity and later became bodyguard to labor leader Samuel Gompers. He had planned to be a professional boxer but changed his mind and became a fireman. He found the going dull, so he joined the Police Department in 1923.

When he retired a few years ago, he bought a big farm in Middletown, New York, decided he'd like to live the life of a country squire. But he maintained a room in the Taft Hotel, because he couldn't remain too far distant from his Broadway. In 1964, while holidaying in Miami Beach, he just "didn't feel right," as he explained later. Deciding the Florida sun was too much for him, he flew back to New York and invaded Toots Shor's. Ford Frick, then baseball czar, settled down with him.

"John," he said, "you're not looking well at all. You go see a doctor." He practically browbeat the retired cop into submitting to an examination. The diagnosis was that he had been suffering from acute and long neglected diabetes, and for the first time in his long career, Broderick was hospitalized. There he worsened, and he suffered a massive heart attack.

In his final two years, he lived quietly at his farm, rarely coming into Manhattan. He had previously been contenting himself with taking care of his nine prize palominos, but with the heart trouble and strict orders from his doctors, riding was now forbidden. So he sold the palominos. "I couldn't stand not being able to ride them. They needed the exercise," he said.

On the night of January 16, 1966, he felt he just had to go into Manhattan for a quiet celebration at Shor's. It was the eve of his birthday, and he wanted some friends near or around him. He left the gathering early enough to return to his farm, and went straight to bed.

He never woke up.

The Dancing Man

On whether Bill "Bojangles" Robinson, one of the great dancing men of the twentieth century, would have been perturbed by the rebellion of members of his race these days against "whitey" I cannot truthfully offer an opinion. For him, the color line rarely existed—and as far as his fellow professionals in show business, it just as rarely bothered them that his skin wasn't as white as theirs.

He earned in excess of $5,000,000 during his long career, but had very little of it left at his death. Bill was a spendthrift and self-confessed gambling fool. He was a consistent loser in a version of ten-card rummy known in Negro circles as "cooncan." One notorious gambler followed him around from theatre to theatre, winning thousands of dollars from him until Little Bo, as Robinson's wife was known, cornered the two of them in Bill's dressing room in a Seattle theatre, pulled a gun (she confessed later it wasn't loaded), pointed it at the gambler and snapped icily, "If I ever see you within ten yards of Bill again, I'll fill you full of holes—git." The fellow got. Then she laid the law down to Robinson, and he promised meekly he'd never touch a card again.

"Did you keep that promise?" I once asked him.

Robinson grinned. "Boss, I sure did. (Bill's favorite salutation was "Boss.") I didn't tech dem cards like I promised. I jes grabbed 'em tight. You couldn't call dat techin' 'em, now could you?"

When Bill was being featured in those Shirley Temple films, the press release pictured him as a gentle, good-natured soul, highly religious, etc., etc. Actually the Robinson we knew was flare-tempered, profane, sulked when crossed, domineering, and had his violent dislikes—among them at the time, Ethel Waters and Stepin Fetchit. When he was celebrating his fiftieth anniversary in show business at the Cotton Club, he introduced Fetchit as "my great pal, a wonderful artist." The dead-panned Step merely bowed with characteristic weariness and refused to step up on the floor. Bill never forgave him for that. It was that same night that he introduced, "my lil' sister, that grand artist, ladies and gen'men, Ethel Waters."

Ethel lumbered, heavy-footed, up to the mike and confessed: "I ain't talked to Bill in a long, long time—'cause we don't like each other none too well—and never has. Jes' the same, folks, I guess it's silly for grown folks actin' thata way. How would you like to hear 'Stormy Weather'?"

Shirley Temple, a sophisticated six-year-old, perches on the author's knee, gazing so affectionately into his paternal eyes. The second after the cameraman shot the pose, Shirley's smile was promptly erased, replaced by a look of disdain as she scampered away. The love affair ended as quickly as it started.

However, Bojangles liked and loved more people than he disliked, and no one was more generous. He used to give away expensive suits, ties, hats and money freely. Everything, in fact, but his shoes. He would spend as much as from twenty-five to sixty dollars a pair—a considerable price for those days. He usually had one hundred pairs available to suit his fancy of the moment.

Bill told me the proudest moment of his life was when John D. Rockefeller, Jr., built a playground project in Harlem after listening to his appeal. The dancing man parking his car at a busy section of Lenox Avenue one afternoon and found the urchins using the running board for a base in playing one o' cat. He asked why they weren't at a playground or at the empty lots. The kids giggled. "We ain't got none o' those things." Bill discovered it was true that there wasn't a playground and that, moreover, whatever big empty lots there were nearby, the Rockefellers owned. So he invaded the office of John D., and sending in his name, he was pleased to be ushered in immediately.

"Look here, Boss," said Bojangles, after a few preliminaries. "I live in your fine apartment house in Harlem and I pay plenty rent. You got empty lots that ain't doin' nuthin', and colored kids got no place to play. Why don't you do sumpin' about dat?" The project was announced formally the following day.

Bill was shot at—and into—several times. On one occasion, he told me, it was during the Spanish-American War. He wasn't a soldier, he confessed—but he was wounded nevertheless. "I'm in this dance hall in Battlebor', No'th Ca'lina," he explained, "and this lootenant is cleaning his gun and it goes off and the bullet hits my knee." But when I inquired just why an officer should pick a dance hall to clean his gun, Bill admitted he "jes couldn't tell."

Another time, in Pittsburgh, he chased after two teen-agers he had seen robbing an old white man. Bill always carried the gold-plated revolver which had been presented to him by the police of Harlem. He fired into the air. A cop emerging from a one-arm luncheon saw Robinson fire those shots, and taking careful aim plugged the dancing man through the right arm.

Robinson's unique dancing routines were imitated far and wide, and are to this day, and his skill made him the highest-salaried Negro star of his day.

Among the special honors that delighted him were his titles such as Special Deputy Sheriff of New York County, Special Inspector Motor Vehicles for the State of New York, Admiral in the Great Navy of the State of Nebraska [*sic!*] and Supreme Honorary Mascot of the New York Giants.

The dancing man was also something of a comedian, but I can't say that some of the quips and gags he offered to regain breath between his stepping around were for Sunday school consumption. Once when I reproached him in print for what I considered an unnecessarily vulgar, almost obscene gag, he phoned. "Boss," he exploded, "no one was in that club who wasn't over twenty-one. And if there'd been kids, they wouldn't get it anyway. What you become, a preachin' man?"

He rarely drank or smoked. In fact, two Alexanders (his favorite libation when he did take a drink) would give him the staggers and the loose tongue. A single cigar gave him, as he described it, a "twirlin' head."

Robinson's weight rarely fluctuated between 160 and 162 pounds through all the years I knew him. He was solidly built, and had no telltale lines of age in his face even in his sixties. He remained as agile as a youth of twenty-one, yet he would eat between five and six quarts of ice cream a day and consume two or three dozen hot biscuits. To celebrate his sixty-first birthday, and his fifty-second year as a dancing man, he ran from Forty-eighth Street to Times Square—backwards!

Of course, there were times when he encountered the prejudice of bigoted whites toward other Negroes, though rarely toward himself—and I am certain he was resentful, yet I never heard him voice the resentment.

There was an occasion, however, at a testimonial dinner in Hollywood for famed Broadway physician Dr. Leo Michel, when Robinson was the only Negro invited. When it came to the seating arrangements, there was something of embarrassment as to where the performer should be seated. Bill, pretending he was unaware of the confusion, said: "I'd kinda like it if I could sit right up there by myself near the piano. I like sitting near a piano—by myself."

Producer Sam Harris, composer Irving Berlin, movie tycoon Jack Warner and half a dozen others rushed forward and insisted they would be offended if Bill Robinson didn't sit at their tables. By that time, the floundering committee had come to its senses and insisted Bojangles be seated at the speakers' table.

He lived well always. His home was a seven-room, luxuriously furnished flat in Harlem, and he was usually driven around in his huge costly Dusenberg by a chauffeur who could imitate every one of his steps. He lavished furs and diamonds on his wife, and she encouraged him, explaining, "They're like money in the bank."

One of his original expressions, which remains to this day in the show business lexicon, was "copacetic," meaning everything is tops, everything is even more okay than okay. One thing, Bill Robinson wouldn't like if he were alive to read this profile is my attempt to report the drawly dialect he employed, for Bill never believed he talked that way.

The great durable dancing star died on November 25, 1949, at the age of seventy-one, but able, almost to the last, to move those wonderful, inspired, twinkling feet with all the graceful agility which had brought him acclaim during his long career.

Bantum Barnum

The fantastic career of Billy Rose, showman, author, columnist, songwriter, theatre owner and financier, has been fairly well covered in two biographies which came off the presses almost simultaneously early in 1968. I have only a few fragments to add. Of a night, for instance, when we sat in a little pub known as Adrian's Tap Room, and a singing lad was chanting "Me and My Shadow." Billy gulped down his ginger ale, wiped a few drops from his lips and said: "I don't remember how many years ago I wrote it, but it was in Al Jolson's suite in the Ritz Towers. There was a big party going on—sixty or seventy people raising the roof, really going to town with plenty of hoopla. So I went into a corner and while the shouting kept blasting in my ears, I scribbled off the lyrics—the lonesomest song I ever wrote."

On another occasion, back in 1946, when I dropped in on him in his apartment in the Ziegfeld Theatre, he asked me to read a column that was ready for the string of papers using his pieces. "Sometimes," he said, "sleeping here in my cozy little apartment in this Ziegfeld Theatre, the ghost of Will Rogers prods me with his spurs and Marilyn Miller does a pirouette and old Ziggy himself asks me to dash off a thousand-word telegram. Then I get to thinking about what I ought to write about tomorrow. Keeps me awake most of the night."

Of course, I knew that though many of the ideas of his columns originated with him, they were actually put together by several "ghosts" with Billy changing a sentence here or there—injecting some of his own colorful phrases.

It was on this night that he also commented on the World's Fair being proposed in London and said he hoped to operate his "liquid slot machine there." When I seemed puzzled, he explained: "My Aquacade, of course."

On another occasion, we were strolling home from Reuben's long after midnight, and passing a familiar citizen of wealth, I commented on his current unhappiness, which revolved about an unsavory divorce action brought by his wife. I added tritely that so many people who had everything—money, fame, etc., seemed unhappy. At this point we came toward the Ziegfeld Theatre. Billy said: "Look at that beautiful building. Think of all the great stars who performed there. And I own it—every brick and tile and proscenium light—free and clear. No mortgages. I could rip off that name, Ziegfeld, and put up my own, if I wanted to. I wouldn't do that. What I'm getting at is I've got money now, I've got property, that mansion of mine, my place in the country, and I think I have fame, too. Louis, I'll tell you something confidentially —I'm not unhappy at all.

But I wondered, as he left me to go home to his big mansion

—a lonely mansion. For Joyce Mathews had left him for the second time—this time, she had insisted, for good.

"Young Man with a Horn"

A few years ago as I was passing by a little Broadway music shop, there came floating out in the gravel-throated voice of Louis Armstrong the then current Number One song hit "Hello, Dolly!" and I stood there and listened along with several others to the recording. Some of us forgot we were on a busy street and applauded.

My memory drifted back to a night some decades previously at the Cotton Club. It was after hours, and the waiters were piling up the tables. In a corner box, we sat with Joe Glaser, manager of many big-time acts, and bullnecked Louis Armstrong, who was even then considered the ace trumpet-man of the world, joined us. I noticed his upper lip was a spongy mass, like that of a prizefighter who has been through the mill. There were millions of little scars like initialed horsehide from years and years of blowing that tube.

Glaser said: "Sit down, man."

Satchmo settled down, almost apologetically. Glaser said: "Pops, good news for you, Vinton Freedley wants you to costar with Margaret Sullavan and Burgess Meredith in *Young Man with a Horn*. How about it?"

Armstrong mumbled, unenthusiastically, "Not for me. I'd do anything for you—you my poppa—but that's voodoo to me. That's a play about Bix. Bix is daid and I don't want no ghosts fingerin' my horn, Poppa."

"Okay, Pops," said Glaser, easily. "I'll sign you for *Swingin' the Dream*—but don't forget, Shakespeare, he is dead, too. Very dead."

"That's solid, Poppa," rumbled the scrapey-voiced Gabriel, "but Shakespeare, he ain't no Bix, not him."

So we plunged into memories of Bix Beiderbecke, already a legend with musicians, although at that time he had been dead only some eight years—dead at the age of twenty-eight, this genius of the horn who was as white as Satchmo was black.

"He was the most," said Armstrong. He insisted Bix had the greatest ear in the business, although he never learned to read a note. At the age of five, it was said, he had listened to a recording of the "Hungarian Rhapsody" and then played it on the piano, flawlessly.

At fourteen, Bix floated around New Orleans, rowing up and down the Mississippi to listen to Armstrong's trumpet notes blasting on the *Capitol,* biggest of the river showboats. Bix would sneak in and sit behind the bandstand, listening and absorbing. After the show, he would take his cheap trumpet and play everything Armstrong had offered, note for note, beat for beat.

"Man," said Armstrong, "it was jes' eerie."

In the years that followed, Satchmo waged many battles of music against Box. En route to one engagement, he recalled how Bix, riding through an Indiana wheatfield on his way to a town with composer Hoagy Carmichael as his companion, stopped the car and played haunting trumpet solos for an hour. "Hoagy tol' me," recalled Armstrong, "It was like he was talkin' to God."

By his early twenties, Bix was going big. He was making plenty of money, living furiously and spending as if tomorrow would not come. Princeton students began collecting his records. Other collegians took up the fad. Despite his big earnings, Bix continued to live in a little room on West Forty-fourth Street, and here the Dorseys, Benny Goodman, Harry James and other top horn players assembled for private jam sessions.

Bix played with the Casa Loma orchestra, but quit when asked to remain for lengthy rehearsals.

"What for?" he protested. "I can't read arrangements." He joined Paul Whiteman, expertly delivering the difficult Ferde Grofé arrangements after listening to them once or twice.

Then, while he was bedded with a head cold, a group of Princeton students pleaded with him to assemble a band for their prom. Ill as he was, he obliged. It was his final performance. Death claimed him shortly after. It might be recorded that during his illness, Whiteman kept Bix's seat in the band unoccupied.

To this day, Louis Armstrong, king of the trumpeters, Bix's tutor and guide, keeps recalling Beiderbecke mournfully and affectionately, and he will assure you solemnly, as he did that night, that Bix's ghost listens in whenever he plays. Satchmo calls it "voodoo."

And as I listened to Satchmo giving out with "Hello, Dolly!" I wondered if somewhere hovering over the music box in the little shop might not be the shadowy wraith of Bix Beiderbecke, perhaps blowing out an accompaniment on a silent trumpet.

The "Discoverer"

The man who prided himself on being the great "discoverer" of talent was a tall, energetic, voluble showman named Nils T. Granlund, usually referred to by his initials, N.T.G. Hailing originally from Lapland, of all places, this former racing driver, flier, pugilist, newspaperman and press agent finally barged into show business.

I didn't know him when he was achieving some modest fame as a radio announcer over Station WHN far back in 1923, but by the time I was reporting on Broadway, he had become established as a dominant cabaret man, one with an uncanny knack of selecting little girls for his chorus lines who were destined for more glorious careers on stage and screen. Among those who credited him with having detected their possibilities were Joan Crawford, Barbara Stanwyck, Ruby Keeler, Joan Leslie, Yvonne De Carlo, Adele Jergens, Marie McDonald, Claire Luce (the actress, not the former Ambassador) and four or five others.

Once, going over his career for a profile I was writing, he asked me not to forget that he had introduced amateur dancing contests into the Loew theatres—the first stage experience of girls who headed later for stardom—and that he had once been city editor of a Rhode Island newspaper at the age of twenty. I never did check further on that. But it was true that he had been a pioneer producer of girly shows at various of the Manhattan night spots—the Hollywood, Paradise, Silver Slipper, Frivolity, among others.

For a time after he left Broadway, he was active on the Coast. Then came the dismal dispatch in April of 1957 that he had succumbed to injuries suffered in a taxicab accident in Las Vegas, Nevada. There was some mystery about his age at death—reports ranged from sixty-five to seventy-two.

King of the Dime Novels

I don't think any Bing Crosby or Frank Sinatra fan ever experienced the thrill that was mine when I first met big, white-haired George M. Patten, who preferred to call himself Gil or Gilbert Patten, and who was even better known to millions of readers of an earlier generation as Burt L. Standish. That was the name under which he wrote those never-to-be-forgotten nickel and dime novels dealing with the adventures of two wonderful young athletic heroes, Frank and Dick Merriwell.

He always seems to be beaming goodwill and cordiality even though, as we became friends, I knew he was more or less strapped for funds—this prolific writer who had written close to fifty million words in his lifetime, a figure he estimated to me himself back in the late thirties.

To me, as to many others who had been ardent readers of Merriwell stories in their youth, he was a legendary figure, and so it was unbelievable to me that he could still be alive—all six feet plus of him—and that I was having a drink with him at Lee Chumley's. He earned so little money out of all those writings that he remained close to poverty most of his life. In the early 1940's he was even on the verge of eviction from his little apartment, so that at the advanced age of seventy-five he sat down and wrote a novel, *Mr. Frank Merriwell,* hoping its sales would yield him sufficient royalties to ease his final years. Unfortunately, the book had limited sales.

Once Patten told me that when he was churning out the Merriwell adventures at Yale, he himself had never come closer to the inside or outside of the university in New Haven than the railroad station at Bridgeport, Connecticut, some seventeen miles away. Some of his earliest pre-Merriwell novels he sold to the dime-novel publishers Beadle & Adams for, he confessed ruefully, fifty dollars each. "Seemed like a soft touch then," he added, "for a young fellow from Maine." Soon he was earning $1,700 a year, and when those earnings soared to $2,700, he married his sweetheart and came on to New York.

When the old house of Beadle & Adams began to slump, his rates were sliced, and finally there was no market for his writings.

"I went broke," said Patten, "and we were even evicted from our little walk-up flat. I remember walking all the way from 116th Street to Park Place without a nickel in my jeans just to collect twenty-five dollars due me for a short story I sold to a syndicate."

Then he remembered he still had one hundred dollars due him from Beadle & Adams. But when he invaded the office to collect, he was handed ninety dollars and told to be satisfied. "I vowed never again to write a dime novel," said Patten.

He didn't keep that vow, for he had to support a wife. Something of a break came when Street & Smith editor Arthur D. Hall, seeking juvenile yarns of distinction, offered Patten fifty dollars a week on a three-year contract if he could deliver a series of acceptable stories at the rate of 20,000 words every seven days. Together they finally picked Frank Merriwell as the name of the hero, because it implied an open, straightforward person, "Merry" and "Well." Patten told me he didn't know just why he decided on the nom de plume of Burt L. Standish. The first Frank Merriwell stories appeared on the stands April 8, 1896. Dick Merriwell was born a few years later.

And Patten's final salary for these runaway best sellers before he quit was 150 dollars a week! And no royalties.

I was sitting with Gil one night in Chumley's in 1933, when Lee Chumley brought novelist Carl Van Vechten over to our table. "I've always wanted to meet you," said Van Vechten. Patten rose and shaking hands with the fellow writer, said, "I want to tell you there's a distinction about your books, a swing to your style that I envy, sir. You are a great writer, and it's a privilege to shake your hand."

Van Vechten, visibly delighted by the posy, said: "I feel flattered you think so. But I would give anything to have the wide circulation you've enjoyed in your lifetime, sir. I still remember the thrill I used to get reading your books those many years ago. I couldn't wait until the next one was out. It's you I envy, sir."

After Van Vechten returned to his own table, Patten said, "Now wasn't that nice of him, a famous writer like him? I wouldn't be surprised if he earns more from his writings in a year than I did in a lifetime. Just a matter of timing, Louis. Besides, how does anyone know the Merriwell stories would have the same appeal these days that they did when I was turning them out. They might say—what's the word?—corny, yes?"

Patten died peacefully in his sleep on January 17, 1945, at the home of his son in Vista, California. He was seventy-eight. *The New York Times* devoted an entire column to the obituary, estimating his books had reached a circulation of approximately 123,600,000 copies!

He Wore Gowns

Once hailed as the "most glamorous woman" on the American stage, the titleholder undoubtedly chuckled all the way to the bank, for actually the "most glamorous woman" was William

Dalton, better known by his stage name of Julian Eltinge. I once asked him how he became a female impersonator. He said, "Well, there was this show the Boston Cadets used to put on—they were something like the Knickerbocker Greys here—and they put me in a girl part, and if you'll excuse the expression, I was quite a hit. I was ten years old at the time. So the next year, they built the show around me. That doomed me, I guess."

As the years trooped by, Eltinge was starred in a series of plays and musicals, chiefly in female roles. At the height of his fame, when his earnings were in the six figures annually, and taxes almost nil, he used to tell friends they would never have to run a benefit for him because he was investing in annuities. Meanwhile, a Broadway theatre was named after him, but the glory of the playhouse, like the glory of Julian's name, faded with the years, and it became a burlesque house.

Eltinge himself remained loyal to his art and to the traditions he respected. He never permitted cheapness to be associated with his name. Even in his final stand, as a member of a group of old-timers, along with Blanche Ring, Gilda Gray and Pat Rooney at Billy Rose's Diamond Horseshoe, he retained the dignity for which he was noted. By this time, all his careful investments had dwindled pitifully because he had converted his annuities into stocks and other deals which faltered.

It is ironic that the curtain of his life dropped March 7, 1941, just twenty-four hours before the final curtain fell on the long-run Diamond Horseshoe show in which he was starred. He was fifty-seven.

Broadway's Hot Toddy

There has never been anyone quite like him—this hustling citizen out of Chicago calling himself Mike Todd after tossing into discard as too cumbersome his real name, Avron Goldbogen. To me, when I knew him in his earlier days, he was someone right out of a movie of the old-time Bowery—in appearance, that is. To get the picture, see him as I used to—his hat at a cocky tilt over his broad head, a cigar usually protruding from a corner of his mouth (he consumed about fifteen a day). His suits were noisy, his walk something of a strut.

Yet, and forgive the punning reference, he was to become not only about the hottest toddy on Broadway, but he was also to gain recognition as a daring showman in most of the capitals of the world.

Quite a citizen, this Todd. He was a reckless gambler, a man who made and squandered millions, who was broke time and again, only to stage amazing comebacks, and he was an ardent wooer of three dominant movie stars, and destined to wed two of them. His exit from the world he loved was as dramatic as his career.

Boarding his private plane in Los Angeles to fly to New York, where he was to be honored by the Friars Club as its "Man of the Year," he went to his flaming death in the Zuñi Mountains of New Mexico on March 23, 1958. He was fifty. Perishing with him were his biographer, Art Cohn, and his pilot and copilot, Bill Verner and Tom Barclay.

Todd was a smoothie, a glib persuader who managed to borrow fantastic amounts, even from tough businessmen, often without signing a note. This despite the fact that he admitted freely he was a compulsive gambler, who without flinching could drop $50,000 in a single day at the races or just as much in a single session of gin rummy. In fact, he once admitted to me that on a train ride out to Hollywood for a quick deal which he hoped would net him close to $100,000, he engaged in a gin rummy game with film producer David O. Selznick, and took a beating for $45,000. And, when he arived in Hollywood, he learned to his dismay that the deal was off.

Todd was scheduled for a career as a pharmacist. In fact he was apprenticed to a druggist when he was barely fourteen. But pills and nostrums held forth no allure to the even then glib, energetic youngster. He tried his skill as a shoe salesman, then became a street-corner pitchman. The legend is that he would stand on a street corner in Chicago with a stiletto apparently protruding from his throat (catsup staining the area was one of his added touches). Crowds would gather, and then his assistant would begin peddling potato peelers. Mike even worked as a shill in carnivals, but at the age of seventeen he came up with a bolder venture. He started a "college" for bricklayers which lured quite a few "students" until they learned that the unions refused to recognize their *diplomas*.

"I was really a petty larceny guy," he once told me, "anything for the fast buck. I never cared for the dough itself, but getting it, especially from suckers in those kid days—that's how I got my kicks."

He invaded Manhattan, determined to make a niche for himself as a producer. His two first offerings, *Call Me Ziggy* and *The Man from Cairo,* were dismal flops. Then he brought in *The Hot Mikado,* starring Bill Robinson, and tasted the glory of his first success. It continued as a prosperous lure when he transferred it to the New York World's Fair, though he envied rival showman Billy Rose's greater moneymaking attraction, the Aquacade. Incidentally, there never was much love lost between the two showmen, although Todd often conceded that "little jerk has the knowhow and you can't take it from him." And Rose on rare occasions would grudgingly admit, "Todd's a great pitchman."

In three short years, Todd was to produce four successive winners: *Star and Garter,* starring Gypsy Rose Lee, *Mexican Hayride, Something for the Boys* and *Up in Central Park.*

It was with the advent of *Up in Central Park* that Mike began to decide there was no glory like the glory of being a party host. He tossed an elaborate hoedown in the Tavern on the Green, had some of his prize guests transported by horse and buggy, and wined and dined close to seven hundred people. All told, the gathering dented Todd's bankroll for close to $15,000, but it was the talk of the town. It may be said that he started something, for, gradually, other producers began hosting big parties following premieres—a practice that continues to this day.

In 1950, he had another box-office smash, *As the Girls Go*—the rumor was Mike had blown his wad again and this time he had to call on his bride, movie actress Joan Blondell, for $80,000.

Then came the showdown, and it did seem that Todd's meteoric career was over. He went bankrupt, with debts amounting to $1,105,616. Mike confessed that he had lost heavily gambling and revealed he had borrowed from persons in all walks of life: among them, Chicago tycoon Henry Crown ($600,000 was his debt to him), movie producer William Goetz ($25,000), shoe tycoon Irving Florsheim, industrialist-millionaire Alfred Strelsin and a dozen others. But he insisted he had repaid the $80,000 he had borrowed from wife Joan Blondell.

The miracle of Todd, whom Georgie Jessel once described as "the con man who became a connoisseur," was that he was ready for his most ambitious venture—the new cinematic process that he named after himself, Todd A-O." Investors flocked to his aid and the first Todd A-O offerings, with Lowell Thomas as one of the narrators, brought a new image into movies.

Mike's first wife was a pretty, dark-haired girl, Bertha Freshman, whom he married when he was nineteen and she was eighteen. They remained married for twenty years, apparently happily enough until Mike began to find new romantic interests. They parted, and it was Todd who filed suit for divorce.

Todd had become smitten with a movie star, Joan Blondell. It was a stormy courtship, and Joan confessed to intimates that half the time she didn't know what Mike was trying to prove. But he still remained the deft smoothie, and on July 5, 1947, they became Mr. and Mrs. in Las Vegas. The marriage continued just as turbulent as the courtship. Finally Joan decided enough was enough, and she divorced him.

By this time, another cinema beauty had caught Todd's fancy. This was Evelyn Keyes, ex-wife of John Huston. I remember Mike would be getting his shave and trim in John Sideri's barbershop which occupied a room on the third floor of plush "21," and there would be Evelyn, seated in a chair watching patiently while Mike would be on the phone, to Barber John's annoyance, phoning all over the country, and often to different parts of the world. It was evident to those of us who patronized the shop that the lovely Evelyn was madly in love. Indeed, to paraphrase an old saying, an actress hath no greater love than to give up her career for a man, and Evelyn did.

And then Todd met Elizabeth Taylor, and he forgot beautiful Evelyn. Mike put as much dedication and drive into his wooing of the glamorous star who had divorced Michael Wilding as he devoted to his flamboyant enterprises, and it paid off.

(Incidentally, Evelyn Keyes eventually married musician Artie Shaw, among whose previous wives had been such other belles as Ava Gardner, Lana Turner, novelist Kathleen Winsor, actress Doris Dowling, Jerome Kern's daughter, Betty, and a couple of others. Evelyn became Mrs. Shaw the Eighth. The two seem to be getting along with each other nicely, for the marriage, which took place in 1956, is still intact.)

It became my lot to break the story of the Todd-Taylor romance. Encountering Liz and Mike in cozy togetherness at Toots Shor's one evening, I said, half in jest, "Is this for real, you two?"

Miss Taylor wound an arm affectionately around Todd's

neck, kissed him on the cheek, looked at me out of those gorgeous violet eyes and murmured, "I love him passionately. He's my man—and I'm his woman!"

Intimates of Liz insist that Burton appealed to her because he was so much like Todd in his dominating ways—something the more pliable and fairly easygoing Eddie Fisher, who preceded him as Miss Taylor's husband, was not.

Todd's final and most ambitious and most successful project was the production of the film version of Jules Verne's *Around the World in Eighty Days,* a magnificently successful movie destined to win five of the coveted Oscars.

Once again he was to be the big party man. He hosted a slam-bang affair in London to which nobility, high society, movie stars and millionaires, as well as a few common people, were invited. For the premiere of *Eighty Days* in Manhattan, he decided only Madison Square Garden was spacious enough, and guests poured in by the thousands for free champagne, hot dogs, hamburgers and even caviar.

This party proved to be a major fiasco. Larcenous waiters demanded payment for the champagne and for the viands. The following day the press directed vitriolic blasts at Todd: "The public got bread crumbs and a circus . . ." "We can well imagine how the Soviets will present a picture to the rest of the world of New York fiddling while the country burns . . ." "Vulgar . . ." "Ostentatious . . ." "Party Shambles . . .," etc.

Todd was hurt—he admitted that to me. "I hate to tell you how many thousands of dollars that taffy pull cost me. I just wanted to give folks a good time, and I get it in the neck," he lamented.

"Wasn't it because you thought it was good publicity for the picture?" I asked.

"Sure, sure, what's wrong with that? Let them call me a wheeler and dealer, but I keep money going into circulation and nobody suffers." And then he added, glumly, "It could have been such a whale of a party!"

Perhaps you may gain an idea of how this energetic citizen operated if I report on one late afternoon with him in 1956—again it was while he sat in John Sideri's barber chair upstairs in "21." The manicurist held one of his hands, buffing his nails while John scraped the Todd chin. To the big-time operator's right sat his pretty secretary, Midori Tsuji, taking notes as Mike dictated—between a long-distance call to Paris and a call from California.

In the meantime, somehow, he managed to carry on a conversation with me.

When the Paris talk was completed, Mike handled the Hollywood call from his home in Beverly Hills where the Yugoslavian Ambassador was lodging. Something about a big party with Mike okaying some of the guests invited, saying "no" to others.

And in between, to repeat, he still managed to answer some of my questions. For instance he said everything had run off smoothly in Russia, where he had been the guest of high functionaries in Moscow, Leningrad and Kiev. It was true he had made arrangements to produce with Russian governmental cooperation and the blessing of our State Department five superproductions in Todd A-O—the first of which would be a collection of the best that the Soviet had to offer in entertainment.

"Show you how far they're ready to go," said Mike. "There is one sequence when I said a few harps would furnish a neat background. They almost screamed. 'A few harps! Mr. Todd, we want you to have our best, all of them.' I asked, 'How many would that be?' They said, '160.'"

On the matter of his projected *War and Peace* picture, Mike said he was confident he would go ahead with it, but admitted the Russians were holding back until they were certain it would surpass anything ever done in pictures. "You know," said Mike. "Todd doesn't do anything unless it's the best."

He was irritated, he confessed, by some printed reports that our State Department had regarded his Russian venture with misgivings.

At this point he yelled, "Mike, come over here," and a slim young man got up from his chair. "You know Mike, Jr.?" Todd said by way of introduction, "Made me a grandpa last week. Mike, show Mr. Sobol that letter. Read that letter, Louis."

Mike, Jr., fished around in his pockets and finally came up with a note from a State Department official thanking Todd, Sr., for keeping the Department appraised of all development and expressing its high approval.

None of this, understand, came over in a continuous flow. Todd was still managing to give directions to the other end on the Hollywood call—and now there was a call awaiting from London.

I started to press Mike for his impressions of Sovietland, conditions there, etc. But there was still another call waiting, and Todd suddenly realized that Midori Tsuji was impatient for him to complete his dictation, so all I got was, "I'll have to talk with you when I get back. I'm shoving off for the Coast tonight,"—and then he was on with this party in London.

The end of Mike Todd came, to repeat, so tragically. Naturally, the big Friars' affair was canceled, and the special gold statuette struck in his honor was sent to his grieving widow, Liz Taylor.

George Jessel, who was to have been the toastmaster, commented: "Whatever his vices or virtues, Mike Todd's talents as a supershowman outweighed them. He ran the gamut from the Gaiety delicatessen on Forty-sixth Street to the Gothic cathedral in France. He could plead like a pushcart peddler and a moment later with the dignity and authority of a Roman emperor."

Prankster

In the winter of 1932, during a social lull that had cast a pall of ennui over cafe society, a mysterious international figure, Don Galeazzo Francisco Busby de Catonay Capodarso of Bombay and São Paulo, reputed to be one of the world's wealthiest and most eligible bachelors, breezed into the New York scene and sent doleful Mayfair into a dither.

When this dream prince, who was reputedly worth 35 million dollars, refused to entertain callers at his elegant duplex suite on Park Avenue, the social lions and lionesses were fit to be tied. For two weeks, his impeccable social secretary, Niccolo de Quattrociocchi, apologetically spurned all appointments for the romantic recluse.

Then apparently shedding his isolationist mood, the wealthy don, through his secretary, announced a gala cocktail dansant in honor of his niece, H. G. H. Maria Grace de Catona Alcazar, and showered a deliriously happy but surprised elite with beautifully engraved invitations.

Society reporters beat out the gladsome tidings. The sagas in printer's ink were varied, but in the main the stories disclosed that Don y Capodarso had been born in South America, kidnapped by the gypsies and taken to Bombay, where eventually he prospered and owned vast estates.

The smart set buzzed with excitement. Hostesses canceled their own parties. Glamor girls broke previous engagements. Multimillionaire Billy Leeds sent his yacht off to the South Seas without him. Picture then the Social Set's homicidal reaction when it discovered the reputed fabulous character was a moronic-looking, stuttering and completely bewildered Bowery bum, hired and dressed for the occasion.

Behind this elaborate hoax was none other than Quattrociocchi whose name for almost a decade had proved the bone in the throats of linotypers. Nicky, an American citizen whose birth certificate acknowledged that he was born in Palermo, Sicily, ranked with such specialists in the gusty jest and perpetrators of practical jokes as Frank Libuse, Vincent Barnett, Hugh Troy, Joe Cook, Marc Lachmann and other former exponents of the decadent art of creating confusion, consternation and discomfort for unsuspecting innocents.

Nicky continued to have his little fling at the shenanigans, though he quieted down after one tragic kickback. That was in the fall of 1937, when he engineered the "chain-letter mystery cocktail party." As hundreds of celebrants who had been invited to the "most unusual party of the season" swarmed the sidewalks and lobby of 480 Park Avenue, by a melancholy coincidence, an attractive dancer, Helen Kim Mont, wife of a well-known designer, James Mont, was ending her life by inhaling gas in her apartment building. There was a panic among the assemblers as the police arrived—and even more panic for Nicky, who had been guilty of the party prank, too—but was cleared of any connection with the suicide.

Nicky opened a colorful restaurant, El Borracho, and demonstrated his imagination by the gimmicks he provided for the decor, including his "Kiss Room," the walls of which were plastered with slips bearing the lip impressions of notable beauties from all walks of life, and placards with quotes about kissing from poets and authors of the past.

Among Nicky's favorite pranks was to drop a stray key into a victim's pocket, usually when the subject was blotto. When the chap sobered up and found the key, as a rule he began wondering and worrying, especially if he was a married man with a jealous wife.

Nicky also made it a practice when he was hosting a party at El Borracho to plant a cheap little imitation pearl in one of the oysters being served, being careful to see that it was placed before one of the women guests. The "lucky" lass would shriek with joy, and Nicky would study the pearl and give it a high appraisal. And not until the lady brought it to a jeweler would she learn the sad truth.

When he finally sold his restaurant, he retired to his native Palermo and devoted himself to a new career of songwriting. When I last heard from him, he was even considering embarking on an operetta score. He also revealed he was homesick, so very homesick, for New York. Three weeks later, in March of 1968, came the news that Nicky was dead.

The Showman Supreme

There may be some who will dispute the claim that Florenz Ziegfeld was the greatest showman of modern times, but no one will deny that he was the pioneer of musical extravaganzas. Even his contemporaries Earl Carroll and George White were never quite able to attain the Ziegfeld stature, although Carroll left a handsome sum after his untimely death in a plane crash. White was reputed to have amassed more than 4 million dollars from his shows, only to dissipate it, chiefly through gambling. Ziegfeld himself died leaving a great name in show business but little in the way of earthly possession.

These days we have had spectacular musicals costing far more than those into which the Great Glorifier poured lavishly of backers' money—offerings that cost anywhere from $300,000 to $600,000 before they get off their feet.

Flo probably could boast of more solid hits than most producers before him, or since, though David Merrick and Hal Prince seem to have found the magic formula, and, in time, their output may better Ziegfeld's, because they're still young and still alive. Ziegfeld's career was interrupted by death in 1932, but what memorable shows he gave us to keep his memory alive, aside from the glorious series of *Follies, Rio Rita, Kid Boots* to *Showboat, Sally, Whoopee, et al.*

He was usually pessimistic before each opening and seemed overwhelmed by surprise as each show clicked and merrily brought dollars into the box office. Thus, just before the opening of *Rosalie,* he complained bitterly to librettist William Anthony McGuire. "This is going to be my biggest flop. I feel it." McGuire shook his head in mock sympathy. "Please," he said, "accept my condolences, in this, your darkest hour of success."

The Ziegfeld stamp on a showgirl immediately made her a Personage. She often went on to stardom—or at least to a certain amount of success in wedding a man of wealth or distinction.

Consider the imposing array: Peggy Hopkins Joyce, Paulette Goddard, Marilyn Miller, Imogene Wilson, Claire Luce, Hazel Forbes, Lina Basquette, June Knight, Gladys Glad, Lilyan Tashman, Marion Davies, Billie Dove—the list is almost endless.

The Ziegfeld touch was magic with the men stars, too, from Eddie Cantor and Will Rogers to Leon Errol and Fred Astaire.

And many, so many, ended up tragically. Gay Ziegfeld butterfly Myrna Darby died of sun poisoning. Olive Thomas (Jack Pickford's wife) took an overdose of a sleeping potion in Paris. Dorothy Dell rode to her death in an auto in Pasadena. Helen Walsh was burned to death in a fire aboard Harry Richman's yacht. Peggy Shannon was found dead at a kitchen table in North Hollywood, a half-burned cigarette still clutched tightly between her fingers. Her closest friend, who had joined the Follies with her, Cynthia Cambridge, once known as "Miss England," was tossed to her death from a horse in Hyde Park, London. Lillian Lorraine sank into dire poverty and lay on the bed of pain for years after an accident in which she broke her spine. Jessie Reed died in a charity ward in a Chicago hospital. Marilyn Miller succumbed to a rare toxic illness.

The stunningly beautiful Hilda Ferguson, at the height of a glamorous career, had two personal maids in attendance and a secretary in addition to a chauffeur whom she garbed in sky blue to match the color of her limousine. Her jewelry was estimated to be worth close to half a million dollars, and she boasted several suitors whose combined wealth would total twenty times that amount. But when she collapsed, an alcoholic at the foot of a dingy staircase in an obscure speakeasy, she was penniless and friendless. She died, lonely, forgotten, in a hospital ward, leaving no assets except a daughter who had inherited her mother's great beauty and who was to wed Canadian multimillionaire Duncan McMartin.

And Will Rogers was to meet sudden death in an ill-fated plane trip with Wiley Post in Point Barrow, Alaska, in the summer of 1935. Will took off on the flight despite the forebodings of Mrs. Rogers, who told him she felt "something awful" was going to happen. Rogers tried to soothe her fears, and finally, as the story goes, said, "Tell you what. I'll toss a coin. Heads I go, tails you can keep me here." When the spinning coin finally settled, heads up, Will grinned and said, "See—I win."

On the other hand, many Ziegfeld graduates fared less dismally. Peggy Hopkins Joyce made a career of marriage—and jewels; Hazel Forbes inherited millions when her husband died, went on to wed the star she worshipped, Harry Richman, only to divorce him later. Ruby Keeler married Al Jolson, then divorced him. Gladys Glad became Mrs. Mark Hellinger. Adele Astaire married into one of the great families of British nobility—became Lady Cavendish, with castles and wealth and social prestige.

Paulette Goddard married and divorced Charlie Chaplin and then Burgess Meredith, and is currently wed to German novelist Erich Maria Remarque, who wrote *All Quiet on the Western Front*. Louise Andrews became Mrs. Arthur "Bugs" Baer, Barbara Stanwyck married Frank Fay, and after their divorce, Robert Taylor, whom she also divorced.

But to get back to the Glorifier himself. In spite of the money that kept coming in from his shows, he spent as rapidly as he earned, and creditors were forever hounding him. At one period, he found himself on the verge of bankruptcy. Will Rogers, walking into his office, saw him writing a letter.

"Hey," roared Rogers. "What's this? I thought you never wrote letters. You've got the reputation for being the champion sender of telegrams. They say without you, Western Union would go under."

"If things keep up the way they are," moaned Ziggy, "I won't be sending telegrams ever again—I'll be delivering them."

Sally, Showboat and *Kid Boots* netted the showman more than a million dollars each, but he lived so extravagantly, spending so recklessly for everything from trinkets to diamonds to huge homes, that even in that period of almost no taxes his bank accounts were always perilously low. He had two gold telephones on his desk, his stream of telegrams averaged eight hundred words each, he traveled always in private railroad cars, carrying numerous trunks, each overflowing with expensive clothes, all of which explains why no one was surprised when it was learned that, to build the theatre which was to bear his name and be his monument, he had to borrow all the money.

After it was completed, and he was being congratulated, he once sighed to Eddie Cantor: "Oh, yes, I'm happy with it, but it has disadvantages. My creditors will know exactly where to find me now." Then he went off fishing, using as usual, gold fishhooks and a silver fishing rod!

Ziegfeld was intolerant of fellow showmen. He felt he was king, and he snubbed both Earl Carroll and George White as upstarts and imitators. I was in the 5 O'Clock Club one night when the band began playing a medley of hit songs from the *Vanities* in tribute to Earl Carroll, who was present. Ziegfeld entered and was being ushered to the table reserved for him when he heard the tunes. He wheeled around, followed by his amazed party, and stalked out.

This intolerance was even extended to that colorful figure of the theatre, George M. Cohan, who in turn resented Flo and his attitude so much that he would never permit a tune from a Ziegfeld show to be played in any theatre he controlled or at which he was playing.

The romances, which ended in marriage first with the piquant Anna Held and later with the vivacious Billie Burke, have become thricetold tales, and indeed, my former *Journal-American* fellow worker Marjorie Farnsworth developed the stories in great detail in her comprehensive history, *The Ziegfeld Follies.* Briefly, for those who still don't know the facts, Flo fell in love with Anna Held when the little French actress was starring in his first musical, *A Parlor Match.* He had imported her after hearing her sing "Won't You Come and Play Wiz Me?" They were divorced in 1921, after Flo confessed he had fallen in love with Billie Burke.

Ziggy first met Billie at a New Year's Eve masked affair. In the traditional "Paul Jones," where men and women form separate lines and march until a whistle halts them, whereupon they dance with the person in front of them, Billie found herself in the arms of a chap disguised as a tattered and bewhiskered tramp. Every time the whistle blew, she found herself opposite the same man—Ziegfeld, who had prearranged it with the whistle blower.

As the romance developed, and because there was no place where Flo felt he could be alone with the little red-haired star, he persuaded her to rendezvous with him at one spot he was certain no Broadwayite or anyone in their circle, would barge in on them—Grant's Tomb.

The Great Glorifier died in Santa Monica, California, on July 22, 1932, of a heart attack, only a few minutes before Billie Burke, rushing from her motion-picture chores in *A Bill of Divorcement* was able to reach his bedside. He was sixty-two.

Another dominant showman became the owner of the Ziegfeld Theatre which was to be the Glorifier's monument—Billy Rose, who was to die even while the theatre was being torn down to make room for a skyscraper business building—the theatre that was to be forevermore Ziegfeld's monument.

The Careless Librettist

Which brings me to William Anthony McGuire, who wrote so many of the librettos for the Ziegfeld hits. Among them were *Ziegfeld Follies of 1924,* which starred Will Rogers; *Kid Boots,* dominated by Eddie Cantor; *Rosalie,* with Marilyn Miller and Jack Donahue; *Whoopee,* with Eddie Cantor again; *The Three Musketeers,* with Dennis King and Vivienne Segal; *Smiles,* with Marilyn Miller and Fred and Adele Astaire; *Show Girl,* with Ruby Keeler and Clayton, Jackson and Durante.

It was quite a combination, McGuire and Ziegfeld. And they had much in common, for both were prodigal spenders. Ziegfeld's extravagances, as I have pointed out, and as the show world in general knew, kept him broke. Few were aware that McGuire struggled through his lifetime trying to catch up with his debts. There was no income, no matter how great, he couldn't live beyond. His money slipped away on the horses, the dice and the wheel.

It was easy for him to get money. Almost any producer was ready to meet his demands for an option on a Bill McGuire script. It is a fact he gave out so many options that he couldn't keep up with them, and the plays were never written. All the time, royalties were coming in in heaps of negotiable currency, for in addition to the Ziegfeld offers, McGuire was the author of some highly successful nonmusicals, among them, *Six Cylinder Love,* starring June Walker and Ernie Truex; *It's a Boy, If I Wuz Rich* (that one starred Joe Laurie, Jr.); *Twelve Miles Out,* with Frank Shannon and Warren Williams.

One day Bill ran into veteran producer Al Woods. "Hey," shouted Woods, "when are you going to finish that play you outlined to me?"

"What play?" asked McGuire.

"You know, the one about the rumrunner who commandeered someone's house on Long Island to store booze."

McGuire, who didn't even recall the plot, said meekly: "Oh, that one! You'll have it soon." He went home, started on the play, actually finished it, and then produced it himself. That was the end of a friendship with Woods.

When he died, it was reported his trunk yielded heaps of unfinished scripts, but I never did learn what became of them. It was fitting, of course, in view of their long and successful association, that McGuire was picked by Metro to turn out the

William Powell comments solemnly on Sobol's sartorial casualness — but insists that hat must go.

story of his pal's career, *The Great Ziegfeld,* which starred Luise Rainer and William Powell.

Clown in a Serious Mood

We were at Toots Shor's, and Jackie Gleason was in a magnanimous mood as he quaffed his ale with Falstaffian gulps and scornfully parried the ribald thrusts of that man-about-town, Host Toots. Jackie turned his broad back on his heckler and resumed: "Just like you say, I was the original pinch-hit kid. When anybody couldn't show up, they put the hurry call in for me, and awaaay I'd go, the dan-dan-dandy fill-in kid. You remember when they got me to come into the Park Avenue when Billy Daniels took sick? Every time someone like Frankie Hyers or Pat Harrington or Jack White couldn't make it at the 18 Club, it was little Jackie boy who stepped in and always saved the day. And for peanuts. Got so the minute I'd hear someone had a scratch or was bleeding from the nose, I'd be over to a joint, ready to go on."

I turned the conversation to his then current hassle with Milton Berle, observing that Berle's rating was dropping while Phil Silvers' was going up. "He's fading. The champ's ready for the towel," jeered a denigrator at our table.

Gleason turned serious. "Don't say that," he snapped. "This guy Berle was up there for seven long years, the Number One man. Seven years! That's a couple of lifetimes in this teevee racket. How many guys you think there are now—name any of them—me, too—who will be up there, blasting away with the funny stuff and holding on to the top like Berle did. I'm not in love with the guy, but he's got it, and he's still Mr. Big in my book.

"Tell you something else. Wasn't for Berle, a lot of us wouldn't have got a break either. When he became Mister Television, those network guys began saying: 'We gotta get comics. They want funny stuff. Let's get funnymen.' Whatever else you say about Berle, don't forget that. And don't count him out, don't ever count him out. He'll be in there pitching for a long time."

The waiter brought over another schooner of beer, and Gleason raised it in salute "To a great talent," he roared. "Me!" Toots Shor yelled "Wotcha ever do, ya bum?" Gleason shouted: "Gave your crummy joint some class by coming in here, ya bum!" Shor shrieked: "Who needs ya?" Gleason finished his beer, wiped his lips and sang out: "Will someone kindly remove this object? Close the cover over him tight.

"As I was saying," continued Jackie, "before I was so rudely interrupted by this bobby-soxer fan of mine, it's no cinch staying up there in this rat race. You have to keep delivering, week after week. And how many can stand the gaff? Tell you something else, some of the funniest guys we got around can't get the break on teevee. Like Henny Youngman and Gene Baylos, Joey Bishop and Jackie Miles. And there's some funny Joes over in the burlesque got more on the ball than some of the big shots that whoop it up on teevee and everyone makes a fuss about them.

"Funniest guy I know is Ben Lessy. Once Sammy Lewis wanted to team the both of us up in Slapsie Maxie's out in L.A. We had the same dressing room. When Ben was dressing, I'd look over at the sad puss of his, and it broke me up. I got cramps from laughing. He looked at me, and he broke up. We went out to do our turn, and we couldn't get nowhere—just kept laughing at each other. So we had to quit."

At this point, Shor broke in. "Funnyman," he sneered, "tell the nice people about Como." [At the time Perry Como on NBC opposite Gleason on CBS was topping Gleason in the ratings.] Jackie murmured "Como, Como? Oh, yes, they tell me it's quite a nice lake in Italy." (This colloquy, or rather monologue, took place in November of 1955, and despite Gleason's gloomy observation, he still remains a top banana on TV these dozen or more years later, as does millionaire Perry Como, although Como has seen fit to reduce his schedule to several major shows a year instead of the weekly grind. As for the comedians Jackie mentioned as having no exposure on TV, one of them at least, broke through to quite an enviable status—Joey Bishop.)

The Eccentric Genius

Few people will acknowledge freely that they are what we term eccentric characters. But Oscar Levant feels insulted if you regard him as completely normal. This sardonic wit, great musician, excellent actor and provocative writer has been termed his own worst enemy, but insists some enemies are more fascinating than boring friends.

I used to encounter Levant when he was part of the Broadway scene, usually at Dr. Leo Michel's place, the favorite drop-in haunt for many Broadwayites. One afternoon, though, when he spotted me seated in Michel's combination living room and reception room, reading a magazine, Levant mumbled, "Can't a patient have some privacy? What are you snooping around for?" He scowled and walked out of the room. But by this time I was accustomed to Oscar's peculiarities and didn't feel offended, and suspected the next time we met he might be gay and talkative and friendly.

For years, Levant cut his sardonic trail through Lindy's, Shor's, Reuben's and other gathering places in Manhattan until he drifted off to Hollywood and mingled with fellowmen at Chasen's and Romanoff's, then chief spawning grounds for savage wits. He convinced one and all in movieland, as he had us in New York, that his was not a gentle humor. He preferred the acid-dipped dirks of wit. As a result, Hollywood saw to it that in casting him for picture roles it would be for portrayals adhering to his reputation as a dour, caustic citizen. In fact, Levant often came to the aid of the scriptwriters by contributing his own dialog.

There are few men for whom Levant had any respect, or has to this day. An exception is Maestro Arturo Rubenstein, not because of his musical talents so much as because Rubenstein is one of the great raconteurs. And, of course, Oscar had great reverence for George Gershwin, who in fact was about the only one that could control the rebellious pianist-wit.

Oscar first came to the mild attention of the public as a

member of Ben Bernie's orchestra, although it could not have been too happy an association, because Bernie, something of a wit himself, used to discourage what he considered Levant's impertinence. Levant once recalled that while with Bernie he was robbed on Christmas Eve of his week's pay. When he arrived at the theatre that night, Clifton Webb, who was on the same bill, was distributing gifts to the boys in the band. Oscar's present was a wallet, and he exploded.

There are many stories that have been told about this eccentric genius—I have chronicled quite a few of them myself through the years—and some of them have been offered anew in the many profiles subsequently written about him. So if one or two of the anecdotes may sound like twicetold tales, I plead they deserve retelling.

For instance, the time he and Gershwin attended a screening of a major film in Hollywood, and the director asked, "How did you like it?"

"It's terrible," snarled Levant.

"Who are you to tell me it's terrible?" screamed the movie man.

Levant sneered. "Who," he demanded, "do you *have* to be?"

His first marriage a failure, Oscar married the beautiful June Gale, and to the surprise of their mutual friends, stormy as the marriage has been on occasions, they still remain a steadfastly married couple. June understands the fellow. Once he complained to a friend he knew that his wife, then pregnant, was poisoning the expected child's mind against him.

"You're crazy, how could she do that?" exclaimed the friend.

Moaned Levant: "I found her writing nasty notes about me—and swallowing them!"

Another man he respected and considered a friend was playwright George S. Kaufman. One time, visiting the Kaufmans, he fancied the playwright had insulted him. Furious, he rose, reached for his coat, buttoned it, and then snapped: "I'm not going."

"Why not?" demanded Kaufman.

"Because," said Oscar, "I have no place to go."

He had never been too careful about money, and before recognition arrived, and some juicy movie contracts, he was usually broke. When Harpo Marx kept begging him to come out to Hollywood and visit him, Oscar wrote back he couldn't because the fare was unavailable. Marx wired: "Come out to the sunshine.

I'll pay half your fare."

Levant wired back, collect: "In that case I'll meet you in Kansas City."

One night years ago, when I entered Chasen's, I saw Levant seated with a well-known but garrulous actor who was noted for dominating conversations. Having finished my meal, I was outside waiting for the attendant to bring around my car, when Oscar ran out.

"Hey, Louie!" he shouted. "What did you have for dinner tonight?"

I told him.

"Well," he moaned, "That's the nearest I'll come to eating tonight. I've been in there with that loose-mouth for two hours and couldn't get in a word to the waiter."

Once, while back in New York on a brief visit, he was walking out of Toots Shor's restaurant when a certain agent with a reputation for shady and sometimes treacherous dealings, came toward him. Levant boomed out heartily, "Hey, Joe, I'm on my way back to the Coast. How about giving me a quick double cross?"

Levant leaped into national fame as a member of the famed panel on radio's "Information Please," where he more than held his own in competition with fellow wits Franklin P. Adams (F.P.A.) and Clifton Fadiman. It was distressing in the years that followed to read of his battles with pills, and his apparently fruitless sessions with psychiatrists—for this is a supertalented fellow whom success has been eager to embrace and with whom many would like to become friends, if he'd only permit it.

I'm indebted to profilist Maurice Zolotow for one story. Back in 1949, Oscar and June were guests at a dinner at the White House. As they were saying their good-nights to President and Mrs. Harry Truman, Levant turned to his wife, and loudly, in tones of bored resignation, said, "Guess now it's our turn to have *them* for dinner!"

Once, at a party, Oscar was urged by guests please to settle down at the piano and pound out a few tunes for them. Levant pleaded a headache, lumbago, fallen arches, and insisted he was in no mood to play. Finally one young woman snapped: "If you don't want to be agreeable and play, Mr. Levant, I'm going to leave this party."

"Darling," murmured Oscar, "That is a most fascinating alternative."

The Saloon Wit

Saloonkeepers and restaurant and night-spot operators are not noted particularly for their sense of humor or their ability to toss out the merrie quip. There is one exception, Nicky Blair, affectionately labeled by intimates as "The Colonel." A dapper, good-looking affable gentleman, through the years Nicky built up a solid reputation for himself as one of the town's keenest wits and almost the equal of the late Florenz Ziegfeld as a connoisseur of beautiful women—not for personal reasons as much as for adornment of his lavish cabaret productions.

Even during the height of his eminence as entrepreneur of dominant cabarets, he would beam as he recalled his starvation days, and how he hustled for the elusive dollar with a ready quip on his lips, and holes in his socks and shoes.

More than anyone else, he is to be accused of starting the Gold Rush for performers when he shelled out to comedian Milton Berle a salary and percentage that averaged between $10,000 and $12,000 a week—an unheard-of sum then for a night-spot performer in New York. This was at the Carnival, and Berle remained on for a record run—forty weeks. Preceding him had been comedienne Martha Raye, quite overwhelmed with her $5,000 weekly salary. After Berle, came the slapstick team of Olsen and Johnson, who were quite content with their $10,000 weekly.

This was the same Blair who in other days winced when he had Berle as an attraction at his Paradise restaurant, and was forced to pay him $1,500 per week, though other stellar lures in some of his previous clubs, Helen Morgan, Ruth Etting, Morton Downey and Helen Kane, never could nick him for more than $1,000.

This amiable citizen who talks like "Bugs" Baer writes, whose wittiest thrusts pierced the Depression gloom when his business was in the doldrums, was solicited by none less than Jack Benny to quit the saloon business and become his Number One gag-writing boy.

Nicky and I started a rather precarious friendship when he barred me from an opening at his plush Casanova Club because I was in brown mufti and the command had gone out that for this occasion only dinner suits or swallowtails were acceptable.

During the Speakeasy era, Nicky had frequent brushes with the impetuous enforcement lads. In 1926, they raided his Texas

Tommy Club with axes, shouts and threats. In 1927, they raided the 300 Club in which Texas Guinan was his partner and star. In 1928, Nicky, then running the original Helen Morgan Club (there was another one later on) went on a yachting trip and came back to find his place padlocked and wrecked because of the overzealous axe-wielding cohorts of Mabel Willebrandt.

It was then that he opened the Casanova Club on the site of the old 300. Among his subsequent stars were Van and Schenck, Jack Buchanan, Jessie Matthews, Ruth Etting, Morton Downey, Ramon and Rosita, and just as Helen Kane was energetically boop-boop-a-dooping, in barged raiders again.

In 1932, he opened the big cabaret known as the Paradise restaurant and operated it until 1939, when the Depression forced him to close the doors. Then he shifted over to the Billy Rose enterprises, becoming general manager for his rival. They parted amicably in 1944, when Nicky opened the Carnival with Toots Shor as a silent, minor-interest partner. Toots, when Nicky was running the Paradise, used to drop in nightly, penniless and discouraged, to gain some cheer from Nicky's wisecracks.

In the dying days of the Paradise, a high-spending playboy, Russell Ryder, used to come in nightly and hand out hundred-dollar gratuities to hatcheck girls, captains, waiters and busboys, although the tab at his table might not exceed twenty dollars. With little money coming in during those final days of the cabaret, Blair used to stand at the door of the washroom, trying to look like the attendant in order to snare one of those century notes.

There was always a close bond between Nicky and Toots Shor, strengthened by the fact that Nicky had married beautiful Joan Burgess and Toots had married equally beautiful although tinier Marion (Baby) Vogt, and both girls had been "classmates" in the last of Flo Ziegfeld's *Follies.*

Another close friend was producer George White, and in the happier years when White was a millionaire, Nicky, in his leisure time between raids, used to follow the sun with him. Once he and White went to Palm Beach and were invited by banker Otto Kahn to be his houseguests. At dinner the first night, after the brandy and cigars were passed, Kahn inquired, "Is there anything else special you boys would like?"

Nicky answered promptly: "Well, yes. How about a little spending money?"

The banker thought that was the funniest remark, and for

the rest of the stay, Nicky was the unofficial court-jester at his parties.

Nicky once dropped into Toots Shor's restaurant with his son Eddie, then about twelve. The lad sought advice from Toots. "Hey, can you tell me why everybody makes such a fuss about Roddie Rockefeller? He goes to my school in Riverdale and he plays on my football team. He plays okay, but shucks, he's no all-American in my book."

Nicky interposed, "Well, his pop is kind of important."

"Important," screamed Toots, making certain that General "Hap" Arnold and General Emmett (Rosey) O'Donnell, who were at the adjoining table, could hear every word. "Lis'n Eddie. I own a saloon. Your pop owns a saloon. Well, this Rockefeller kid's pop used to own a saloon right down the block a bit across the street, the Rainbow Room. You wanna know somethin'? The joint is closed. The kid's pop couldn't make the grade as a saloon-keeper."

Nicky drifted into the restaurant business finally when he opened the Blair House. For a while, his personal popularity brought in the customers, but the dining-out New York populace is fickle, and finally this venture went on the rocks.

It was while he was hosting the Blair House that Nicky started distributing a "business card" poking some good-natured fun at two then new and much-publicized additions to the collection of restaurants in Manhattan, Trader Vic's and The Forum of the Twelve Caesars. In part the card advised: "When in New York visit Traitor Nick's—enjoy the exotic booze. For your special parties may we suggest our private room—The Collossear Room of the 6 Caesars (capacity 40 Romans). Dine with the living Caesars—Irving Caesar (songwriter), Sid Caesar (TV star), Little Caesar (Edward G. Robinson), Caesar Salad (king of all salads), Morris Caesar (804 6th Avenue—Cleaning & Dyeing). We are not connected with any other Traitors."

Currently, as I write this, Blair is still pouring out his witty sallies as host of one of the entertainment rooms at the Eden Roc Hotel in Miami Beach.

Broadway Doctor

We have many novels and films about physicians, chiefly

about the homespun experiences of country doctors. However, Hollywood has neglected the story of a physician who never drove a horse and buggy over country roads to bring a new life into the world, or braved sleet and flood to mend a broken bone. But what about the Broadway doctor, and one in particular, Dr. Leo Michel? His was a different type of saga. For close to sixty years he devoted himself to the temperamental children of show business. Surely, as the bereaved wife in *Death of a Salesman* cries out about Willy Loman, attention must finally be paid to such a person.

His countless patients and friends who were devoted to the kindly though highly erratic physician, a frustrated showman, himself, included such diversified citizens as Damon Runyon, society columnist Maury Paul (the original Cholly Knickerbocker), illustrators Harrison Fisher and Henry Clive, songwriters Lew Brown, Buddy De Sylva, Arthur Swanstrom, champions Jack Dempsey and Max Baer, producers Sam Harris and George M. Cohan, comedians Eddie Cantor, Phil Baker, Oscar Levant, Georgie Jessel and many others.

The story of Doc Michel would revolve in part around the obscure performers whom he first encouraged to keep trying, on whose behalf he hounded producers into giving them a break, of the many to whom he shelled out his own money so that they might take singing or dancing lessons.

The love interest, of course, would be furnished by his long-run courtship of musical comedy star Ada Mae Weeks, about whom he would occasionally comment: "I have been in love with five girls in my lifetime—all of them were Ada Mae." When she finally married Count Castegnaro of Venice, Michel for a time wooed comedienne Vicki Cummings.

Adventure, humor, pathos, thrills, mystery—all the ingredients are there for the book or the play about the good doctor. There was the time he rode a freight train through a howling blizzard into Boston to prevent a morose young star from killing herself. Once a man walked into his office and asked how much he would pay for a human head, and before the startled Michel could answer, started to slash his throat with a razor. The doctor fought with him for more than an hour and finally quieted him. Then he talked him out of trying to commit suicide. He soothed estranged couples, paid out of his own pocket for the hospitalization of impecunious chorus girls, supported actors down on their luck and often secured roles for them. As I have mentioned elsewhere, his was always open house at all hours of the days. During his office hours, folks dropped in anyway, lounging around in the large living room and helping themselves freely from the bar.

Some outstanding song hits were composed on Michel's piano. Vincent Youmans, Arthur Swanstrom and Ray Henderson tapped out the first threads of tunes destined for world acceptance while on friendly visits to the hospitable medico. Michel once had a canary (a present from Ada Mae) which was consulted by the tunesmiths as some people consult astrologists and fortune-tellers. You played your tune, and if the canary picked up the melody, you were almost assured of a hit. If the canary remained mum, then you might just as well discard the melody, and start all over again.

Lorenz Hart got the inspiration for the Rodgers-Hart *Babes in Arms* musical from a casual conversation he had with the doctor. One incident concerning a pearl necklace furnished Mark Hellinger with the plot for half a dozen columns, with variations. The striking mural over the bar in the doctor's living room was painted by Henry Clive in the Rubaiyat motif. It was Harry Hershfield who named Michel "Angel of Broadway"—corny, perhaps, but a fairly accurate description of a man who sacrificed the major part of his fortune aiding folks on the Lighted Thoroughfare.

Once Ziegfeld's dance director, Seymour Felix, decided turnabout was justified, and after several rebuffs, finally persuaded the doctor to have dinner at his home, warning, since he knew Michel's habit of being surrounded by people, to come alone. At seven o'clock, four strangers dropped in. "Is Doc Michel here yet?" they asked. At seven thirty there were nineteen uninvited guests. At eight o'clock the doctor himself arrived, with six more friends. By eight thirty, there were close to a hundred people crowding into the Felix household. Michel had hinted casually to everyone he encountered that the Felixes were tossing a dinner for him and said, "Come up if you have nothing to do."

The distraught director finally telephoned Reuben's to cater a special banquet; then he phoned a few musician friends to come quickly to make up a little orchestra—and the party roared on. The following day the Felixes left for an extended cruise. Understandably, they didn't even bother to send the good doctor a postcard.

Michel and I often dueled on the golf course, especially during summer weekends at the famed Catskills mountain resort

Grossinger's. In his late seventies the sturdy doctor still managed to beat me time and again, though I was some thirty years younger. Even at eighty, he was still playing golf and still taking in his daily swim at the City Athletic Club.

Tragedy marred his final years. His only brother, a lawyer, Joseph Michel, and a woman companion were murdered in Acapulco, and the spark went out of the bighearted physician. He died not too long after, in October of 1960, aged eighty-five.

The Ageless Belle

There has rarely been a gayer member of what is termed Cafe Society than the bubbling chatterbox Fannie Ward, who, even in her late seventies, always entered a night spot or a party with the bounce of an eighteen-year-old. Hers was never the most quiet voice in the room, and you could hear her most intimate conversation two dozen yards away. She always dressed like a young deb, and her hats were the type best described as being heard as well as seen.

She was probably among the first women to undergo plastic surgery to remove telltale wrinkles. Her face-lifts were repeated periodically, but she kept insisting it was merely a proper manipulation of muscles—with an occasional use of a "Siberian snow face-mask." She often hailed me when I entered the Stork Club or El Morocco, always hinting she had some choice bit of gossip to tell. Actually, it was usually something right out of the morning tabloids.

Miss Ward, who had appeared in quite a number of plays in New York in the nineties, married a wealthy British diamond dealer and moneylender, Joseph Lewis, in 1898, but divorced him in 1913 and married an actor, Jack Dean. This was evidently a happy merger, for they were inseparable during the years when I began seeing them around. Dean rarely spoke and merely sat quietly and listened while Fannie as usual talked on and on. When he died in 1950, she was missing from the usual night haunts for months, and it was reported she had become a bit melancholy. Some years previously, similarly, she had gone into seclusion when her daughter, Lady Plunket, was killed in an air crash. And I recall that was the only time I had ever heard her speak with despair. "I've lived too long, too long," she said.

But when she returned to the night frivolity after that mourning period, Fannie Ward was back on the same rounds, as much of a chatterbox as before but now insisting she was going to write her memoirs. She must have been on the threshold of the eighties by then—at least in the late seventies—and her face, despite the "treatments," was showing the ravages of age. But she retained the old-time vanity. One night at El Morocco she called me over. "I haven't told anyone," she whispered, "But have a drink to me, this is my birthday. I'm seventy." This was back in 1951, and recalling she had once told me she was born in 1872, I started to ask whether she wasn't a bit confused in her mathematics, but I checked myself in time.

Six months later, Fannie Ward, the "eternal soubrette," was dead. Some papers gave her age as eighty-two, others, more kindly, placed it at "approaching eighty." But Fannie was beyond caring. Her personal possessions—furs, gowns and her bed with cherubs hovering over the head—were sold at auction with only a few bidders present. The auctioneer was an impatient fellow who probably never had met the vivacious Fannie. "Let's get on with it," he kept shouting. "I want to get rid of this junk, but fast."

The Kingfish

This is an hitherto untold story about the late Huey Long. At a gathering in Manhattan, he had met a lovely young artist, Cleanthe Carr, daughter of a one-time well-known cartoonist, Gene Carr. Cleanthe, a few days later, executed a derisive caricature of the Louisiana dictator, and comedian-accordionist Phil Baker, a friend of both, had decided Long ought to view the drawing and persuaded him to accompany him to Cleanthe's apartment. So the Senator, his tall bodyguard, Phil and Peggy Baker and I drove over.

Not without considerable trepidation, the young artist brought out the caricature. It presented Huey, his hair in wild disarray, his ample mouth distorted cavernously, his hand flourishing dramatically, his nose snooted up almost piglike. He was evidently supposed to be engaged in one of his vehement harangues. I shuddered as I studied the picture, and Baker groaned to me, "Why didn't I keep my big trap shut?"

Huey stared at the drawing for almost two minutes in silence and then let out a war whoop. "By God," he roared, "by jiminy Hellfire, if that ain't the best I ever seen. Honey, that sho' is something, now ain't it? God, that's blankety-blank, ahma-a-zin'! No foolin', you didn't do that yo'self? Yo' must love me!"

The Kingfish continued. "I remember I was to a dinnah party, and the gal sittin' on my left, she kept kinda glarin' at me and scowlin', and all of a sudden, she reached for a bottle. So help me, she reached for a bottle and was just goin' to make a pass at me and ah caught her arm. 'What!' ah asked her, 'What in fool's name yo' want to hit me with the bottle for, you fool chile?' ah sez to her. And you know what she sez to me, she says, 'Huey Long, I guess it's because ah love you!' Well, ah didn't know that lady and ah don't know you too well but lookin' at his ma-ar-velous libelous picture of me, ah guess it's because yo' love me, honey."

A nice friendship blossomed between Cleanthe and the Kingfish, and it led to a literary alliance—that is, Huey commissioned the girl to draw the illustrations for the book which he had just completed, *My First Days in the White House*. Cleanthe completed most of the drawings in five days, and during that period she and the Senator were in constant conference. The one which aroused the most enthusiasm on the part of Long revealed him, as President, in session with members of his Cabinet: Herbert Hoover sitting stiffly, plum-faced and looking straight ahead, William Borah whispering into Long's ear while he gazed in amusement at Franklin D. Roosevelt seated sadly in a corner, with Al Smith in turn casting disdainful eyes in Rossevelt's direction.

On his return to Louisiana, the Kingfish phoned Cleanthe two or three times daily, cautioning her to be careful of her diet, to shun cigarettes and "Hey, don't pull yo' punches on those pictures. Keep them hot, chile!"

Early in September of 1935 he phoned from Louisiana, and his voice conveyed he was deeply depressed. Cleanthe told me she had said to him, "You sound low. Anything wrong?" And he answered: "Chile, there's nothing wrong with me—nor with the world. Everything's fine—ah'll be back in New York, and we'll celebrate the book. Jus' talk to me now and tell me somethin' funny, hey, chile."

Cleanthe didn't hear from him again or ever see him again. Six days later, Huey Long was shot to death.

13

Stories Out of a Grab Bag

I DON'T KNOW WHETHER novelist John O'Hara resumed cordial relations with Ernest Hemingway before the latter's tragic death, but for some years there had been a coolness between them. George Jean Nathan once revealed to me just what had brought about the rupture. It seems Hemingway and O'Hara were in a Third Avenue saloon when John proudly displayed a blackthorn cane that had come from Ireland. "This cane is solid, unbreakable," he insisted. "It's like the Irish themselves—solid, unbreakable."

Hemingway said, "Let's see that stick, John." And then placing it in back of his shoulders, snapped it in two. "Nothing is so solid that it's unbreakable, not even the Irish," he said with a grin. According to Nathan, O'Hara went white, bitterly denounced Hemingway, and turned his back on him to indicate they were no longer friends.

Months later, while Hemingway was in Ireland, he bought a blackthorn cane, and on his return to New York, he sought out O'Hara and presented it to him, with appropriate belated apologies. John was highly pleased, and all seemed well with the two again. "This one," said O'Hara, "is even sturdier, I can see. I'll have this one with me for the rest of my life."

"Well, then," I interrupted Nathan, "I guess, they're pals again."

"No, not at all," replied the critic. "What happened then was this. Hemingway said: 'Let me feel that stick again, John.' John handed it over. Hemingway said: 'As I've been trying to convince you, John, for your own good, nothing is unbreakable. Not the Irish, not the British, not the Americans—not the spirit—not even this solid stick.' And he placed it back of his shoulders and promptly snapped it in two!"

Mr. O'Hara, according to Nathan, failed to appreciate Mr. Hemingway's "philosophy." Hemingway apparently lost one of his admirers forever.

Back in 1925, before socialite Ellin Mackay became Mrs. Irving Berlin, she wrote a piece for the then struggling *New Yorker* magazine. It revolved about her generation of society. From Hollywood came a bid to editor Harold Ross offering $50,000 for the movie rights, half of which would go to the magazine, the other $25,000 to Miss Mackay.

Ross phoned her. "It's a lot of money," he said, "and we certainly here at *The New Yorker* could use it, the way we're going, but if you want my friendly advice, let's not accept it."

Surprised, Miss Mackay asked, "But why? I don't understand."

"Because," said Ross, "the honest truth, if you can take it, is the article had nothing in it of movie value. So they're giving us that fat sum for one reason—they want to exploit your name. You don't want to go through life with that on your conscience—selling out your fine name, do you?"

Ross's fatherly admonition evidently swayed young Miss Mackay for, whether reluctantly or not, she agreed to forget the tempting bid.

The legend has persisted that Franklin D. Roosevelt's favorite melody was "Home on the Range," and it is a fact that the late President himself, when you asked him quickly to nominate his favorite tune, would just as quickly reply, "Home on the Range." Some twenty years or so ago I exposed the reason F. D. R. had a pet song.

When society orchestra leader Meyer Davis and his band were invited to play at a White House party, the publicity man Harry Sobol wrote to Roosevelt's secretary, Marvin McIntyre, requesting that he advise as to the President's song preference. McIntyre wrote back that as far as he knew the President had no particular choice. The press agent did have one, himself, however, and so he decided that "Home on the Range" fitted the Presidential personality and planted advance stories to that effect.

So it was that at the party when Roosevelt entered the room with Eleanor, the band struck up the tune. F. D. R., who had read some of the advance stories, tapped his case enthusiastically and roared: "Fine, Meyer, fine. I love that song." During the entertainment later, Eddie Peabody gripped his banjo and scraped out his lively version of the melody. After that the world—and Roosevelt himself—were convinced that "Home on the Range" was the one song that the President really did favor.

The spin of the wheel, the toss of the dice, the breath of the wind—take your choice of a dozen clichés indicating that Fate is a fickle jade, hey, hey! There was a blind chap who wrung your heart as you listened to him in front of theatres singing medleys from the musical offerings being featured inside as he accompanied himself expertly on his accordion.

On this particular night, he was in front of the Alvin Theatre delivering the chants from *Porgy and Bess* when George Gershwin, composer of the memorable score, emerged. Gershwin himself told me the story. He felt deeply moved, and prodded by a sudden impulse, started toward the singing musician to ask some questions. The woman who invariably accompanied the man—it may or may not have been his wife—darted toward Gershwin, took him by the hand and brought him over to the blind man.

"Booshe," she whispered, "feel. This is George Gershwin."

The accordionist without sight groped until his hands felt the composer's face.

"George, you know who I am?" he asked. "Try and think."

Gershwin hesitated.

The blind man said, "Goldfarb. Remember P.S. 25?"

Gershwin shivered involuntarily. He remembered.

"We were classmates," he revealed, as he told me the story. "You can't imagine how I felt. We were about twelve or maybe thirteen at the time, and already Goldfarb was quite a pianist. I envied him and asked him maybe he'd be good enough to take me to his piano teacher. He did, and I took lessons from his teacher. I had great ambitions in those days, but his were even greater—and rightly so, for he was, and I imagine he still is, a true musician."

Blindness darkened Goldfarb's life, and he ended up a street musician, usually concluding his evening concerts with his former classmate's song "I Got Plenty of Nuthin'."

It was probably the most unusual wedding in Manhattan's romantic history—the marriage, January 27, 1941, of Kapa Davidoff and beautiful Lubov Brunelle. The ceremony itself, adhering rigidly to the Russian ritual, took place at the Russian Orthodox Church on Madison Avenue at 119th Street. Grand Duchess Marie acted as "foster mother" to the bride. Those are the cold facts.

The warm, romantic, bizarre and cockeyed facts are these. Kapa Davidoff was once the husband of attractive Tamara Geva, ballerina and actress, who married Kapa after she had divorced choreographer George Balanchine. Before his marriage to Tamara, Kapa's wife had been the lovely Lucia Davidova. When Tamara and Kapa split, she and Lucia became intimate friends, and not infrequently Davidoff and his two ex-wives made the rounds as a happy threesome.

So it was natural that, before deciding that Lubov Brunelle should be his third bride, Kapa conferred with both Tamara and Lucia and won their wholehearted approval. And, of course, they were among those present at the wedding.

Kapa Davidoff was not a conventional man. For the nuptial reception and celebration after the wedding ceremonies, his good friend, the champion horseman Prince Soltan Guirey, a former Caucasian officer in the service of the late Czar, transformed his huge riding academy, Boots and Saddles, on Ninety-first Street, into a festive hall.

There, following the ancient Russian custom, which decrees that the mother of either bride or groom shall greet the newlyweds by offering the traditional bread and salt, Grand Duchess Marie herself, as "foster mother," was at the entrance to the riding academy, with a huge tray covered with thick slices of black bread and small pinches of salt. The party sizzled with gaiety. There was food and there was drink. Vodka and champagne flowed as freely and generously as a spring freshet. Toasts were murmured or roared and glasses were smashed.

To those who were not acquainted with them, Kapa introduced his lovely bride and his beautiful ex-brides.

"Meet," he would say, "Tamaraska, my wife. She was my second wife."

Or: "Have you met Lusha, my wife? Not today's wife. My first wife."

And Lubov Brunelle Davidoff, Kapa's third beloved, nodded in blushing approval.

The party grew even gayer.

Tamara Geva and Lucia Davidova each locked an arm with Kapa Davidoff and pulled him to a corner. Tamara said: "Kapa, now you are again a husband. Now again you have a wife, a beautiful, understanding, lovely wife. Be kind to her, Kapa."

"Yes," implored Lucia. "Lubov is so nice. You are lucky to have someone so nice and quiet like Lubov. Be good."

"What's the matter with you?" demanded Kapa Davidoff. "I love Lubov. I am mad for Lubov. She is my wife, my darling, my precious, my beautiful wife. What kind of talk is this—be kind, be good?"

(This colloquy as I present it was revealed to me by Tamara, herself.)

Suddenly the little conference was interrupted by shouts and applause. There, on the back of a white horse was Lubov Brunelle in her flowing bridal gown of white, riding straight toward them. Another guest leaped upon the horse's back. He stood upright precariously, waving his glass of champagne and roaring for a toast to the bride. They rode around the transformed rink, Lubov gaily flourishing her bridal veil, tossing kisses, smiling at one and all while the unknown cavalier, still managing to stand on the horse's broad haunches like a circus trick-rider, kept shouting his toast.

Kapa studied his bride with prideful swimming eyes.

"Isn't she," he asked Tamara Geva and Lucia Davidova, "the most wonderful wife a man ever had? She is my heart, my life."

A tall young man holding a glass of champagne in one hand and vodka in another passed by Tamara two or three times, on occasion shaking his head and asking querulously: "Why—why?"

The party lasted until late the following morning, and as Tamara Geva left, she suddenly recalled that Bride Number Three, Lubov Brunelle, was one of the backers of *Cabin in the Sky,* which Tamara's first husband, George Balanchine, had staged. Then it was she realized there should have been another guest to complete the bizarre cycle—Ballerina Vera Zorina, who had succeeded her as Balanchine's wife, and George himself. Later she learned they had been invited but had sent their regrets.

These then are the warm romantic, bizarre and cockeyed facts about a Russian wedding which took place in our town.

Maury Paul, who was the original Cholly Knickerbocker of the Hearst papers, was no respecter of lofty personages. He often tossed good-natured ribbing in the direction of the queen of the social set, the dowager Mrs. Cornelius Vanderbilt. For a time, he kept referring to the beige fox fur piece which always adorned her in public appearances. He called it a "poor, overworked pelt" and hinted that the "union of fox fur pieces should rebel."

One night at the opera, Mrs. Vanderbilt encountered Maury. She urged him to step closer and give her a hand, which gallantly he did. Whereupon she took off her fur piece and maneuvered the head so that it bit into the columnist's hand.

"That," she snapped, "is the way one 'overworked pelt' feels about your insults."

Maury managed to get an item out of the incident, however, for Mrs. Vanderbilt went on to explain that actually she possessed seven beige fox neck furs, all created for her by a famed Parisian furrier. "You speak of unions," she said, "well, let me tell you this. Each of my fur pieces works only one day, and then gets six days' rest."

Not all of Charles MacArthur's plays were what might be termed Broadway smashes, and he had less than glowing illusions about any of his contributions to the theatre. He once told me he had refused to read a single review of his short-lived trifle *Johnny on a Spot,* but had asked George S. Kaufman whether any of the notices had been in the slightest degree perhaps constructive.

"Charlie," answered Kaufman, dourly, "truthfully, none of them was constructive. Perhaps, the word should be 'destructive.'"

"I always felt," said MacArthur, "that a playwright with a bad play is like a ballplayer who has just struck out—only in this case the umpire throws a bat at him."

Incidentally, on the night of the opening, which was just after the attack on Pearl Harbor, MacArthur encountered George Jean Nathan at the Algonquin. Nathan, who hadn't dealt too kindly with the play, said, "Hello," but Charlie triumphantly waved a newspaper at him, exposing a screaming headline on page one—"MacArthur Expects Vicious Attack!"

The late Tommy Manville, Jr., much-wedded multimillionaire (eleven wives), was a citizen who adored publicity during most of his bizarre career. There was a time when he phoned me and asked what I would suggest as the best way to obtain the services of a good lawyer. Without stopping to think, I advised, "Why don't you advertise?" and promptly forgot the matter. A few days later in most of the Manhattan newspapers appeared a full-page ad to the effect that the services of a good lawyer were sought—signed, "Tommy Manville, Jr."

Shortly thereafter, Mr. Manville sued me and my paper for 5 million dollars—the top figure ever demanded to that point in a libel suit. This was after our entry into World War II. The charge was that I had impugned his patriotism by observing in my column that "It would be nice if Tommy Manville, Jr., would allocate some of the money he is spending for baubles for blondes to the fund being raised by our paper to buy a battleship."

The case was tossed out of court, with the judge observing acidly that it was shameful to have the court's time preempted by such a silly suit.

A week later, I encountered Manville in "21," and was endeavoring to brush by him when he grabbed me by an arm and exclaimed with great geniality, "Hey, Louie—you're not snubbing an old friend, are you?" Icily, I asked how could I consider him a friend after that libel suit. "Oh," said Manville, cheerily, "My lawyer told me we would get publicity all over the country—Page One headlines—if I sued for five million dollars." Then he added sadly: "Not a single paper reported it—not one. That Eli Johnson gave me a bad steer."

"Eli Johnson!" I exclaimed. "Was that the lawyer you got through the newspaper ads?" And Manville nodded. It just so happened that Johnson and I had been classmates in Crosby High in Waterbury, Connecticut, and in his senior year, in fact, I had helped him bone up on his Latin so he could pass the exams. Johnson later explained to me ruefully: "I knew the case didn't have a chance, but I didn't see that it could do you any harm, except to give you a little publicity as well as Manville. I had to do something for the big fee he was paying me."

One could get maudlin, I suppose, and squeeze out a tear over the changes that have occurred on Broadway, in Hollywood, or for that matter in Chicago, St. Louis or even Rome, London and Paris. It's a phony sentiment at best, and nostalgic yearnings are only a synthetic anodyne for current frets.

Nevertheless, some months ago as I strolled along Broadway, I did recall a conversation I had once with an enterprising showman, Joe Moss, who was quite a dominant figure in our town as the operator of two of our more exciting cabarets, the Hollywood Restaurant and the International Casino. It was a discussion in which not only were staggering figures mentioned—the profits he anticipated, the salaries he was willing to pay—but in which he also expressed his pride in the fact that so many of the big stars of the entertainment world were eager for engagements in his cabarets. He mentioned the rise to greater glory of two of his former attractions, Rudy Vallee and Alice Faye. But he didn't mention the name of one vaudevillian who had been presented to him by an agent as a worthy performer—a lively young comedian who wanted so much to headline one of the bills in either night spot. Moss had told the agent he doubted that the fellow had sufficient prestige or even talent to be a draw.

Raising money at a benefit for the Red Cross Flood Relief Fund, which the author sponsored, we find this group quite happy with the results. *From left to right:* the late Joe Moss at whose cabaret, the Hollywood Restaurant, the benefit was held; the late Ted Husing, radio sports commentator; Ethel Merman, Bob Hope and Sobol. Moss was one of the town's pioneer cabaret men. His other place, the International Casino, was reputed at the time to be the most opulent in its decor of any cabaret in America. Both places are memories—replaced by clothing stores.

Some years later, the two big cabarets passed out of Joe Moss's control, and out of the Broadway scene. Joe himself drifted from one enterprise to another. He had been recognized as the dude of all nightclub men of his time, patronizing the best and most expensive tailors, so it was ironic that the buildings which had housed the cabarets eventually were occupied by ready-to-wear men's clothing stores.

And what started me recalling my talk with Moss was running into the very young comedian he had rejected, standing in front of where once had been the Hollywood Restaurant. He was studying the clothing display—and passersby stared at Bob Hope, some with awe.

Some twenty years ago at a cocktail party at the Hampshire House, I watched a beautiful woman in action. Around her crowded magazine editors, columnists, men and women radio and television commentators, authors and a few high dignitaries from the cinema world, most of them pouring out their admiration for her. Women present conceded she was easily the most fashionably attired among them and envied the manner in which she wore her expensive outfit. One movie critic asked me if I didn't think she looked "positively radiant under that positively thrilling hat" and of course I answered, "Positively!"

The slim, beautiful, enchanting woman was a top-flight movie star, and the party was being held in her honor. But I went back in memory a decade or so and remembered a dowdy, stoutish, fumbling young girl, never too sure of herself. She was trying to get a foothold in Broadway then, hoping for something that might lead to recognition instead of passes by obscure louts who saw her only as a girl in the chorus who might welcome their amorous attention.

One of her nightclub bosses, Lou Schwartz, suggested that she change her name, Billie Cassin, to something a bit more flossy. So she became Lucille LeSueur. She began going through a strenuous dieting regime, slimmed down drastically and finally landed a small part in a picture in Hollywood. Everyone knows the rest of the story.

What puzzled me on this night at the Hampshire House when she was being honored was that the now big-time Hollywood star had a haunted look—as if she suspected it was all so temporary. And even to this day, when I run into Joan Crawford, she still seems to have that same haunted look. I still don't understand why.

This is the tale about a dancing lad and a literate girl and how their romance blossomed. He was a tall, skinny "Reuben, Reuben, I've Been Thinking" type of chap who tossed himself around in gravity-defying dances so you'd think the big hayseed would break his precious neck or at least a kneecap. The girl was pretty, had a sharp wit and was filled with ambition. I took her one night to a literary party that Horace Liveright was hosting at the time when he was one of the town's leading book publishers. As we mingled with prominent authors, the girl remarked that some day she hoped the man she married would be a writer. "I'd get behind a fellow like that and push him into working and turning out worthwhile stuff," she insisted. "A woman can do a lot for her man besides baby him."

Well, this did seem like a threadbare and corny bit of philosophy, and I told her so. Some weeks later, at a night at Dr. Leo Michel's place, this girl sat down and played the piano and sang out happy little songs with lyrics she had authored herself. This dancing fellow, who was just about coming along then in show business, was there that night, and they met for the first time. I can't say, because I don't know to this day, whether they made much of an impression on each other, but I do recall that I asked the girl later if she had seen him work. "Sister," I said, "if you want to see educated feet in action, you ought to catch his act." She sniffed and said haughtily something to the effect that "It's the educated mind that appeals to me."

They met frequently thereafter, usually at Doc Michel's, for as I have mentioned elsewhere, his combined apartment and office was the gathering place for so many of us those days. It was evident that these two, the dancing boy and the witty girl from California, weren't hitting it off too well, chiefly because she of the many talents was aloofish, and he was shy. There was a book-writing citizen present one night, and after a few drinks it was really a treat to watch him put in his pitch for the lovely lady. They sat around, and whenever I edged close, I would hear the talk swirl about Bernard Shaw and George Gershwin, H. G. Wells and Beethoven's sonatas. I thought, well here she is, right in her proper element—and here's just the fellow for her. An up-and-coming author, a bachelor, or rather to be accurate, a free man by virtue of a recent divorce. This was Romance in the making, a good match.

I lost contact with the principals for a time. The author was busy with his newest book. It became a best seller, and sold for a handsome sum to the movies. The dancing lad was growing more important in the show world. And the girl, if she did get back to Doc Michel's, apparently picked nights when I had engagements elsewhere.

There came, though, some months later, a night when the dancing lad was starring at Nicky Blair's Carnival. As he leaped across the stage, swinging those long, loose arms around, crashing to the floor on his knees or stepping lightly into a nostalgic throw-back to a soft-shoe beat—with the crowded room pounding palms and roaring approval, I spotted the girl of the many talents. The fellow who wrote books wasn't with her—just a few close friends.

After the show, she went backstage to join Ray Bolger, the lad of the educated feet. And the girl, Gwen Rickard, asked him how soon he'd be ready for their two thirty snack at Reuben's. She had every right to ask, for she was now Mrs. Ray Bolger.

[Editor's note: I debated whether to identify the principal in the following story but decided not to for she is still active—and very, very sensitive.]

There was a night when a one-time glittering star was seated at a tiny table with an escort in what was then labeled "Siberia" in El Morocco—the old El Morocco when the late John Perona was the suave host. It was a section to which tourists were usually directed. The former star seemed fretful, and the man sharing drinks with her observed with dismay that she was paying little attention to his remarks.

In the woman's glorious past, there had been something about her that was imperious and arrogant. This night, in contrast, her manner was one of self-doubt, even humility, and the man was pleased because it served his purpose. He was not out with her to pay amorous court but rather he was seeking to interest her in the publication of a series of her memoirs in which prominent names were to figure.

But the former star, so enthusiastic on her way to El Morocco, was inattentive, visibly annoyed. She mumbled: "There was a time I would come in here they would give me the best table. Now they've forgotten me."

Her escort excused himself and went over to the Round Table, where Perona was seated with a few cronies. He explained hurriedly. Perona summoned headwaiter Angelo and gave him a command. Angelo nodded. A few seconds later, he personally escorted the pair to a table against the wall on the Right Side of the room—a table next to mine. After they were seated, Perona himself came over to chat with the woman.

Now a noticeable change came over her. Her eyes sparkled. She was gay, voluble, excited. There were audible whispers from tables close by. Some neighboring patrons recognized her. The agent was pleased. Now he could conduct his negotiations with a contented actress. He ordered wine. This was like old days. Again she was the famed *femme fatale* of the silent screen, for whose attentions film idols had fought. She was the glamorous figure who had dominated Louella's and Hedda's columns, whose beautiful face had decorated covers of the fan magazines. She had even been front-page news because of her romantic link with a famed screen lover.

From my table adjoining, I watched and eavesdropped as the man with her talked earnestly. Dollars and cents entered into his pleas and explanations. But the more he talked, the more aware he became that things were not the same now. His companion was undergoing a transformation before his very eyes. Her shyness, diffidence, humility and self-doubt had vanished. The imperious manner of those other days had come back. There was self-confidence and arrogance in the very toss of her lovely head.

"You can see," he said, "how this will work out. We should get busy on it right away."

She looked at him coldly and distantly—this much I could see. According to what the agent told me later, there was ice in her tones, and behind each word she uttered he could feel that those other memories were parading in regal procession. Now she was the queen again—no longer snubbed by headwaiters.

"I really must think it over," she said, and turned from him to indicate the interview had been presumptuous on his part. He sipped his drink glumly.

"What was the use?" he commented later. "I knew I was licked."

Years later, I saw her in Romanoff's in Beverly Hills with two other women. She was still attractive and she seemed happy, perhaps because here she was on home ground. People still remembered.

Not too long ago, as we both dashed across Fifty-seventh Street and Broadway, trying to get over before the green lights changed, a performer and I stopped long enough, once we had deposited ourselves safely, to chat briefly. He told me he was heading west for a night-spot engagement, and I wished him luck.

After we parted I recalled that in other years I used to enjoy him in that nest of nostalgia, Bill's Gay Nineties, where he was a merry singing lad, offering his carols in something of the Jolson manner with a bit of Harry Richman tossed in. He looked always like the typical song-and-dance man out of the movies and the storybooks. And there came to mind something he had revealed to me.

For many years he and another performer were a vaudeville team but never quite made the Big Time. My singing lad became enamored of a pert little girl on the bill at one of the out-of-town theatres, and his frantic courtship of her promised for a time to end in marriage. But then he began to fret about abandoning the free and easy life of a bachelor.

So one night, when he had an aftertheatre date with the girl, he pleaded a headache and asked his partner to take on the assignment. The partner agreed. And not to prolong this, he and the girl fell in love and dated frequently thereafter whenever they happened to be on the same bill. The man finally told his partner he was going to marry the girl and was awarded his full blessing. They wed shortly after.

This broke up the partnership, because the young couple teamed up, and our singing man went on his solo path. Here is what is so rarely believed in typical Broadway stories, but this is the solemn truth. The team of newlyweds began to collect fame as they rolled along. Folks found the Dulcy-like naïveté of the pretty young woman hilarious and refreshing. In fact, as time went by, the young husband seemed content to act as a bit of a stooge for his wife, although those in show business knew that most of the clever material was actually written by the fellow. Their fame kept increasing when they acquired their own network radio program. Now they were truly Big Time and were among the hottest and highest-paid acts in vaudeville when they could spare a recess from radio. And then the movies beckoned, and their reputation became international.

But our singing man who decided to skip the date with the girl who might—he was never really to know—have married him, what about him? Why, he just kept going, chanting his gay little songs, and when vaudeville faded out, he went into night spots. Never a headliner, but he didn't seem to care. And, to repeat, the last time I heard him those years ago was when he was having his run at Bill's Gay Nineties.

I occasionally wonder whether it would have fared differently with Billy Lorraine if he had kept that appointment with the pert, pretty, prattling little Gracie Allen that night instead of sending his partner, George Nat Burns!

Claques at the opera have become virtually extinct. But they flourished in other years, and even the greats among the singing stars pressed them into service to applaud and cheer and start enthusiastic uproars.

I recall one case of rebellion on the part of an operatic star, Rosa Ponselle. As she told the story, she was approached by a man who proclaimed himself *chef de claque* and offered the services of his group.

"How much?" asked Miss Ponselle.

"For three curtain calls—and they'll be good and loud—one hundred and fifty dollars," she was told. "For each additional call another twenty-five dollars, and we'll want fifty dollars for shouting 'Bravo' at the end of the performance."

"Suppose," said the singing lady, "I just don't want your services?"

The man stared at her icily.

"In that case, Miss Ponselle," he assured her, "I'll have fifty men at the opera house tonight and they'll hiss you off the stage!" The star stared back at him just as icily and snapped, "Just you try—and see what I do!" and turned her back on him. Her performance that night was rewarded with the usual applause and cheers—but no hisses.

Another tale comes to mind—although this one may be purely apocryphal. An enthusiastic admirer of Lily Pons gathered his own little claque to cheer Miss Pons and became annoyed when he noticed that one gentleman seated across the aisle didn't seem to join the general enthusiasm. He neither applauded nor lifted his voice in cheer. The volunteer leader during the first intermission, approached the aloofish fellow and demanded: "What's the matter, don't you like Lily Pons?"

He crept back to his seat, humble and embarrassed when the

answer was: "I like her very much. I'm her husband, Andre Kostelanetz."

There was a time when Alec Woollcott had one of his periodic "mads" against the Algonquin set, and *New Yorker* editor Harold Ross, in particular. Ross decided the Town Scold ought to be pacified. As a "conciliatory" gesture, he went over to Huber's Museum on Forty-second Street where, whenever he put a nickel into a slot of one of the machines, turned a disk and pulled a few levers, out would leap a bright yellow or red pencil with the desired lettering on it. Ross put in one hundred nickels, manipulated the revolving disk and the levers and received one hundred pencils, with naughty insulting words spelled out. Every day for one hundred days, editor Ross sent the sulking Woollcott an "insult" pencil until he finally cried "uncle," and returned to his seat and his companions at the Algonquin Roundtable.

Harry Richman once snared a huge marlin off Bimini and brought it back to the night spot in Miami Beach where he was starring at the time. I happened to drop in with Eddie Cantor, and Richman came over and started to tell us of his battle with the big fish and what a beauty it was. "I have it here and I'm going to get it mounted," he said. "Just wait a few seconds," and he summoned a captain and asked him to fetch the marlin he had brought in earlier that day.

The captain and two waiters returned with the marlin—a marlin which had been cut up in dozens of portions by the chef and spread out on several big platters! Richman was not in his best singing form that night.

Most entertainers have no illusions about why they often receive invitations to parties. They realize the host or hostess expects they'll pay off for being granted the exalted privilege of mingling with the invited guests by singing a song or playing the piano or giving out with a few jokes. Which is why so many performers send their regrets.

Veteran comedian Lou Holtz once told me about an invitation to a bash. At the time he was touring vaudeville with a unit consisting of singer Gertrude Niesen and a pianist just coming into his own as a composer, Harold Arlen, and a stooge comic, Benny Baker. For the act, Holtz received some $5,000 a week—a goodly sum in those days—out of which he distributed salaries to the members of his little group.

One afternoon, he received a call. The name of the man on the other end of the phone meant nothing to him. Would Mr. Holtz and his little company please honor him by turning up at the Central Park Casino at midnight for a little party?

"Sure, brother," chirped Holtz. "For $2,500." To his surprise, the answer was: "Fine, I'll expect you at midnight."

So the little troupe journeyed over to the Central Park Casino. Holtz told a few of his well-worn stories and waved his cane in the direction of Miss Niesen and Arlen. Miss Niesen chanted a couple of songs with Arlen accompanying her on the piano. Baker filled in with his stooging bit. By two in the morning, stuffed with food, drenched in wine, showered with attention and acclaim, Holtz felt something of a heel and decided to be magnanimous about the whole deal. He made up his mind to tell the host he was kidding about wanting pay.

He edged over to him, but before he could have his little generous say, a check was pressed into his hand. "You'll find it's $3,000," he was informed. "You forgot to mention about pay for those fine people in your company."

The thoughtful host, incidentally, was the very social Anthony Drexel Biddle.

I must make mention of another party—this one in Beverly Hills. Harry and Dorothy Jameson were giving it in honor of Peggy and me, and Dorothy assured us she was inviting a flock of people we knew, among them some performers. I said: "Now, Dorothy, under no circumstance call on them to do any entertaining. They're friends, and I want them to remain friends."

"Of course, darling," reassured Mrs. Jameson. "We're all just getting together for fun. I understand your position perfectly."

It was a jolly party and the libations and the cuisine, perfection. Suddenly, without bidding, one of the guests, composer Jule Styne, sat down at the piano and began playing. Then Ethel Merman sidled over and began singing while Jule accompanied her. Then Eddie Fisher and Debbie Reynolds, newlyweds at the time, offered a comedy singing and dancing routine. Lisa Kirk got impatient and took over. It went on that way for the remainder of the evening.

I kept on protesting, hypocritically: "Say, we didn't expect any of you to do this, we really didn't." But even as the words

You may have to look twice to be convinced it isn't Debbie Reynolds smoking that long stogie held between the fingers of the author. She and Eddie Fisher were reputed to be among the happiest of Hollywood couples at the time. Below Eddie is Mrs. Bob Considine, and the cut-off profile is that of Joan Crawford. In the dim background, seeming to stare over Debbie's shoulders, is Richard Kollmar, then married to the late Dorothy Killgallen.
Photo by David Workman

tumbled out, Frank Sinatra was beginning to sing. The honest truth is I'd have felt disappointed bitterly if these performers had not gone on. I loved every minute of the entertainment.

One night some decades ago, as a companion and I were walking along Fifth Avenue, we noticed that though a freezing breeze was lashing out from the northeast, a hardy little group stood patiently watching as workmen lifted a noble elm (this was when these trees were being imported from Connecticut) and set it into its lodging place on Fifth Avenue. It was a long and laborious task.

From out of West Fifty-second Street shuffled the elderly Negro minstrel Sam, who used to patrol the section, playing a guitar. As he neared us, my companion grabbed him, took him aside, whispered into his ear, placed some folding money into his free hand. The slim white gentleman and the colored musician came back to the group around the tree. Sam thrummed his guitar and my slim companion sang Joyce Kilmer's "Trees."

Then as Sam played my companion followed with "Woodman Spare That Tree." Everyone present applauded, and a few of the more generous started a collection which they handed to my friend, who solemnly turned it over to Sam. He walked with me, exclaiming: "That was great, wasn't it? Can't remember having more fun."

My skinny companion was Hoagy Carmichael, composer of so many song hits—"Star Dust," "Lazy Bones," "Thanks for the Memory" and many others, including "I Get Along Without You Very Well."

The late literary agent Mark Hanna and I were invited by the lady of the diamonds, Peggy Hopkins Joyce, to a midnight cocktail party in her suite at the Waldorf. We arrived early and Hanna, a chronic gumchewer, placed a fresh slab in his mouth and started chewing away vigorously. Miss Joyce stared at him with something of dismay.

"Mark," she said petulantly, "you're such a nice fellow, but I wish you wouldn't sit here chewing gum. I have some awfully nice people coming—Tito Schipa, for instance. Tito's a genius and all that, but I don't think he'd understand about your chewing gum."

Hanna said, "Peggy, I have chewed gum in the best circles, but if that's the way you feel about it, okay, okay." And he got rid of the wad.

Five or six guests arrived, among them the opera star. And it was quite obvious that his meal had been spiced by garlic and onions. After a few moments conversation, Hanna flagrantly reached for a slab of gum and began chewing and started to walk away. Tito Schipa clutched him by an arm. "Mr. Hanna," he said, looking about furtively, "Can you spare another piece of gum, yes?"

Although I had become impressed with the rare buffoonery of Danny Kaye and the promise he had of advancing to the top echelon in show business, it wasn't until he was being featured at a night spot, La Martinique, in March of 1941 that I became aware of a quiet but expressive-faced young woman who was his accompanist, a dark-haired, smiling-eyed girl. I noticed that before Danny embarked upon any number, he first looked inquiringly at her, waited for either a nod of approval or disapproval, and that even as she played the piano, her eyes never seemed to leave him but followed every movement. And her lips silently formed the words he was singing or speaking.

I learned that night that she was Sylvia Fine, Danny's wife, and that if ever there was a Svengali and Trilby in benign reverse, this was a rare instance, for not only was she responsible for the involved and striking arrangements and most of his original material, but also it was she who rehearsed him until she was satisfied with his gesturing and posturing, his enunciation, his facial expressions, his timing, etc. And, always, she remained modestly behind the scenes.

Danny often confessed as his career progressed that he had to fall back truthfully on the cliché, "All that I am, all that I hope to be, etc., etc., etc."

Jack Benny told me that when he was traveling abroad some years ago, he dropped into a cafe in Budapest. His companion told him that here assembled outstanding musicians who played because they wanted to play, not for the sake of the money they might earn. Benny said he was quite impressed. At one point, he was introduced to a violinist who bowed casually and started off promptly to another table. Embarrassed, Benny's Hungarian companion called the artist back.

"Hermann," he said, in mild rebuke, "maybe you didn't understand. This is Jack Benny. He is the famous star of radio and movies. Do you know how much he earns? Fifteen or maybe twenty thousand dollars a week. A week, you hear?"

The violinist shrugged his shoulders. "Does he," he asked, "like what he is doing?"

Cartoonist-columnist Irving Hoffman settled down at a table in "21" with George Jean Nathan and *Esquire*'s editor, Arnold Gingrich, and remarked that he had just bought a copy of a portable edition of F. Scott Fitzgerald stories and observed that John O'Hara in the foreword took a slap at Sinclair Lewis for writing not for literary appreciation but for money.

"That's nonsense!" exploded Nathan. "Red Lewis has never written just for the sake of monetary compensation."

Said Hoffman mildly: "I read something similar about Lewis in another book."

"Oh, tut, tut," said Nathan, "you never read any such thing."

Said Hoffman: "But I have, and by coincidence, I have the book with me. Let me read part of it. It says here . . ." and Hoffman read off a paragraph in which the author, in commenting on Lewis' novel *Mantrap,* insisted: "it would need only a cameraman standing behind it and a peroxide blonde in front of it to make a popular moving picture," and concluded with the observation, "and made no bones of what he was doing, but frankly announced to anyone who would listen that he was, to use his own locution, 'turning out a swell piece of cheese to grab off some easy gravy.'"

Nathan grinned. "Irving," he said, "you win. You should have been a lawyer."

The quote was from the *Intimate Notebooks of George Jean Nathan.*

Clare Boothe Luce is credited with debunking the legend of Stalin's great drinking prowess. She branded it a myth and a fraud. As the story went, when she was covering one of the Big Three huddles shortly after World War II, Clare noticed that the Russian dictator's drinks were not poured from a bottle of vodka but from a special decanter. She insisted she would like a sip from the same container that was reserved for Red Joe. There was considerable reluctance but finally, at a nod from Stalin, an attendant yielded, and Clare, along with others drinking the next toast, did it with the special vodka. Actually, she found it a mild minty drink, the kind you could consume in great quantities without even feeling a tingle. So the story went that, apocryphal or not, that was the reason the hardy Stalin had been holding his own at the big he-men drinking jousts that were so widely publicized.

Eddie Cantor had a special painting executed revealing Debbie Reynolds dressed as a cute puppet and perched on Eddie Fisher's knee. This was when the two were reportedly the happiest young couple in filmland. The Cantors had the painting hung over their fireplace in their Beverly Hills home.

After the parting, when Eddie began courting Elizabeth Taylor and the two frequently visited with the Cantors, Eddie Cantor, when he knew that they were coming over to the house, would take the picture down and substitute another. Similarly, when Debbie was scheduled to come visiting, down would come the painting.

One day, Debbie wanted to know why the picture wasn't up —had the Cantors gotten rid of it? When she was informed, no, they still had it, she begged them to give it to her—price no object.

"Why would you want it?" asked Cantor.

"I always thought it was so cute," said Debbie. "Besides, when the children grow up, I want them to know their father as he was when I thought we were so happy together."

Once when I asked the late boisterous, outspoken, hard-drink-

A conference between Jimmy Stewart and the author. The three lads in adjoining seats seem far from impressed.

ing playwright Brendan Behan what languages he spoke, he replied: "Gaelic, English, Yiddish and Rubbish." He told me he was bitterly disappointed with New York's Irish. "Even on St. Patrick's Day," he grumbled, "they don't drink Irish whiskey. They go for Scotch, and you know where that comes from." He said he had taught Jackie Gleason to count ten in Gaelic. "Now the lad boasts he has mastered the language. Let him count to fifty before he says that."

When an abbreviated version of *Naughty Marietta* was presented at the Pierre's Cotillion Room, I noted in my column that Behan sat without blinking, winking or drinking, from which I gathered this operetta was not his particular dish of corn—particularly since there was, unlike Behan's own current play *The Hostage,* not a single four-letter word in the entire Victor Herbert offering.

Two days later came a mild protest from Behan on a postcard: "Louis, contrary to your report, I love *Naughty Marietta.* I am the only member of the gathering that could have sung 'Ah, Sweet Mystery of Life,' only I wasn't asked. Victor Herbert, like me, was a Dublinman, and in 1920 was president of the United States Friends of Irish Freedom."

In one of its issues, the show-business publication, *Variety,* accorded Behan's tongue-in-cheek review under "New Acts," noting that the playwright had made an appearance at Harry McGurk's Jagger House, made a little speech in Gaelic and then sang a couple of Irish songs.

Up until the news came of his death, an Eighth Avenue pub displayed this sign in its window: "Brendan Behan Slipped Here. . . ."

14

Letters—and Some Postscripts

HENRY DAVID THOREAU LAMENTED: "I have received not more than one or two letters in my life that were worth the postage." Ironic, isn't it, that this despiser of mail was honored with a postage stamp bearing his likeness?

I have been more fortunate than Thoreau and find myself in complete disagreement with his dismal denigration of correspondence. Through the years the mail has delivered communiqués that have afforded me delight, amazement, sometimes resentment and, frequently, information and news fit to print. Or they have offered a springboard for observations. And in many instances, though the letters have contained nothing too profound or provocative, they have stirred up memories.

I started saving letters as far back as the late twenties, and I am submitting a few here out of the hundreds from my files. Starting off with a brief note from Carl Sandburg, the offerings in this chapter include communications from a wide range of personalities of the past and present—among them J. Edgar Hoover, the ill-fated Maxwell Bodenheim, late war correspondent and author

Quentin Reynolds, former musical comedy star Claire Luce, George M. Cohan, Groucho Marx, Irene Castle, Howard Hughes —as well as his uncle, the late author, Rupert Hughes—Arthur Godfrey, Robert L. Ripley, Lucius Beebe and Jim Bishop. So many others.

JUNE 24, 1959

DEAR LOUIS SOBOL:

May I express my thanks for the bouquet you so generously tossed at my rather enlarged feet. It was an enjoyable party and I was happy to have a chat with you and meet your very pretty wife. Perhaps we shall meet again.

Yours,
CARL SANDBURG

My first meeting with the poet, musician, folk singer, biographer, lecturer and ex-newspaperman was on the occasion of his eighty-first birthday on January 6, 1959. My apartment-house neighbor, Ethel Smith, the concert organist, had gathered a few dozen of us in her large apartment to help Sandburg celebrate. She had called upon the skill of Theodore of the Waldorf and his artistic aides for a huge sculptured likeness of the guest of honor, carved in ice to take its place alongside the huge birthday cake. By 2:00 A.M., the ice bust had melted until it was almost wafer-thin, yet the poetic face of Sandburg remained miraculously intact as if neither time nor the elements could efface the lasting impression this man made on all who knew him and respected him.

Lincoln's dedicated biographer smiled when I suggested that after his full and busy life he might be looking forward to years of ease and perhaps plain idleness. He revealed at that time he was in the process of completing the second volume of his autobiography, which he expected to title *Ever Winds of Chance*. I recalled that he had written the foreword to Harry Golden's best seller *Only in America*, and I remarked that Golden was far less fluent on Jack Paar's show than in his literary offerings.

"He's like me," commented Sandburg. "He chokes up in front of those monstrous cameras."

Earlier in the evening, June Havoc had sung a few of Sandburg's poems set to music. Humorist Sam Levenson offered his whimsical comments on family life as he knew it as a child (years later, he was to expand his observations into a book, *Everything but Money,* which topped the best-seller lists for months). Hostess Ethel Smith came through with her musical contributions, and then Sandburg settled back and began singing some of his folk songs, accompanying himself on the guitar—but not before taking time out to praise Levenson.

"He is truly the outstanding American humorist of today, in my opinion, at least. He lives up to the tradition of Bill Nye and Artemus Ward." Then, noticing Alicia Patterson (late publisher of *Newsday*), he paused between numbers to recall that her father and he were pals in the old Chicago days. "We were in the Socialist Party together," he recalled, "and we left it at about the same time."

At the beginning of the evening, actress Peggy Wood introduced herself to the poet. "I was once married to John Weaver," she said. Sandburg nodded and said, "A fine writer he was. And you are still as beautiful as you always were," he added chivalrously.

The world's outstanding guitarist, Segovia, sat quietly in a corner. Sandburg embraced him. "I have an ulterior motive," he confessed. "We have a recording together. Long-playing, of course."

He seemed highly pleased as he surveyed the guests, and at one point, he murmured, "It's really flattering—all these folks coming out in this bitter cold for this party for me." Among those he surveyed, in addition to the folks I have mentioned, were Lawrence Langner, cofounder of the Theatre Guild, actor Conrad Nagel, conductor Andre Kostelanetz, actresses Stella Adler, Paula Lawrence, Jessie Royce Landis and her husband, Gen'l Jeff Seitz, and actor Kevin McCarthy.

Before I left the party, I asked Sandburg whether he still retained his high opinion of the daily newspaper, and recalled a quote of his, "The first page today has human stuff in it that puts novels in the discard."

Sandburg smiled gently. "This would be a lost, dull world without the daily newspaper," he said. "You mustn't forget I was once a newspaperman myself."

ATLANTA, GA.
OCT. 1, 1936

DEAR MR. SOBOL:

I have just received a clipping of your column of Sept. 24th in which you mention my book, *Gone With the Wind.* I must write and correct an error in it. I am confident the error was no fault of yours but does an injustice to a charming young lady and I feel it should be corrected.

You state that "Scarlett O'Hara" in the book is modeled after Miss Betty Timmons of Atlanta. Certainly that is not a compliment to any girl. "Scarlett" was not a very nice person. I am not personally acquainted with Miss Timmons (she is not my niece nor is she a relative of mine) but I know many of her friends and know she is a girl of charm and beauty and character. "Scarlett" was not the same type of person as Miss Timmons—and so fine a girl should not be compared with her. I did not take the character of "Scarlett" from anyone, living or dead.

Sincerely,
MARGARET MITCHELL

My answer to the novelist:

MY DEAR MISS MITCHELL:

The whole business is rather embarrassing in view of what you have written, for I obtained the information directly from Miss Betty Timmons, herself. The chivalrous conclusion is that Miss Timmons, who has an outside possibility of stepping into the "Scarlett O'Hara" role in the picture, may have been inspired by some overzealous press agent.

FEB. 20TH, 1940

DEAR SOBOL:

I liked your "Mr. New York" piece—it was good. It represented thought, imagination and good reporting. But I am wondering if you are quite right on the average New Yorker's literary and cultural tastes. I doubt very much that he subscribed to the various magazines to which you refer. I think on the whole he is satisfied with *The Saturday Evening Post* and *Collier's.* In place of *The New Yorker,* he reads the gossip columnists.

I think he even suspects the Book-of-the-Month Club—and what does he want books for when he has the newspapers. He listens to "Information Please" for the ad-lib stuff. Incidentally, to be dogmatic, for a moment he agrees with me that "Information Please" no longer seeks to become informative but has become a humorous program (sometimes). He is reasonably sure of one or two laughs a night from Levant and F.P.A. He marvels at Kieran's knowledge of natural history; he likes Fadiman's easy control, but he thinks the questions are deliberately intended to pin his mental ears back, and so when he wants to sell himself a little by feeding his ego, he turns to easier quizzes.

He has another characteristic—your Average Mr. New York—he loves parades and he likes to look at what he calls the big shots, irregardless [one of his slips] of whether they are the big shots of sports pictures, business or crime. He has a healthy curiosity that makes him want to know this type moves, breathes and walks and talks.

Once in a while he is emotionalized by demagogues or blatherskites, but presently his sound sense asserts itself and decency returns to him. He has one major fault: the swiftness and savagery of life in the city has made him a worshipper of success which he spells with a dollar sign. At the same time, he has quite an understandable and wholly human relish for those of the mighty who are found with their pants down.

Your Average Mr. New York has a sort of suspicion of manners. That causes him to be somewhat impolite when he is unexpectedly spoken to, but he is good hearted and always tries to be helpful. If the other fellow is surly, so is he, but if the other fellow is nice, he is, too. These are just some of his characteristics. They have to do with his intrinsic qualities. I suggest you describe him by outlining these extrinsic qualities. What does he look like? How does he talk, etc.? Of one thing I am sure: he isn't half as well dressed as are the women in his family. They have a New York air; he hasn't.

As ever,
HERBERT BAYARD SWOPE

Swope's letter, some portions of which I saw fit to print in my column, brought in dozens of protesting notes from readers who described themselves as "Average New Yorkers" but disagreed vigorously with his description of them. Some accused the former editor of being snobbish in his outlook—of gazing down at fellow citizens from his ivory tower perch. There are others who wrote in that Swope's observations were quite accurate. I published some of the letters—forwarded most of them to Swope, who seemed quite delighted at the uproar he had inspired.

LONDON
Nov. 4, 1940

SUGAR LIPS:

It was great hearing from you, Louisher—and some encouraging news from Marcus. Grand news about the revived interest in the Gibbons picture. I've just finished a book, *The Wounded Don't Cry*—Dutton is publishing. Have a proposition from Walter Wanger to write a film based on the Eagle Squadron here but doubt if I'll have time. I'm trying to write one now for David Niven (Captain Niven, if you please). Grand fellow, Louisher. He's been working in the war office—important job, too—but now they have asked him to take a three months' leave and do a picture. He was reluctant at first. All he wants to do is to fight, but it was a direct order, so he asked me to write it—said he'd play any part at all. I'm working on an angle trying to glorify the AFS [auxillary firemen] who are taking the worst beating of anyone. But I'm leaving in a few days for Cairo and don't know if I can do Niven's thing first. Incidentally, come to think of it, I'm working for *Collier's,* too, so all other stuff must be incidental.

Working conditions are pretty difficult. It's hard working at nights as I've always done. At first we just ignored the guns and the bombs, but I find you can take only so much of it. After a month of the constant pounding, you can't ignore them anymore. If you are working and you hear that whistle and it sounds close, you run into the corridor to get away from the flying glass. There are new types of guns shooting every night, and sometimes you can't tell the difference between them and bombs exploding. When you work at night, you are always unconsciously keeping one ear cocked for the next one. You don't get to sleep until pretty late—not by choice—you just can't sleep with the guns going unless you are in an underground shelter where you can't hear them. I don't use the shelters. I never lived in a kennel and I'll be damned if I'm going to die in one.

Have you run into Bill Stoneman of the *Chicago Daily News* yet? He's around town—left here a few days ago for the States. There is a real reporter, Louisher. We all think he's the No. 1 man of us all—it's unanimous. Get to meet him and know him —it'll pay off.

Nothing you've heard or read about the horror of night bombing is exaggerated, but despite it we do have some fun here. There are a lot of grand guys—men like Christiansen, the editor of the *Express;* Frank Owen of the *Standard;* Nat Gubbins of the *Sunday Express;* and our fellows: Stoneman, Bob Low of *Liberty,* Ed Beattie of the U.P., Ray Daniels of *The New York Times* and Uncle Ed Angley of the *Herald Trib.* A great, great bunch of reporters, and they take a hell of a beating but certainly stand up to it.

The tough thing is getting home at night if you've been working in the office. There are no cabs during a raid, and I've got just about the only driver in London who drives at night. So mostly the lads have to walk home, and walking home in the blackout with shrapnel coming down and a few bombs whistling is not having a waltz with Hedy LaMarr. Yet fellows like Ed Beattie and Red Mueller of INS and others do it every night.

I'm going to Cairo because I think England has won the Battle of London and that the Germans will try somewhere else. Oh, we'll keep on taking a beating for a while, but even after seven weeks of the hammering, London is still standing up. Not even London Bridge is falling down. But you'd be surprised how little important damage has been done. This is Nov. 4th—shops, workers, flats, churches, hospitals have been thoroughly shellacked, but the ministeries and the real military objectives are pretty much intact.

The people of London certainly can take it. It is as though Jack Dempsey died and they cut his heart up in seven million pieces and grafted a piece into each Londoner. They just get mad when their homes fall down on them; they never even entertain the thought of surrender. If Hitler ever conquers this island, he'd have to spend the next eleven years burying the dead, because everybody here is willing to die if he can only get one crack in first. They are grim and determined. How the hell did we ever lick them in 1776? When you see men like David Niven, whom we always knew as a nice affable pleasant fellow to have a drink with, not only ready but sincerely honestly willing to get killed if he can get a punch in first, it makes you think we are all mad because Hitler didn't try the invasion. He'd have gotten the surprise of his life.

I'm afraid you wouldn't like it here. You couldn't get a decent martini, and Sobol is no good without his martinis. The only Vermouth left is very tired old Vermouth and apparently Vermouth doesn't improve with age. There are no lemons or limes so we can't have cocktails that need lemons or lime. And there is very little brandy. Mostly we drink gin and lime juice and soda—and it's not bad.

Has this reached New York now? What are the British soldiers doing? They are still knitting socks for the civilians of London. Say hello to Mark]Hanna] and Sherman [Billingsley] and Toots [Shor]. Dying to see his new place, I hear he has a nice blue-plate special for seventeen dollars.

A kiss for Mrs. S.
Your pal,
QUENT [Quentin Reynolds]

I continued to get these lengthy communiqués from Reynolds all through the war action, and it amazed me that he could find the time, for he was turning in his pieces at *Collier's*, working on another book, occasionally appearing on radio abroad. Marcus, to whom he refers at the start of the letter, was Mark Hanna, our mutual literary agent. Quent and I had outlined the career of Floyd Gibbons for a film, and the interest at the time seemed encouraging, but we never got to sell it, nor can I recall that there was ever a picture made based on Gibbons' career.

FEB. 24, 1940

DEAR LOUIS:

Re your recent paragraph in which you quote the skepticism of Huntsman Jordan and Engineer Frank W. Kravigny over the genuineness of shrunken heads, may I have my say? It is true the heads of small monkeys have been extensively used, the flat nose of the monkey being pinched outward until it resembles a human nose. A number of these so-called shrunken heads have also been made of rabbit skin, the face part of the "head" being shaved and tanned, leaving eyebrows and lashes and pressed and moulded into human shape.

I have some seven genuine shrunken heads, and when you come over to my home in Mamaroneck next time, remind me to show them to you. I'll also show you the difference between original and faked specimens. For that matter, at the Museum of the American Indian at 155th and Broadway, there are two entire shrunken figures—one of which is a white man. Also the shrunken heads at the Museum are quite authentic.

Indeed, remarkable life-like shrunken heads continue to trickle out of the mysterious Amazon jungle where the Jivaro Indians furtively practise the grisly art discovered by their ancestors.

Just so you'll know,
ROBERT L. RIPLEY

One of the Believe-It-or-Not man's closest friends was accordionist-singer Gypsy Markoff, and on March 19, 1943, shortly after the crash of the United States plane in Lisbon carrying, among others, a flock of performers, some of whom perished in the wreck, I received a long detailed letter from Gypsy describing the terrifying experience. In part:

I am trying to write this with a fractured shoulder. My right ankle is also fractured and sewn up to the knee. They picked glass pieces out of the plane and everything imaginable out of my head and forehead and my ear was practically torn off, just hanging on by a thread of skin. I am scarred behind the ear and neck. I will, of course, need plastic surgery.

Everyone here in Lisbon is wonderful. I have a private room and day and night English nurses. The American minister visited us today. I knew him well as he was in Egypt when I was there. The American legation and consulate and their wives have been simply wonderful—constantly visiting, showering us with flowers, candy and cigarettes.

Most of my things are gone, including my new silver fox coat, but one thing they found floating in the river were my pictures of Bob Ripley. Won't he like that as a believe-it-or-not?

Today Stanton Griffis came from London and cabled for a new accordion for me. About fourteen people were saved out of thirty-five besides me—and I do not even swim. I thought I had a life preserver cushion but it wasn't at all, and yet, believing it was, I managed to keep afloat and swim to the rescue ship with yelling to Yvette [another performer] for moral support.

She was alongside of me and kept shouting: "Keep going, Gypsy. Keep going!" Her voice kept me alive, and she, of all six of us, is not even marred or bruised—not a scratch on her. She is our official manager and very good at it, too. Do tell her mother not to worry—she is okay—except she needs the hairdresser and we were told one is coming to take care of her today.

Lorraine Rognan's only injury is a slightly fractured ankle but her husband was lost—imagine how she must feel. And Tamara Dreisen—that beautiful girl—Tamara who first introduced me to you at the Club Abbey—she went down. Jane Froman is badly hurt—so badly. I doubt if she ever will walk again.

In May, Robert L. Ripley hosted a come-home party for Gypsy at his Mamaroneck home, and at one point there was a phone call from Governor Herbert Lehman. "Tell Gypsy," he said, "I am the man who helped her cut her steak and even comb her hair during the clipper flight back. I salute her again for being a better soldier than I am. I took the same trip back that she did and the doctor ordered me to bed and told me to stay there for at least twenty-four hours and here she is, already going to parties."

Gypsy Markoff beat off her woeful injuries and returned to her show business career. Bob Ripley died of a heart attack on May 27, 1949, leaving an estate estimated in excess of a million dollars. Among the honorary pallbearers at the elaborate funeral were: Captain Eddie Rickenbacker, Hearst corporation president Richard E. Berlin, William Randolph Hearst, Jr., book publisher M. Lincoln Schuster, General Jimmy Doolittle, illustrators Howard Chandler Christy and James Montgomery Flagg, Lowell Thomas, former heavyweight champions Jack Dempsey and Gene Tunney.

NEW YORK
MARCH 4, 1941

DEAR LOUIS SOBOL:

Would you mind informing your friend, Mr. Lawlor of San Francisco, that neither Sam Harris nor myself are at all interested in his opinion of us. Nevertheless we should like him to know that the controversy being carried on in your column regarding the selling of newspapers for the 'quake sufferers of San Francisco in 1906 might possibly change other folks' opinions which we highly value. The facts are that the *New York American* promoted the idea of selling the papers from the truck and that Sam Harris and I, along with several members of the staff, spent an entire day on the truck and covered the greater part of the city disposing of an entire special edition at anywhere from five to one hundred dollars a copy.

Whatever the amount collected was I have no idea, as the moneys were turned over to the *American* immediately and put, as I understand it, into a common fund. The thing was not done as a publicity stunt nor were Sam and I looking for any certificate of acknowledgement. It was all arranged by the newspaper's staff and we were called upon to assist.

We did the same for the *American* at the time of the *Titanic* disaster, and, if my memory serves me correctly, we paid something like $5,000 for the first copy of the special edition. I am sure Mr. Hearst himself will vouch for us and I am pleased to read that you think we're a couple of square guys.

GEORGE M. COHAN

Cohan was referring to San Francisco's Jack Lawlor's skepticism of a paragraph I had devoted to Cohan and his then partner

Harris, in which I stated they had helped sell autographed copies of the *New York Journal* (Cohan insisted it was the *American*) on street corners, raising some $12,000 for the benefit of the quake sufferers.

In part, Lawlor wrote:

> I covered the Mayor's office here for the *San Francisco Chronicle,* following the Fire—and since all the money for relief from all over the world passed through this office, I certainly would have known about it if any had been earmarked from Cohan and Harris. It would have been a story when stories were scarce on account of the Fire and Quake so overshadowed everything that ordinary news was a bore. In fact, if it is so, why was it along in 1907 and 1908, when Cohan and Harris showed here at the Van Ness Theatre, no mention was made by them of the funds. It would have been good publicity.

My postscript to Jack Lawlor's note was: "Mister, I can't tell you, but in any controversy, my money is on Cohan and Harris."

And indeed, later when I probed, just to satisfy my own curiosity, I learned that the two theatrical biggies had peddled those papers, raising considerable money. Other theatrical folks of the era were also pressed into service for the cause.

NEW YORK
MAY 10, 1941

DEAR LOUIS SOBOL:

Thanks for the little reference to my humble self. I have often called myself an "expired poet." I do not know how poetry can survive two World Wars. It is too much for one generation. The little preface to which you refer is absolutely sincere. I think Virsing has written an admirable book. He is a distinguished economist, a brilliant journalist, the editor of the *Münchener Neueste Nachrichten* [Munich] for which I write—as well as a personal friend.

Within a few weeks I shall send you another little book which will probably interest you more, although it may make you angry. It is called *The Seven Against Man*. You wrote sometime ago you saw me walking briskly on Fifth Avenue; I did not see you or I would certainly have interrupted my goose step to chat with you.

Cordially,
GEORGE SYLVESTER VIERECK

The poet-novelist was referring to a few reproachful lines I had offered in the column a week previously: "The pity of it is that so brilliant a writer as George Sylvester Viereck is—perhaps I should say, was—now devotes himself to insipid propagandistic piffle for the Nazis. They even have him writing prefaces for the publications of the propaganda mill, Flanders Hall, which offers pamphlets against "ruthless Great Britain."

Viereck was the author of twenty or more books (*My First Two Thousand Years* was a runaway best seller) as well as some excellent poems—his *Nineveh and Other Poems* drew high praise from the critics. In fact, James Huneker insisted they were "shot through with the splendors of Heine, Swinburne and Keats." A few months after his letter to me, Viereck found himself in trouble with the federal authorities—they accused him of being a German agent who did not report his propaganda activities.

Years previously, I had interviewed him in the spacious living room in his Riverside Drive home, and noticed some half dozen pictures of Kaiser Wilhelm, most of them bearing affectionate inscriptions.

"He is a great man," commented the author, "Someday the world will realize the true sincerity, the greatness, the unselfishness of the Kaiser. Yes, I am pro-German and always will be, but I defy anyone to question my love for America or my patriotism. It was a mistake for America to plunge into the war [World War I]. She gained nothing—nothing at all except the hate of her allies who owe her money."

Viereck went on to prophesy that Germany would rise again. "Someday," he said, "There will be another leader, not as kindly as the Kaiser, but shrewder, colder, ruthless, perhaps. That day must come, and Germany will go on to its rightful place in the world. The next time, I hope fervently, America will mind its own business."

Then he filled my arms with books—books he had authored —several of them containing eulogies of the Kaiser.

Viereck started his propaganda activities when World War II broke out—before Pearl Harbor. He was finally indicted in March of 1942 and sentenced to serve from two to six years as an unregistered Nazi agent, although he wasn't imprisoned, after taking an appeal, until a year later. He was paroled in 1947, still maintaining stoutly that once the United States had entered the war, his loyalty was to America.

The sad irony was that while he was serving his sentence, his son Corporal George Sylvester Viereck, Jr., who had been decorated for gallantry during battle, was killed in action on the Anzio beachhead in March of 1944. Another son, Sergeant Peter Viereck, also served with our forces. In fact, he had enlisted a few days after the attack on Pearl Harbor.

353 WEST 57TH ST.
MARCH 16, 1938

DEAR LOUIS:

If I have not worn your kind heart to shreds—PLEASE do send that little note to Jules Brulatour about me. You know how to word it so as not to implicate yourself and yet put in a good word for me, as I am in dire distress now. I so wish you would strain a point, Louis, and do this for me for which I would bless you. Unless something happens I am now headed for what looks like the final round-up. I am trying night and day to get something without avail. If Mr. B. would let me have a moderate amount, I plan to put most of it in ads for editing work—and have a good chance of survival. Please do this for me.

Faithfully,
STEVE CLOW

I came to know Steve Clow in the early thirties when he shuffled into my office and handed me a few pages of nostalgic reminiscences and wanted to know if, in the event I could use the material, I might pay him something—anything. He seemed overwhelmingly grateful when I handed him fifteen dollars. Thereafter, he would either come to the office for a little "loan" or send me a plaintive letter, pleading for five or ten dollars to tide him over. I learned later that Mark Hellinger was similarly approached from time to time, and was far more generous in the sums he donated.

Clow's wasted career came to an end on June 6, 1941, in a charity ward at Bellevue. Once the top chronicler of Broadway's romances, tragedies and scandals in the era preceding the gossip columnist of the newspapers, Clow was king in his own narrow and slightly sordid walk until he made the mistake for which society never forgave him—blackmail. He expiated his sin in prison, and the gay life he had known when he ran his little magazine, *Broadway Brevities*, came to an end. Thereafter there were endless days of hunger, humiliation and disgrace. In another of his final letters to me, he offered thanks for another minor loan and hinted that at last a break for the better seemed imminent. He was certain he would not have to trouble me again and would, in fact, be able at long last to repay the loans. Death took him four days later.

Clow was always promising to write about *fin-de-siècle* Manhattan, about Allen Street when it was, in his words, "the port of missing nymphy, in the full penumbra of 50 cents lubricity." Of Fourteenth Street, as he put it, "when Tom Sharkey hung over the bar of his saloons." Of Lüchow's and "its sacrosanct odors of Pilsner where Frank Harris used to berate the waiter about his delayed amontillado while eating buns from an ambulatory cardboard box."

He told me he was present when Harry K. Thaw sent three bullets into the body of Stanford White at Madison Square Garden in 1906. He claimed to have been a friend of Bat Masterson and Alfred Henry Lewis, often sitting with them in the little side room at Shanley's on Forty-second Street, draining the glass-bottom mugs of their ale.

He never did get to write that book, and the only writing he did were those appeals for loans to the few people who felt sorry for him.

A handful of former friends did turn out for the funeral—friends who saved him from the humiliation of a pauper's grave. Among them were former columnist S. Jay Kaufman, Village poetess Juanita Clivette, Evelyn Nesbit Thaw, and, ironically enough, Maxwell S. Mattuck, who had been the prosecutor responsible for his conviction.

BEVERLY HILLS
JUNE 6, 1951

DEAR LOUIS:

A Mr. Fred Allen has sent me your column of May 21st in which you state that: "Groucho Marx, Fred Allen and Goodman Ace—all talking but not a single one cracking a smile throughout the meal."

This item, although slightly slanderous, won't get you a letter from my attorney but I must say it isn't true. We did sit rather glumly through the meal, but at the conclusion of the dinner when Goody Ace picked up the check I laughed hysterically for twenty minutes.

Yours,
GROUCHO MARX

Three wires:

ELKTON, MD.
NOV. 15, 1940

DEAR LOUIS:

Happy to tell you that Bill Smith and I were just married.

ETHEL MERMAN

(The marriage was dissolved within a few months, and Miss Merman went on to marry in succession and divorce newspaperman Bob Levitt, airline tycoon Bob Six and cinema star Ernest Borgnine.)

YUMA, ARIZ.
SEPT. 4, 1937

DEAR LOUIS:
We were just married and wanted you to be the first to know. Love.

ALICE AND TONY MARTIN

(After a few years, Alice Faye and Tony were divorced. She went on to wed bandleader and occasional comedian Phil Harris. Tony wooed and wed the lovely Cyd Charisse. Both couples have been happily married ever since.)

NEW YORK
OCT. 24, 1951

DEAR LOUIS:
There is no truth to the items about my telephoning Milton Berle a couple of times a day for advice. It so happens that with the exception of a birthday party a few weeks ago for our little daughter, at which we hardly spoke, Milton and I have not seen each other for a long time and not been out together since last March. Once and for all I would like to say that there is not the

slightest chance of a reconciliation. Milton is a fine person but I don't love him.

JOYCE MATHEWS

(After Joyce had married Milton Berle, divorced him, remarried him and divorced him again, she wed Billy Rose, only to follow the same pattern. She divorced Billy, then remarried him, then divorced him again. Rose, after a brief marriage with Doris Warner of the movie clan, began hinting he and Joyce might wed for the third time, but his death ended that hope. In his will, he made it clear he had not forgotten her, bequeathing her a one-million-dollar trust fund.)

THE GOTHAM
MAY 4, 1950

DEAR LOUIS:

I was delighted to be back in my dear New York again as the unnoticed, not to say, uncrowned, Queen of the May. But I was shocked to find that you, usually so accurate and reliable, had fallen for a fallacy.

In your column you wrote that George Washington played the zither and said so in a letter to Martha from Valley Forge. If I were a humorist I might term that letter a Bally Forgery. For Martha burned all of George's letters that she could find. Two only escaped her and one of them was written when he was made Commander-in-Chief and left Philadelphia to join the army. He promised to be back in the fall but it was eight years later. No letter from Valley Forge to Martha is in existence and there is no evidence whatever that he ever played a musical instrument.

The matter is of no great importance except as proof that even you are human and can make a mistake. As one who never makes anything else, I welcome you back to the ill-known human race.

Always affectionately yours,
RUPERT HUGHES

NEW YORK, N. Y.
FEB. 3, 1941

DEAR LOUIS SOBOL:

The repercussions from your reference to me, along with the little-girl photograph, began almost before the first edition was off the press. Neighbors slid cuttings under my door; friends, acquaintances and strangers telephoned; gong went the Sobol bell.

And now a query: I am doing a book called *Self Portrait*. Since it is to be literally that, photographs are in order. I have been on the trail of the one you used in your column for months. It is almost the only child-picture of me I know anything about. I am wondering if there is some way I can borrow, beg, steal or even buy the plate from which your newspaper print was made.

Meanwhile, dear Louis Sobol, even though travel-stained with her journey through this strange interlude, the adult version of that little girl remains,

Admiringly yours,
FANNIE HURST

FEDERAL BUREAU OF INVESTIGATION
WASHINGTON, D.C., MARCH 11, 1942

DEAR LOUIS:

I thought your reference to the Bruce Minton article in *New Masses* was very well done. As you have pointed out so emphatically in the past, the Bureau has been the target of some 57 varieties of smears. I have been referred to as being radical, Fascist-minded, and frankly I expected to be blamed sooner or later for the blowing up of the Battleship *Maine* in the Spanish-American war. However, we must realize that in public life and in carrying on the work of the FBI, we can expect brickbats of those engaged in un-American activities if we do our work well. The people of America certainly would have cause for alarm if the *New Masses* were to start commending the FBI instead of criticizing it.

With best wishes and kind regards,
EDGAR

THE WHITE HOUSE, REGENTS PARK
LONDON, N.W. 1, JANUARY 15, 1965

DEAR LOUIS:

It was so good of you to "resurrect" my name in the list of Fred Astaire's dancing partners. I was in fact, his first partner, after Adele married and we did *Gay Divorce* (I still think Cole Porter's "Night and Day" in that production the best tune he ever wrote) in New York. I was delighted, too, that Fred used the dancing routine in "Night and Day" suggested by me when he filmed the play. Due to an accident on the stage during the run of *Gay Divorce,* my dancing days were soon over but the good Lord opened a wider door to me—the legitimate theatre where, after all these years I am still trying to become a good actress.

By strange coincidence, the first film Fred did—with Joan Crawford—was an episode from my life story, written by James Warner Bellah. The film was *Dancing Lady.*

As ever
CLAIRE LUCE

MARCH 8, 1944

DEAR LOUIS:

Forgive a pal if he tells you you were wrong about Caruso being the first to sing George M. Cohan's "Over There" at the Friars' dinner with Raymond Hitchcock as toastmaster. But don't feel badly, others made the same mistake before you. To set you right, Nora Bayes and Irving Fisher first sang "Over There." Cohan had brought it back stage at the 39th Street Theatre where Nora was doing an intimate show called *Songs We Love,* and George said to her, "Nora, I've just written a song I'd like you to try, I want to see if it's any good." Nora put it on next and it was a big hit. She used it in vaudeville after that.

Caruso did sing "Over There" sometime later at the Friars' dinner you mention. It was George M. Cohan, though, who was the toastmaster, and Hitchcock was one of the speakers—as were Rennold Wolf, music critic William J. Henderson, Victor Herbert.

Ever thine,
JOE LAURIE, JR.

NEW YORK
FEB. 17, 1941

O, DEAR LOUIS:

Why did you who have always been so kindly refer to me as "faded star." How unfair of you. While making the Ziegfeld picture, I had an offer to make another for another studio and also a tour for 22 weeks on a contract that would have netted me $250,000. I was cut out of the picture, the contracts were not signed. I found it hard to get work—so I went off to Mexico and

> Sahara Desert—then Billy Rose signed me on at the Diamond Horseshoe and you know I was quite a success, and that more good 4-figure offers came in. Why "faded star"?
>
> GILDA GRAY

I felt quite penitent—and in a later column, recalled her glorious past when she was literally the toast of the town.

Gilda Gray died on December 24, 1959, and she would have been happy over the glowing obituary salutes. In my own tribute, I commented that

> ... It was like a penny thriller, this story of the little immigrant girl who emerged from a bawdy bistro where she twisted her gelatinous slimness in a provocative cooch and chanted her ribald blues as drink-sodden habitués leered and guffawed and applauded. The cooch gradually resolved itself to a dance—to be forever labeled "The Shimmy"—and the little immigrant girl was able, out of the fabulous earnings that began to accrue, to pay $175,000 for a showplace at Oceanside, Long Island, a magnificent mansion with pillared porches, shaded by a baby forest of locust trees.
>
> Here the Sheba of Shimmy Shakers dwelt and held court in those bright happy-go-lucky years of the twenties when her star was among the brightest in the theatrical heavens—when she was first the friend and later the wife of Gaillard Thomas (Gil) Boag who, more than any others, was said to have guided her to her dazzling success. Gil died not too many months ago, completely out of touch with his former wife.

Gilda, blonde, blue-eyed, lithe, electrifying torso-tosser, was the Big Town's Glamor Girl Number 1 long before the descriptive had come into usage. She "inspired" performers to shake their shoulders and their hips and many scores of singing lads and lasses to chant the "St. Louis Blues," "Beale Street Blues," "Memphis Blues" and other jazz chants which she had popularized.

Ziegfeld had her working for him for some three years. He labeled her the Golden Girl and paid her $3,500 a week. I don't know how much money Gilda had left out of her fortune when she died, but I don't think it could have been much. For when I saw her at the time she was content with trifling pay as one of the group of old-timers in Billy Rose's Diamond Horseshoe, I found her living in two drab little rooms in a midtown hotel, her entire personal staff consisting of two canaries—this Golden

Girl, who in her heyday had three press agents, a private secretary, two personal maids, a butler, a housekeeper, a cook, two chauffeurs, a gardener, a gardener's helper, and three housemaids.

Gail (Gil) Boag died early in March of 1959. During his marriage to Gilda, O. O. McIntyre wrote a highly sentimental tribute:

> He reads the Mother Goose jingles to her which she slowly and patiently spells out letter by letter. She has learned to form letters in a childish amateurish way—and the letters spell words that are symbols of her love for him and her own happiness. On one of her recent birthdays, he presented to her a de luxe edition of *Robinson Crusoe* with the loving inscription of hope that she would soon be able to master its pages. A rope of pearls was beside the book, but when he came home, it was the book that she held while her eyes glistened with gratitude.

Some years later, after their divorce, Gilda, referring to O. O. McIntyre's posy for Boag, exploded: "It's the bunk. Gil was no angel. Don't let anyone tell you I was happy in that marriage. For all he did for me, he got paid—and well. I wasn't his meal ticket —I was his banquet ticket."

Gilda always insisted she had given Gil $150,000 in divorce settlement, as well as their Long Island estate. The mansion, when last I heard about it some years ago, had been converted into an undertaking parlor. The Shimmy Queen, to repeat, died on December 24, 1959—nine short months after Gil Boag was laid to rest. To the end, I don't think Gilda Gray ever thought of herself as a "faded star."

DEC. 7, 1942

DEAR LOUIS:

I am not at all pleased with your recent statements about me in your *American Weekly* piece. For the past fifteen years, newspapers have dished up a lurid, distorted, largely untrue account of happenings in my life and those of certain women during the three years between 1928 and 1931. I was not arrested or even questioned by the police during those years, yet you never mention the utter lack of evidence of wrong-doing on my part, and you and your paper, year after year, picture me a libertine-knave and airy Don Juan.

Can't you finally drop this stale malice and really aid me in obtaining work, or leave me alone? My ninth book of verse was printed this year, yet you ask when will I go back to writing. If you can give me nothing but exaggerated sneers and wild nonsense I wish you would remain silent concerning me.

MAXWELL BODENHEIM

But the truth was I based my piece strictly on what had been revealed in practically every newspaper in New York through the years—as well as some information Bodenheim personally had conveyed to me on occasions when I sat with him in one or another of the Village gathering places.

In his book *My Life and Loves in Greenwich Village,* published in 1954, shortly after his tragic death, Bodenheim himself confirmed most of the statements I had made. By that time, it was no secret that this talented poet and novelist was an alcoholic and broke. He and his wife, Ruth Fagan, were slain in their dingy quarters on Third Avenue on the night of February 7, 1954, by a vagrant dishwasher, Harold Weinberg, who made a full confession. According to the self-confessed slayer, Bodenheim in a drunken stupor had awakened to find him, Weinberg, making love to Ruth and had attacked him, whereupon Weinberg shot him to death with a rifle, and because Ruth Fagan had gone to the defense of Bodenheim, Weinberg stabbed her fatally with a hunting knife.

(In November of 1967, Weinberg, having spent some thirteen years in Matteawan was believed by the doctors to have recovered his sanity and to be eligible for a new trial. But as he marched into the courtroom, he suddenly began shouting wild incoherencies, even accusing his own court-appointed lawyer of having committed the murders, and so, on the judge's orders, Weinberg was recommitted.)

GARDEN OF ALLAH
HOLLYWOOD, CALIF.
Nov. 19, 1938

DEAR LOUIS:

In the same column today where you mention that "words of horrified protest shriek to be released" over some political imbroglio three or thousand miles away [Ed.'s note: He was referring to a paragraph revolving about Hitler and the movements of his Nazi hordes which were eventually to lead to World War II!], you nominate Gene Cavallero as of the Colony *Club.*

May I suggest that outrage and horror in Main Street is worth more than a war in Europe and that for my favorite New York columnist not to know the difference between the Colony *Club* and the Colony *Restaurant* suggests that you haven't been eating in the right places.

The Colony Club is a private premises sheltering a posse of elderly beldames, the *social* equivalent of, say, the Union League and the social parallel of the waiting room at Grand Central. The Colony Restaurant is the most distinguished eating place in North America. Mr. Cavallero owns part and works at the latter.

Louis, Louis, you must rise above Fifty-second Street if you are to be the complete New York reporter. Yours in a California high mist which is laying sleet on the highways and beating in the roof with hailstones.

LUCIUS BEEBE

TEANECK, N.J.
OCT. 25, 1952

DEAR LOU:

I am truly humbled. No one ever referred to anything I have ever written as "brilliant." Instead of inflating my Irish ego, it had the opposite effect: I felt saddened. Twenty-five years ago, I would have given an arm if Frank Carson or Harvey Duell of the *News* had said it, or Emile Gauvreau of the *Mirror*. But they never said it. And perhaps, to be just, it was never deserved and it may not even be deserved now. But you wrote "brilliant," and for the rest of my life I'm going to insist that that was exactly what you meant.

Come to think of it, the only word of praise I can ever remember came from Charlie Barth, the night editor of the *Mirror*. He is a quiet guy, as you know, the last in the world to praise or condemn. My final assignment on the *Mirror* before leaving for *Collier's* magazine, was to cover the execution of Eli Schonbrun and John Cullen in Sing Sing. If you recall the case, a stout German refugee woman, Susan Reich, had refused to give them a diamond ring and they (Madeline Webb was involved, too)—had strangled her with piano wire and had cut the ring off her finger.

When the execution was done, I wrote the story—as all reporters do—exactly as I had seen it. It was filed at the Western Union office in Ossining and, because of the war, two girl operators bugged it to New York. When the last take was in, I noticed that one of the girls was crying. At that moment, the machine chattered and she took a message from Barth. It was addressed to me. All it said was: "Well done."

I never forgot it and I shall never forget what you wrote about the book.

Best,
JIM BISHOP

I thought his was rather a handsome letter in return for the few words of praise I had bestowed upon Bishop for his biography *The Mark Hellinger Story*. Incidentally, in one chapter, Bishop wrote: "Most of the wise men of the editorial staff had figured Louis Sobol would be brought over to the *News*. Sobol was on a dying sheet (*The Graphic*) but not for long. He was picked up by the New York *Journal*, where his dissertations on nostalgia would become famous . . ." So now in turn I had to write a note of appreciation to Jim.

Actually for the records, Colonel Hause, the managing editor of the *News*, did send for me with a bid to become the gossip columnist on the morning tabloid. His idea was to have me run a daily column of gossipy shorts. Since I was beginning to experiment with so-called "think pieces" occasionally and becoming averse to the daily grind of one-liners, I turned the invitation down. A few months later, as I have recorded in an earlier chapter, I went over to the *Journal*.

DECEMBER 6, 1932

DEAR MR. SOBOL:

I have read in your column the misstatements concerning my unfortunate husband, Nijinsky, and assumed you made the said statements unwittingly. Wouldn't you care to have the true facts?

Mesdames Pavlova, Karalli, Karsavina had finished the Imperial School in St. Petersburg years before Nijinsky graduated from there. They were his partners—not his pupils. Nijinsky had no pupils except myself and his sister, Bronia, also a graduate of the Imperial School.

Unfortunately, he became mentally deranged in 1919. Ever since he has been nursed under my supervision—the first seven years at home—since then in a sanatorium in Switzerland. He has been under treatments by so eminent psychiatrists as Prof. Bleuler, Jung, Kreplin and Wagner-Jauregg. Their names alone are sufficient to show that Nijinsky has never been mistreated or chained. He has neither hypnotized himself or anybody else. Never did he believe or behave as a horse or any other animal.

At the performance you refer to in your column, Nijinsky was accompanied by Serge de Diagilew, my sister and the nurses. My only aim these years has been and still is, in spite of tremendous sacrifices to provide Nijinsky with the proper care and to lessen his sufferings.

With best regards to you,
ROMOLA NIJINSKY

What I had written in part—and what Mme Nijinsky had hastened to insist were not the facts, was as follows:

There was a time when Nijinsky's very appearance on a stage in any European City was the signal for hysterical applause. As he grew more successful, he became mysterious and morbid. He plunged deeply into the study of occult sciences and soon acquired the power of hypnotism. At first he experimented on his friends. It was great fun—better than the ordinary parlor tricks—making a dignified prima donna crawl around the room on her hands and knees in the belief that she was a puppy, for instance.

But Nijinsky sought greater achievements in this newly discovered occult realm. He decided to hypnotize himself, and came the day when newspapers throughout the world ran headlines informing: "Nijinsky Hypnotizes Himself"—"Nijinsky Believes He Is A Horse"—"Nijinsky Hopelessly Insane."

Since then the foremost physicians and scientists have endeavored futilely to bring him out of his self-afflicted trance. Recently Balieff of the Chauve Souris took him to the Opera de Paris where, manacled to his seat, he watched his protégée Karsavina, dance for him. Music, gaiety, applauding crowds on all sides—but this tragic figure, chained to his seat, remained as a stranger, insensible to what was taking place. Karsavina, from the stage, smiled at him and for him. Only his wildly staring eyes greeted her. She wavered a bit and then swooned in the midst of her performance. The curtain was rung down.

Now all this—most of which Mme Nijinsky disputed—came to me in a long letter from Paris from one who had known Nijinsky well, and who wrote he had been present at the incident at the Opera de Paris. Nevertheless, in all fairness, I ran Mme Nijinsky's letter in the column.

The great dancing genius, ill-fated through so much of his

life, died in London on April 8, 1950—with the long-loyal wife Romola, at his bedside. Ironically enough, in his last few years he had evidenced signs of recovery from his schizophrenia and in fact had attended a television rehearsal of the ballet of the French National Opera, seemingly in good health and in good spirits. But that evening at his home in Surrey, he complained of a severe headache. Mrs. Nijinsky summoned a physician who decided to move him to a London clinic. A few days later he died there—aged sixty. The ailment was diagnozed as nephritis.

LAKE FOREST, ILL.
APRIL 6, 1964

DEAR MR. SOBOL:

I read your items that I had taught Arthur Murray special dance routines and that he subsequently applied for a job at Castle House.

I never taught anyone how to dance except Mr. William Randolph Hearst, Sr., who needed very little advice from me as he was naturally a very fine dancer. Mr. Murray, in spite of his earlier claims to the contrary, never had a job at Castle House. Mrs. Hubbel, who ran the dancing school at Castle House, was never an admirer of Mr. Murray and wouldn't welcome him instructing at Castle House where the standards were high and our teachers were debutantes—and the male teachers what might be called "male debutantes."

Vernon Castle taught a few lucky applicants, dancing a few hours a week, but with his home at Manhasset on the water, it was too hard to get him away from his dogs, horses and speedboats to teach many hours a week, in spite of how handsomely it paid.

Sincerely,
IRENE CASTLE

Checking, I was advised that one of Murray's earlier drumbeaters had built up this minor legend about the dancing man. Subsequent press agents had occasionally repeated the story, until it may be very probable that Arthur Murray himself came to believe it truly was so. Just as the late FDR finally came to believe that "Home On the Range" was actually the song he favored above all others.

CHARLOTTE, N.C.
OCT. 3, 1959

DEAR LOUIS SOBOL:

Upon my return from Israel, I found about 60 or 70 copies of your column of Sept. 12th. These subscribers of mine up there seem to be a little worried about your reference to the *Exodus* review in one of my recent issues.

A correction. The *Exodus* review was written by my son, Richard, and signed, as usual, R. G., and while I personally may have disagreed with some of his observations, I do not interfere.

Another correction—your statement that *The Carolina Israelite* review was the only critical stab. The original reviews were not too enthusiastic, and certainly my son's (he reads books for CBS) was far more gentlemanly than the one in *Commentary,* the official publication of the American Jewish Committee. And of course the reviews in Israel were far from satisfactory.

Mr. Uris has done a tremendous job. During five weeks in Israel I saw hundreds of American tourists using *Exodus* as a guidebook, and when a man can achieve that with a novel, he has done a tremendous thing.

You and I would cringe at the thought that anyone would have to "excuse" literary criticism, but I thought that these facts are pertinent.

Sincerely,
HARRY GOLDEN

NEW YORK
FEB. 19, 1940

DEAR LOUIS SOBOL:

Congratulations and a hearty hand-clasp. With your permission I would like to use your brilliant column of yesterday along with my "appreciation" herewith enclosed, in a little booklet to pass along to my sales force and to clients. What you have written deserves to be read by every man and woman in America, and of course we all know there is nothing deader than yesterday's newspaper, so I would like to put it in more permanent form.

I wouldn't be at all surprised if, after I had printed it, other firms through the country would want to send it to their salesmen. It has often happened in the past with things I had written myself where the circulation ran into many thousands.

I hope someday to know you personally. It so happens that Jack Lait was lunching with me at the Tavern the day he met you to talk over your going with the Hearst organization. You of course will not recall, but he introduced us and then went over to a side table with you.

In those day we all gathered at Koenigsburg's table at the old Friars Club—Koenig, Gortatowsky, Joe Connolly, Jack Lait and myself. And of course Billy LaHiff and myself established the now famous corner table at the Tavern. Since Billy's death, I have not been in the Tavern—and of course, the old Friars—as compared with the new—is no more—and since I never did go to nightclubs I've missed meeting and getting to know you personally.

Cordially,
JAMES W. ELLIOTT

I was a bit flattered by this note—and it brought back a memory. Years previously, when James Elliott was being hailed as the nation's Supersalesman, one of his alluring advertisements made me discontented with my meager pay as a Connecticut newspaperman. I was impressed with the visions of success and prestige that were in store for young gentlemen whom Mr. Elliott might find eligible for berths in his vast, prosperous organization.

So I splurged for train fare to Manhattan, attended one of Mr. Elliott's meetings, and was duly impressed. Mr. Elliott, however, was not impressed with me, for when I got to him and timorously expressed a yearning to become one of his supersalesmen, the master, after a quick and piercing survey, snapped something to the effect that he should prefer to have me write him a letter, stating in full my qualifications.

I did write the letter but received no reply, and finally and sadly decided that Mr. Elliott had no place for me in his cast of brilliant young men.

I am submitting portions of the column which struck the fancy of the late master salesman—and which he did reissue as he promised in several thousand handsomely printed booklets:

One More Round: Of the many statements the late James J. Corbett made through his colorful career, only one has stuck with me during the years. "What," he was asked, "was important for a man to become champion?" Corbett replied: "Fight One More Round."

Corbett was a pugilistic champion, but there have been champions in other fields, and the same may be said of them—they have been able to fight "one more round." Thomas Edison, seeking a proper filament to light his incandescent lamp, failed month after month, but one day his efforts were crowned with success, and the world was gifted with the electric light. He had fought "one more round."

S. N. Behrman, one of America's outstanding playwrights, turned out manuscripts for eleven years before he finally sold his first play. At this time I forget the number of stories Fannie Hurst wrote before the first was accepted. Somerset Maugham was a failure for eleven years, earning in all that time the gross sum of five hundred dollars. A producer needing a play to fill in while he was looking around, dug Maugham's forgotten *Lady Frederick* out of a desk drawer. Maugham became the toast of London.

Thus I went on—mentioned Ulysses S. Grant, Dr. Paul Ehrlich and his Magic Bullet (605 previous failures to find the successful formula—the 606th a success—and so it was labeled with that number). I brought in Enrico Caruso, who persevered for almost a dozen years, studying at night while he worked in a factory during the day.

I mentioned others—Walt Disney, for instance, whose first series of animated cartoons, "Oswald the Rabbit," was a dismal failure. But then came "Mickey Mouse." I referred to Robert L. Ripley (Believe-It-or-Not) who was fired from the first three newspapers on which he worked; O. O. McIntyre, dismissed as a copyreader from the *Evening Mail;* H. G. Wells, discharged after one month as a drygoods salesman. I recollect that the first time George Gershwin played the piano in a theatre, the audience laughed him off the stage. As a composer, he wrote almost one hundred tunes before selling his first for five dollars.

And so on and on, ending with Carrie Jacobs Bond, semi-invalid, trying to run a rooming house, selling hand-painted china—even singing songs in vaudeville. A failure at everything. All the time, trying her hand at writing songs, which the publishers spurned, and then she wrote "The End of a Perfect Day."

OCT. 2, 1936

DEAR LOUIS SOBOL:

My sincere thanks for your letter. As Moran and Mack used

to say, "perhaps I shouldn't have mentioned it." In any event let's forget it. I quite agree with you it would be a mistake to print anything more about it. If my letter to Bill [Hearst, Jr.] will lead to you and I becoming better acquainted it will at least be worth something.

All my friends, without exception, read your work as regularly as they eat. [How could I resist that bit of flattery!] Perhaps this is why I became upset about the item which I mentioned.

Incidentally, I noticed you wrote the other day that Mark Hellinger had a nice deal for some picture work. This does not startle me in the least. I am surprised you fellows have not gotten on the gravy train before. Personally I would rather depend on one good newspaper writer, who, through experience, has a real insight into the human drama that makes up everyday life, than on all the so-called specialists rolled in one.

With best wishes,
HOWARD HUGHES

The lines which had offended the then quite youthful young millionaire were as follows: "Howard Hughes in a crumpled white linen jacket but a fresh-looking creamy-white doll clinging to his thinnish arm, hovers uncertainly in the Paradise lobby Tuesday night until headwaiter Albert Berryman steers him to his party."

I meant it innocently enough as an observation, but Hughes misconstrued the "hovers uncertainly" as implying he might have been drinking, which was far from my intent—and also, because of the reference to the "creamy-white doll," that I was cataloging him as something of a playboy.

Hughes, despite his high opinion of newsmen as worthy of assignments in the movie industry, never called upon me to come to the aid of the movies, although perhaps that may have been because I never appealed to him for a berth when he became a power in the cinema world. We did get on fairly cordial terms after our slight misunderstanding. There was one occasion, at the time he was being seen around with Lana Turner, when I encountered the pair in El Morocco, and invited them to join me and my wife at an opening at the Latin Quarter.

Lana was all for going, but Hughes shook his head firmly, insisting that it was gay enough at El Morocco. And presumably it is even gayer in Las Vegas, which he now practically owns. As one comic put it, Hughes has adopted for his theme song: "This Land Is Mine."

VIRGINIA CITY, NEVADA
JULY 22, 1958

DEAR LOUIS:

Your column on the vanished boulevardier of a few days ago inspires this communiqué. You base your hypothesis on the theory that a boulevardier is a happy dog who doesn't believe that we work to live or live to work and then cite myself amongst a group of characters known to work like dogs for a living, as eager beavers as ever came down the pike: Jules Glaenzer, Serge Obolensky, John Perona, Conrad Hilton, Mark Hanna. To be sure, you mitigate this working stiff category with some public nuisances and freeloaders, Windsor and Rubirosa, but these no-gooders would never have made the Boulevardiers' guild in any time or place except your mistaken selection. Neither of them has the moral stamina demanded for the calling.

The truth of the matter is that the climate of the United States and New York especially is unsuited to the boulevardier and has been for nigh onto fifty years. You have to go back to Berry Wall, Center Hitchcock, Richard Canfield and the elder Barrymore, well before your or my time (except Berry Wall, whom I used to know in Paris in the early twenties) before you can encounter the leisured expert in sumptuous but honorable living tempered by wit and tolerance.

Possibly the boulevardier can exist today in New Orleans of the cities in America. Certainly the late Lyle Saxon was in the great tradition even though times were tough on him toward the end. I remember well how, long after he had ceased to have occasion to dress for the evening, his man Joe still set out his silver-buckled dancing pumps at dinner time even though Saxon was dining in a cafeteria. Nor would the old gentleman ever allow common waiters to serve him in public. Joe stood behind his place and passed the dishes to him as was proper.

There never were any real boulevardiers in my time in New York, even though Odd McIntyre and I and Charlie Towne may have approached this status. We were all too busy chasing a fast and somewhat harder buck for really dignified indolence.

As usual, your severest critic,
LUCIUS BEEBE

I quote some excerpts from the column that lured Beebe's own analysis.

> I have forgotten just when and how I became acquainted and infatuated with the descriptive, "boulevardier." It could very well have been from some treatise by James Huneker or perhaps a passing reference by O. O. McIntyre, but when finally I acquired a column, I endowed certain gentlemen around town with this particular posy.
>
> To me, the true boulevardier was (and is) the gay fellow who adheres firmly to his epicurean tastes and fastidiousness with the steadfastness of a Christian martyr. I knew he was to be found not only along our Fifth Avenue and in the purlieus of Park Avenue, but he was the fellow you would be most likely to encounter on the world-famed boulevards and at the watering meccas of the world—in Nice and Deauville, Mittersil' and Monte Carlo, parading debonairely, gambling like a gentleman and wooing the great international beauties.
>
> These lads were the connoisseurs of the flavored dish and molded silks and cheviots, the expert wine tasters, the gents who bowed to the tradition of George Bryan Brummell. They followed the sun, and few of them believed that we work to live or live to work.
>
> But here let me inject my melancholy note—there are so few of them around. Where there were so many to liven up a paragraph or two in other years, too few now devote themselves to passionate discussions of the correct tone of Burgundy that should accompany a boned squab stuffed with pâté or argue into dawn the merits of vin Rhone or Vouvray for summer consumption or mourn the incorrect cut of a lapel or the correct height of a collar.
>
> I would pick Serge Obolensky as a survivor—although quite disloyal to the clan, for he does work and work hard as a hotel host. But he does know his scoff and his vintages, and tailors swoon when he enters their establishments.
>
> Lucius Beebe was a self-avowed boulevardier in other years, but now he wears cowboy hats and boots and silver-buckled belts and works at being a newspaper publisher. And though he will still come through in the grand manner when he invades Manhattan and spends as much as a hundred dollars or more for dinner for two at the Pavillon or "21" or the Colony, nevertheless he must be counted among the deserters.
>
> Jules Glaenzer is still with us, but he has abandoned the ranks of the lavish party givers, is a rare frequenter of the night

haunts, and no longer is perturbed if the salad isn't tossed to his liking.

I went on to discuss Aly Khan, Conrad Hilton, John Perona and Mark Hanna among others. "There are some," I also insisted, "who will maintain that the Duke of Windsor rates the big 'B' and others who would include Errol Flynn and Mike Romanoff."

"I cannot," I concluded, "in all conscience include the fabulous Greeks—Onassis, Goulandris and Niarchos, for great wealth and sumptuous yachts aren't the qualifying essentials, and there isn't a single newspaperman who rates the nod currently—not since the passing of O. O. McIntyre."

SEPT. 15, 1937

DEAR LOUIS SOBOL:

I have never met you but I do follow your column—let me be honest, when I can spare the time. I did read the handsome little tribute you paid my book—although having authored it, I cannot agree with you that it might have been cut one-third and would thereby, to quote you, gained more momentum. But again, thank you—and I will not turn critic, in retaliation, and suggest you should cut your column pieces by one-third to gain momentum.

Yours,
THOMAS WOLFE

I finally met the distinguished novelist one night in "21" shortly before his death. What impressed me is that when the introduction was made, he rose. At the time I wish he hadn't done that, for Mr. Wolfe was six feet and some five or six inches tall—and I am just barely able to reach five feet five inches—and Mr. Wolfe had the grip of a man of height and brawn. For days after, I fingered my way painfully over the typewriter keys with only the left hand.

JULY 3, 1938

DEAR LOUIS:

It was nice talking to you the other afternoon—and you seemed quite interested in what Lew [Fields] and I had to tell you about those other days when I guess you might say we were riding pretty high. I don't suppose anyone knows more about those glorious nineties than Lew and I except, perhaps, Bill Brady and Dan Frohman. It was in 1898—maybe you weren't even born then—that we engaged Lillian Russell and she was with us for many years. In 1905 I started Flo Ziegfeld in the girlie biz. And back in 1896, Fields and myself started the modern type of girl show on Broadway and we were the first to burlesque current plays and now I see they're going to do it in pictures.

As ever,
JOE WEBER

Those slapstick comedians, Weber and Fields, had been in long retirement, of course, when I arrived on the Broadway scene, but I had read so much about their career that I was a bit awe-stricken when I first met them. Thereafter I sought them out at their usual lunching place, the Astor's Hunt Room, and lured many rich paragraphs from them dealing with show business and personalities of the past. Lew Fields was to become the proud father of three talented offspring—one was the late playwright, Joe Fields, who gave us *Doughgirls, My Sister Eileen,* and *Junior Miss,* and was also collaborator with Anita Loos on *Gentlemen Prefer Blondes;* with Oscar Hammerstein II on *Flower Drum Song* and with Jerome Chodorov on *Wonderful Town.*

His other son, the late Herb Fields, collaborated with his sister, librettist Dorothy Fields, on many hit musicals—among them, *Annie, Get Your Gun, Up in Central Park, Something for the Boys, Mexican Hayride* and others, besides *Present Arms* and *Panama Hattie* and *DuBarry Was a Lady,* this one with Buddy De Sylva.

As for Dorothy Fields, she turned out the lyrics for close to five hundred songs—many of them outstanding hits, such as "I Can't Give You Anything but Love, Baby," "I'm in the Mood for Love," etc., and, of course, in more recent years, the spirited songs in the musical *Sweet Charity,* which starred Gwen Verdon.

Before his death in 1941 at the age of seventy-five, Lew Fields had lived long enough to take bows for the success of his three children.

CHICAGO, MAY 15, 1945

DEAR LOUIS SOBOL:

I want to assure you my eyes smarted, too, when I read the

comment in your column of your visit to the old-time silent movies. Some of the best years of my life went into those old-timers. I loved them then, I love them still. They will abide with me until my course is run.

Yours as ever,
WM. S. HART

There must have been thousands of other folks from coast to coast who felt that little pang when they read that William S. Hart, the two-gun hero of the silents, had died on June 22, 1946. What a hero he was to us, and in what awe we held him! I struck up a friendship with this boyhood hero of mine in later years, and we carried on quite a correspondence. He was a sentimental old fellow and a softy, which you'd never suspect from those films. And every time he wrote a book, he'd send me an affectionately inscribed copy.

I always thought that the one actor who came closest to filling his boots was the late Gary Cooper. Like Hart, tough as he was in many of his pictures, he, too, was a gentle chap, a softy. I remember how Cooper charmed the women in our party one day in Cannes when he left his table at a restaurant to come over to say hello. The last time I saw Bill Hart was in Jack Dempsey's restaurant when it was on Eighth Avenue, a year or so before his death. The last time I saw Cooper was at the Colony about six months before he died. He looked years younger than his age that night, and there was no indication of the dread ailment that was to fell him, nor anything in his manner to indicate he knew his days were numbered. Yet we were informed that even then the doctors had revealed to him the nature of his illness.

APRIL 5, 1963

DEAR LOUIS:

I must confess that I did think your crack about my failure to rise to the occasion at Basin Street was a bit on the snide side, if not entirely called for. During my 36 years in show business, you and I have encountered one another no more than half a dozen times at most. The reason, of course, is obvious: I don't frequent the spots on your beat. However, let me set you straight —so you'll realize how little you can depend on getting your information second hand.

Peggy Lee is one of the very few performers who could ever

get me into a nightclub. Her Serene Highness reigns over her subjects with such supreme authority as to place us all under her hypnotic spell. One forgets completely the torture of the place: the smoke, the reek of alcoholic breaths, the redolence of the perfume mixed with the sweat due to the horrible humidity, not to mention the libidinous intertwining of one's lower limbs with those of complete strangers of either sex or both, under the table and on either side. Nevertheless I will go anywhere, anytime and pay any price to watch Miss Peggy Lee at work. Then I go home and play all twenty-one of her albums.

So I went to see her the other night. Benny Goodman, despite your informant, was not present. At least, if he was, he did not make an appearance on the stage that night.

Down near the end of Peggy's midnight performance (it was now 1:30ish), she announced a very dear friend of hers was in the audience someplace. She couldn't see him, she said, because of the spotlights in her eyes, but she could FEEL his presence. She was most gracious. She said she wanted to introduce him, even though she knew that he hated the procedure, because "our friendship means so much to me." And she introduced me.

I received one of the warmest receptions ever accorded me in my career, and I was thrilled beyond measure because I never dreamed that nightclub habitués in New York had much use for a guy who does a daily radio program at ten o'clock in the morning and makes only infrequent television appearances these nights. Then Peggy asked if I would sing with her. I demurred with thanks, saying, "Oh, no, thank you, Peggy dear. I want to hear more of YOU." She said, "Oh, I don't mean for you to come up here on the stage. I mean . . ." but she never finished. The audience roared approval of the idea and urged me up. I said, "Peggy, do you remember the duet we did on my program the other day?" She nodded, and I made my way to the platform.

We sang the duet. Peggy sings "Talk to Me" whilst I sing "Kiss Me Once, Kiss Me Twice, Kiss Me Once Again," which is a perfect countermelody. It happened that it came off beautifully and the audience was obviously pleased. We got a tremendous hand and there were cries of "more, more, more!" which is where we, being seasoned showmen, left them.

And that's the way it really was, Louis.

Most cordially,
ARTHUR GODFREY

This lengthy protest by Godfrey was inspired by a few lines in my column in which, from information furnished by a zealous drumbeater, I wrote: "Benny Goodman climbed on the stage at Basin Street East, grabbed a clarinet and offered a half-hour concert gratis—contributing to the happiness of the patrons—especially to the owners. Goodman for free is always a joyous event for night-spot hosts. Another customer present this particular night, enjoyed it immensely but didn't offer to join in with the band—Arthur Godfrey."

Reproaching the press agent for misleading me on Benny Goodman's presence, I was informed indignantly that he had erred only in that he had presented Goodman and Godfrey at the same session, instead of a night apart. Some good came out of it all, however—Godfrey invited me to be a paid guest on his radio program.

FOREST HILLS, N.Y.
APRIL 26, 1938

DEAR MR. SOBOL:

Your paragraphs in the *Journal-American* two weeks ago were read to me. In it you wrote you had done ghost writing for me among others. I resent such a statement—it conveys a gross misrepresentation of facts.

It is true, in 1924, Mr. Leslie Fulenwider asked me to write a brief article daily for Famous Feature Syndicates. I furnished him with material I had already written and which only needed shortening to suit his purposes. This was done with the understanding that the articles should stop when the material was exhausted. After a while, to my great chagrin, I discovered that although the items I sent Mr. Fulenwider had been used up, yet the articles were being continued. I telegraphed him to suspend the articles. Several years later I wrote thoughts on immortality under the heading of death notices for Famous Features Syndicate.

I can't understand your reference therefore to "ghost writing" for me.

Sincerely,
HELEN KELLER

In my letter to Miss Keller I explained that her pieces had been turned over to me while I was with Famous Features, and that part of my chores was to rewrite them so that they would appear to be new thoughts by the famed, remarkable woman who had not permitted her triple affliction—deafness, muteness and blindness—to keep her from being as active—if not more active—than most people without any of her handicaps. And I was careful thereafter not to refer to the rewrite job as "ghost writing" for her. I have never been sure that she ever forgave me—in spite of my explanatory note.

Aug. 26, 1965

Dear Louis:

I have been dwarfed by Studs Lonigan. Even you, when you make reference to me, bring in my Studs Lonigan background. Now for years I have given much time to Irish studies—literary, historical and political. But the only Irish phenomena editors want me to be known by is "Studs Lonigan."

Since 1957 I have published over three hundred pieces. Only one of these was about Studs Lonigan. One, *Communism and Military Power,* has been praised by senators, a well-known military writer and an army colonel.

Slowly and gradually you will be able to notice this—American publications and publishing houses giving credit to foreign sources for the original publication of writings of mine.

Editors and others engulfed me with Studs Lonigan. In consequence I have outwritten the American publishing industry and now have at least 60,000 pages of mss. and/or collected writings which I think should eventually, and some sooner, go into book publication.

I have been crippled from a fair competitive opportunity by being treated as an ignorant loogin—but eventually I will live to see a laughingstock made out of many people.

Cordially,
Jim Farrell

Some two years later, came this postscript:

The battle is over. I have now more than enough work to do that I am able to present a variety of parts of my future writings which will provide the public with all that it needs to judge my enemies and detractors—and myself. . . .

Frankly, I was mystified by these notes and others, for I always believed James T. Farrell was held in high regard by critics, and his numerous fans, like myself, found his *Studs Lonigan* and other novels absorbing reading. Indeed, despite his own denigration of the novels that propelled him into fame, it is a fact that these books have lodged him among the literary elite—though in late years, according to his letters to me, he would prefer more attention to his poems.

Despite correspondence between us, oddly enough Farrell and I have never met.

15

Along the Newsbeat

I LIKE NEWSPAPERMEN. Perhaps it's because I used to be a newspaperman myself once. I look forward to mingling with the members of the craft, and I have even been known to sit tolerantly while a fellow columnist boasted of some of his more recent exclusives. What I like about the men of my business is that 90 percent of their conversation is shoptalk, and a newsman's shoptalk, like show folks' talk, is the most fascinating talk there is because it covers the world and the people in the world.

Most newspapermen have had at least one exciting adventure —certainly a series of adventures if the reporter has been a war correspondent. Some have flirted with death. I know one chap who bears the scars of three bullet wounds because he was mistaken for a federal agent during Prohibition days. I know another who lost his wife because his editor assigned him to entice some important and incriminating information from a political boss's girl friend. So he proceeded to make love to the girl, got the information and the letters, but lost his wife, who just didn't understand.

Once in my own early newspaper career when I was state editor for the *Waterbury Republican,* touring with a photographer, we came across the body of a man, scarcely hidden by the roadside brush—the body of a missing cab driver who when last seen had a young couple as his passengers. The body was bullet ridden. The couple was apprehended later in Upstate New York and sentenced to a long prison term. But the story got minor play, although ordinarily this would have been Page One news in our town of Waterbury. The reason it was dismissed so lightly was that President Harding died that very night, and the front page of the *Republican,* the following day, was given over to his career, the details of his death, etc.

Many newsmen have known what it is to be threatened. Winchell for a time was forced to travel with a bodyguard. Gene McHugh, night editor of the *Daily News,* was taken for what threatened to be a "ride" by the late Jack "Legs" Diamond, but he talked himself free. I was threatened with annihilation by a mob man named Jerry Sullivan because of an item I had written about his leader. The late Lee Mortimer was beaten up by Frank Sinatra, and Jimmie Fidler was punched in the nose by the late Errol Flynn. The late Dan Parker received several threats on his life when he was exposing nefarious characters in the fight game.

That's why, to reverse the cliché, you meet the most interesting newspaper people, and I like them for their small talk and their big talk, for their recklessness and their enterprise—and even for their chronic threats to quit the business. They rarely do except when the business quits them, as it has so frequently with the folding of so many newspapers throughout the country in recent years.

"Feudin' and Fussin'"

For years, to my chagrin, a humiliating canard was spread far and wide to the effect that Louis Sobol was one of the gentlest of the Broadway columnists who, rather than write an offensive line or paragraph, would remain silent. Fellow columnists and other writers, whenever referring to me, employed the descriptives "amiable," "mellow," "kindly," "never attacks," etc., etc., *ad nauseam.*

Well, for an "amiable," "mellow," "never attacks" newsman, it is a matter of deep puzzlement to me that I have been involved in a series of feuds, and chiefly with fellow writers. Let me tell you about them.

As far back as 1931, when I transferred my department from the *Graphic* to the *Journal,* I found myself embroiled in a quarrel with Ed Sullivan. Ed, having succeeded me on the *Graphic* (and in my final column, I had welcomed him warmly to the spot), decided in his first column to announce he would not indulge himself or his readers in petty "back-fence" gossip and expressed his scorn for keyhole journalists and keyhole journalism. Whereupon I parried back and freely drew on Shakespeare to the effect that "empty vessels make the most sound." I labeled the paragraph "The Ennui of His Contempt-oraries."

Columnists Earl Wilson and Sobol listen as columnist-TV host Ed Sullivan recalls early days with the author on *The Evening Graphic* when he was the sports columnist, and Sobol was the Broadway paragrapher and drama critic. At the "March of Dimes" dinner honoring the author as "Man of the Year" (May 7, 1962).

The return blast didn't sit well with Ed, and at a theatrical opening a few nights later, during the intermission, he grabbed me by the lapels of my jacket and threatened to commit mayhem right there and then. However, perhaps because of folks milling about, he restrained himself but not without a few more vehement threats. But as the years passed, Sullivan's resentment faded and so did mine. We forgot our differences and gradually returned to a friendly basis again and remain good friends to this day. In fact, in an autobiographical piece for the *Ladies' Home Journal* in 1967, Sullivan freely expressed his regrets over the incident.

A feud with Walter Winchell erupted some years later. Winchell, surrounded by a few press agents, hailed me as I was about to enter the Club Abbey. "Hey, Louie, come over here, I want you to hear this," he shouted. I was coming down with the flu at the time and was in a sorry mood. "You want me, come over here," I barked, and walked into the club.

That started a coolness between us that lasted for years—with both of us sniping at each other on our respective pillars. In addition to bitter little exchanges in our respective columns, Walter dispatched acrimonious notes to me from time to time. For instance, on December 1, 1931, I received a communiqué in which he scolded:

> That was certainly third-rate trying to even a grudge with me—that frame you plotted with Bide [Bide Dudley was then drama editor of the *Evening World*]. You even told other radio commentators "Howz it you didn't hear of my Lucky Strike offer?" You owe an apology to Dudley for giving him such a false steer to exploit your ambitions.
>
> Get a big radio contract, all the more power to you, but don't try to do it the way you tried in the *Journal* on Monday.

A note from Lord, Thomas & Logan and Mr. Hill (George Washington Hill) to me at the studio read: "There is absolutely no foundation to the statement in the *Evening Journal.* No approach whatever has been made to Sobol."

Another similar note came early in April and a copy of one he had sent to Jerry Wald, then radio columnist of the *Graphic,* again insisting I was undermining him by telling folks I was on call to succeed him on the *Lucky Strike* hour.

Actually, while still on the *Ludwig Baumann* hour over WOR, I had been signed on a weekly retainer to be ready to step into Winchell's *Lucky Strike* program if and when a situation arose. The situation arose a few weeks later, when Winchell suffered a temporary breakdown. I took over the *Lucky Strike* hour thrice weekly, beginning on April 19, 1932, and continued until, under a new policy, Jack Pearl came in with his Baron Munchausen routine for one of the three-a-week sessions, Walter O'Keefe on another, and Winchell came back to host the third.

Then one evening when the New Year's Eve festivities were

at their height in the Stork Club, I spotted J. Edgar Hoover and Clyde Tolson at a table and strutted over to wish them holiday greetings, and noticed that Winchell was also at the table. Hoover said, "You two know each other, of course." Winchell grinned, and sheepishly I murmured, "Happy New Year, Walter!" and he wished me the same. I sat down with them—and joined in the general conversation. The feud was over.

There is a postscript to the three-way discord among Messrs. Winchell, Sullivan and Sobol. As I have recorded, my brouhaha with W.W. and Ed subsided after a few years of sniping, and we became quite friendly. But Winchell and Sullivan continued to hiss each other for some thirty-five years or so, which is something of a mark to shoot at, I should think. And then one night, in September of 1967, Winchell arrived in town, mellowed and apparently imbued with the feeling of good fellowship, and he spotted Ed and his wife Sylvia in Dinty Moore's. He walked over to their table and began chatting with them as if he and Sullivan had been intimate lodge members. And that epochal feud was over, too, and indeed, a few nights later they were together at El Morocco.

I happened to be at another table with my wife. Winchell "commanded" me to join him and Sullivan. Then he shouted over to the photographer, Bill Marks, and the three of us posed cordially for several pictures—the three feudist graduates of the *Graphic*—for, to repeat, Winchell had inaugurated the column on the tabloid, I succeeded to the department when he moved over to the *Mirror,* and Sullivan succeeded me when I shifted to the *Journal.* The picture might be labeled, "Two Millionaires and a Pauper," for it's no secret that both Winchell and Sullivan have amassed tidy fortunes.

Indeed, to indicate how the quarrels that seemed so momentous to us in those earlier years have become something to reminisce about and even to laugh over when we remember how serious they appeared to be, both Sullivan and I and our wives were nominated by Winchell to become members of the board of his pet project, the Damon Runyon Cancer Fund.

My long-standing friendship with George Jean Nathan ended, much to my dismay, because of an apparently innocuous line in my column. Nor were my repeated attempts at appeasement with the critic successful. I had written "To George Jean Nathan, every bad play is another Hiss trial." Entering "21" a few nights after, and finding Nathan at his usual corner table, I greeted him amiably, only to be treated to an icy stare.

"Something wrong, George?" I asked, puzzled at this unaccustomed coldness.

"Don't ever speak to me again," he snapped. "I don't ever want to speak to you." He waved to a waiter. "Waiter, bring me some holders for my cigarettes."

Bewildered, I pressed on, seeking the source of his indignation.

"I resent your impugning my integrity as a critic," he exploded. I finally drew from him the explanation. It was the "Hiss" line that had offended him. I tried to tell him it was merely a bit of a bad pun and actually intended as a compliment. But he turned his back on me to indicate he wanted no more dealings with me.

I decided to let him enjoy his dour little mood. The following night, certain he would have calmed down, I greeted him again in "21" with "How are things, George?"

He stared right through me.

A few nights later, at a theatre opening, he had an adjoining seat, and Peggy, whom he had always seemed to hold in high and affectionate regard, tried to start a conversation with him. He turned his back, and I finally realized all attempts at a reconciliation were futile.

To his dying day, George Jean Nathan snubbed me openly and never spoke to me again.

Perhaps my most bitter falling out was with Westbrook Pegler, who, fumbling about during his ordeal in the courtroom as a defendant in the Quentin Reynolds libel suit, attacked both Damon Runyon and me as being "unreliable" newspapermen. This was his retort when attorney Louis Nizer read excerpts from some of our columns which applauded Reynolds as an able and dedicated reporter.

Pegler's attack on me was a puzzler. I had received so many kindly notes from him through the years—letters of approval of certain columns which appealed to him, and one letter in particular, brimming over with soft, warm, sympathetic sentiments following the death of my wife Lee in 1948, that I couldn't understand this turnabout.

I finally wrote him a brief note expressing my puzzlement

Eavesdropping on three gentlemen of stature: Barry Goldwater, Louis Nizer, famed lawyer and author of best sellers, and William Randolph Hearst, Jr. Goldwater was aiming for the Presidency at the time, Nizer was mentally counting up his last royalty checks and Hearst was insisting he didn't want to be vice-president. The author was hoping his long cigar would last through the dinner.
Photo by Bill Mark

and received in turn a rather hysterical reply from which I offer this extract:

> I knew that in reasonable time you would provide in your column absolute proof of my comment, under cross-examination, to which you took exception in the way of the whole brood of professional bellyachers who moan for "minorities" but lynch any decent American who is dedicated to Truth, Human Dignity and the Constitution. Whoever has the manhood to strike back at this encroaching evil is "paranoid" and "psychopathic" [I had not used these words—nor was the tenor of my letter in that direction]. You made the quite expectable charge that I had "blown my stack." In plainer words, I am insane, etc.
>
> I wonder if the Jews were "paranoid" and "psychopathic" and whether it would have been correct and humane to sneer that they had blown their stacks when they were squawking to Heaven that Hitler was doing them dirt. The anti-Jews used to resort to sneers but I have never agreed with them. If you were consistent, you would now concern yourself with equal ardor and fury to rebuke those who have duplicated in the courts of the United States the desperate plight of the Jew in the People's Courts of Adolf Hitler. I know now, from personal experience in my own country, what a leering mockery a Jew had to endure in the guise of Justice in the Nazi courts.
>
> As to Sinatra, you know his records as well as I do. I have contempt for any newspaperman who abuses his prerogative and trust to exalt this man and exculpate him in his endless es-

> capades. [I had written a paragraph in praise of Sinatra.] And you know very well you do not speak for any substantial portion of American newspapermen. I watched a whole corps of Broadway-Hollywood journalists making a social time with the Hollywood riffraff when Browne and Bioff were riding high and never saw a syllable on the subject from any of them. That comes under the subject of "checking the facts."

Nevertheless, I continued to retain a high respect for Peg's writing skill, though in complete disagreement most of the time with his ideology. And when, on occasion, he indulged himself in a sentimental or nostalgic column, he had no greater fan, despite the fact that we were no longer on speaking terms.

Which brings me to the temporary rupture of friendship with Leonard Lyons, who had been a consistent and productive contributor to my department before being awarded a column of his own. Leonard decided it was unethical for me to appear in vaudeville and permit stars to come onstage for ad-lib performances. Since most of the performers used to join me as a lark—without invitation—I struck back, accusing Lyons of ingratitude, recalling how often I had introduced him to various so-called celebrities. We remained cool to each other for quite a time, but we resumed amicable relations when he fathered the first of his four sons. In this instance, as the buoyant new papa stood waiting for someone at the cigar counter in "21," I went up to him and congratulated him on the big event. We shook hands, and Sobol and Lyons resumed their cordiality.

The story of my rift with novelist John O'Hara stemmed from nothing I had written or done to offend him. He was in the Stork Club, seated with his late wife, a most charming woman, when I entered and was assigned the table next to him. At this period, O'Hara and I had been more or less pals and had even traveled to Hollywood together, years previously. We also had the same literary agent, Mark Hanna, so imagine my consternation when John glared at me as if I were an unwelcome stranger and finally spoke. "You're a whore," he rasped, "A Hearst whore." I thought he must be pulling my leg and that this was due to something I had written he might have disagreed with, and which he would now proceed to argue out good-naturedly with me.

There was nothing good-natured about him, however. He simply roared repetitiously: "You're a Hearst whore!" His wife, visibly embarrassed, tugged at his arm to stop him, but again he hurled the accusation at me, only this time in louder tones. So I rose and moved to another table. We have never exchanged another word since. But maybe I am a bit on the mellow side for I do read everything he writes, and I do happen to think he is one of our top storytellers.

I come now to the great war correspondent Floyd Gibbons, who stopped speaking to me, and it was only some months before his death that I learned the reason. I went up to him one day in Jack Dempsey's restaurant and insisted on learning why he had a beef against me. It seems that I had reported him at the bar in "21," "alone—and looking forlorn." He resented that. He had felt at that particular point in his career the world was closing down on him. He was no longer delivering his staccato talks over the radio, he had no lecture commitments and he had been doing no writing. Highly sensitive at all times, it was his opinion that I was trying to convey subtly that his friends had deserted him. I am not quite certain—and never was able to be certain—that I convinced him that night in Dempsey's that what I had written was not intended as a slur but simply as an observation.

A humorist whom I have esteemed highly took offense about a paragraph which actually was intended to extol his talents. Milton Berle had written a book entitled *Comedians Don't Laugh,* in which he named his personal choice for the ten greatest humorists of our times. The name of Arthur "Bugs" Baer was not among them so I commented: "There may be some among us, for instance, who would like to vote for Mr. Arthur 'Bugs' Baer, whose crisp wit has been none the less effective because of the profound thought behind each apparently farfetched quip." To this day I have never been able to understand how this could be offensive to Baer, but he complained to my editor, Bill Curley, who in turn relayed to me Baer's displeasure and hurt. However, in this instance, though neither of us mentioned the matter, we ran into each other too often and with mutual friends to permit the coolness to endure.

Herbert Bayard Swope nourished his peeve for a long, long time. I first became aware that suddenly I was not the most popular citizen with him personally, when one night, in "21," he spurned my outthrust hand and snapped in no obscure phrasing just why he no longer considered me a friend. There was always something definite about Mr. Swope's assertions which never left a doubt in anyone's mind. The offending line which drew down his wrath was this: "Just for a change, instead of a statement by Herbert Bayard Swope on racing, opera or the publishing business, I'd like to read one by his brother, Gerard—known as the Silent Swope." In this instance, I felt perhaps H.B. had a just grievance, and I sent him a note of apology. When we met again months later, he seemed quite cordial, and I took it for granted all was forgiven. But I never was sure.

Back in the years when I wore a dual mantle of columnist and drama critic, I made light of a play by fellow critic Bide Dudley. Bide, who only a few days previously had ripped a newcomer's play to shreds, didn't appreciate the integrity behind my adverse review, and it was months before he would nod to me at opening nights, by which time his play had long been consigned to Cain's warehouse.

I rest my case—although I have several more examples to offer, to convince one and all that apparently, despite the evil rumors—many of them printed—branding me "amiable," "non-malicious," a fellow who "has never been involved in feuds"—I have had my fair share of disagreements. Could any other newsman boast that he had been sued for the unprecedented sum of five million dollars for libel? But as I have recorded it in more detail elsewhere in these chapters, that was my distinction, with Tommy Manville, Jr., launching the suit.

About a Few Editors

It is a somber fact—by no means to be considered significant, however—that of ten editors under whom I have served in one capacity or another during my newspaper career, all but two have passed away—three by violent death. I remember most of them with kindly feelings, for they were tolerant, understanding and, indeed, helpful. There were a few exceptions, but why harbor resentment against the dead?

My first editor was a slim, fast-spoken, energetic chap named Timothy Barry. Hiring me for my first newspaper job on the *Waterbury* [Connecticut] *Republican,* he tolerated my early fumbling about, good-naturedly advised me that bodies were "interred" not "interned" and that he preferred "buried," and cautioned me and other fledglings not to refer to a simple fire as a "holocaust."

He had resigned from the paper to become executive secretary of Waterbury's Chamber of Commerce shortly after I entered the army during World War I, and it was while I was at Camp

Jesup in Atlanta, Georgia, that a copy sent me of the *Republican* revealed the sad news that Tim Barry had died of injuries received in a trolley crash. He had been something of a hero, for despite his injuries, he had helped save other victims.

After the war, when I returned to the *Republican* as state editor, then sports editor and occasionally acting city editor, E. R. Stevenson had succeeded Barry as editor. He was a Lincolnesque type in appearance, who used to drawl out rather ruefully that a one-time college classmate had handed him a script of a novel to read and comment upon, and that he had returned it to him with the observation that it was "rather weak stuff." Then Stevenson would chuckle and add: "That was Sinclair Lewis—the manuscript later became a book I guess we all wish we had written, *Main Street*."

Louis Weitzenkorn came over to the *Evening Graphic* from the *Morning World* to succeed editor Emile Gauvreau, who had shifted to the *Daily Mirror*. Weitzenkorn was bristling with ideas—among them what he considered his chief mission: to transform the screaming, sensational tab into a dignified sedate daily. One of his first steps in that direction was to relieve me of my duties as a drama critic. He brought in the erudite Gilbert Seldes for the post. He also urged me to drop gossip from the column and to concentrate on literary personalities and other "worthwhiles." I preferred to ignore his advice and continued covering night spots and restaurants and plays and shoveling out minor items about show folks. Weitzenkorn later offered his opinion of "yellow journalism" in a spirited little melodrama, *Five Star Final,* after he had left the *Graphic*. In March of 1943 came the wire dispatch from Wilkes Barre, Pennsylvania, that he had perished in a fire.

In the late twenties, I went to work for Famous Features Syndicate. An eccentric named Leslie Fulenwider, originally from Birmingham, Alabama, was the boss. He was an aloofish gentleman, lavish in his praise when things went right, but cold and sadistic when they did not.

It was at this stage of my career that I became a "ghost writer," alternating with a fine newsman, Don Garden, on those sordid little "Peaches" Browning and "Daddy" Browning first-person revelations that proved such circulation lures for the *Graphic,* the *New York Journal* and other papers around the country. I also ghosted some of Queen Marie's personal philosophies, and revised blind-mute Helen Keller's offerings, as well as pounding out the first-person stories of Charlotte and James Mills, daughter and father respectively of the murdered Eleanor Mills of the Hall-Mills double-slaying tragedy.

One day, Fulenwider summoned me to his office. He asked me politely how things were at home. I told him not too happy, for both my wife and daughter were quite ill. He shook his head sympathetically, murmured, "Isn't that too bad?" and then announced curtly that he had decided to dispense with my services—that very day—adding that I would find two weeks' dismissal pay in my envelope.

Taken aback, I asked him what he found wrong with my work.

"I find it entirely satisfactory," he conceded, "but I don't like you. Our personalities clash."

Fulenwider dropped from a plane to his terrible death some years later. The papers said it was not known whether he jumped deliberately from the aircraft, whether his parachute had failed to open—or whether he had known in advance that the "chute would not open."

Ted von Ziekurch, who succeeded Weitzenkorn on the *Graphic,* was undoubtedly one of the hardest-working newspapermen I ever encountered. And one of the most lovable. In addition to his harassing *Graphic* chores, he also edited a Macfadden tabloid in Philadelphia, wrote the sports column for it, commuted daily between Manhattan and Philly, and still found time to turn out special articles and fiction for magazines. Von Ziekurch restored me to drama-critic status and even suggested that I also become supervising editor of the drama pages and the movies as well. It was shortly after I moved over to the *Journal* that I learned that the hard-working newsman, then editor-in-chief of a major magazine, had dropped dead at his desk.

Similarly, another energetic executive was Seymour Berkson who, when he became editor and publisher of the *Journal-American,* decided, like Weitzenkorn, that my column should abandon its chitchat formula for "think" pieces—and even paragraphs about the fashion world. As in the previous instance, I demurred, and a coolness arose between us. But I must say, in all fairness, that when I did turn out some special pieces or some paragraph that struck his fancy, Berkson promptly sent me a memo of praise.

A fatal heart attack felled him while he was in San Francisco.

Along with Tim Barry and Ted von Ziekurch, my most pleasant memories cling to the late Emile H. Gauvreau, who, as has already been indicated, planted me in the much-coveted dual berth of Broadway columnist and drama critic of the *Evening Graphic,* and the late William A. Curley, who was my editor for so many years on the *New York Journal* and the *Journal-American.*

Curley spurned ivory-tower status. I never had to phone his secretary to set up an appointment when I wanted to see him. The practice was to barge in on him almost daily for a chat, which he seemed to relish. He was interested in the gossip of the day and made inquiry when some blind item puzzled him, requesting identification of the personalities involved. I took him often on a round of the town, and if some nightclub performer met with his favor, he would phone me the following day and suggest that it might not be amiss to give the artist a little boost in the column.

Such raises as came along with the renewal of my contracts were at his suggestion to the general management—without first advising me in advance that he was responsible for the boost. His favorite night-spot operator was Sherman Billingsley, and my only brief falling-out with Curley came when Sherman expressed annoyance to him about some other restaurant or other, in which case editor Curley would suggest that perhaps I ought not to accord space to the offending rival of the Stork Club.

Free and easy access to the editor's office vanished when Seymour Berkson took over after Bill Curley's death. Nor for that matter, though he was a far more amiable gentleman than Berkson, did his successor, Joe Kingsbury Smith, welcome intrusions unless he issued the summons or unless an appointment was made in advance.

On the other hand, Bill Hearst, Jr., managing editor Sam Day, and his successor, Paul Schoenstein, were easily accessible, and so was Walter Young while he held the post of the *Journal-American* publisher. And equally so was the late Joseph V. Connolly when he was head of King Features Syndicate. I toss a fragrant posy in the direction of all these bosses who didn't take their lofty status too seriously.

Requiescat in Pace

Bernarr Macfadden's *Evening Graphic* gasped its final breath on July 7, 1932. The end came almost without warning. I was by this time safely ensconced on the *New York Evening Journal,* but the news came as a bit of a shocker, for like so many of us who had left the rowdy little gazette—Winchell, Sullivan, Jerry Wald, Norman Krasna, cartoonists Gus Edson and Will Gould—we were all grateful for the showcase it had provided for our wares. And some of us would bow down, if not in reverence, at least in something of a sentimental salute to the rakish little sheet which never adhered too closely to the truth if a snappy headline meant a prod to the circulation. When a cameraman's lens or an artist's fancy couldn't catch enough excitement, the *Graphic* whipped up a lulu of a fake composograph. Some old-timers may still recall that honey in which "Daddy" Browning was on his hands and knees in front of his plumpish bride, "Peaches," while a little balloon like those used in cartoons indicated that he was barking an affectionate "woof-woof." I remember, of course—why not? I ghosted most of those lurid Browning confessionals.

The *Graphic* used to create its own fiction. It was authored by an energetic, prolific little genius named Lewis Allen Browne who could knock out 5,000 to 10,000 words at a sitting—words of fact and fancy built around some dominant figure of the day who had figured in a bit of scandal. It made for racy reading but it also brought on some libel suits. Among the thinly disguised stories was one about Earl Carroll, another about Babe Ruth, still another about the socialite Kip Rhinelander, and one was in the works on Flo Ziegfeld—but he had gotten word to the Macfadden hierarchy that he would sue and sue heavily—so that particular fact-and-fancy story was abandoned.

In the period before Emile Gauvreau tapped me to succeed Winchell as columnist and drama critic, I was managing editor of the *Graphic* syndicate—with Winchell, Ed Sullivan and my own column the principal features. I also contributed occasional editorials and paragraphs for Gauvreau's column, *Hot Off the Griddle*. And when Winchell was barred by the Shuberts, I covered the plays in the Shubert houses.

The *Graphic* had the first female city editor in the history of New York newspapers, a young woman named Laura Vitray. She was one of the several successors to Frank Mallen after he left the *Graphic*. Later Mallen was to write a fairly definitive history of the *Graphic* under the title of *Sauce for the Gander*. He figured quite importantly in my career for he was responsible for bringing me to New York. Mallen, hailing originally from New London, had liked the sports column I was conducting in the *New London Day* in addition to my chores as city editor.

There was a rather sprightly girl reporter named Rhea Gore, and we soon learned that she was the estranged wife of actor Walter Huston. One day, a tall gangling lad came into the city room and Rhea embraced him and kissed him and proudly proclaimed this was her son. And that was my first meeting with John Huston. For a time he was a member of the staff—a very short time, indeed, for though a fine writer, somehow, his reporting didn't measure up to the *Graphic* standards, and he was fired. John Huston went on to become one of moviedom's great directors, producers, writers, and actors, and now he has a fabulous castle in Ireland, a few millions in his bank account—and no regrets about a dismal newspaper past.

Few of us had any illusions about the *Graphic*. We knew that compared with most of the other newspapers in town, it was a tawdry whore—but always a fascinating and exciting one—and like many a fallen woman, it commanded a fierce loyalty from us, though perhaps not too much respect. Frankly, there was a place for a paper like the *Graphic* in the razzle-dazzle era of the twenties and sprouting thirties. As I have recorded earlier, it was a crazy, pleasure-loving period, dominated by the illicit speakeasies and murderous hoodlums who were arrogant with more spending money and more power than they had ever dreamed of. It was an era of crackpots, show-offs, floozies, playboys, great showmen like Ziegfeld, Carroll and White, and exciting murder trials. Radio and the newfangled talking movies were giving us new celebrities, and the Broadway columnist was coming into his boastful own. And there were hundreds of new millionaires who believed the Wall Street ticker tape—millionaires who became paupers just as the thirties crept in.

But the advertisers were not too partial to a scandal sheet, and the story was that the Macfadden venture had lost between 10 and 12 million dollars. The future looked even less promising, and so the tabloid was abandoned. There were occasional rumors that the *Graphic* was to be revived under new ownership. But they remained rumors. Nor have any of the imitators that have sprung up from time to time ever been able to achieve the same impact with the reading public.

Since I was attached to the *Evening Journal* at the time, I can't actually describe the emotions of the employees of Mr. Hearst's other paper, *The American*, when it was merged with the *Journal* in 1935. Most of the dominant byliners of the morning paper were absorbed in the family of the evening paper, and so were many of the reporters and subeditors.

But I do know that as soon as the word got around on the *Journal-American* in the middle of 1966 that a merger was in the works with the *World Telegram,* and, later, that the *Tribune,* too, was to be included in the marriage, there was general dismay. Some of us, of course, were informed early that we were to continue on the new paper and that a former *Journal-American* man, Frank Conniff, was to be the editor. This seemed reassuring until the actual merger took place later in the year. It became apparent that the *World Telegram* staff men were dominant, even though a Hearst man was the editorial chief.

The zest of the *Journal-American*—the exciting presentation of its news stories and features—disappeared. It did seem as if the more stodgy elements of the *Tribune* and the *World Telegram* were afforded precedence. My column and Winchell's were sluffed off, reduced to a thrice-a-week schedule with limited space. Joe Dever's bright society chitchat was finally eliminated, as were Bert Bacharach's homespun tidbits. Only the woman's page, edited by the brilliant Phil Leff, retained some of the old-time spirit with its authoritative fashion column by Eugenie Sheppard and Suzy Knickerbocker's saucy reports on the social set. Jimmy Cannon and Red Smith kept the sports pages alive, and Leslie Gould and Sam Shulsky put life into the financial section.

Managing editor Paul Schoenstein was kept in his post at the merged newspaper, Bob Considine, Bill Slocum and Jim Bishop retained their positions on the page opposite the editorial, and Jack O'Brian kept his six-days schedule as Broadway columnist. But it was no longer the same. There was not the *esprit de corps,* the good-fellowship, we had enjoyed through the years on the *Journal-American.* The *WJT* had all the *joie de vivre,* the togetherness, of a rolling mill. It was no longer fun, and it had a depressing effect on what was being presented to the public. It was not a paper that the late William Randolph Hearst would have tolerated.

His *Journal-American* had been a big, bountiful reading bargain. Not only was its presentation of news and features exciting but it boasted a formidable array of writing stars and cartoonists who had a tremendous number of loyal followers. I'm making no attempt to list them, but I do want to make some mention of some of the glamorous darlings who decorated our fashion department, for most of them fared so beautifully. Josephine Hughes became one of America's foremost fashion arbiters. Betty Betz married Canadian multimillionaire Frank McMahon and is one of the outstanding hostesses of Palm Beach. Florence Pritchett became the wife of Earl E. T. Smith, our former Ambassador to Cuba (lovely and brilliant Florence who was to die much too young). Nancy Holmes married millionaire Chris Holmes (after she divorced him, he wed the great beauty, Arlene Dahl and she, too, divorced him). Peggy Shannon married Hearst executive Charles Gould, now publisher of the San Francisco *Herald-Examiner*. Robin Chandler went on to wed film actor Jeffrey Lynn. When that marriage was dissolved, she had a successful career in Wall Street before giving it up to become the wife of our then Ambassador to Spain, Angier Biddle Duke.

Many of the thousands of the former *WJT* employees are still jobless—a few have drifted into other fields. One night in October of 1967, I entered a cab as I left Danny's Hideaway. The driver hailed me cordially with "Hi, Louie." And when I answered in some uncertain tones: "Fine, how are you?" he said: "Don't you remember me? I'm——" and he mentioned his name. "I was on the *Journal-American* with you. I'm one of the guys didn't get to the new paper. So I've been hacking." Then he named several others of the old *Journal-American* staff who had become cab drivers.

Damon Runyon

Death relieved Damon Runyon of his cancerous agony on December 10, 1946. Could he have read the glowing send-off by fellow newsmen, he might have been a bit skeptical, because Damon had no illusions about his popularity—and cared less. As Bill Corum put it, nobody really knew the fellow. No one actually hated him, and those who didn't like or love him at least respected him, and many regarded him with considerable awe.

I do know that Winchell did love and respect him, and has continued indefatigable in perpetuating the noble memorial to him—the Damon Runyon Fund. Another who idolized him was the portly show business agent Paul Small (he was once married to Estelle Taylor after her divorce from Jack Dempsey, and later to Lillian Schary, sister of producer-writer Dore Schary). Small, one of Runyon's most consistent companions in the writer's later years, practically overwhelmed him with his solicitude, and he made it a practice, sometimes to Runyon's annoyance, of saving the little notes Damon wrote out in conducting a conversation after he had lost his speech.

Some others for whom Runyon had a genuine affection and who returned the affection were Leo and Clara Lindy, whose Broadway restaurant was the locale for so many of his short stories. Writer Gene Fowler and Chuck Green, after whom he patterned one of his characters, were also genuine mourners when Runyon passed away.

But the truth is, there were many who, though respecting Damon's talents, were not too partial to him as a person. He didn't lend himself easily to friendship—was too often suspicious of friendly gestures—especially after he became successful and world famous. But he did have a preference for what we term "characters"—pugs, petty larceny men, some ballplayers, some boxing managers.

It was a blue day when a surgeon's knife, striking at his malignant throat affliction, removed his power of speech, for Damon loved to sit around talking with cronies while he consumed his countless cups of coffee. Now, with speech gone, he had to write his little messages. Some of them became collector's items, for as time went by, he developed a style in these which went in for the extreme in terseness.

Thus one night during the intermission of a pretty dismal play, seeking to learn my opinion of the turkey, he scrawled out his inquiry.

One word: "Nu?"—Yiddish for "Well?"

On another occasion, I in turn asked what he thought of a certain musical. Damon scribbled: "Big yawn."

When I moved over to the *Journal,* there was no space on the *Journal* floor, so I was assigned an office on the fifth floor, which was *New York American* terrain (this, of course, was before the two papers merged). Runyon dropped in on me one day and commented: "Hope this office brings you luck. It was mine for a while." Then he said with something of pride that *Collier's,* which was using his short stories, had upped the price to $1,500 per (later, he was to command from $2,500 to $5,000) and had asked him to contribute a minimum of twenty a year. Elated, he had worked all night on one, had rushed it to the magazine and had just received word from the editor that it was one of his best.

"Now that you're batting out that fiction for the big dough, I suppose you'll be quitting this newspaper grind," I said.

Runyon shook his head. "If I gave up a steady job, I'd be

writing for scared money. It's like playing poker with scared dough—you usually lose."

On another occasion, sitting with him in Lindy's, I inquired: "Damon, why did you wait so long before you began turning out these short stories?" His reply: "I was building up background."

We met often at Dr. Leo Michel's apartment, the gathering place for many of us. On one night, Runyon acted aloofish. I thought he was simply in a mood, but finally he said icily: "I read your stories in *Collier's*. Why don't you develop a style of your own instead of stealing mine?"

The fiction pieces to which he referred were written in present-tense style, but not in slang nor in any way reminiscent of Runyon's pattern, but he thought the present tense was imitative. I cited examples of writers far back—long before Runyon had begun his prolific output—who had employed the device—even pointed out that Ring Lardner fancied that style in a few of his stories. When, some weeks later, I submitted another of my fiction pieces to *Collier's,* Fiction Editor Kenneth Littauer informed me that he couldn't use it because he had received too many complaints from Runyon, and after all, *Collier's* didn't want to offend one of its prize authors. So I peddled my story to *Redbook.* However, Damon's displeasure with me didn't last too long, and whenever I was in Miami Beach, he usually invited me to his island home, and when we happened to be in Hollywood at the same time, we frequently made the rounds together.

Runyon was one of the most immaculately attired members of the newspaper fraternity, and he was especially a fancier of footgear. He possessed at least a hundred pairs—some of which he had worn perhaps only once or twice—and usually he had some friends break them in for him. He was not without his grudges. And he forgave rarely. Columnist Leonard Lyons once wrote that he saw Damon turn his back on a man he had always considered an old friend—inseparable in the days when Runyon wrote a column for the *New York American.* To lift from Lyons':

"Are you angry?" I asked.

"He was arrested in an arson case when his factory burned down," said Runyon.

"Is that why you're angry at him?" I asked.

"Well," he explained, "I always resented their finding the *American*'s sports section soaked in oil."

Once Sherman Billingsley asked Runyon why he didn't write

a magazine piece about him. Runyon scribbled a note: "Might." He approached *Cosmopolitan* magazine and was told with enthusiasm by the editor, "By all means." It was the last magazine article Runyon was to write. Ironically enough he didn't live long enough to see it in print.

Army of the Legendary

Which reminds me. A group of us sat around Toots Shor's one night shortly after Runyon's death, and I think it was sports columnist Bill Corum who opined that the late columnist and short-story writer had now joined the army of Legendary Figures of the newspaper craft. Naturally, other candidates were thrust forward.

Thus the names that came up included O. O. McIntyre, Don Marquis, W. O. McGheehan, Heywood Broun, Richard Harding Davis, Ernie Pyle, Floyd Gibbons.

It was then that Corum said glumly: "Yeah—they'll be legends all right, all right, but if they were alive and walked into Toots's tonight, nobody would faint away in excitement. They wouldn't cause a real stir. Not like Joe DiMaggio or Babe Ruth or Jack Dempsey, say, or movie guys like Clark Gable or John Wayne or Valentino, if Valentino were alive. Or dolls like Marilyn Monroe or Greta Garbo or Joan Crawford. They'll be legends, too."

Ted Husing nodded his head in glum agreement. "I've seen them crowd around Milton Berle or Arthur Godfrey, but I don't ever remember anybody crowding around Runyon or Pegler or even you, Bill."

We discussed the whys and wherefores that contribute to making personalities steam up the atmosphere or become conversation pieces, and we concluded it depended on showmanship, which might take many forms.

Thus, Jimmy Walker, who certainly was not the most effective mayor of New York, joined the legendary ranks—and stirred up a buzz whenever he entered a public place—because of his witty sallies, the recklessness of his early personal life, his chronic tardiness and for half a dozen other reasons.

At any rate, after the debate, one of us piped up: "We're sitting with a legend right now"—and pointed to Toots Shor. Shor grinned and nodded in full acquiescence. "I can drink any crumbum here right under the table," was his gracious acceptance of the honor.

A Bad Actor

Of the various court trials I was assigned to cover as a columnist who might be expected to furnish lighter touches and sidelights, none produced more personal enjoyment, for want of a better word, than the Fritz Kuhn sessions. But it almost ended disastrously for me.

Kuhn, a stalwart six-footer and rather handsome, was Adolf Hitler's arrogant *Gauleiter* in the United States—national leader of the German-American Bund. He headquartered in New York, and I often spotted him in one or another of the restaurants—one night, in fact, at the bar of the Stork Club. He was in civies that evening, but usually he strutted about in a Nazi uniform, affecting boots and spurs, and carrying a swagger stick. Then came his downfall. He was indicted for grand larceny and forgery. Seems he had been diverting Bund monies to pay for his merry and amorous flings about town.

It was early in November, 1939, that he went on trial. It occurred to me that everyone seemed to be having a pleasant time in the stuffy General Sessions Court. And I so reported. Not only Bund Fuehrer Kuhn, who kept chewing gum and occasionally permitting a smile to caress his thin lips, but Judge Wallace, who every so often tossed out a crisp ad lib. I described him in my dispatches as having somewhat of a resemblance to Jean Hersholt in the role of Dr. Dafoe in the film dealing with the Dionne quintuplets.

The judge kept interposing his own sharp remarks constantly during the proceedings. Thus, when a young jury prospect named Curtenius Gillette, Jr., was being subjected to defense counsel Peter L. F. Sabbatino's quiz, chiefly on his racial and patriotic prejudices, Wallace interrupted to remark that ten years hence nobody would know what happened at the trial—and a hundred years hence nobody would know that "we are assembled here, that we happened at all."

As the trial ran on into its third week, I reported that "it is still the great box-office attraction, and has shaped itself into something very much like one of those dear old Tyler revivals.

That is, with a cast of great many stars with one- or two-line parts —Mayor La Guardia, District Attorney Tom Dewey, Police Commissioner Valentine, and, of course, Kuhn and the judge."

I commented further: "And if programs had been issued, there would undoubtedly have been this footnote: 'For one appearance only maybe, J. Edgar Hoover. Reserve your seats for Monday's appearance.'"

I observed that the D.A., Tom Dewey, summoned not as prosecutor but as witness, had quite a fat part. His were the dramatic lines of the day, I insisted, "and he made the most of them. Nor did he overplay his role. It was a telling performance and there were times when he brought the audience to its feet, figuratively speaking. 'It is difficult to say I have hatred for the Bund,' volunteered the D.A., 'Rather, I should say, contempt.'"

At this point the script called for Judge Wallace to interrupt: "The personal feelings of the District Attorney are not to be considered in the case."

From my aisle seat I watched defendant Kuhn, and I thought he did well with his silent role. He shrugged his shoulders, rubbed his broad chin with his right hand, took off his glasses, wiped them, scowled for a blinking second, put his glasses back, and then started doodling upon the pad of paper in front of him. A fine piece of pantomime, worthy of that other delightful clown Jimmy Savo.

At any rate, my dispatch continued in this vein. After the trial was concluded and Kuhn was sentenced to a prison term, Judge Wallace announced that he was taking under advisement holding one of the newsmen for contempt—admitting later that he meant me for my frivolous treatment of the proceedings, especially the piece to which the *Journal-American* had awarded a three-column boxed head: "*Cherchez la Femme* or Trial of 'Fuehrer Fritz.' All-Star Smash Hit Going into 3rd Week. Hate! Love! Passion! Furniture! Cast of Notables!"

Apparently Judge Wallace had a second thought on my dereliction, and I remained out of a jail cell.

As for Kuhn, after his prison sentence and deportation to Germany, he was imprisoned at Dachau. He escaped and, after the war, sank into obscurity, working in his final days in a small chemical plant in Munich where the Nazi Party was born. He had had many women in his life, as the court trial revealed—though he was never divorced by his wife. She was at his side during his dying days, and it was reported he had begged for her forgiveness for his extramarital transgressions. But that didn't prevent his final mistress, waitress Hedwig Munz, from also visiting him. Kuhn's end came on November 14, 1951.

Short Story with a Moral

Anxiety mingled with embarrassment as distinguished members of the committee assembled in Oklahoma City to honor an Eastern newspaperman, James D. (Red) Horan, assistant managing editor of the *New York Journal-American*. The committee kept stealing glances at their respective wristwatches. Seventeen governors from as many Western states had arrived, chiefly by train for the big occasion. But the governor selected to make the principal address and formally present the much-coveted Western Heritage award was missing—and the deadline, 6:00 P.M., was only a minute away.

This was late in January of 1962, and the West had been lashed by furious winds and a snowfall that had reached blizzard proportions. The missing governor was scheduled to arrive by his favorite conveyance, a C-47 National Guard plane. It was overdue, and the anxiety mounted.

But at ten minutes to 6:00, into the big hall of the Skirvin Hotel, walked Montana's Governor Donald G. Nutter, and he was hailed with cheers, so relieved were the dignitaries and friends. And at 6:00 sharp, as scheduled, Governor Nutter presented the award to Horan in tribute to his fine novel of the West, *The Shadow Catcher*—published, coincidentally enough, by Crown, publishers of this book you are reading now.

Jim is a prolific writer—a newspaperman who, after a long day at his desk at the *Journal-American* with in-between self-imposed assignments taking him on some crusade or other, would spend his evenings pounding away at his typewriter, turning out one book after another—among them *Desperate Men, The D.A.'s Man,* and others including his more recent one of 1966 a fascinating novel, *The Right Image,* all of these also published by Crown.

The ceremonies completed, Governor Nutter chatted amiably with Horan and his wife, Gertrude, remarking at one point that he thought Jim looked a bit on the pale side. "You city folks don't get enough of the great outdoors," he said. "Now I tell you what. I can't let you go back East until you get a bit of real living in real he-man's country—Montana, the greatest state in the Union, bar none. Yes, sir, you and your lovely lady are going to fly back with me in my great little plane—and we'll get up one whale of a party."

While Horan was fumbling about for a reply, Mrs. Horan came to the rescue. "Thank you very much, Mr. Governor, but Jim and I will do no such thing because the only flying he's going to do is back to the *Journal-American* office."

The governor took the rebuff good-naturedly. "You just don't know what you're missing," he remarked. "Maybe some other time, hey? Why, just a ride in this plane I use would make it worthwhile."

Jim told me later, he was tempted. He is a lover of the Far West and its traditions. For a time he debated with himself whether he should wire managing editor Paul Schoenstein and ask for a few days more leave so he might enjoy the Montana experience in the company of the Governor and a party of high dignitaries. But Mrs. Horan was adamant, and finally and with great reluctance, he told Governor Nutter he would have to ask for a rain check. He did have to fly back to his chores.

Jim was at his desk the following day when he was handed the melancholy dispatch:

> Wolf Creek, Mont. Jan. 25: Gov. Donald G. Nutter, two aides and a crew of three, died early today when their plane apparently was ripped apart and slammed into a mountainside by the extreme turbulence. Gov. Nutter, 46, who survived 62 combat missions in the Pacific during World War II, perished in the burning wreckage of a Montana Air National Guard C-47 in a rugged snow-covered area of west-central Montana.

Papa Hemingway

Few writers of our generation have inspired the type of affectionate as well as sincerely mournful farewells from newsmen that Ernest Hemingway received after his tragic death. The reason was simple. Papa Hemingway was a pal of newsmen. He liked them and he was friendly to columnists. He insisted he admired what they wrote day in and day out, which was quite a compliment when we consider his own writings with their wider and certainly greater literary appeal. The lads of the Fourth Estate kept seeking him out from time to time and always found him ready to welcome them, to drink with them, to chat with them, and to answer their questions freely. He became a close pal of several, especially Leonard Lyons and Jimmy Cannon. In fact, when they didn't seek him out, he would go out of his way to contact them. He was a self-appointed host—and a hospitable one—to any newspaperman visiting Cuba.

While I cannot in all honesty say I knew him as well as did other confreres, I still cherish a note he scribbled off one night in the Stork Club at a particularly low point in my personal life—with my wife, Lee, close to the death which finally claimed her.

"Would you care to come over and cry it out? I'll listen," was what the note said.

Nothing profound, but it was effective. I stopped being sorry for myself—for a few hours, at any rate.

An Okay from Variety

For several months after I assumed the columnar mantle on the *Graphic, Variety's* mugs kept insisting I was a small-town upstart trying to fill a pretty big man's shoes, those of a favorite of theirs named Winchell. *Variety* kept sniping at me, and it was discouraging. Then one night at the old Chateau Madrid, Jack White asked me whether I'd like to meet Sime Silverman, the big boss of *Variety*. The white-haired, handsome publisher was sitting at a long table, surrounded by some friends and a few members of the *Variety* staff. Sime seemed friendly enough, but I felt ill at ease in view of the steady bombardment by the theatrical paper.

Then I remembered something, and from my wallet I pulled out a little card and quite dramatically thrust it at Silverman. He beamed. He passed the little card around, and then he exclaimed: "Why didn't you let us know you were one of us? What kept you quiet?"

Thereafter, though I don't think my column improved perceptibly, I was rewarded with the kindest notices from time to time, a friendly attitude that persists to this day, and I count many of the staff members from Editor Abel Green down as among my friends. The little card was signed by Jack Conway. It conveyed the information to one and all that Louis Sobol was the duly authorized New London, Connecticut, correspondent of *Variety*. It had been issued to me back in the days when I was city editor and sports editor of the *New London Day,* and was moonlighting by contributing to *Variety* as well as occasionally to one or another of the New York newspapers.

Frustration

I must record one defeat. That was when I attempted to interview Greta Garbo one night back in 1940. I was prodded by the thought that this would be quite a triumph, in view of the frustration encountered by so many newsmen who had tried to get the Aloof One to open up. Garbo was eating salad—with a spoon—and chatting away buoyantly with Gaylord Hauser, the diet expert, who reportedly was wooing her at the time. Their table was in an obscure corner of the upstairs room at "21," and I had spotted the pair and decided that since she seemed to be in an unusually amiable mood, this was my opportunity to approach the Swedish Sphinx.

Adjusting my tie and assuming my most winning manner, I made a circling approach, thinking to obtain my objective by a flanking movement. Perhaps if Miss Garbo had been alone I might have succeeded, but Hauser was manning the barricades and stopped me cold with one of his dietician's spinach-juice stares.

After shaking off the icicles, I entreated Bob Kriendler of the "21" hierarchy and a diplomat from shiny boots to hair oil, to intervene.

"What?" snapped Hauser, at Bob. "Can't you see Miss Garbo is in a highly nervous state?"

(Miss Garbo still was calmly eating her salad with a spoon.)

"No, no, no!" I heard Hauser shout, and then he announced that a newspaperman would spoil Miss Garbo's evening completely.

(Miss Garbo reached for another spoonful of salad and calmly crunched.)

Mr. Hauser had a final say. "No, no, no, no!"

Bob Kriendler turned to me.

He says "No!" he said sadly.

Three columnists toast a newcomer to the field. *Left to right:* Sobol, Arthur "Bugs" Baer, Dorothy Kilgallen and Walter Winchell. I had stepped into the spot left vacant by the death of O. O. McIntyre, and Dorothy had been lifted from her reportorial chores to succeed me as conductor of "The Voice of Broadway." She was to go on to even loftier status as a radio commentator and dominant panelist of the long-lived "What's My Line" show—only to die tragically at the height of her booming career.

The Unsung

The managing editor, the city editor, the star reporter, the columnist have had their days and nights of glorification in short story and novel, in the movies, television, and on the stage. But it seems to me someone ought to turn the spotlight on another member of the newspaper clan, the fellow we call the feature editor.

An alert feature editor, spotting an item that Jacqueline Kennedy, say, is affecting a drastic new hairdo, will assign a reporter to dig up clips about other former First Ladies and new styles they may have inspired in coiffures or even dress—may even order more intense research, bringing in queens of the past. A public enemy of an almost forgotten era goes on trial or passes away. No time must be wasted. The morgue must yield its rewards in clips and pictures, and shortly there is a series and again we read of the Capones and the O'Bannions, of the Colisimos and the "Dutch" Schultzes, and so on. The whole gory period is resurrected with references to the machine-gun fire, bombings, bodies stuffed into burlap bags, corpses encased in cement.

A few days later, perhaps, there will be a milder piece, or even a series dealing with the favorite midnight dishes of famed operatic thrushes, all because in an interview Lily Pons may have hinted she likes a plate of beans before retiring for the night. An actor confesses ruefully that he never had a real home, but always it had been a hotel room or a suite. A natural, this—and we are treated to the happiness of other performers who have real homes or to the sad stories of actors who wistfully concede having a home like other folks has been denied them.

Sometimes the feature is taken over by the managing editor or the city editor or one of the assistants. Thus, it was managing editor Paul Schoenstein of the *Journal-American* who decided that there might be an interesting story in two brothers who, starting almost from scratch, have become the chief rivals of Conrad Hilton and his associates in hotel operations—the Tisch brothers, Larry and Bob, who control such major inns and motels as the Regency, Warwick, Americana, Summit, Squires and others in Manhattan alone, as well as the famed Mark Hopkins in San Francisco, the Ambassador Hotel in Chicago, the Americana in Miami Beach and the Americana in Puerto Rico—also a chain of theatres, including Loew's. I drew that particular assignment —just as it was decided by Publisher-Editor J. Kingsbury Smith that since Dorothy Kilgallen had succeeded me as the Broadway columnist when I was moved into the O. O. McIntyre spot, that following her tragic death, I should write the series covering her meteoric career as columnist, author, radio commentator and TV panelist.

Frankly, if I owned a big newspaper, I would assign one man exclusively to develop ideas for features. For I am the type of reader who wants my daily ration of news caviar along with the ham and eggs and who reads his spot news over his coffee and muffins and then turns to the features while smoking his cigar. In fact, for years I've made it a practice to clip well-written special articles and file them.

Incidentally, there are other men I would recruit for the working staff if I were ever to become boss of a Big Town newspaper—reporters from small-town gazettes. This is not a hint to editors of metropolitan papers to fire their star prima donnas and immediately place ads for reporters with previous training on whistle-stop weeklies. Some fine newsmen never worked on any but big city papers, and some didn't even start out as office boys but crashed right into the delicate craft as full-fledged newspapermen with police cards from scratch.

But as a rule, the lad getting his start in the business with a job smack off the reel on a metropolitan sheet has two strikes against him. He may go on for years without ever writing a word of copy—just scooting around digging up the facts of the story while a reporter on the other end with the earphones does the actual weaving together of the piece, the sweating over the typewriter. Or the good rewrite man, restless as a cooch dancer's hips, might want to get into the open and ferret out a yarn for himself, instead of having to take the other fellow's few hundred words for it.

There have been police reporters on our New York papers who never have had the opportunity of covering anything else, and court reporters who would sacrifice an arm to chase a four-alarm fire. There are feature writers with by-lines and high salary checks who would fumble and flounder if asked to turn in a simple obituary or cover a gambling-house raid. They would toss all the big words in the *Thesaurus* at the story, spice it or sob it up, but never assemble the facts so that the reader would have a clear picture of a situation. Feature writers, for the most part, usually want to impress one and all with their smartness. That goes double in spades for us who have conducted columns.

To get back to the small-town boys. The assignment sheet for the day may have the reporter covering obits, police, fires, frats, lodges, a section of town, a church meeting and four to half a dozen special stories. He will not only dash around getting his facts, come back to the office, get busy on the telephone, but he will settle down at the typewriter and pound out his little pieces: perhaps a column of obits, perhaps two sticks (four inches) on the church meeting, two or three minor fires for half a column of copy and so on, until it's nothing for the cub in a small town to turn in from ten to fifteen pages, double-spaced. Easily from 3,000 to 5,000 words.

As a fledgling gains experience, he draws new assignments. He covers courts and politics, a murder and a fatal hotel fire or sometimes even an execution. He writes peppery, crusading stories. He begins taking a turn at the desk writing heads. He learns a little about makeup. He has closer contact with the men in the composing room and in the pressroom than any of the reporters who work in big cities.

In my own case, as a young reporter on the *Waterbury Republican*, I had just written what I thought was quite a stirring story on a local murder when the city editor told me I would also have to take on the sports beat for a few days because the sports editor, who was the entire department, was holed up with the grippe. That didn't mean I was relieved of my other chores. So, in addition to the regular beat, I found myself covering a baseball game in the afternoon, a fight which took place that week, wrote or rewrote about three columns of sports news, edited six columns in all, wrote the heads and saw the page to bed. In between, I turned in my other stories.

When I became a New York byliner, I just barely managed to squeeze out some 1,200 words in my earlier days on the *Graphic* and the *Journal*—800 when the column assumed a new format—before collapsing with a press agent holding on to each typewriting hand and a loyal secretary fanning me with a bottle of Scotch or the promise thereof.

But getting back to the small-town newsman. Earnest, ambitious young reporters—always with an ear open to a call from the Big Town—they certainly are thorough newspapermen, and I'd match any one of them after his tough schooling, with the best of our stars of the Big Town.

Not Like the Movies

Those of us who once were "working newspapermen" until we were relegated to the background as "specialists" or "columnists," chafed a bit everytime we entered the city room and sensed the excitement whenever big stories were breaking. I employ the word "sensed" because as a rule there is no rushing about, no shouting, no barking of commands, no frenzied huddles of editors and subalterns—not at all the uproar you have come to expect after viewing city room scenes in the movies or on the stage.

The excitement is there, though, and apparent to any who have worked as reporters or on the desk. Big stories pop out of the day's hopper daily—and Names. The supreme essentials of stirring drama are a daily mixture: murder, retribution, retaliation, tragedy, humor, intrigue, spies, plots and counterplots, atomic threats, scientific discoveries, suicides, holdups, political chicanery.

The news editor or managing editor sits at one side of the "horseshoe" or "rim" and makes quick decisions under the pressure of changing editions. Shall it be a one-line streamer, or two? Ninety-six point or 144, 120 point condensed or 120 Gothic caps? The 120 point condensed is more flexible if big type is to be used as you may squeeze twenty-three letters and spaces into it, but only eight in 120 Gothic. There is always the struggle for short words, for the telling word.

The city editor seems to be sitting calmly enough, yet at the moment he has two or three reporters assigned to a new and baffling murder. Photographers are scattered all over town. He wants a new lead from a rewrite man on a startling political development. The phones at his side ring constantly. He asks the mayor a question direct, and he explains to the editor-in-chief why a certain story was treated the way it was.

The copyboys bring the flimsies or copy fresh from the teletypes. The next piece of perhaps only half a dozen lines may mean the upset of some portion of the world, the death, natural or by violence, of a dictator. In recent years there haven't been so many occasions for the woefully expensive extras as there were during World War days, and perhaps not so much of the daily city room turmoil as it was back in those years when some balance had to be maintained between city and national events and the war. Yet, even then, I recall there was no considerable excitement or rush. Always there seemed to be surface calm.

Those of us who contributed our daily trivia were forced to stand on the outside looking in, something tugging away inside us to be part of what was going on in the city room every minute. We poked handsome words about in a soup of trivialities while there was that constant foreboding of unrest about the world, the pessimistic hints of another war brewing or the fumbling attempts to maintain the peace. We tried to snare meager consolation from the thought that in our vague trifling way, perhaps we, too, were contributing to that necessary balance without which the current woes of the world, real or threatening, would have nothing to relieve it by way of lighthearted contrast. Occasionally as we wandered aimlessly through the saloons, something occurred that seemed momentous, and we hastened to the office or plumped down at the typewriter at home to write out the story, or else to recount it over the telephone to a rewrite man. If our by-line appeared on it, there was a thrill and the feeling of fulfillment. Once again we had become part of the city-room crew. A reporter again! Happy, happy word. Reporter!

Star Makers?

There is not too much excitement left for the Broadway historian who invades the same nightly gathering places, mingles with the same familiar habitués, turns up at the premieres of plays and pictures, even though he endeavors to inject glow and enthusiasm into his reports. But there are periods of reward, especially when he correctly predicts that an obscure youngster is destined for stardom. Even the synthetically enthusiastic press agent experiences a thrill when, to his own amazement, the obscure client on whose behalf he has been issuing buoyant bulletins comes through to become a Name.

Every so often, I used to receive plaintive appeals please to spare a little time to listen to some young bootblack or store clerk with a voice "like Caruso's" or to study songs turned out faster than you can clear your throat by some stenographer or men's room attendant. And though I usually expressed my regrets, I often wondered whether I was not missing the chance to become a discoverer. The bootblack might have become a Mario Lanza, the men's room attendant another Irving Berlin.

After all, wasn't I the fellow who tried to discourage Betty Hutton from risking her luck by shifting from musical comedies to the movies after Buddy De Sylva had issued his call? Would I have given two coppers for the chances of a not too photogenic citizen who was entered in one of those marathon dance contests? How could I foresee that in time he would become a top-drawer singing ace, Frankie Laine. Or that the winner of a Charleston contest would become Ginger Rogers, star of stage and screen. Or that a handsome horn-blower in a band would become Tony Martin. Or that another skinny singing vocalist with a band would become the Frank Sinatra who dominated columns and feature pages.

For the Broadway and Hollywood columnists, it is the great American pastime—uncovering an obscure bud and helping her or him blossom under the sun of ballyhoo. Winchell, invading a rowdy little haunt in Miami Beach, thought a middle-aged singing woman really something and tossed his printed posies her way. Roberta Sherwood became a night-spot star.

I will not venture to intimate that I, by virtue of my faith and persistency made a star out of a girl who used to operate a lift in Chicago, but she always gave me credit for a notable assist, a lass named Dorothy Lamour. Actually a combine consisting of a girl press agent, an aggressive radio talent man and a cafe man, Sherman Billingsley, contributed their bit. But horn-blower and singer Louis Prima does insist that the paragraphs in praise of him when I caught his act in a New Orleans nightclub were responsible for attracting the attention of a Manhattan operator who brought him on to the Famous Door, and after that he sailed on to fame and fortune. Similarly, because I happened to be the only newsman present when Ethel Merman made her professional Broadway debut at Les Ambassadeurs and turned in a glowing report, she had always credited me with being her "discoverer."

It was a newspaperman who had the satisfaction of having his judgment vindicated—the late Billy Wilkerson, publisher of the *Hollywood Reporter,* watching a dream puss brooding over a black and white in Schwab's drugstore, he approached the girl and asked her name and address. Later, he urged Director Mervyn LeRoy to contact her. Mervyn did, liked what he saw, tested her, assigned her to a minor role in a picture, *They Won't Forget* (she ran up or down a flight of stairs), and nobody did forget Lana Turner.

It was cartoonist and then columnist Irving Hoffman and a press agent named Joe Russell who detected possibilities in a girl understudying Tallulah Bankhead in a play. They delivered compelling sales talks to film producer Hal Wallis—after which Hoffman steered Wallis, as if by accident, to the Stork Club. Here, by coincidence (arranged by Hoffman), Wallis spotted an attractive-looking miss and asked Hoffman whether he knew her. The cartoonist looked very surprised for a second or two and then exclaimed, "Well, waddaya know—that's the girl I mentioned to you," and introduced Wallis to Lizbeth Scott. After that Wallis took over—starred her in several of his pictures.

Gossip Is Salable

At one point in my career when I thought I had been graduated from the ranks of the gossip columnists to the status of a more dignified historian, I directed a few jibes in the direction of the chatter boys. But gradually I had to concede, the gossip mills grind fast and furious in this country, and even sedate journals cater to the demand of the public for newsy morsels pertaining to folks in the spotlight.

So more meekly this time—and with less disdain—I know that

one moves around town and hears and sees. Comes then the business of putting two and two together, but the more wary veterans, having learned by experience, that not everything the ears hear and the eyes see may balance with what is the actual truth, skirt around it neatly by naming no names—merely hinting. These are the so-called "blind items." Then, when and if the story does break, the columnist finds himself in the happy position of being able to boast that as of such and such a date, he was the first to have broken the news.

It is true, nevertheless, that many outstanding beats, domestic, financial or political, have first been aired in one or two lines in a column. What became Page One news concerning Grace Kelly and Prince Rainier, Ingrid Bergman's affair with Rossellini and the subsequent breakup years later, Rita Hayworth's romance and marriage with Aly Khan and the severence of that tie, the Clark Gable–Kay Spreckels alliance, Tyrone Power's elopement with Linda Christian, the Marilyn Monroe–Arthur Miller story, and so many others have first come to the knowledge of the public through one column or another. Even that Billy Rose had become the largest shareholder in A.T.&T.—and, of course, the first hints of his various marriages—and the split-ups.

The late Tyrone Power chats with the author between takes. I met him for the first time when he had a role in Katharine Cornell's starring play *Romeo and Juliet,* and I recall he told me that though he came from a distinguished theatrical family he wasn't too certain he wanted the stage as his career. But shortly after he was signed by 20th Century-Fox, and apparently his discontent ended as his career sizzled along to its heights.

It is a fact, "blind items" seem to fascinate the readers. They provide a guessing game. Even as hip a character as Abel Green, editor of *Variety,* once stopped me in the Stork Club to inquire whom did I mean when I wrote that a certain "famed movie star's marriage was on the rocks," etc. And when I once insisted "right now there are three big stories ready to break wide open in this town," I received a querulous note from confrere Earl Wilson: "Why," he demanded, petulantly, "doesn't somebody tell *me*?"

When the "blind item" begins jelling, the next step is to mention the names. First cautiously, with much evasive and protective wordage, and then boldly asserting that it is a truth. After which each columnist tries to beat the other into print proclaiming that the public read about it first in *his* department.

The urge to know what's going on with this biggie and that honey is nothing new. It dates back to the era before the Pharaohs, before the Bible was anything but a handful of facts and rumors kept alive by the better storytellers. Who knows who first spread the whisper about David and Bathsheba or hinted that King Solomon was fooling around?

I know this. From the loftiest to the lowliest among our citizenry there is none who doesn't want to know all the intimate details of what is what with his neighbors. Whenever women or men gather, the newsy tidbits are exchanged. Seeing these gossip morsels in print seems to place the stamp of authenticity on them. And as most columnists have learned, gossip is a highly salable commodity.

He Had It Made!

Among the members of our craft who heeded the call to the gold mines of Hollywood was Mark Hellinger. Once when we were spending a few weeks in movieland, Hellinger, with a bit of embarrassment, even with something of apology in his voice, invited my wife and me to have dinner with him and Gladys Glad at his cozy little hacienda. I could not understand Mark's embarrassment until we arrived at the massive portals leading to extensive, manicured grounds—and then I knew. For as if by magic and with no assistance of human hands, the gates opened to permit our car to enter. Pinkish and bluish lights played their symphony on the gentle waters of the swimming pool not quite as large as Lake Erie. A mile of housefront greeted us. Formal gardens and

In an expansive mood, the late Mark Hellinger, having surrendered his columnar portfolio to become a Hollywood writer and producer, outlines his next project to the late movie star Linda Darnell, and his wife, former Ziegfeld queen, Gladys Glad, and the envious author.

rock gardens, half a mountainside in the rear and a smallish Yosemite Valley in front—we glimpsed this in a few seconds before entering the mansion.

"Pappy," said Mr. Hellinger, in small voice, blushing boyishly crimson. "Now, you understand. On your sacred word of honor, promise, you will never tell the boys back home."

That night when my wife and I returned to our little hall bedroom and lighted the gas lamps, there was a look in her eyes which I had never seen there before, and there was polar coldness and contempt in her manner. She spoke to me only once.

"Newssss-paperman!" she hissed.

Oh, Well, Money Isn't Everything!

Newspapermen are better paid these years, though I doubt if there are more than a dozen top-drawer reporters across the span of this country who can produce a weekly paycheck to equal the fee of a fair-to-middlin' performer in a nightclub or on a television show—the exceptions being those few of our calling who fatten their weekly take-home pay with extracurricular exertions through radio, TV or magazine outlets.

I can recall back in my celluloid collar days when we would sit around in the city room after hours and listen with bated breath and envy to the fabulous tales of New York newspaper aces drawing as much as $100 to $150 a week. It seemed utterly unbelievable.

When the late Irvin Cobb's pay on the old *Evening World* was boosted to $160 a week, the awed comment spread to every newspaper shop in the country. It was true, but Cobb, himself, later pointed out that his paper didn't want him to get an inflated head over his staggering income, so it was arranged that he receive $99 from the *Evening World* and $61 from the *Sunday World*.

Seems the Pulitzer-owned papers in those days had a ruling that employees receiving $100 or more in salary were paid by check at the window designated for executives only. All others had to stand in line with office boys, run-of-the-mill reporters, clerks and copyreaders at the more crowded and less exclusive window. This, Cobb used to confess ruefully, was quite humiliating to him—now that he was a big moneyed man—having to queue up with the "lesser fry."

He Spelled It with an "e"

For some months after I first assumed my columnar mantle, a bit of confusion arose that brought on a few complications to Bernard Sobel and me. Though the spelling of his name was different, I would receive bills intended for him. And vice versa. Or some girl would phone pleading with me to get her a break with Flo Ziegfeld, for Sobel was the drumbeater for the Great Glorifier and his shows.

There was some embarrassment, too, in later years when Bernie began turning out his books on the history of burlesque, his theatrical encyclopedias and other works. Then I began receiving effusive notes of commendation as the author of those books. Even to this day, there are some people who believe that the late Bernard Sobel and Louis Sobol are one and the same.

Incidentally, Bernie had one great love in his life—the statuesque Ziegfeld beauty, Frieda Mierse—but her love was directed to comedian Ed Wynn. It was an open secret, the romance between the two, and it endured for years. It culminated in marriage in June, 1937, after Wynn's wife Hilda, daughter of actor Frank

Keenan, divorced him. But as often happens, marriage ruined the great romance, and not much more than a year or so later, Frieda divorced Ed claiming there was too much difference in their ages. She was twenty-seven then, Ed fifty-two.

As for Bernard Sobel, he remained a bachelor until his death, March 12, 1964.

Twice-Told Anecdote

Newspapermen pride themselves on their sophisticated outlook and cherish few superstitions. But it is a fact that in newspaper offices, there is an unwritten rule against whistling. I am a whistle-hater from far back, and there used to be a subeditor who occupied an office across the hall from mine who used his pipes unceasingly, usually giving out with popular torch dirges of the day which depressed me.

One day, I invaded his office and said: "Jim, did you ever hear the story—you must have—of Lord Northcliffe and the kid who went whistling by his office one afternoon?"

"If it's a good story, tell it to me," he said.

"It goes something like this," I went on. "Northcliffe barked: 'Hey, you boy. Draw your pay. You're discharged.'

" 'You can't fire me,' said the boy. 'I work for Green & Dixon.'

" 'What do they pay you?'

" 'Twelve bob a week.'

" 'You start work for me tomorrow—twenty bob a week.'

"The kid reported on the next morning. Northcliffe gave him a big smile. 'You work for me now, son, right?'

" 'Yes, sir,' said the boy.

" 'Good,' Northcliffe snapped. 'You're fired.' "

My neighbor said: "I like the story. Never heard it before. I gotta remember it."

I went back to my office. A few seconds later, emanating from my neighbor's office came his whistling dirge of "Moanin' Low."

Success Story

By 1940, Hollywood's Jimmie Fidler's annual income as a radio commentator and columnist had been estimated at close to $200,000 annually, but in 1932, Fidler's income was considerably less. I was in a position to know, for at the time he was my personal Hollywood correspondent at a weekly salary of $75, his wage for furnishing me with a few morsels for my thrice-weekly "Lucky Strike" broadcasts over WEAF and affiliated stations across the land. He was quite solicitous then about my progress as a radio commentator and Broadway columnist, for if I fell by the wayside, so, too, would his income.

He had no need of me or my fee by 1940 and thereafter. He had become a radio personality himself and a widely syndicated columnist, and he boasted a Hollywood estate with a swimming pool, two dogs, a contract for a picture role—and most of his hair.

The Forgotten Cartoonist

In an earlier book of mine, *Some Days Were Happy,* I dwelt briefly on a long-forgotten cartoonist, Carl E. Schultze. Now I'd like to present the complete story.

Back in April of 1935, I ran a line to the effect that Schultze, creator of the highly popular comic strip "Foxy Grandpa" which was originated in the *New York Herald* at the turn of the century and then moved on to the *New York American* and other Hearst papers, was reported eking out a meager living drawing posters for Y.M.C.A.'s.

Two days later came a letter from Schultze, confessing that for more than a year he had lodged at the Twenty-third Street Y.M.C.A. turning out cards and posters for the branch. "But," he added, "things look brighter now, and I'm planning to modernize the old character and give him new life in book form."

In the same mail arrived a note from Karl T. Marx, Secretary of the German-American Conference Relief Committee, advising that the veteran cartoonist had applied at the office for help and been assigned to interview applicants for jobs.

I was filled with melancholy over the plight of an artist who in his day ranked with the top-drawer cartoonists—as readers of my generation certainly should recall—for many of us had been ardent fans of the genial, philosophical character Schultze had created.

A week later, another note arrived from Schultze. "Your 'Voice of Broadway' certainly started something. The latest is the Associated Press which came in here yesterday with a fine hurray

—pictures and everything. From the quiet tranquil life, I have suddenly found myself in a whirlwind of activity—a sort of dust storm—but gold dust. Even if none gathers down around me, I've certainly got the old works tuned up and am happily on my way. Anyway I have known for quite a few years past the things most worthwhile in life and haven't a single kick to register. Life can always be good—it's silly to mind the bumps."

And, indeed, feature stories appeared in several of the Manhattan newspapers, detailing his earlier career, praising his acceptance of his current obscurity and financial distress. He was sixty-nine then.

I lost contact with the fine, cheerful old gentleman until one day in January of 1939, while I was on the Coast, accumulated mail was forwarded to me, and among the items was a postcard from Schultze with a brief little message. "A smile from Foxy Grandpa. So nice to be alive with nice people who are alive. So happy days." It was signed with a drawing of Foxy Grandpa—and then Schultze's own signature.

The card was dated January 12. It reached me January 19, the very day that the newspaper carried the news of the artist's death of a heart attack at the age of seventy-two. According to the obituaries, the once dominant and high-earning cartoonist had been subsisting for a year or so on a $95-a-month job as an illustrator in the reading materials project of the WPA.

In Tribute

I cannot dismiss this chapter without paying some tribute to a remarkable chap, eighty-three-year-old Harry Hershfield, humorist, cartoonist ("Desperate Desmond," "Abie the Agent," *et al.*), columnist, author, afterdinner speaker, club man (he's Shepherd of the Lambs, and president of the Circus Saints and Sinners). It was Harry, who, when I became Broadway columnist for the *Evening Graphic,* graciously started to introduce me to prominent people around town, eminent newsmen, politicians, Mayor Jimmy Walker, judges and some show folks. He, himself, for a brief period, had been columnist for the *New York Journal,* the post I was to assume two years later.

It was Hershfield who supplied me with original anecdotes and little gags to brighten up those early columns, a practice he never abandoned for almost forty years thereafter. To this day, you cannot run into the amazing octogenarian without being rewarded with a fresh, humorous story, created out of his own fertile imagination. A fellow could fill a book with his offerings.

He is my apartment house neighbor, occupying a studio suite, whose walls are crowded with superb paintings by masters, past and present—a collection, he, himself, estimates may be worth close to a million dollars.

I'm going to content myself with only one anecdote—not by him but about him. Harry Hershfield and Al Hirshfeld, the distinguished theatrical illustrator and caricaturist, met at the opening of a play, *The Life of Reilly,* in April of 1942, their first meeting in some eight months. Harry said: "I keep getting praised for your wonderful caricatures." Al said: "I have been getting by on many of your famous jokes. But for a week, at least, this will identify me," and he pointed to a gaping molar space in his upper jaw.

Harry grinned. "That's what you think," he said, and opening his mouth revealed the identical empty space in his own lineup of teeth.

Humorist Harry Hershfield and comedienne Beatrice Lillie apparently are highly amused merely studying the face of the author who, alone, seems determined not to be caught unawares by the cameraman.
Photo by Hale Haberman

16

"*When Good Fellows Get Together . . .*"

I HAVE NEVER BEEN WHAT YOU might term a "joiner," and so, unlike several of my confreres, I resisted the impulse to apply for membership in the leading clubs of show business—the Friars, for instance, the Lambs or the Players. And, of course, I knew better than to try for the Union, Racquet or any of the University Clubs, or some dozen others I might mention.

However, there were five fellowships whose special enticements I couldn't resist, namely the Hoyle Club, Société des Knisteres, Artists & Writers, Skeeters, and Silurians. None of these boasted its own clubhouse at which a member might seek refuge. (You've seen movies in which the man of the house after a squabble with his lady fair, storms out, shouting: "I'm moving to the club.") No, these groups merely got together occasionally for amiable camaraderie.

The Hoyle Club, for instance, had a limited membership and convened once a week, usually in a suite at the Algonquin Hotel. Its mission was not too lofty. We assembled for poker sessions. Though it was against protocol for more than seven to gather for action any night, often there would be additional members, content to kibbitz and to share in the usual midnight repast.

Among those who held a franchise permitting them to play were playwrights Howard Lindsay, Russel Crouse, Arthur Kober, composers and lyricists George and Ira Gershwin and Billy Rose, columnists Heywood Broun, Franklin P. Adams, Paul Yawitz, Sidney Skolsky, and this reporter, publicists John Peter Toohey, Howard Benedict, Theron Bamburger, and Congressman Kenneth Simpson.

Eventually a Hollywood branch was organized, convening at the Players Club. Its consistent members were usually composer Jerome Kern, playwrights Clifford Odets and Marc Connelly, actor Charles Coburn and librettist Morris Ryskind, and because they had shifted their activities to the Coast, a few ex-members of the New York branch, especially Ira Gershwin, Benedict and Yawitz. And, of course, when any of the Manhattan contingent was on holiday or assignment in Hollywood, he was eligible to join in the sessions.

As a matter of record, it was at these poker duels that Crouse and Lindsay developed the affection for each other that led to their highly successful partnership as collaborators and producers of some of Broadway's notable hits—and it was from one of the sessions of the Hollywood branch that Jerome Kern, according to legend, in a depressed mood because he had not raked in a single pot during the entire evening, departed for home, sat down at the piano and began tinkling around until out of it all emerged a little number that, with the lyrics by Oscar Hammerstein II, was later to be sung and played around the world—"The Last Time I Saw Paris."

Nor do I forget the night when Billy Rose violated all our rules by bringing along his wife, comedienne Fanny Brice, and pleaded with us to let her participate. Chivalry finally won out, though I must confess that two of us, Arthur Kober and myself, held out quite a while but in the end yielded, too. Kober undoubtedly at evening's end might have wished that he had "stood" in bed—or at least that the famed comedienne had—for there came a point during the action when he drew two cards to find himself in the proud possession of a full house. Eventually, the rest of us dropped out of the bidding, except Miss Brice who met every raise and added her own boost. Finally, Kober smiled and murmured: "It's getting late, Fanny, and besides this pot's just big enough to suit me. Against my better judgment, but because I admire you, I'm only going to call."

He spread out his full house. Miss Brice slowly, with her face quite expressionless, exposed her own holdings on the green baize —a royal spade flush! It was the first, I confess, I had ever seen in all my poker playing to that point.

In my column a few days later, in what I considered an innocently joshing little paragraph referring to Miss Brice's triumph, I concluded, "I still think she plays poker like a woman." She never spoke to me again, and Billy Rose never joined Hoyle Club gatherings again.

On another occasion, Kenneth Simpson was among the players. This was during the final days of the Roosevelt-Willkie campaign when Simpson, something of a power in New York State Republican circles, was a candidate for Congress. We were playing a round of stud. Simpson, with a pair of queens revealed, kept warning Crouse who was displaying treys. "Drop out, Buck, you know you can't win."

On the next and final turn of the cards, a king dropped to match another king for Simpson, giving him two pairs. But Crouse's next was a third trey.

As he raked in the pot, he said: "Congressman, someday you may become President of the United States. When you do, remember that three unobtrusive treys—representing the common man—kicked your high-hat kings and arrogant queens right in their homely faces. Let that guide you through your political career."

After the game, I walked along for a few blocks with Simpson. "Want to know something?" he said glumly, "What happened tonight in poker is symbolic of almost everything in life. Just when I get to the point of winning, I usually get kicked in the face, just like Buck Crouse's crack about the treys and the kings and the queens." A few weeks later, Simpson was shorn of his power in Republican circles, but he did manage to win his seat in Congress, and political reporters hinted he was headed for great national achievement. A month later, came the "kick in the face" —death.

It was Crouse, incidentally, who became the phrase-creator for our set. Thus, whenever a pair of kings was bested by a lowly grouping of treys and deuces, Buck always shouted: "You have been trey-deuced." When a player triumphantly slapped down jacks and eights, Crouse invariably announced, "Boys, Jackson Heights."

Once when Lindsay and Crouse were in Hollywood, they were honored with a farewell poker session. So successful were the visiting lads, the chips piling up into huge towers in front of them, that they canceled their train reservations and remained on for six more farewell sessions. Then reluctantly, they caught the Super Chief and sped home to New York. Their winning streak continued there, though in another field. For, shortly after, their newest play opened—one of the season's outstanding hits, *State of the Union*.

The Hoyle Club had certain rituals. Thus when a player was forced to buy a second stack of chips, everyone rose and sang out joyously: "Happy Birthday to You, Happy Birthday," etc. The purchase of a third stack was the signal for the chanting of "Good-bye Boys, I'm Through." On one occasion, the lads authorized a special gathering, where players were obliged to wear red false beards and not to remove them until one or another uncovered a full house.

On one of the evenings, Arthur Kober, then a theatrical publicity man, sighed as he reflected that it had been a losing night. "The little woman won't like it," he moaned. "No money to bring home for our breakfast of caviar and champagne. Helpless little girl, she depends on me." The Kobers' idyllic marriage broke up in later years. Kober became a successful playwright. *Having a Wonderful Time* was one play that yielded him a handsome fortune. As for the "little woman," Lillian Hellman, she broke through her domestic chrysalis to author some of the great plays of our era: *Children's Hour, Watch on the Rhine, The Little Foxes, Another Part of the Forest* and other offerings for both the theatre and the movies.

There was one session of the Hoyle Club Arthur Kober didn't attend. This was the day he was married again. He sent the boys the following wire: "Sorry, I can't join you tonight as there is no way of bettering the perfect hand I am now holding."

I finally dropped out of the Hoyle Club when I discovered my stubborn opponents never were convinced when I raised on a deuce in the hole that I had anything but a deuce in the hole. They were so consistently right, I finally decided there was no career in bluffing. The Hoyle Club, with so many of its original members among the departed, is a thing of the past. But its joyous memories linger on.

Even more exclusive than the Hoyle Club was the Société des Knisteres consisting of five members: *Variety* editor Abel Green, literary agent Mark Hanna, anecdote collector Hal Horne and his rival, publisher Bennett Cerf, and myself. One night back in April of 1946, we convened for a serious objective: to expand the membership roster and to consider the applications of a dozen candidates.

The meeting was held in the apartment of young millionaire Armand Deutsch. We had accepted his invitation chiefly because he was noted for the Lucullan feasts offered by his cook, and also because he was famed for his rare brandies, rare etchings, imported Havana cigars—and even light and humorous conversation.

Mr. Deutsch's wife at the time, Actress Benay Venuta (who was later to marry actor Fred Clarke and then divorce him, too), having warned the guests not to spill ashes on the priceless rugs or scratch up the family heirlooms, departed. But not before receiving a telephone call from her closest friend, Miss Ethel Merman advising that *Annie Get Your Gun* would not open as scheduled because some mishap had occurred on the stage of the Imperial Theatre. Ordinarily this would have tossed a pall on the meeting until a poll revealed that none of those foregathered had invested a nickel.

Candidate Joe Laurie, Jr., comedian and author of show business books, started the afterdinner round table session by recalling boyhood days on the Lower East Side, especially the occasion when he drove a horse and wagon loaded with manure up snooty Fifth Avenue, chasing all the patrician barouches off the thoroughfare. He also recalled a minor racket when he collected two cents each from his cronies on the promise to point out fallen women. He took the paying guests over to a neighborhood bank and assured them solemnly as each woman passed that she was among the "fallen." He lost face when one of the boys recognized his aunt.

Candidate Abe Burrows sat down at the piano and solemnly intoned, as his keys pounded out the accompanying symphony, the sad plight of the "Girl with the Three Blue Eyes" and the citizen who walked "Down Memory Lane" with not a thing to remember and not a thing on his mind. Candidate Burrows also satirized Norman Corwin's air preachments and rambled a bit about the patriotic Armenian who fell at Concord—and remained, under the Red, White and Blue—still an Armenian.

At this point, Candidate Harry Kurnitz, fresh in from Metro's slave mill, recalled a genial uncle, who brooded because as a pants presser he was a distinct failure. Seems he was unable to lift or apply the iron efficiently. He was fated to be assigned only to plain pressing—the boss refusing to permit him to apply his talents to fancy creases or involved pleats. It was quite mortifying to the family, Candidate Kurnitz announced mournfully.

Host and Candidate Armand Deutsch held forth in a reminiscent mood, too, about his first effort to be a businessman. Armand dwelt in an elaborate mansion outside of Chicago and, at the age of eleven, announced firmly that he was going to open a lemonade stand in front of the vast estate. His grandfather, Julius Rosenwald, multimillionaire head of Sears, Roebuck, gathered the family in formal conclave and finally decided this was a step in the right direction.

The following morning, young Deutsch was prepared for the great enterprise. To his delight, he found an ornate stand with a rainbow-hued canopy overhead, set up near the driveway. Hovering near was the family butler, diligently stirring a caldron —not of lemonade but of orangeade. On the surface floated orange peels. The golden liquid was spiced with crushed strawberries and drifting grapes. Whenever a prospective patron drove near, Armand hailed him, delivered his selling talk and the butler brought a glass of the nectar over while Armand collected. At the end of a few hours, he had a dollar and a half clear profit, the orangeade was gone, the sun disappeared behind the clouds and the butler disappeared with the empty caldron while an army of maids busied themselves washing the glasses and the gardener and his helper began cleaning up. "Let's face it," insisted Deutsch, "Can you think of a more comfortable way to start out in business?"

At this point, Jack Forester, just back from Paris and out of the OSS, told some stories—particularly one about the fatal Lisbon crash in which some entertainers had lost their lives—including Singer Tamara Dreisen, and in which singer Jane Froman and accordionist Gypsy Markoff had been so woefully injured. He revealed that as soon as the word had spread that the big plane was down, Nazi agents and Allied agents in Lisbon began frantic efforts to gather in the pouches that contained important diplomatic communiqués. The Portuguese authorities also took a hand in trying to prevent any trouble between the warring factions. The Americans finally won out and retrieved all the pouches but one, which went to the bottom of the sea.

And so the session of the Société des Knisteres proceeded on until the early postmidnight hours, and then a secret conference of the five charter members was held. All candidates had been blackballed, including host Deutsch. The Société des Knisteres was to continue the most exclusive social club in the world.

The Artists & Writers Club, as its label indicates, was originally organized to gather certain members of the literary and art sets for occasional dinners and chatter, though often outsiders were admitted to our esoteric clan. Usually, we congregated in the upstairs dining room of "21."

Sports columnist Grantland Rice, one of the original organizers, was president. After his death, cartoonist Rube Goldberg succeeded him. Goldberg usually was the master of ceremonies at our gatherings.

An account of just one meeting may convey some idea of what took place at these sessions. This one took place on December 7, 1944, and, of course, since December 7 was a memorable date in our history, there were solemn toasts to our fighting lads, and Rube thereupon introduced a special guest, Captain Frank Farrell (later to become a New York columnist). Farrell recounted how fellow Marines had fought and died to gain yards of terrain—of the terrible death toll in the Pacific areas not revealed in press accounts. By acclaim, he was voted in as an honorary member of the club.

Then we turned to lighter subjects. Artist James Montgomery Flagg revealed his minor problems when he began painting that famous and much-discussed mural of the Dempsey-Willard fight that was to be hung in Jack Dempsey's restaurant.

"I didn't even know how sensitive some folks could be," he lamented. "Why, this fight was held back in 1919, and I painted in some folks who never were at that fight simply because Jack thought they were important and should be included. Do you know something? Some of them, and I'm not kidding, actually squawked because they didn't like the seats I put them in! And my friend Damon Runyon told me he wasn't too sure he even liked the people I put next to him in that painting."

Producer John Golden was another speaker. He discussed old-time chaps who drew and wrote and got together occasionally for fun and light imbibing. Among those he mentioned was that cartoonist genius, Dick Outcault, who had created the popular cartoon, "Yellow Kid." He said Outcault hadn't originally intended that the "kid" should be yellow, but there was a slight mishap in the coloring process. Golden confessed that it was he who used to write the balloon captions for the cartoon. "I got more of a kick out of them," he insisted, "Than when I wrote 'Poor Butterfly' years later."

"Well, William Randolph Hearst came along and coaxed Outcault to bring 'Yellow Kid' over to the *Journal.* Whereupon Joe Pulitzer, irked by this theft of one of his artists, had a certain newcomer imitate the strip, and for quite a while we had two 'Yellow Kids' running. Everybody in the business considered this highly unethical, and in fact many of the boys stopped talking to the young imitator artist.

"The years passed, and I became a producer. One day my secretary came in and said there was a man outside to see me, and, of course, as you must guess, it was the ostracized cartoonist. By this time, I wasn't as peeved with him as I had been in those earlier days, so I told the girl to show him in.

"He said: 'Look here, John Golden, you don't have to be so high-hat with me. I don't do any silly cartoons anymore. I move around with the best of them. I paint kings and queens, and I get more for a single painting than I did for a whole year's cartooning. So don't be so stuck up with me. I'm just as important as you are.'"

Golden went on to tell us that indeed the fellow had become as important as he claimed. He was George B. Luks whose paintings were hung in national museums around the world, and whom James Huneker once described as "a Puck, a Caliban, a Falstaff, a tornado."

This inspired emcee Rube Goldberg to advise the assembly that someday his own elaborate if not too delicate mural in the gent's room in the Monte Carlo Club might attain for him equal acclaim. (I often wonder what happened to that naughty mural, for the Monte Carlo Club vanished from the scene years ago.)

I do think I should mention some of the members who also attended this particular December session. Among them were illustrators and cartoonists Otto ("Little King") Soglow, Dean Cornwell, Arthur William Brown, Russell Patterson, Syd Hydeman, Paul Frehm, Bradshaw Crandell, Ham Fisher, Willard Mullin. Others were Frank ("Bring 'Em Back Alive") Buck, playwright Phil Dunning, photographer Hal Phyfe, detective Ray Schindler, tennis ace Francis T. Hunter, publicist Ted Saucier, lexicographer and poet Wilfred Funk, millionaire and bandleader

Roger Wolfe Kahn, who was later to become one of our more daring test pilots.

In the late fifties and early sixties, the club's interest drifted to golf, and the only dinners held now are those following one of the tournaments. Many of the original members died until merely a handful are still listed on the roster. After all, fellows in their seventies and eighties favor their rheumatic bones—and golf is not for them. Rube Goldberg, eighty-four, remained on as president, though, until last year when he insisted upon retiring and Bob Considine, vice-president, was moved up to succeed him. Joe Willicombe, Jr., a Kings Features executive, is currently secretary-treasurer of the club.

The Skeeters was organized in 1951 by sportscaster Ted Husing. Its mission was and is no loftier than those of the other clubs that claimed me as a member. About twice a year we assemble and either by bus or train—and occasionally by yacht belonging to one or another of the wealthier citizens of our group—journey to the Monmouth or Garden State tracks for a day of racing. And once a year, there is a dinner—also at a restaurant owned by a member—either Toots Shor's or "21." That is still the annual schedule.

Permanent secretary is Walter Kennedy, currently professional basketball czar, before that Mayor of Stamford, Connecticut, and before that publicist for the Globe Trotters and chief aide to Husing when the latter was announcing major sports events. Of the original members, Humphrey Bogart, cartoonist Ham Fisher, football coach Herman Hickman, Husing, sports columnist Bill Corum, Jules Lack, hotelman Jimmy Hart, restaurateur John Martin and Joe Eckhouse are among some twenty who have passed away. (Fisher who created "Joe Palooka" was to die a suicide. Lack, a carpet tycoon, was shot to death by a jealous husband.)

Originally, the membership roster was limited to fifty, and a "secret" steering committee elected applicants from a long waiting list to fill vacancies left by death or expulsion (members who missed three successive gatherings were automatically ousted).

Currently, it is a diversified collection of citizens from all walks of life who enjoy the distinction of being Skeeters. Among them are: Gene Mori, president of Hialeah and Garden State race tracks; Robert Sarnoff, president of RCA; Sonny Werblin, former co-owner of the football Jets; restaurateurs Toots Shor, Charles

Berns, Tom Saxe, Jr., Maxwell Kriendler, and Gene Leone; and among others are Walter Kennedy, of course; Walter Young, former publisher of the *Journal-American;* retired jockey Eddie Arcaro, former film stars William Gargan and Don Ameche, hotelman Seymour Weiss, columnist Bob Considine, bankers Horace (Hap) Flanigan and James A. Farley, Jr., industrialists Joseph A. Martino, Russell Feldman, Bernard Relin, David Marx and Harry Gould, retired General Emmett (Rosy) O'Donnell and Colonel Tony Story (he was General Douglas MacArthur's pilot), John Daly, Frank Folsom, Milton Rackmil, head of Universal Pictures and Decca Records; Admiral John Bergen, publisher Sander Simon, Irving Mitchell Felt, chairman of the board of Madison Square Garden and top kick of many multi-million-dollar enterprises; Abel Green, editor of the leading theatrical publication, *Variety;* Paul Screvane and others.

Serious subjects are zealously avoided when this mixed, though not necessarily mixed-up group gets together. Huddles are chiefly over the advisability of following the choices of professional handicappers or tips volunteered by track attendants. At the dinners, aside from a standing silent toast in tribute to the memory of the departed members, the speeches are frivolous, and any attempt at being serious is usually booed.

There was one night, though, when Bob Considine rose to his feet to demand in all solemnity that we consider how lacking in purpose our club was. He insisted that we cease to be a lighthearted, self-centered aggregation and begin devoting ourselves to *Weltschmerz,* improvement of social conditions, and so on and so on. At a subsequent dinner, he rose again and humbly begged the collective apology of all members for his misguided attempt to steer us to worthy objectives. "I've decided," he announced, "that the good fellowship we enjoy is boon enough in itself. I ask forgiveness."

Toots Shor promptly suggested that we drink to "Rabbi Considine" who had finally seen the light and had promised to mend his ways. To indicate that he really reformed, Bob rose and rattled off a few inconsequential but merry stories. So inconsequential, I can't recall a single one of them.

Among the more select of the press clubs is the Society of the Silurians. None is eligible to membership unless he has been a New York newsman, cartoonist or illustrator for a minimum of twenty-five years. On the other hand, he need not be actively engaged in newspaper work to gain membership. It is sufficient, if before he retired or entered into another field, that he had done service on the staff of a Manhattan paper.

There is always a big turnout for the annual dinners and occasional in-between affairs, with some notable tapped as chief speaker. But it is not the dinner, itself, nor the speaker, which makes these gatherings attractive to many of us. It's the shoptalk, and especially the anecdotes offered by the old-timers who remember back to the days of Herbert Bayard Swope and Irvin Cobb or that irascible city editor Charles Chapin, who was imprisoned for killing his wife.

Thus, I was fascinated by one story told me by an aging Silurian, and I quote him, as best as I can, from memory:

"I sat one day chatting with Irvin Cobb in the Twentieth Century-Fox's commissary," he said, "and with a straight face he told me this story. He said he had been in Catalina Island and had dozed off in a boat. He had a beautiful dream in which a gorgeous mermaid wound his fisherman's line gently around her head, and, lo, the line became a string of precious pearls and the hook a crown of gold and diamonds. Cobb said that, unwilling to let the treasure sink with the mermaid, he began pulling her toward him.

"He woke from his dream and there he found, standing almost upright on its tail in the waters, a colossal whopper of a marlin which must have weighed at least 400 pounds. Cobb let out and pulled in, he whipped and he panted and he swore and he prayed. Slowly he began to win his fight, and then, when the prey was almost at boat's side, the line snapped.

"'What then?' I asked him.

"Cobb continued in that dry, almost one note voice of his. 'Well, sir, that marlin stood again on the water's surface and loud and clear from it came a scornful laugh—a woman's laugh!'"

Another yarn old-timers among the Silurians like to recall is that of the reporter who submitted a story to city editor Chapin which ran a full column about what ordinarily should have been dismissed in a single paragraph—the discovery of a body floating in the East River. "The murky waters of the East River," he wrote, "yielded today the swollen body of an unidentified man," and so on. Chapin was delighted with the piece. On the bulletin board, he posted a notice which advised: "Here was a man who built a poignant story from so ordinary an event as the discovery of a body in the river." From then on, every "floater" inspired paragraphs that featured "the murky waters," etc.

So Chapin posted another notice informing the staff that henceforth any story mentioning "murky waters" would end the *Evening World* career of the reporter. Unfortunately, one of the boys away on his vacation did not read the ultimatum and, upon the day of his return, submitted a story of a drowning, adhering to the "murky waters" formula. Chapin fired him, barking, "When you can explain what 'murky waters' are and why you used the phrase, maybe you can come back to work."

The reporter walked into the nearest saloon. He returned three hours later and walking up to Chapin, spat out: "I'll shell you why sh' Eash River hash murky wa'rrrs. Ish becaush she hash to float pash Harlem, shash why." The usually irascible city editor, for once, was amused. He put the errant reporter back on the payroll.

Another story I heard at a gathering of the Silurians (when I asked Herbert Bayard Swope was it true, he replied: "It's so long ago—but I do think there's some truth to it"). It seems that Swope, before he became managing editor of the old *World,* was assigned to escort visiting Prince Louis of Battenburg on a tour of Manhattan's night life. At one point of their wanderings, they landed in the colorful saloon known as "Nigger Mike's," then on Pell Street, where the proprietor, eager to demonstrate his hospitality, spurned the Prince's proffer to pay the check. Whereupon the saloon's singing waiter also politely declined a handsome tip.

Swope, so the tale goes, was so impressed with the waiter's gesture that he made it the core of his feature story the following day. True or legend, it is a fact that, to the end of his days, Swope remained on the closest of terms with the former singing waiter—known now as Irving Berlin.

To repeat, these were the five clubs in which I could claim membership. But I must make reference to another group I did not belong to but nevertheless found myself invited to many of its annual affairs.

It's been years since I attended my last Illustrators Club's shows, but the memories linger on of the Rabelaisian skits, of the pretty girls who occasionally dispensed with even the protective fig leaves, and of one evening back in May of 1948 when the "ladies" of the ensemble, rouged and in abbreviated chorus girl costumes, included cartoonist George "Jiggs" McManus, actors Henry Fonda and Paul Douglas, former New Jersey Governor Harold Hoffman, photographer Hal Phyfe, comedian Peter Donald and a few others—all of whom had been transformed into fetching "dolls" by artists Russell Patterson, Arthur William Brown, Al Dorn, Otto Soglow, Norman Rockwell and Gladys Parker. Indeed, I remember another of the shows in which the principal stripper who divested herself down to a G-string was the aforementioned cartoonist, pretty Gladys Parker.

On another occasion—this was when the annual show was presented at the Heckscher Theatre back in November of 1935—the proceedings were rudely interrupted as gendarmes suddenly appeared on the stage. Those of us assembled waited for them to go into an act, but Herbert Bayard Swope came upon stage and rather indignantly pointed out that these were genuine policemen who were arresting the undraped girls, whereupon several judges in the audience got up and beat a hasty exit. Mr. Swope, in fact—as did Peter Riley Cooper—demanded that under the circumstances everyone present should insist upon being arrested, too.

Magistrate Thomas Aurelia freed the five girls after the defense lawyer pointed out that the penal code condemning immoral stage presentations absolves actors, employees and stagehands from blame. Whereupon, when the judge handed down his decision, some twenty or more illustrators and cartoonists, who had risen early in the morning, contrary to their usual schedule in order to be in court to lend moral support to the girls, broke into cheers. Incidentally, the charge was that Section 1, 148 of the Penal Code had been violated, but Subdivision D, which the lawyer quoted, saved them. It had been put into the ruling at the suggestion of Theodore Roosevelt when he was governor. Ironically enough, through the years, despite this saving clause, many performers have been arrested and convicted for immoral performances.

One evening I had playwright Sidney Kingsley as my guest at an Illustrators' show. I recall one scene where Artist Al Dorn brought upon stage for ad lib performances Dean Cornwell, Gilbert Bundy, Russell Patterson, Roy Spreter and some others, then called upon a few "amateurs" from the assembly to join them, among them Lieutenant Colonel Greg "Pappy" Boyington, Bert Wheeler, Jules Glaenzer, Marc Connelly and that old sleuth,

Ray Schindler. Artist Bundy, who had been with Boyington in Tarawa, had him stick his head through an aperture in a backdrop—and made a hasty sketch of him.

This was back in 1945—and it afforded Harry Hershfield an opportunity to tell several of his favorite twice-told tales: Of the man, for instance, who came home unexpectedly and found his wife kissing his best friend. The best friend said: "Look, we're grown-up men. Let's not be silly about this. We'll play a round of rummy for her."

The husband said, "Okay, but just to make it interesting, let's play for a penny on the side."

Unabashed, Harry told other stories bravely, perhaps brazenly, like his oldie of the man who bragged he feared nothing and was dared to thrust his right arm into the jaws of a ferocious lion. Ever since, Harry said, he has been known as "Lefty."

Later, I said to Hershfield: "Man, you really gave them some whiskered beauts."

The humorist grinned. "They laughed, didn't they?" he said. "Let me tell you something. You've gone to vaudeville shows, and a clown does a pratfall and you roar. Then maybe a year or two later, you catch his act again, and again he does the same pratfall—and again you roar. Good stories, like good acts, never get moldy."

17

"Eat, Drink and Be Merry . . ."

I WILL NOT SAY THAT NOWHERE in the world does the populace prefer to dine out as extensively as it does in Manhattan, but it is safe to volunteer that no metropolis on the face of the globe can boast a wider assortment of culinary offerings. Not Paris nor Rome, not London nor Madrid, not anywhere. On some side arteries between Eighth and Third avenues from the Fifties to Forty-second Street, you may gorge yourself on delicacies indigenous to France or South Africa, Spain or Argentina, Italy or Germany, Turkey or Russia, China or Sweden, Japan or the Polynesian Islands.

It is a fact that within ten blocks of the Times Square district alone you may have your spicy shish kebab, pompano *papillotte, canapé marquis,* beef stroganoff, shark's-fin soup, fish, sirloin grilled over hickory-log fire, sauerbraten, *crêpes suzettes,* terrapin Maryland, *ossi buchi con risotto,* ham and eggs, *ching-yu, huevos Malaguena* or *ghivesi calugarese, poi,* fried chicken Southern style—foods and combinations of food that the prodigious gluttons or epicures of olden days never dreamed existed. In Manhattan, they are yours for the asking, with sauces and garnitures to make the mouth drool.

Once when I deplored my own lack of appetite and wondered whether it wasn't a case for the doctor, I looked over and saw Greta Garbo at "21" placidly and contentedly nibbling away at lettuce, celery and a sliver of cheese, and immediately decided that perhaps I had been overeating anyway, but my discouragement returned when a few nights later at Lindy's I watched Irving Berlin pack away a steak the size of an elephant's tail-rest, and some months previously, also in Lindy's, I had watched in dismay as J. Edgar Hoover forked huge chunks of steak tartare.

At Toots Shor's, Joe DiMaggio, looking almost haggard, before my very eyes once consumed two huge orders of prime roast beef—and there was that night when I watched in wonder at Reuben's when the sensitive-looking Ingrid Bergman dug with gusto and visible delight into a mountainous corned beef sandwich and followed up with a generous slab of apple pie.

My opinion of the fragile Duke of Windsor went up a bit when I saw him reach for his leg of chicken and gnaw at it, just like us common folks whose pillowcases boast no royal crest. None of that dainty slicing away with a knife but just a good, healthy chewing away as he gripped the bone with his once regal fingers. Mind you, this was at the snooty Colony, and ever since I have joined the unabashed ones who use digits instead of silver.

I have been in Lüchow's and watched those bosom pals, the late George Jean Nathan and the late H. L. Mencken, tucking away a huge *Pfannkuchen* with *Preisselbeeren,* washing it down with goblets of lager while the orchestra delivered a concert of ancient Viennese tunes. There was also a time I sat in Peter Luger's over in Brooklyn, waiting for the delivery of my tenderloin, medium well, smothered in onions, and amused myself in the interim surveying Messrs. James J. Walker and Gene Fowler arguing to determine who would pay the check. Mr. Fowler lost, but the ex-Mayor grabbed for the tab anyway, and perhaps it was at this point that Fowler made up his mind that someday he would devote himself writing the biography of Jimmy—which he did, as we all know who read his fascinating book, *Beau James.*

It has been my rare fortune to have dined in famed restaurants throughout the country: Hollywood and San Francisco, New Orleans and Chicago, Miami Beach and Palm Springs, Atlanta and New Haven, as well as in Rome, Venice, San Juan, Rio de Janeiro, Havana—also at lunch carts, railroad-station counters and airport dineries, in hotel grills and automats, and you would think out of this grueling experience of eating out, I should be among the nation's outstanding gourmets.

The sad truth is I still stick to the bare essentials and steer clear of chef's delights and so-called heavenly sauces. I dislike game birds, antelope chops, buffalo steaks, venison and eels. In fact, I have got to a point where there is no thrill at sitting down at a restaurant table at all, to a point where I envy all those who have the good fortune and good sense to dine in their own homes, surrounded by their own circle of friends.

Nevertheless, my columnar chores prodded me into frequenting eating places. Gradually, as far as Manhattan was concerned, I began limiting my invasions to those restaurants offering potentialities as news sources—"21,"—the Colony, the Stork, Whyte's 57th Street, Lindy's, Dinty Moore's, Voisin, Sardi's, Harwyn, Eden Roc, Toots Shor's, The Tavern, Reuben's, Danny Stradella's Hideaway, Bill Reed's Little Club (and later Barberry Room), Lüchow's, Leone's, Pen and Pencil, Gallagher's, Kippy's and perhaps a dozen others.

Thus, though I can't recall what my dishes were that night in "21" a few years ago, I do remember vividly a happening that had nothing to do with the menu. The well-known literary and talent agent, Irving Lazar, bridling under the needling of film producer Otto Preminger, who was accusing him of having sold the film rights to Truman Capote's best seller, *In Cold Blood,* to producer Richard Brooks (Preminger insisted Lazar had promised him and Frank Sinatra first bidding rights), rammed a glass into Preminger's forehead. It made for a sizzling Page One story. After all, two columnists, Sobol and Jack O'Brian were first-hand witnesses.

There was another night in "21" in 1941 when I settled down with Rosie Dolly and her millionaire husband, department-store heir Irving Netcher. It was a bit of a celebration, but I don't remember whether it was the birthday of one of them or a wedding anniversary. However, the guests had departed and the three of us were left. Rosie recalled some of the bizarre highlights of her show-business career partnered with sister Jennie—recalled, too, some of her fantastic winning streaks at roulette and *chemin de fer* in Deauville and Cannes, including two occasions when she broke the bank.

"But I always said Jennie is the luckier one," she said glumly, "I'm a piker compared to her when it comes to luck."

She turned to Netcher and purred: "Dahleeng, you married the wrong Dolly sister. Jennie's the one. She has the pep and such a nice disposition—everything. She wears clothes better. Me, I worry all the time. About everything, and nothing. Jennie, she laughs at the world, nothing worries her. With her disposition, she would live to be a hundred."

Some two weeks later, came the dispatch to our *Journal-American* office, from Hollywood: Its first lines read: Jennie Dolly, forty-eight, of the once famous dancing sisters was found dead by hanging yesterday in her fashionable apartment. Detective Lieutenant Bryon Diller said: 'It is undoubtedly suicide.'"

Colorful Jack Kriendler, cofounder of "21" with Charles Berns, is long gone, and now his brother, World War II hero Marine Colonel Bob Kriendler has taken over together with his brother Pete and Charles Berns's brother Jerry as well as a Kriendler nephew, Sheldon Tannen, and "21" is probably among the more popular eating places in the world under their collective guidance. The roster of consistent patrons is out of *Who's Who*: statesmen, diplomats, governors, stage, television and film notables —multimillionaires and even some plain folks who can afford the prices and want to eat good food in style.

Evenings have always been lively at Danny's Hideaway. I remember when Tony Curtis and Janet Leigh decided it was just the place for the reception following their wedding. Perhaps no

Today's ruling hierarchy of "21" dining leisurely after the midnight rush has subsided. *From left to right:* Sheldon Tannen, with the chef perched solicitously over his shoulder, sportsman Pete Kriendler, former newsman Jerry Burns, and Marine hero, Colonel Robert Kriendler.
Photo by The New York Times

pair of stars could boast a more distinguished choir—reading from left to right, it consisted of Perry Como, Dean Martin and Jerry Lewis (they were still partners at the time), Frankie Laine and the five DeMarco Sisters, with Dick Stabile conducting. The song they offered was Irving Berlin's sentimental "Always." It was an occasion for the young couple to remember always, perhaps, but unfortunately, some years later the ideal marriage came to an end.

When in town, Danny's is one of the chief gathering places for the comics Jack E. Leonard, Red Buttons, Jack Carter, Alan King as well as for visiting cinema stars, especially owner Danny Stradella's idol, John Wayne. In fact, one night, Danny, beaming as he spotted three favorite he-men of the movies and stage at separate tables, Wayne, Robert Preston and Forrest Tucker, waited until they were through with dinner and then invited them to join him at the Copa Lounge, where to the amazement and amusement of those of us who went along, he initiated them into the intricacies of the then popular Twist. Watching these four squirming, perking and twisting was something a cameraman should have recorded for posterity.

An amazing little fellow, this Danny Stradella, who started out as a boxer in the bantamweight division, won a prize in one of the Harvest Moon dancing contests, and is a frustrated cowboy who envisions himself in chaps and boots astride a mustang, two guns flanking his holstered hips as he rides off to battle murderous cattle rustlers. In his daydreams he is John Wayne or Marshal Dillon, which may explain his occasional far-off look when a patron complains about the location of his table in the preferred Celebrity Room where Oscar Award winners smirk out of their frames on the walls.

He also pictures himself something of a modern-day "Diamond" Jim Brady as he hosts parties of from twenty to forty at opening nights—usually at Jules Podell's Copacabana.

There is perhaps no more colorful assembly place than Jan Mitchell's Lüchow's, one of our oldest restaurants, and it boasts Liquor License No. 1, obtained just when Prohibition came to an end. To list folks who gather there, especially on Sunday nights, is just to read off page after page of *Who's Who in America,* the *Social Register,* and the various motion picture and stage publications.

Mitchell's own parties in the Lillian Russell room on the second floor have brought together the elite of town, for he delights in gathering the town's dominant personalities, particularly after a glittering theatrical premiere. Jan is one of the more astute businessmen of our town, who has become a millionaire since taking over Lüchow's—not only because of his other restaurant ventures, notably his acquisition of the Longchamps chain, control of which he sold a year or so ago for hefty capital gains, and of another ancient and historic eating place, Charles in the Village.

Invade Lüchow's on a Sunday night and you will more often than not find other table occupants to include Senator Jacob Javits and his attractive wife Marion, newspaper publisher Samuel Newhouse and his Mitzi, columnists Leonard Lyons, Earl Wilson, Frank Farrell, Bob Considine and their wives, Gloria Swanson, a flock of judges and politicians—as well as any number of stage and film stars.

Jan Mitchell beams as he surveys his distinguished assembly, and perhaps it's only my imagination, but the founder, August Lüchow also seems to beam from his framed portrait on the wall.

As for the ebullient Toots Shor, "adviser" to Presidential hopefuls, football coaches, baseball biggies and movie stars—and his famed gathering place, books and magazine articles have been devoted to him and the activities boiling daily in his restaurant. I have already touched on him and them in various preceding chapters so I can dispense at this point with further comment.

One of the nation's plushier dining establishments is the Colony Restaurant where the adjoining table may be occupied by the Duke and Duchess of Windsor or some member of the Vanderbilt or Rockefeller family, or of the Henry Ford dynasty. Emerging from the Prohibition days it has flourished as a haven for gourmets, and though the wine flows freely, no patron dares to show the signs of overindulgence, for let him stagger out or emit uncouth drunken remarks, and the doors are barred to him forever. Some customers have been known to sulk for weeks if their favorite table is preempted.

It is difficult to believe that, at the beginning, this elegant eating place, while still in the same building it now occupies on East Sixty-first Street, shared the converted town house with a gambling room supervised by the ill-famed Arnold Rothstein. At that time, the restaurant was operated by a night-spot man named Joe Pani, and Gene Cavallero was his captain. Joining forces and finances with *maître d'* Ernest Cerutti and the chef, Alfred Hartman, Cavallero became one-third owner of the restaurant, and eventually sole boss.

A year or so ago, now a millionaire with a beautiful estate in Lago di Garda in northern Italy, and an equally opulent home and grounds in Long Island, the senior Cavallero went into semi-retirement, dividing his time between the two estates while Gene, Jr., is now in full charge, after having served a long and rigorous apprenticeship.

It was in the Colony that Mayor Jimmy Walker introduced me to a tall, somber-faced man and his attractive wife. "You two really should get to know each other," said Walker. "Louis, this is O. O. McIntyre, a fellow in the trade." How was I to guess at the time that years later, after McIntyre's death, William Randolph Hearst, Sr., would send out an order to his editors that my column was to replace Odd's thereafter. The shift was of comparatively short duration, for I was too saturated with Broadway and Broadwayese to be a suitable successor to the amiable Odd, and so at my request I regained my Broadway column.

Another preferred dining lure is Whyte's on Fifty-seventh Street, companion place to the other and original Whyte's in downtown Manhattan, both owned by the enterprising Ray Hopper, who has a popular and handsome young George Macris as his chief aide and general manager. My partiality to Whyte's Fifty-seventh Street may be due, perhaps, to the fact that it is in the building in which I dwell—an inspiring convenience as it has proved to fellow tenants like Harry Hershfield, Earl Wilson, Lisa Kirk, Ethel Smith, Jack E. Leonard, Conrad Nagel and others.

Some years ago, while in the restaurant, three men were at the bar engaged in a loud discussion of ballplayers, past and present. One debater was insisting Christy Mathewson was the greatest and after him Mickey Mantle, while another held forth for Joe DiMaggio. The third agreed they would be remembered through the years, but none as vividly or with more respect for his prowess than Babe Ruth. Finally, one of them whom I knew approached me—"Who do you think will always be considered the greatest ballplayer of them all?"

I said: "Tell you what. See that lady over at that table? You ask her."

"Okay," he said, good-naturedly, "You just won't talk. I get it," and went back to the bar.

But I really meant it. For the lady surely had a definite opinion. She was Mrs. Babe Ruth.

Lindy's continues to prosper as a restaurant, but something of the old allure has vanished with the disappearance from its

A serious nonpolitical huddle between Robert F. Wagner, then mayor of New York and now ambassador to Spain, and the author.

The Sobols at dinner with Senator Jacob Javits and his wife Marion. Not once during the evening did the senator inquire whether we had voted for him. This was at the Harwyn Club, which has faded from the Manhattan scene. But there has been no fading out of the energetic senator.
Photo by Bill Mark

patronage of the colorful characters who inspired Damon Runyon to employ the restaurant as the background for so many of his stories. Leo Lindemann, affectionately hailed as Lindy, is long gone, and so is his wife Clara, who because of his patience in listening to tales of woe, was referred to as "The Magnificent Ear."

Songwriters, song pluggers, show folks and even eminents like the late Bernard Baruch and J. Edgar Hoover and Clyde Tolson were frequent diners, and there were occasions when Hoover might be seated not more than a booth or two away from a high-number Public Enemy. And always, listening and observing would be Damon Runyon, whose large portrait still hangs in a dominant spot on one of the walls. For years, Lindy's was the favorite dining place for Irving Berlin, and it was in Lindy's that the comics of the day assembled to heckle one another. A few of the newer breed still prefer it as their daily meeting place.

It was in Lindy's one night in 1959, sitting with Jack Benny, when the comedian opened up. "Here I'm sixty-five," he moaned, "Good Lord, in five more years I'll be seventy. I feel like hissing young guys forty or fifty. Golly, I remember I was in Earl Carroll's *Vanities*. I was just married to Mary and was pulling down $1,500 a week. And was that big money to me. Then they wanted me to join Fred and Adele Astaire in *Bandwagon* at the same figure. The Astaires were the tops. I thought—in a show with them, I don't want anything better.

"So I went to Carroll—and asked him to release me. He said: 'Don't be silly. Why should I let you go?' "

"I said this was my big chance. I even offered to give him $500 a week out of my pay for as long as I was in the Astaire show, which meant I'd be working for a lot less. Carroll said: 'No.' Then I got desperate, I said: 'Look, Mr. Carroll, you let me go and I'll hand you over the whole $1,500 a week.' For nothing I was willing, just so I'd be with the Astaires. Carroll said, 'No.'

"So I stuck with the show, and suddenly everyone is talking about a radio team, Gene and Glenn. They were really going hot. I said to Mary, 'This radio, that's the future. Look, I've been in vaudeville and in this Earl Carroll show, but how many people know Jack Benny or talk about him? I've got to get on radio.' I'll say this for Mary—she didn't say: 'You're making good money in show business. Why take a chance?' Nothing like that. She said: 'If it'll make you happy, go ahead and try for radio.'

"So once again I went to Earl Carroll. I said I'd like out. He said: 'You got a better offer?' I said no, but I wanted to see if I could get into radio. This time Carroll said: 'Okay, Jack. The show's about to run itself out. You can leave.'

"So I stepped out of my $1,500-a-week job. But there were no radio offers. My money began to run out, and I began to kick myself for being such a damn fool. Just married and no job—not even a vaudeville engagement.

"And then I went on for a guest shot for no dough. It was Ed Sullivan's little radio show, and an agency man heard me. A couple of months later, I had my own radio show. Now people began to know there was a Jack Benny, and that satisfied my ego.

Believe me, the money was small at the start, and I could have pulled more by going into a show or concentrating on vaudeville.

"Since then I've had a lot of luck. And now here I am sixty-five—going on seventy—and what do I do? Beat my brains out playing engagements in a few night spots, like in Vegas and Miami Beach. I'm silly enough if a show came along I might even try a whirl in that. Crazy, isn't it? I should be taking it easy. The TV show is enough work. What is it? The ham in me? You have no idea how hammy I am. Take my violin concerts. I don't get a nickel for myself out of them—it's for charity—but now I really want to be a good fiddler.

"I'll say this, too, for Mary. My success hasn't changed her. She goes out and spends as much money now as she used to spend when we didn't have any money."

Just then a young chap came over, pleading for an autograph.

"How old are you, son?" asked Benny.

The chap answered: "Twenty-four, Mr. Benny."

Jack glared at him. "Get away from me before I kick you in the face—twenty-four! I feel sick." And then he grinned as he scrawled a little sentiment on the menu for the young man.

Sardi's, the famed restaurant patronized by actors, producers, directors, screen stars, theatrical agents, authors, politicians and tourists, has, among its attractions, its gallery of caricatures, chiefly by the late Alex Gard, but many since his death by Don Bevan who, incidentally was married to the daughter of former screen star Nancy Kelly and playwright Jack Kirkland.

Gard's background was draped in mystery. As he told it to me, his actual name was Kremkoff, his family's fortune had been lost during the Red Revolution, he had managed to pick up the loose threads again by becoming an actor in Bulgaria, followed by happier years in Paris where he painted and designed floats.

His contract early in the career of Sardi's provided that he, as the party of the first part, was to furnish caricatures suitable for the restaurant and that Vincent Sardi, Sr., as party of the second part was in turn to furnish meals suitable to Gard—two meals a day for one person or one for two.

Gard's first caricature was of comedian Ted Healy. His last, as far as I can determine, was of Oscar Serlin, producer of *Life with Father.*

There is usually a bitterness in the Gard caricatures if you study them. Yet none matched him for his genius in conveying to paper with a few pencil strokes the characteristics of his victim. Of him, truly, Confucius might have said: "One picture is worth ten thousand words—wicked words."

So cruel and unflattering were they that Helen Morgan wept when she saw hers. My wife always refused to sit at a table where she would face mine. Katharine Cornell vowed she would never return to the restaurant unless Gard made certain changes, above all removing the cigarette dangling salaciously from her lips. Drama critic John Anderson would never sign his.

Subjects were asked to sign the distorted portraits in the gallery usually referred to by caricaturist-writer Irving Hoffman as "Gard's Chosen People." Playwright Sidney Kingsley's scrawl was "There's a divinity which shapes all ends." John Barrymore's solemn inscription was: "To be or not to be—but why worry?" Boris Karloff scribbled: "He said I look like Boris Karloff." Collaborating playwrights Russel Crouse and Howard Lindsay, in a rare double pose, wrote: "That's a very good likeness of my partner."

It had been a practice of the elder Sardi to hang associated personalities close to each other. He never permitted romance to be shattered on his walls—no matter what chasms of differences arose between the principals in real life. Thus Frank Fay and Barbara Stanwyck, who met and wooed in the restaurant, continued after their divorce to face each other amiably on the wall. And kept snugly together also were Douglas Fairbanks and Joan Crawford, long after their marriage had dissolved, and Claudette Colbert and Norman Foster, too.

Subjects who fell into disgrace usually had the caricatures removed to make place for some upcoming personality. Thus, in her sorrier days, Lillian Roth's portrait was stored in the basement. When she bounced back so beautifully and was featured in *I Can Get It for You Wholesale,* the caricature was dusted off and restored to its place on the wall with a little ceremony at which Miss Roth shed a few tears, and explained them away by insisting, "I always cry at hangings."

The gayest nights—sometimes turned to sadness—are immediately after a theatrical opening when First Nighters gather and wait for the performers, producer and director of the offering, applauding them as they enter. Then all wait around for the first reviews, and that's when a sad note is often injected if the notices turn out to be unfavorable.

In more recent months, a new restaurant, Kippy's, has caught the fancy of the dining public. It's founder was Joe Kipness, a former dress manufacturer, who first turned theatrical producer when he partnered with Monte Proser in offering a hit musical, *High Button Shoes,* which starred Phil Silvers. Kippy's, with its decor dominated by relics of Revolutionary days, is on the site formerly occupied by Ruby Foo's and previously by the King's Terrace. (Recently Kippy's was sold for the reported sum of $1,500,000 to Ira and Harold Koenigsburg, owners of a rival restaurant, Chandler's.) Kipness remains co-owner with Art Schindler of the Hawaii Kai which features a Polynesian cuisine and a seafood place, and of Joe's Pier 52 on the premises formerly housing the Hickory House.

Almost next door to Kippy's is Gallagher's, the steak house founded by Helen Gallagher and her husband Jack Solomon. Helen and Jack have been claimed by death but Gallagher's continues to prosper under the ownership of Jerry Brody and the supervision of its general manager, Dick Conlon. Here the walls are lined with pictures of sportsmen, past and present, as well as stage and film stars. Conlon is quite a rare personality himself, an avid golfer with a low handicap, and a professed gourmet who likes to sample the dishes offered in the eating places of rival establishments. Loyal patrons at Gallagher's include former boxing champion Rocky Graziano, columnist Jimmy Breslin, Madison Square Garden's headman, Irving Felt, songwriter Frank Loesser as well as actors and actresses who may be appearing in productions on the street—West Fifty-second.

Incidentally, Jack Solomon, even when Gallagher's was an assured success, decided he and Helen should have another place. He launched The Flying Trapeze, which certainly had something new to present—actual trapezes hung from the ceiling on which every so often performers would go flying through the air with the greatest of ease. It didn't last too long, however—another place to add to the Tombs of Broadway.

But this is by no means intended as a guide to the restaurants of New York for that would require a book in itself. And indeed, there have been scores of volumes published through the years devoted to the histories and virtues and menus of the thousands of eating places scattered around our metropolis.

For that matter, the hotel dining rooms would have to be discussed, including the few remaining supper clubs that still

This scene built up to no suspense. The author is congratulating the great film director, Alfred Hitchcock—not on his most recent offering—but on the fact that he had successfully dieted off some thirty pounds of excess avoirdupois, and Hitchcock couldn't have been more pleased than if he had just been handed an Oscar.

The late Sherman Billingsley and the author settle at a table in the Stork Club to study a few pictures Billingsley was planning to include in his book. Death claimed him before he could complete his memoirs, but his daughter Shermane is working on the project.

feature entertainment, such as the Americana's Royal Box, the Plaza's Persian Room, the St. Regis Maisonette and the Waldorf's Empire Room. Come to think of it, that about covers the hotels—for here too, we must note the change from former years when there were more than a dozen of the town's inns offering entertainment along with leisurely dining.

Getting back to restaurants, just briefly: Dinty Moore's has had a long and colorful career, for instance, and there are any number of luxurious eating places such as the Four Seasons, The Forum of the Twelve Caesars, Leone's, Caravelle, Grenouille, Chez Vito with its parading violinists and operatic singers; Asti's, also with a group of opera singers; Voisin, a favorite dining place for Perle Mesta and the Kennedys, among others; the Stage Delicatessen operated by the witty Max Asnas and patronized by comedians, columnists and stage stars; and many other places but I am calling a halt except to accord just a little space to some obscure bistros.

There is something of Paris which is rowdy and earthy in these dimly lit, low-ceilinged haunts sprinkled through the brownstone sectors of our West Forties and Fifties, chiefly between Eighth and Ninth avenues. Unlike the garish taverns of the upper East Side where even the Gallic-tinted titles on the front doors appear anglicized, these bawdy *boîtes* are as saucily Parisian as the tilt of M. Chevalier's straw skimmer. You find no carpet on the floor, nor are there doormen with gold braid splashed like omelettes across their chests. Ask for *crêpe suzettes,* and you receive a look of chilled disdain.

Inside the smoke hangs from the ceiling like floating cotton, the accents are shrill and an accordion occasionally wheezes plaintively. Brandy is a favorite libation. As for the cuisine, few of the places boast formal printed menus—you take your beefsteak and you like it. There is even a rumor that in some of these places you may order that Montparnassian delicacy (though I will not vouch for this)—horsemeat! You must be content, the rumor persists, to eat it drugstore style, that is to say, as a sandwich.

Naturally, for relish, what else but plenty of horseradish.

Quite a contrast with an establishment also featuring a Gallic cuisine—Le Pavillon. This was easily the most expensive dinery in our town when its founder, the late autocratic Henri Soule, was the host. After his death, Claude Philippe became its chief operator for a time, and then a new syndicate came into possession, headed by a popular young restaurateur, Stuart Levin, who has managed to restore Le Pavillon as a prestigious eating place, luring the gourmets anew.

Something else as a final postscript. In other days it was considered that the chief function of restaurants was to serve good food and liquors. But gradually a change took place as, one by one, some of the snootier spots began to diversify. For instance, "21" has on display, in addition to imported cigars, neckerchiefs, lighters, various household utensils, canned foodstuff and best sellers among the books. Reuben's features perfumes, cosmetics, and candles. Lindy's offers an imposing line of chocolates as well as delicacies, cakes and pies for retail sales. In the Colony, you may pick out jewelry in the display cases, ranging in price from $50 to $20,000 and higher.

Which reminds me of the time when El Morocco, during the reign of the late John Perona, also had cabinets in its lobby displaying jewelry. Paulette Goddard kept studying a beautiful bracelet—priced, if my memory is faithful, at around $15,000. Her husband, novelist Erich Maria Remarque, was in Switzerland at the time but was expected to arrive in New York within a few days. Paulette wanted to consult him before making a move toward the purchase. Two nights later, when she was back in El Morocco, the movie star gave a little cry of dismay. The bracelet was no longer on display. It has been bought for an unmarried lady by her very much married lover, one of Manhattan's quite prominent Wall Street brokers.

18

Memory Montage

AND NOW OTHER LITTLE MEMORIES cluster in a jumbled montage as I try to separate them. For instance, that of a slim girl in a tight red velvet gown, parting full sensuous lips as she laments, "Don't know any reason why he treats me so poorly," etc., etc., Libby Holman offering the unforgettable melancholy chant "Moanin' Low." Libby subsequently was to be oppressed with tragedies: one husband dead from a bullet wound, suicide or murder, it was never determined; another dead from an overdose of sleeping pills; and a beloved son found frozen to death in a crevasse on Mount Whitney. "Moanin' Low," indeed.

Here's a low-ceilinged dive in Harlem, the Clam House, with dark faces punctuating the heavy fog of smoke like polka dots on a veil. Why should I remember a crippled genius there strumming a dirge on a one-stringed cigar-box guitar—fellow by the name of Boston Charlie?

A night at Les Ambassadeurs, and a tall, horse-faced man at the rope bars my entrance. "All sold out, bud," he snaps. Meekly, I explain. "I'm Sobol. I'm here to cover this opening." He turns his back on me and says to a sinister-looking associate: "This a phony make?" and the thug studies me sourly. Just then, Jimmy Durante, coming to the entrance, spots me, identifies me, and reluctantly the two give their okay. The tall man, Larry Fay, a formidable racketeer of the era, was later to go to a violent death.

And a night in the old Hollywood restaurant and Abe Lyman is leading the band in "Me and My Shadow," in tribute to the song's lyricist, Billy Rose, who is seated with me. Billy begins asking pertinent questions about Eleanor Holm. How am I to know at the time he was to marry her shortly?

A welcome home party for a famous cartoonist, Billy de Beck, and I meet for the first time some other distinguished artists noted for the comic capers of their characters—Rube Goldberg, George McManus, Milt Gross. Also a fellow named Bob Ripley (Momoto, famous Japanese, can swallow his nose"—"There is no lead in a lead pencil").

I escort a group of big businessmen to Harlem to Dickie Wells's place—and I couldn't have staged anything better—for shortly after we are settled, we see one character start to slash his girl with a pocket knife, and then two burlies stamping their hoofs into the assailant's face. We get out in a hurry, for one of those with me is the late department store emir, Bernard Gimbel, another is William Robinson, later to be president of Coca-Cola and a few others of like prestige. They probably looked back on that night with secret glee.

There is the session at the Eden Roc restaurant which I was certain would produce a provocative diversion, for the guests on my radio interview show were pianistic humorist Victor Borge and the equally voluble Sonja Henie. But this time, they both clammed up, and I sweated freely trying to coax more than monosyllabic replies to my questions. Not until the program was over did both open up, but it was too late.

Pretty heiress Gloria Vanderbilt, then a recent bride, barges into "21," pirouettes daintily like a paid model to display a full-length mink coat. Married to Pat DeCicco, she exclaims: "Pat just gave it to me for a present. It's the first time in my life anyone ever gave me such a gorgeous present." A truly happy girl, though we ponder about her happiness over the gift, for with her millions she could have bought herself mink coats to fill a warehouse.

An afternoon for cocktails at the spacious residence in Rome of then Ambassador James D. Zellerbach. A gracious host, he apologizes for not having us stay on for dinner, explaining he is

Did You Ever See a Dream Looking? Well, here's Sophia Loren gazing first soulfully at a photo of the author—then, apparently disillusioned, turning away in bitter disappointment.

The author congratulates a couple of newlyweds, Sonja Henie and socialite Winthrop Gardiner. The sad postscript is that the marriage ended a few years later, and the former ice queen went on to wed Scandinavian industrialist Niels Onstad.
Photo by Hal Phyfe

busy packing, setting off the following day for what he terms a "bonus furlough" back to San Francisco. "I can't remember," he says, "when I have looked forward so much to a vacation—not even when I was a kid—as these five or six weeks I have coming to me. I'm keeping my fingers crossed, with the President heading for Europe. It may just be he might also drop in on Rome, although I haven't heard that he plans to, but if he does, I guess that means cutting my holiday short and getting back here in a hurry."

I sit with Frances Williams at the Club Richman while Harry Richman is singing his songs, and she confesses the romance is over, but that she would never stop loving that man. Of course, by this time, we all knew Clara Bow had entered Harry's life. So Frances drifted on to new loves—and to death, which caressed her much too early in her career.

An August afternoon in 1956 at André Dubonnet's villa at Cap d'Antibes. Porfirio Rubirosa, unshaven, in loose blue slacks and a gray sports shirt, sits in a low chair strumming a guitar and singing a soft serenade of Mexican, French and Italian chants to an audience consisting of my wife, Peggy, and a most beautiful young girl in the skimpiest of bikinis, Odille Rodin. It is evident that Odille is his latest romance. And, of course, soon after they became Mr. and Mrs. he goes to his violent death in his racing sports car.

Later that afternoon, driving through the narrow Eden Roc thoroughfare, we spot a familiar figure walking briskly alone—a vision to behold, crimson slacks, a beautiful Urban-blue silk sports shirt, and a sunset orange ascot. We stop the car and yell out "Hello," and the fellow grins as Peggy remarks on his lively getup. "I get rid of all my complexes this way," he says. "Better than getting loaded," and Gary Cooper proceeds on his way.

It is 3:00 A.M. in Venice and we have prevailed upon a gondolier who is putting his craft away for the night to take us on a brief cruise up the Canal, persuasive bait being a handful of lire, triple his customary fee. Former Olympic swimming champion Eleanor Holm, one of our party, decides as we are drifting along that she'd like to dive into the canal for a swim—clothes and all. Two men plead with her not to, and finally, though reluctantly, she yields to our pleas. The two men are columnist Earl Wilson and this writer—and later we stare at each other in utter disbelief, and I urge Wilson to kick me, and kick me hard. For here could have been a delicious story, not only for our columns, but for the news wires as well.

Jane Wyman is to the right of me at a dinner party in Beverly Hills and reminds me of the night I escorted her to the nightclub debut of a young singing lad at the Riobamba back in the early forties. "I was so impressed with him," she recalls, "that I went back with some friends a few nights later to hear him again. After his show, I told him that when and if he ever came out to the Coast, I was going to have a big party for him so he could meet a lot of folks from the film colony. And I did. It was quite a party, but he was so shy, I recall—so awfully shy." She was referring to Frank Sinatra, of course, who tossed off that shyness in quick time as success embraced him.

That reminded me of the debut at the same Riobamba not too long after of a tall singing lad with an overly prominent hooked nose. But what a thrilling singer. He had no stage presence and offered no toss-away chatter between songs. He just stood there stiffly, even shyly, and sang beautifully. A few years later, this was a performer on his way to stardom, no longer shy, full of self-assurance, and offering witty ad libs—a drastic change that had come over him after a bit of plastic surgery that had altered the shape of his nose. Dean Martin.

Helen Morgan's quavering voice unloading "My Bill." Helen of the big sad eyes and the expressive hands. The lass who had us all spellbound in *Show Boat*—whose career I had followed and covered through the years, and the melancholy that filled me as I began to observe her increasing addiction to the brandy bottle and the gradual deterioration of her voice quality—until that night in Loew's State Theatre when she presented such a pathetic figure as the notes failed to register in key.

An opening night some twenty years or so ago for George Abbott's *Snafu* at the Hudson, and looking up to the left, I spot Nancy Carroll and Haila Stoddard together in a box with playwright Jack Kirkland. Two beauties, both applauding a talented youngster in the play, Patricia Kirkland. A quartet to give those of us who knew them something to ponder about. For Nancy was Kirkland's first wife, and Haila was his current wife but apparently a happy threesome on this occasion. Nancy, of course, was Patricia's mom, so there was a common bond on this occasion.

George Hamilton introduces Lynda Bird Johnson to Peggy and me. We exchange a few perfunctory remarks, and then a grayish-haired fellow clutches me by the arm and says: "I remember you, Louis, but I know who you think I am. You think I'm Buddy Pickford, but I'm not. I'm Buddy Rogers, still married to Mary Pickford." He chuckles over his little joke, and I chuckle with him, and it isn't until Peggy and I walk away that it occurs to me that this palatial home in which George Hamilton is hosting the party in March of 1966 for Lynda Bird once housed Buddy's wife, Miss Pickford, when she was married to Douglas Fairbanks. And I recall, too, some dyspeptic observations by a few Hollywood columnists that after the so vital, extrovert Fairbanks, they could not see how Mary Pickford's marriage to young Buddy Rogers could endure, especially since she made no secret of the fact that she was older than he. More than thirty years have passed since their marriage in 1937, and now there's nary a whisper that it won't last until death do them part.

A get-together with a former publicity man who had collaborated with me on a screenplay, *Need for Each Other,* which we sold to Warner Brothers. Impressed by his share of the generous loot, he decides he must eventually become part of the lush Hollywood scene. So I endeavor to convince D. A. Doran, then story editor of Paramount to consider him as an apprentice, but nothing comes of my attempt. Now here he is, Ernest Lehman, one of the top-flight producer-writers in filmland: who produced the Liz Taylor-Richard Burton co-starrer *Who's Afraid of Virginia Woolf?* and wrote the screenplay for *Sound of Music,* who adapted *The King and I* and *West Side Story* for our screen, who turned in the original script of *Executive Suite* and who wrote and produced the film version of *Hello, Dolly!*

I encounter Rudy Vallee and Alice Faye at Reuben's back in 1934, shielded from vulgar stares by a huge screen with snakes writhing down the center. I ask bluntly is the rumor true that they are about to become Mr. and Mrs.—or the other rumor that they are secretly wed. Miss Faye merely grins, but Rudy seems slightly annoyed and snaps: "It's you fellows who start the rumors." Of course, it does prove to be only one of those things, as Alice goes on to marry Tony Martin and then, after that marriage breaks up, comedian-musician Phil Harris. And Rudy finds happiness elsewhere, too.

And in that same year, as we study the leader of the orchestra at the Casino de Paree—thinnish, high cheek-boned face, sad eyes, the thought comes that he is slowly moving on to join the echelon of the more dominant bandleaders: Paul Whiteman, Harry James, Vincent Lopez, Tommy Dorsey, Glenn Miller, *et al.* But he never does, for Hollywood sees different potentialities for him, and be becomes one of the successful film character actors. Leon Belasco.

A night in honor of veteran Ted Lewis at the Latin Quarter, in observance of his thirty-fifth year in show business. Onto the stage climbs a gray-haired, stoutish lad to dance nimbly to the strains of "Sweet Georgia Brown"—George Raft. He is followed by Pat O'Brian roaring out the Notre Dame song and then offering his version of the Ted Lewis favorite: "When My Baby Smiles at Me" with a suspicion of tears in his eyes as he sings the song directly to his wife at ringside—and then announces proudly that he meant every word of the lyrics, for he had just become a papa.

Here we are in the ballroom of the Beverly Hilton in Beverly Hills at the Variety Club's dinner in March of 1966 honoring Prince Philip of England. Joey Bishop, alternating with Cary Grant as emcee, remarks lugubriously, "Imagine me and His

Highness together—the Prince and the Pauper," and Philip exclaims: "I'm both," and is rewarded with a howl of appreciation. Cary Grant, in his sixties, just become a recent father, also invites a roar when he murmurs: "Say, isn't that funny about John Wayne?" who in the same age bracket had also become a father.

For a change, as Georgie Jessel and this writer sit in Toots Shor's, our conversation takes a serious trend when I remark: "I must say—you're about the best afterdinner speaker and toastmaster we have around today." Jessel doesn't put up a modest protest. Instead he concedes: "Maybe you're right. Want to know why? There isn't any competition to speak of anymore—I mean among show guys. Someone who can get up on his feet and talk and hold his audience. Jack Benny? I'll buy him. Bob Hope? You've got something there. Johnny Carson? I won't object to him. Who else?"

I mentioned a few others. Jessel snorted. "They're funny when someone writes their script. They talk what others write for them. Don't let's include amateurs. Look who you had in the old days—Willie Collier, Nat Goodwin, Raymond Hitchcock, Wilton Lackaye, Henry Dixey, Francis Wilson, Louis Mann—giants, that's what they were. Quick on their feet with the speech. And, oh, yes, De Wolf Hopper."

I throw in the name of lawyer-author Louis Nizer. "We're discussing show folks," protests Jessel, "not politicians or guys like that. Say, no one could top Adlai Stevenson. Want to know how I learned my lessons about speaking—learned it early? When I was ten years old, Joe Weber and Lew Fields used to take me over to Rector's, the Knickerbocker Grill, Delmonico's, and I sat around with open ears and listened to those professionals give out with the good and happy talk. Great training."

And at luncheon at "21" with Pulitzer playwright Sidney Kingsley, I remark: "You work for years on a play. Is it because you only find inspiration at certain intervals?" Kingsley says: "I wish you'd stop blowing that cigar smoke in my face. I've stopped smoking. No, it has nothing to do with inspiration. I mull an idea in my mind sometimes for six or more months before even starting to write. Then, somehow, while I'm writing, the whole idea changes. Meanwhile I keep doing research. I put in more than a year researching for *Detective Story*. I'm never satisfied with the first draft, and not with the second either. After I think I have the play whipped, I let it lie around for a few months—read it over—and usually change it again."

I say, "Saroyan wrote *The Time of Your Life* in three weeks."

Kingsley says: "I'm picking up the tab for this lunch—did Saroyan ever do that?"

The final curtain descends upon *The Little Show* back in 1930, and to my amazement, instead of the expected half-empty house with yawning bitter-enders, the rows are packed solid with such luminaries of the day as Beatrice Lillie, Marc Connelly, Franklin P. Adams, Alexander Woollcott, Howard Dietz, Edna Ferber—and many others. These are some of the "fans" Libby Holman, Clifton Webb and Fred Allen face, and they put on a performance that tops their opening night show. And as they start to take their bows at show's end, pennies begin to clatter upon the stage, not pennies from Heaven but coppers tossed by the folks in the audience—Dietz had distributed bags full of the coins. Solemnly, the stars on stage stoop to pick up the pennies and bow in mock gratitude.

It is a night late in February of 1947 and some of us have turned out for the opening of a new night spot, Billy Reed's Little Club. It is a must for me, for Billy as a ballroom dancer with Louise Mele had been featured on one of my early Loew's State Theatre shows back in the thirties. For the opening, Billy presents a then unknown singing girl, a wholesome-looking lass—the kind usually referred to platitudinously as "the girl next door." We all find her delightful, this shy young beauty who seems so timid as I endeavor later to draw her out in conversation. Doris Day—our first glimpse of the future movie star.

Twelve years later, in celebration of the anniversary, there is another night at the Little Club. This time there is no Doris Day. Only Billy Reed, himself a substitute, as he makes a little speech while cutting the birthday cake, and then steps into a brisk little dance. No movie star, Billy, but the assembly this night might have pleased any star. For among the crowd are Louis Jourdan, George Raft, Elaine Stritch, Ben Gazzara, Gig Young and Elizabeth Montgomery, Sir Cedric and Lady Hardwicke, Darryl Zanuck with Juliette Greco, the Leland Hayworths, Martin Gabel and Arlene Frances, Gregory Ratoff, and dozens of others.

We are at the Tennis Club in Capri—this is in September of 1959—and a middle-aged woman with an interesting if not particularly attractive face, settles down at our table, chatting away gaily with several of the dinner guests. Our host and hostess, Prince Paolo and Princess Marcella Borghese introduce her to us —the name sounding something like "Countess Shanny." After she leaves, we are informed she is Mussolini's daughter Edda, who had been married to Count Ciano. When I express chagrin because I might have wangled a paragraph or two out of her, Princess Borghese consoles: "She wouldn't talk to you now, anything interesting, anyway. She has just finished her memoirs and they will appear here in *Oggi* and then in a book. She needs the money, and won't give out anything for free."

Another evening with the Prince and Princess in July of 1960—at dinner in the ancient ancestral Borghese Palace—a shack of some two hundred rooms in the heart of Rome, but most of it now converted into an exclusive club for a limited number of members. Some of the Borghese family still occupy apartments in the Palace, and most of the paintings, tapestries and furniture remain as they were centuries ago. In a big room, which has been converted into a library, there was an empty portion of wall space which it was felt should be filled with either a tapestry or painting. Prince Borghese tells us he had suggested there were hundreds of canvases in the cellars out of which one might be found to take up the space. After considerable digging around, one was unearthed, in perfect condition, ancient frame and all. It now covers most of a wall, practically dominating the room.

"It was a few months," said the Prince, "before any of us thought of really studying the painting and learning the identity of the artist. If you go up there now and look, you will see for yourself, it's by Tintoretto. It's probably worth half a million dollars—perhaps more—but we have other paintings here worth that much, all dug up from the cellars. None of them is for sale—not yet. And we have no idea how many down there all this time have been bruised and ruined."

Early in 1941 in the colorful little bistro bearing the name of the owner, Janet of France, Janet escorts me over to meet a thinnish, bright-eyed chap dipping his spoon into onion soup after first having pushed crumpled bread into its pale, yellowish thickness. "This," explains Janet, "is Monsieur Belbenoit"—and I recognize him from pictures of him I have seen in the newspapers. Julius René Lucien Belbenoit, who had escaped from Devil's Island, the French penal colony, and had written a best seller *Dry Guillotine,* about his harrowing experiences. It was difficult to believe that this calm, pleasant-mannered man had undergone the agonizing torture and privation described in his thrilling biographical account. Belbenoit in his book had confessed even to eating man's flesh!

Between spoonfuls of his soup, he expressed his happiness at being not only free but also able to dwell on a street of so many restaurants, Fifty-second Street, and to be able to be where there was so much food and be able to walk in and order food as he wishes when he wishes.

For endless days and endless nights he had died daily in the Hell that was his prison isle. His faith had left him—Heaven was something well-fed men and women could have their sentimental dreams about. But now much of his faith had returned, he said, for surely this was Heaven enough, this amazing America—especially Fifty-second Street where there was so much food available.

Moss Hart and I sit in the lobby of the Beverly Hills Hotel and he reveals that for years he has been beset by many fears and complexes which his mind tells him are foolish fancies, but he cannot shed them. So he has been having sessions with a psychiatrist, and he feels he is going to be all right.

"It isn't the treatments, but it's the doctor who has cured me, I think," said Hart. "He told me I could cash in on my fears. He was a fan of mine, he said, loved what I had done in the theatre and suggested I had great material in just the things that were bothering me. So I've been working on something—I think we'll have music in it. In fact, I've been so busy working on it, that all those crazy thoughts haven't bothered me once."

A bit over a year later, I am attending the exciting opening night of the project Moss had referred to, one of the theatrical triumphs of the season of 1941, *Lady in the Dark,* starring Gertrude Lawrence and featuring quite a talented young man who went on to great stardom himself—Danny Kaye.

An afternoon, during my precolumnar days when I mount a flight of stairs in New Brunswick, New Jersey, to enter a drab little apartment to interview James Mills whose attractive wife, Eleanor, a choir singer, had been murdered with her lover, the Reverend Edward Wheeler Hall. The trial is on at the time—a case which dominated the front pages of newspapers throughout the country—and I want to wrest from the frail, meek little man, some revelation as to how he actually felt about the tragedy.

To one question that I direct at him: "Did you ever at any time suspect what was going on?" He replies quietly: "She was such a pretty girl, so pretty. And me . . ." he shrugs his shoulders . . . "I'm just a janitor." Poor Mills, for the most part he remains almost forgotten and ignored, managing only to earn considerable space when death claims him in 1965 at the age of eighty-eight.

Naturally the obituaries revived all the sordid details of the memorable case.

So much else crowded into this memory montage. That thin, shabbily dressed Parisian waif, Edith Piaf, sobbing out her Gallic chants in the Versailles restaurant . . . Joe E. Lewis at the Copa lamenting the fate of poor little February denied the full quota of thirty or thirty-one days . . . Frank Sinatra's voice cracking in the middle of a number—I've forgotten at which night spot it was —and the immediate conclusion by all of us that this fellow was through. In debt and his marriage to Ava Gardner a shambles, etc., etc.—some in the show-business world were so certain the lad who has risen to such meteoric heights was doomed to a quick descent to comparative oblivion.

Here is Rudy Vallee, then starring at the Villa Vallee, insisting he is planning to give up his singing career to enter politics.

I have a feeling of melancholy whenever I come across this picture, for the divine songstress on my right is the late Edith Piaf and, next to her, the late cinema star Linda Darnell.

This was back in 1930 when he was at the height of his fame as a crooner. "I expect to marry if the right girl comes along, by the time I'm thirty-two," (he was twenty-three at the time) he says. "And then I'll go into politics. I've always had the ambition to become a senator, but of course you don't become a senator overnight, and I know it will be necessary to start at the bottom. I may go back to my home town in Maine and settle down there and run for a minor office. I don't want to remain a crooner all my life. If I'm lucky as I've been up to now, I'll be well fixed by the time I'm thirty-two, and then I can devote myself to politics. It has always been my belief that men who devote themselves to politics should do so from sheer desire to serve the public and not for any personal gain."

Rudy never had his ambition fulfilled—and perhaps, currently in his sixties, he may wonder whether he might not have been credited with setting the pattern for others in show business if he had followed those early ambitions, now that a former dancing man George Murphy is a senator and a former actor, Ronald Reagan, a governor.

To repeat, so many memories come to mind—so many I have not attempted to include—but it is time to write "30" before the reader becomes too weary.

INDEX

Note: Page numbers in italics refer to photographs.